OUR SOLDIERS AND THE VICTORIA CROSS.

ROSS L. MANGLES, ESQ., CARRYING A WOUNDED SOLDIER TO THE BOATS ON THE MARCH TO THE RELIEF OF ARRAH.

OUR SOLDIERS,

AND

THE VICTORIA CROSS.

LONDON:

S. O. BEETON, 248 STRAND, W.C.

(TEN DOORS FROM TEMPLE BAR.)

OUR SOLDIERS

AND

THE VICTORIA CROSS.

A GENERAL ACCOUNT OF THE REGIMENTS AND MEN
OF THE BRITISH ARMY:

AND STORIES OF THE BRAVE DEEDS WHICH WON THE PRIZE

"For Valour."

EDITED BY S. O. BEETON.

With Frontispiece and Title-Page printed in Colours,

SIXTEEN FULL-PAGE ENGRAVINGS, AND ILLUSTRATIONS IN THE TEXT.

LONDON:
WARD, LOCK, AND TYLER,
WARWICK HOUSE, PATERNOSTER ROW.

LONDON:
SAVILL AND EDWARDS, PRINTERS, CHANDOS STREET,
COVENT GARDEN.

TO THE READER.

THIS book is written for Boys. The majority of the articles were expressly prepared for the "Boys' Own Magazine," and the interest which their appearance excited, coupled with the favourable notices they won, encouraged the Editor to publish them in a connected form.

Boys—worthy to be called boys—are naturally brave. There is not, so far as we are aware, any etymological connexion between the words *boy* and *brave;* but there *is* an association of ideas, which if it does not make the terms interchangeable, is still strongly suggestive of their being one and the same. The expression *brave* man is easily understood, but to us, *brave* Boy looks like a pleonasm. A man has experience. He has tested—if there be any good thing in him—his courage in the rough exploits of the world's campaign. He has tilted, mayhap, with Quixotic chivalry against windmills, and in the encounter has been discomfited; he has awakened from his bright dream to a sad reality; he has been tempted to turn prosaic—inclined sometimes to beat his sword into a sickle, to gather in for his own special use the golden wheat from *anybody's* cornfield, and to make those late foes of his—the windmills—grind up the corn to make *his* bread. Now he is no longer brave. His views of life are taken from a new point of sight. He smiles at the *boy's* enthusiasm, and counts himself wise in his *man's* selfishness. But a man who has done battle, who has been thrown in the lists, who has been ready to mount and splinter lance again, who in the gaining of experience hast lost nothing of the Boy's boldness—such a man is *brave.*

The drift of these remarks is that experience may ruin a Boy's "pluck"—may give him the vulpine sagacity of Reynard in place of the courage of Leo Africanus.

But a Boy is brave. Youth is the season of confidence. "Your *young* men shall *see visions*" while your "*old* men shall dream dreams." What visions are those which rise up before the young—what brave words to speak, what brave actions to do—how bravely—if need be—to suffer! "The young fellows," said an old soldier to the writer, "are always pushing forward in a battle charge—they are in a mighty hurry to smell powder—*the veterans fall into the rear!*" Do they?—ah, well, 'tis the lesson, perhaps, of experience! But is it better than the Boy's eagerness to be foremost?—is it not—answer, brave hearts—better to die planting the colours on the wall, than to share the spoil which others have won?

This is the leading thought in this book about Soldiers—it is meant to keep alive the bravery of youth in the experience of manhood. The Editor of the book is very sensible of the incompleteness of the work. He knows that it is defective in many places, but it is honest. A good many of the papers were written by one who was then far away on a foreign station doing brave service; some of the papers are the work of dead hands. The articles have been put together as carefully as circumstances would allow, but there has been an anxious care on the Editor's part to retouch as little as possible the work of absent contributors. He offers the book to the Boys of England—not as the best piece of work that can be done—but as a volume they will read with delight and keep as a *souvenir* of pleasant hours. He is of opinion that anything which helps to make Boys more in love with true courage is good work done—he believes that bravery excites bravery, just as iron sharpeneth iron; and so he has confidence in this book being useful—a record of brave deeds that shall make its readers echo the words of King Harry—

"If it be a sin to covet honour,
I am the most offending soul alive."

CONTENTS.

INDEX

TO

ENGRAVINGS AND ILLUSTRATIONS.

LIST OF ILLUSTRATIONS IN THE TEXT.

OUR SOLDIERS AND THE VICTORIA CROSS.

CHAPTER I.

OUR SOLDIERS AND THE VICTORIA CROSS.

IT has been our lot in life to live very much among soldiers, and we like to write and talk about them. We hope that our readers will not be averse from hearing something of a class in whom we have all a common interest. It is true that English boys are not quite so warlike in their tendencies as French; they neither worship *la gloire* nor dress like manikin *soldats*. Swords and guns are not their only playthings, nor are feeble imitations of sanguinary contests their only pastimes. We here delight in all manly games and sports, for which French men and boys have little taste, and we thus acquire a muscular development and hardiness of frame which enable us to bear any amount of fatigue. It was a saying of the grand old Iron Duke that all his battles were won on the playground at Eton; by which we suppose he meant that his officers, most of whom were Eton boys, received there such a physical training as fitted them to be heroes in the strife. Still, it is one of those epigrammatic sayings in which truth is sacrificed for effect; for what could the duke, with all his officers, have done without the brave privates who composed his forces, and to whom he rendered justice on another occasion by saying that with such an army he could go anywhere and do anything?

A chaplain belongs, of course, to the non-combatant class in the army. It is not his duty to appear in the field, or to take part in battles. He has to remain at the hospital, and to administer the consolations of religion to the wounded and the dying; but he is precluded by his profession from being present at, or taking part in, any battle.

It is for this reason, perhaps, that we have always had a certain pleasure in listening to soldiers as they fought their battles over in hospital, and recounted their experience to one another. It was all strange and new to us, as, we dare say, it will be to most of those who read this book.

The soldiers of whom we speak all took part in and survived the Crimean war. Their manly breasts are all adorned with the different medals awarded to them; two of them wear the Victoria Cross. One early object of our curiosity was to ascertain what are the sensations or feelings of a soldier on entering battle, or being exposed to fire for the first time. Now, the answer we invariably received will, perhaps, take some of our readers by surprise. They felt nothing of that warlike intoxication ascribed to the old Vikings on the eve of the combat; they had none of that strange joy ascribed by the patriarch to the war-horse at the sound of the trumpet, nor were they exactly afraid; but there was a certain uneasy sensation experienced by all as the bullet whizzed past the ear, and comrade after comrade dropped, sometimes with a sharp cry of pain, sometimes giving no sign.

This feeling some of them graphically described as similar to that which a bather experiences before plunging into the water: *ce n'est que le premier pas qui coûte;* after the first dip Richard is himself again. But our readers are not to suppose that the soldier shows the same hesitation in advancing to charge as the bather on the brink of the stream. If he did he would be a coward, and be scorned by all his comrades. To make the two cases parallel, we must suppose a thousand bathers rushing forward to the stream at once. Now, though an individual bather standing alone might stop short on reaching the water, and pause before taking a header, a thousand bathers rushing forward at once, would plunge into the water without hesitation. The dread of shame, of exposure, of ridicule, would nerve the least courageous for the final leap. There is, moreover, such a strong feeling of sympathy diffused among large bodies of men acting in concert that the strength of the stronger is imparted to the weaker. Now, it is the same with soldiers advancing to the charge. All of them feel the cold shiver like that of the bather approaching the water, but they march shoulder to shoulder, and with them are some old soldiers who have been under fire before. The younger ones are encouraged by their example, and many a lad who has trembled on first smelling powder has proved himself a hero in the fight.

We have read in books that soldiers sometimes weep while fighting hand to hand and sorely pressed—not tears of cowardly terror by any means, but such tears as the strongest of men will shed in hours of fierce excitement. Wellington wept as he embraced Blucher after the Battle of Waterloo. This, indeed, has been denied, but it is not difficult to believe it true. There are moments in the lives of all men, even the most reserved and self-contained, when the hidden fountains of feeling well over and find an outlet through the eyes, and we should not think a whit less highly ot our soldiers did they shed a few tears of valiant rage while victory was still doubtful. But these tears, we suspect, are purely imaginary. For ourselves, we never met with a single soldier who confessed that he had shed tears himself, or seen others weep. We are sure that they would not have denied it if they had yielded to any such weakness, for, as a class, soldiers are the most truthful of men. All with whom we conversed agreed in affirming that our men were very quiet while fighting hand to hand with the enemy. There would be occasionally a shrill cry of pain from the wounded, or a short cry of triumph from the man who struck down his opponent, but generally, all the dread work of the battle-field was done in silence. All admitted that the most fearful sound during a battle was the cry of a wounded horse; it was so like that of a human being in his death agony—shrill, piercing, heartrending. The horses seem to become almost human in the hour of battle, to share in all the wild passions of the combatants, and to exult equally in the hour of victory.

But while our men fought in silence, the Russians were very noisy both in advancing and in fighting. They uttered the most savage yells, as if they thought to inspire our men with terror by the mere noise they made. They soon discovered that Englishmen are not so easily frightened; but they still continued to shout from mere habit. Their officers also encouraged them in this custom, giving them, moreover, drink to make them pot-valiant. Notwithstanding this, we have always heard our soldiers frankly speak of the Russians as "foemen worthy of their steel." Brave men, we know, learn to respect one another even in the field, and the Russians are certainly one of the bravest nations in Europe. They still retain, however, many of the characteristics of savage life; they have not yet learned to act on the old Roman maxim, "*Debellare superbos, parcere victis.*" They often bayoneted our men when left defenceless and wounded. It is but just to add that they expected no mercy when left in the same condition, and seemed overwhelmed with surprise when our men treated them with the same generous tenderness as though they had been comrades instead of foes.

There are sometimes strange traits of character exhibited during the excitement of battle. Men may have been living under restraint for years, and come to believe themselves to be very different from what they are. Xenophon relates a story of a Greek soldier who, in consequence of a wound which had affected his brain, forgot the language he had spoken for many years, and began to express himself in his native tongue, which, before this accident, seemed to have entirely faded from his memory. Something analogous to this occurred at the Battle of the Alma, in the case of a sergeant of the Guards. He had once been much addicted to swearing, but had been enabled to vanquish this and other evil habits, and for many years had been looked up to by his comrades as a man of exemplary character. His company, while charging up the heights of the Alma, was surrounded by the enemy, and, after suffering severe loss, was obliged to retreat. In vain the poor sergeant endeavoured to rally them. He was borne along with the current. Overpowered with shame and rage, he gave way to a sort of madness, and swore such fearful oaths that we have often heard the men of his company say that it was something awful to hear him. Those who occupied the same tent with him relate that he spent most of the night after the battle in prayer, and was often heard sobbing like a child. He never spoke of the strange outburst of that day to any of his comrades, and they had the delicacy to avoid all allusion to the subject; but it was observed that he was more humble, kind, and considerate in his bearing towards them than he had ever been before. He survived the war and returned to England, where he enjoyed the respect of all who knew him, and was never known to indulge in the habit which gained the mastery over him at the Alma. He is now dead, but his surviving comrades speak with a sort of awe of the incident we have related.

One soldier of the Guards became raving mad at the Alma. It happened in this way:—The Russian fire struck down several of the men as they were advancing. The soldier of whom we speak was a young lad who had never smelt powder before. By his side was a comrade who belonged to the same district, and had enlisted at the same time. The latter was hit by a cannon-ball, and his brains were bespattered over the face of his friend, who became frantic, roaring and shouting like a madman. He imagined that his comrades were the enemy, and that he was fighting hand to hand with them. The whole company was thrown into confusion, and he wounded some of his comrades before he could be disarmed. He was conducted to the rear, fighting and struggling the whole way. The surgeons pronounced him to be a dangerous lunatic, and he was strapped down upon one of the beds in the hospital, with a sentinel to watch over him. That sentinel told us that he was never entrusted before or since with such an unpleasant duty. Owing to the shock which the brain had received, the poor madman could not rest for a moment. He fancied himself in the thickest of the combat, fighting with all the energy of despair, and swearing that his comrades should be avenged. He continued in this raving condition for about twenty-four hours, when, with the exultant cry of "Victory!" he expired. A similar incident occurred at Inkermann: in this case, also, the soldier survived only twenty-four hours.

Soldiers rarely feel much pain at the moment they receive their wounds, unless these be very severe, in which case they suffer much from thirst. There is one very gallant friend of ours—a non-commissioned officer—who was shot through the ankle in crossing the stream at the Alma. He knew not that he was wounded till the battle was over, but thought that his foot had got entangled among the vines in crossing the valley, and that he had sprained the joint. A good soldier never likes to go to hospital when there is any hard fighting, and our friend kept "a quiet sough," as they say in the North, about his wound, and marched at the head of his company as if nothing had happened to him. His courage and endurance were rewarded: he was present at, and took part in, the Battle of Inkermann, where his gallantry attracted the notice of the commanding officer, on whose recommendation he obtained the medal and pension for distinguished conduct in the field. He was wounded also on this occasion, but his hurt was of a far more serious character. He was shot through the head: the bullet literally entered at one side, and came out at the other. He felt a sharp, stinging pain, and remembered nothing more till he regained his consciousness in hospital, and was surprised to learn that he had been some weeks under the doctor's hands. He suffers no inconvenience from his wound now, except occasional dizziness and half-blindness after any excitement or exposure to the sun. Such a man in the French service might have risen to the rank of field-marshal, and obtained a name in the page of history. Well, after all, the great thing is to do our duty well in the position we occupy; and our friend, as sergeant-major of his distinguished regiment, is happier, probably, than if he had had greatness thrust upon him.

Though soldiers recover from their wounds at the moment, they are often very dangerous afterwards. The brain is often injured, and the disease goes on till the man loses his reason, or drops down dead. A poor fellow was hit on the crown of the head by a piece of shell in one of the trenches before Sebastopol. He was stunned at the moment, but thought so little of it that he did not even report himself wounded. For eight years he felt no pain, but one day, while on guard, he was seized with a sudden giddiness, and became insensible. He was conveyed to hospital in a cab, and on recovering his consciousness he found that he was suffering the most intense pain on the crown of his head. His sufferings were very great; the only relief he could obtain was through the application of chloroform.

We write all this knowing that English boys feel deep sympathy with, and profound admiration for, our soldiers, and to show that their powers of endurance, when disabled, equal in heroic worth their gallantry upon the field.

Not all our readers, perhaps, have seen the Victoria Cross. It is not very beautiful nor very valuable in itself. A fac-simile of it appears at the commencement of this chapter. It is a simple piece of bronze, shaped like a cross, and its intrinsic value may be about threepence. Its intrinsic value! but who can tell the price a soldier puts upon it? He had rather have that piece of bronze on his breast than be made a Knight of the Garter, and have his banner hung up with those of the other K.G.'s in the Chapel of St. George at Windsor. To obtain that small piece of bronze of the value of threepence he will lead the forlorn hope, be the first to storm the breach, and ever ready to expose his life to any danger. The Victoria Cross is as much to a soldier as the *gage d'amour* the knight-errant in the days of chivalry received from his lady-love, and swore never to part with. The pledge of her affection might be a soiled and tattered glove, worth even less than the cross "For Valour," but it was dearer to her lover than life itself. O that the day may never come in this country when we shall judge of things by the Hudibrastic principle—

"The price of anything
Is just as much as it will bring!"

for badly then will it fare with Old England. When our soldier come to value their crosses at threepence each, the price they wil fetch at a marine store, we shall not long survive as a nation. Bu there is little danger of such an eventuality. There are things— God be thanked—which we *do* love and value more than life itsel —things which gold can *not* purchase. The Victoria Cross is one of them; and we are about to relate how three gallant officers o one of our most distinguished regiments came to be decorated with the priceless meed "FOR VALOUR." One was a commissioned officer; the other two were sergeants. Though different in rank, they were equal in bravery; their bravery was equally rewarded. Most people —thanks to Mr. Kinglake's history, and other sources of information —are now tolerably familiar with all the details of the Battle of the Alma. They know how the gallant Welsh Fusiliers, after forcing their way to the heights, and seizing the colours on the Russian battery, were so cut up by the enemy that they were forced to retire. They fell back in obedience to orders. It so happened, however, that as the word, "Fusiliers, retire!" was given, the Scots Fusilier Guards were charging up the heights, and the officer in command of them, hearing the order, thought that it was intended for his own men, and commanded them to fall back. This fact is not mentioned by Mr. Kinglake, but there are many witnesses still alive who heard this second order given, and acted upon it. Now, it is very difficult to retire before an enemy without falling into confusion; and it so happened that the Welsh Fusiliers came rushing down like a torrent. One gallant regiment opened their ranks, allowed them to pass through, and then closed again; but the Scots Fusiliers were not so fortunate. They did not open their ranks, because they received no order to do so, and were already falling back, when the crowd of Welsh Fusiliers came rushing upon them, broke through their ranks, and threw them into disorder; and, in the midst of this, the Russians made a dash at the colours of the regiment.

Now, it is not needful to dwell on the fact that it would be as disgraceful for an English regiment to lose its colours as it would have been for an old Roman centurion to have lost his shield. The

for badly then will it fare with Old England. When our soldiers come to value their crosses at threepence each, the price they will fetch at a marine store, we shall not long survive as a nation. But there is little danger of such an eventuality. There are things—God be thanked—which we *do* love and value more than life itself—things which gold can *not* purchase. The Victoria Cross is one of them; and we are about to relate how three gallant officers of one of our most distinguished regiments came to be decorated with the priceless meed "For Valour." One was a commissioned officer; the other two were sergeants. Though different in rank, they were equal in bravery; their bravery was equally rewarded. Most people—thanks to Mr. Kinglake's history, and other sources of information—are now tolerably familiar with all the details of the Battle of the Alma. They know how the gallant Welsh Fusiliers, after forcing their way to the heights, and seizing the colours on the Russian battery, were so cut up by the enemy that they were forced to retire. They fell back in obedience to orders. It so happened, however, that as the word, "Fusiliers, retire!" was given, the Scots Fusilier Guards were charging up the heights, and the officer in command of them, hearing the order, thought that it was intended for his own men, and commanded them to fall back. This fact is not mentioned by Mr. Kinglake, but there are many witnesses still alive who heard this second order given, and acted upon it. Now, it is very difficult to retire before an enemy without falling into confusion; and it so happened that the Welsh Fusiliers came rushing down like a torrent. One gallant regiment opened their ranks, allowed them to pass through, and then closed again; but the Scots Fusiliers were not so fortunate. They did not open their ranks, because they received no order to do so, and were already falling back, when the crowd of Welsh Fusiliers came rushing upon them, broke through their ranks, and threw them into disorder; and, in the midst of this, the Russians made a dash at the colours of the regiment.

Now, it is not needful to dwell on the fact that it would be as disgraceful for an English regiment to lose its colours as it would have been for an old Roman centurion to have lost his shield. The

Captain Loyd Lindsay, Scots Fusilier Guards, saving the regimental colours at the Alma.

colours are usually intrusted to one or two subalterns and several sergeants, who form a sort of guard of honour over them, and are held responsible for their safety. When they are in danger the bravest men in the regiment rally round them, and it is held unworthy not to follow them wherever they are seen. They are the same to our soldiers as the white plume of Henry of Navarre was to his men, or the bronze eagles to Rome's Tenth Legion. Knowing this, officers have sometimes thrown the colours into the very midst of the enemy, sure that their men would die rather than lose them. No sooner, therefore, was it known that the colours were in danger than the bravest men of the regiment tried to reach them, but only a few succeeded. They did not come too soon; the men intrusted with the colours fought like lions, but one officer was struck down, and only two sergeants survived the fearful contest. But the colours were safe, and the men might proudly say, with Francis I. after disastrous Pavia, "*Tout est perdu, hors l'honneur.*" The regiment wiped out the memory of the misfortune at the Alma (it was no disgrace to obey orders) on the bloody field of Inkermann, and a grateful country did not forget the men who loved their colours better than their lives. The officer who was struck down died of his wounds on the voyage home; Death was envious of the honours that awaited him. The other officer still survives, and wears on his breast the cross his sovereign bestowed upon him. He is, or will be, one of the wealthiest men in England, but we are sure that he values that small piece of bronze of the value of threepence more than all the money he has at his banker's.

"Money is round, and rolls away,"

but the memory of a brave action has never perished.

But gallant deeds are the same whether they be done by officers or by men; and the two sergeants demand notice who were also, for the part they took in this affair, decorated with the Victoria Cross. We should not dwell upon their history if it were not that it points a moral, though it does not adorn our tale. Both of these sergeants were fine, handsome fellows; one of them is six feet two inches in height. When they returned to London, and walked forth in the streets, decorated with the memorials of their bravery, their appearance naturally attracted much attention. Foolish people stopped them in the street, and invited them to drink. Now, no man of sense or good-breeding will drink in this way with soldiers, and no man of good feeling will tempt soldiers to drink. Those who thus invited our sergeants, we believe, meant no harm, but only wished to give the sergeants a cheerful glass, and to make them fight their battles o'er again. But soldiers who know how to resist the enemy in war are not always proof against temptation in times of peace. These two Victoria Cross men fell into irregular habits, such as could not be tolerated in the case of non-commissioned officers; every effort was made to save them, but in vain; their irregularities became so glaring that they were reduced to, and have ever since remained in, the ranks. They are steady enough now, but it is felt that they cannot be trusted, and they are not likely ever to regain their former rank. It seems very hard that brave men should lose their position through the mistaken kindness and thoughtlessness of their admirers, and we hope that those who feel sympathy with soldiers will find some better way of expressing it than by giving them drink. These two men, though serving in the ranks, have still much influence over their comrades, and that influence, we are glad to say, is generally exercised for good. The possession of the Victoria Cross carries with it a pension of 10*l.*, which cannot be forfeited through misconduct; the pension for distinguished conduct in the field is 15*l.* per annum.

Many small pledges of affection were found on the persons of our soldiers who fell on the battle-fields of the Crimea. Sometimes a lock of hair, or a photograph, or a last letter from home, or a small Bible or Testament, was found concealed beneath the tunic of a dead soldier. Many of them carried their Bibles with them to the field as a sort of talisman to protect them from danger; and there is a well-authenticated case of one soldier having had his life saved from the bullet, which would otherwise have reached his heart, having lodged in his Bible. We should think that book would become a precious relic in his family, ever to be prized, never to be parted with, for it was literally the Word of Life to him. Another was found with his right hand so firmly clenched that it was difficult to open it. He had allowed the blood from his wound to flow upon his hand, so that, on closing it, his fingers became, as it were, cemented together. Inside the hand were found several sovereigns he had saved from his pay with the intention of remitting them to his wife at home. His last thought was, probably, of her, and her heart must have been touched when she received the money he had saved for her with his heart's blood. Another man, who died of his wounds in hospital, had recourse to a singular expedient to save his watch, which he wished to be sent to his father in some remote country village. It was known that he was possessed of a watch, and there was no small uneasiness among the hospital orderlies when it could not be found after his death. Search was made for it in vain, and suspicion naturally fell upon the orderly who had been with him when he died. As this man, however, had always borne a good character, and there was no direct evidence against him, he was allowed to retain his situation, which must have been anything but a comfortable one. About ten days after the death of the soldier the mystery was cleared up. The effects of a dead soldier are usually sold by auction, and the proceeds, after paying all demands, remitted to his relations at home. It so happened that this man was possessed of a pair of good boots (a rare piece of good fortune in the Crimea), and these were purchased by a comrade for a few shillings. The purchaser, in trying on the right boot, found some obstacle in the toe which he imagined to be a pebble; on shaking it out he discovered the missing watch. The dying man, in the delirium of his last struggle, had contrived to secrete it in the place where it was found. It would be difficult to assign any reasonable motive for such an act; it was probably done in a moment of unconsciousness.

Commodore Wilmot has told us a good deal in his book about the King of Dahomey's Amazons. These female warriors form his body-guard, and are three times as numerous as the men, whom they surpass in strength and bravery. They are very skilful in the use of fire-arms, and carry gigantic razors for shaving off heads—a very unladylike amusement, as all will allow. Now, in this country we have no regularly organized army of Amazons, though there is no saying what we may soon have in these days, when there are so many suggestions for the employment of female labour. It may be a prejudice on our part, but we confess we should not like to see nice young ladies firing off blunderbusses, or shaving off people's heads. Still, women have been found serving in the ranks, both in France and in England, without their sex being discovered, and a good many soldiers' wives accompanied our forces to the East. It is painful, but truthful, to add that most of these adventurous females had to be sent home, for reasons which we had rather not specify; four only were allowed to remain. These well-conducted Amazons weathered all the dangers of the campaign, watched over their husbands in the field and the hospital, did all the marketing, without knowing a word of "the foreign lingo" spoken by the natives, passed through many perils, and returned to relate their "accidents by flood and field" to their admiring friends.

Soldiers, as we have said, are very patient while enduring physical pain. A hospital presents a fearful scene on the day after a battle. It is surprising that no artist has selected such a subject to illustrate the horrors of war. Our army surgeons are brave men, or they would lose their presence of mind amid such scenes, for it requires less courage to kill than to heal. Every form of physical suffering is to be seen there; but a groan is rarely to be heard. It is only during the amputation of a limb, or the probing of a wound, that a sharp cry of pain is sometimes wrung from the sufferer, who generally turns aside his head, as if ashamed of such unsoldierly weakness. Wounded and dying soldiers like to be visited by their chaplains; they often say, "We have led a bad life; can there be any hope for us now?" They may have been bad men, but they are always truthful: they never try to make themselves out to be better than they really are. Their last thought is generally of home. Often in India and the Crimea a dying soldier has said to his chaplain, "You will write and tell them all about it. I hope I have done my duty, and nothing to disgrace my name." If our chaplains did nothing but soothe the last hours of our soldiers, their mission would not be altogether in vain; and no class of men are more grateful for kindness, as our nurses in the East will testify. And here we detract not from the excellent intentions of those ladies in saying that, from want of previous training, they were, as a class, disqualified for the work they undertook; yet we have always heard them spoken of by the men with the deepest respect. We have baptized many a Florence Nightingale, and the feeling cherished towards this lady in the army is almost analogous to the Mariolatry of the Italian peasantry: it borders on idolatry. "Shure she is not a woman, but an angel of mercy," said a poor Irishman whom she had nursed. "I could kiss the very earth she threads." There are many others equally grateful, though less demonstrative and poetical in the expression of their gratitude. Florence Nightingale and the Queen are the two patron saints of the British Army. Our soldiers have not yet forgotten how her Majesty visited them in hospital on their return from the Crimea, and showed her sorrow and her sympathy as a woman best can show it—by her tears. And, after all, be we queen or soldier's wife, drummer-boy or commander-in-chief, we are all members of the same family, with the same great heart beating within our breasts. One touch of nature makes the whole world kin. Our Queen wept for her wounded soldiers, and there was many a soldier wept for our Queen when the great sorrow overtook her. Such tears are not lost; they bind us all together, and give us a deeper insight into that great law of love taught by Him who did not esteem it a weakness to weep at the grave of a friend.

CHAPTER II.

THE GUARDS, OR HOUSEHOLD TROOPS OF ENGLAND.

ROM the earliest times, when standing armies were needless, inasmuch as every human unit that made part of a nation's total was more or less a soldier, and was ready and willing to buckle on his harness and fight at the beck of the ruler to whom he owed allegiance, to the present day when the army and navy estimates are the *bêtes noirs* of every would-be politician who prefers money-grubbing to national honour, the chosen head or chief magistrate of every nation—no matter what his style and title may have been, or may be—has always had a select body-guard at his command, partly as a mark of distinction and honour, and partly for the special defence of his person against malcontents at home and enemies abroad.

To this rule Victoria, by the Grace of God, Queen of the United Kingdom of Great Britain and Ireland, and Empress of Hindostan, is no exception, and could our eyes be gratified with a review in which the "household troops" of all nations took part, from the *Cent Gardes* of Napoleon III. to the Amazons of His Brutality of Dahomey, it would be seen that there are none superior to the British Guards.

The Guards, or Household Troops of England, consist of six regiments, three of cavalry and three of infantry. The three regiments of cavalry are styled respectively, the First Life Guards, the Second Life Guards, and the Horse Guards, or Oxford Blues; while the three regiments of Foot Guards are known as the First, or Grenadier Guards, the Second, or Coldstream Guards, and the Third, or Scots Fusilier Guards. These six magnificent regiments of cavalry and infantry are—and it is just and right to say so, though it be said with the pride of an Englishman—unequalled in the world, whether it be in appointments or soldierly bearing, in physical strength or majesty of stature, in dash or discipline, unflinching endurance of hardships or superb indifference to death—which last, by the way, are qualities common to all British soldiers and sailors at all times and under all circumstances.

The First and Second Life Guards owe their origin to a troop of eighty Cavalier gentlemen who were enrolled in Holland, on May 17, 1660, as a body of Life Guards for the protection of the person of Charles II. against the conspiracies that were said to be forming in England to assassinate him as soon as he set foot once more on English soil. The number of this body-guard was raised to six hundred before the king quitted Holland; but after the Restoration had been effected, several gentlemen retired from the service to return to their homes in the country, and it dwindled down to two troops—one of which remained with the king in London, while the other went into garrison under the Duke of York at Dunkirk. The attempt, however, of the "Fifth Monarchy Men" to overthrow the king's authority in 1661 led to the recall of the Duke of York and his troopers, when the corps of Life Guards was raised to five hundred men, and divided into three troops—the first being called His Majesty's Own; the second, the Duke of York's, as before; and the third the Duke of Albemarle's.

No change was made in the constitution of the Life Guards, with the exception of the addition of a fourth troop after the Duke of Monmouth's rebellion in 1685, until October, 1693, when the Horse Grenadiers, who had hitherto been attached to each troop of Life Guards—just as a company of grenadiers formed part of almost every infantry regiment in the British service until a few years ago—were embodied and formed into a separate troop, distinguished by the title of the Horse Grenadier Guards. It should also be stated that the Scots Life Guards and Horse Grenadier Guards, which had been raised after the Restoration to act as a guard of honour to the Lord High Commissioner and the Scottish Parliament, were marched to London, and incorporated with the English Life Guards shortly after the union of the two kingdoms.

In 1745, after the defeat of Prince Charles Edward—otherwise styled the Pretender—at Culloden, the four troops of Life Guards were reduced to two; but the establishment of the Horse Grenadier Guards, which now consisted of two troops, remained on the same footing. This continued until June 25, 1788, when the two troops of Life Guards and the two troops of Horse Grenadier Guards were embodied into two regiments, the former bearing the title of the First Regiment of Life Guards, and the latter that of the Second Regiment of Life Guards; and no further alteration has been made to the present day, except in the number of companies in each regiment, and the numerical strength of the companies.

The third cavalry regiment of the Household Troops—the Royal Regiment of Horse Guards, or Oxford Blues, as it is familiarly called—was originally a body of horse that had been raised by Cromwell as a body-guard, and had been retained after his death to act as a guard of honour to the Parliament and General Monk, who then bore the title of the Lord General. After the Restoration the whole of the troops that had been in the service of the Parliament were disembodied; but the officers and men of the Lord General's troop of horse were immediately formed into a new regiment, which received the title it now bears, and was placed under the command of the Earl of Oxford. With the exception of alterations at various periods in its numerical strength, no change has taken place in the constitution of this regiment from the time of its enrolment for the service of Charles II. until the present time.

Of the three infantry regiments of the Household Troops, the First, or Grenadier Guards, although it takes precedence of the other two regiments in point of rank, yields to the Coldstream Guards in priority of enrolment. This regiment was incorporated at Brussels in 1657, having been raised at that time by the Duke of York for the service of the Spanish crown in the Netherlands. It consisted of about four hundred men of all ranks, the majority of whom were gallant, reckless, royalist gentlemen, who had fought and bled for Charles I. and his son Charles II. in the Civil War, and had followed the fortunes of the latter and his brother, the Duke of York, when they were driven from England, and obliged to take refuge in France, from which country they were also expelled when peace was made between Louis XIV. and Oliver Cromwell in 1655. The regiment was cut to pieces before Dunkirk in 1658, when that town was taken from the Spaniards by the French troops and the soldiers of the Commonwealth; but it was reorganised two years subsequently by Lord Wentworth, who then assumed the command. In 1662 it was ordered to repair to England, where it was incorporated with a regiment known as the "King's Regiment," commanded by Colonel Russell, under the title of the "First Regiment of Foot Guards." It did not receive its present appellation of the "Grenadier Guards" until after the battle of Waterloo, when it was thus distinguished in commemoration of the glorious charge in which its officers and men broke and routed the veteran Grenadiers of the far-famed French Imperial Guard—the last charge of the British line on June 18, 1815, which decided the terrible struggle of that eventful day in favour of the English arms, and crushed for ever the power and *prestige* of Napoleon I.

The regiment known as the Coldstream Guards derives its origin from a regiment of the Commonwealth that served against the king in the Civil War under the command of General Monk. It takes its name from Coldstream, a small border town in the south of Berwickshire on the left bank of the Tweed. This town formed the head-quarters of General Monk for some time before he set out on his march for London with the view of effecting the restoration of Charles II., and it was here, indeed, that this movement was projected and matured. During his sojourn in this town in 1659, Monk may rather be said to have reorganised and recruited his old corps, originally called "Monk's Regiment," than to have raised a new one, as it is commonly stated, and, having surrounded himself with a body of troops on whose fidelity he could rely, he commenced his march towards London on January 1, 1660. On his arrival his soldiers were employed in repressing the tendency which was evinced by the citizens of London to dispute the authority of the Parliament then sitting. Immediately after the Restoration the forces of the Commonwealth were disbanded by Act of Parliament, but Charles had resolved to add "Monk's Regiment" to the

Household Troops that were then forming for the defence of his person against the attempts of the more desperate republicans who still cherished a bitter hatred to the monarchical form of government, and the soldiers, having laid down their arms on Tower Hill as a mark of obedience to the king's authority, and in token of their dissolution as a regiment of the Commonwealth, immediately took the oath of allegiance, and sprung into existence anew as an English regiment, under the name of "The Duke of Albemarle's, or Lord General's Regiment," which appellation was changed to that of the "Coldstream Guards" about 1670, after the death of Monk, in remembrance of the place where he had prepared for the enterprise which it was his good fortune to bring to such a happy issue.

The precedence of the Grenadier Guards over the Coldstream Guards was established by a general order, dated September 12, 1666, in which it was directed "that the regiment of Guards (composed of the two regiments of Foot Guards, commanded by Colonel Russell and Lord Wentworth) take place of all other regiments, and the colonell take place as the first foot colonell; the General's Regiment (the Duke of Albemarle's, or Coldstream Guards) to take place next."

The Scots Fusilier Guards were placed on the roll of the English army, and first shared the duties and privileges of the Household Troops, shortly after the union had been effected between England and Scotland, in 1707, and it was found unnecessary to retain them any longer in Edinburgh, where, in conjunction with the Scots Life Guards, they had acted as a guard of honour to the Lord High Commissioner and the Scottish Parliament, besides rendering efficient service in the various continental wars in which England had been involved during the latter part of the seventeenth century.

The Scots Life Guards were established in Edinburgh in 1661, a single troop having been enrolled in that year, to which a second was added about two years after, to assist in the maintenance of order and the enforcement of the Episcopalian form of worship, which the covenanting Scotch, especially the Lowlanders, cordially hated. It is probable that the Scots Foot Guards were enrolled at the same time, as it appears that after the suppression of the risings in Scotland in 1667, and the peace that was concluded in that year with Holland, all the regular Scottish forces were disbanded, with the exception of the two troops of Scots Life Guards above mentioned and the regiment of Scots Foot Guards.

Space would fail us entirely if we attempted to notice even a tithe of the thousand and one battles and exploits in which our Household Troops have signalized themselves. We can, indeed, only mention the few hard-fought fights, the names of which are blazoned in scrolls of glowing gold on the regimental colours of these regiments, in memory of the battle-fields in which they have won such a glorious meed of honour and renown at the priceless cost of life and limb and liberty; and we must abstain from making more than the briefest mention of the services rendered by detachments of the Life Guards and Coldstream Guards, who acted as Marines on board the English fleet in 1665 and 1666, under Prince Rupert and the Dukes of York and Albemarle (some fifty years prior to the addition of the splendid and distinguished corps that is now known as the "Royal Marines" to the British army), and at the battle of Solebay in 1672; the gallant deeds of the same regiments before Maestricht in 1673, under the Duke of Monmouth and John Churchill, afterwards Duke of Marlborough, the services of the Grenadier and Coldstream Guards in Flanders, in 1678, under the same generals; the share that these regiments had in the occupation of Tangiers in 1680, in conjunction with the Spanish troops, and the subsequent battles with the Moors; the battle of Bothwell Bridge, in Scotland, with the rebel covenanters, in which the Scots Life Guards and Foot Guards bore a conspicuous part under the Duke of Monmouth; the frustration of the attempt of the same nobleman to wrest the crown from James II., by the untoward battle of Sedgemoor, in which all the regiments of English Life and Foot Guards were engaged; the campaigns against France in the Netherlands, in 1689 and 1691, the last of which was followed by the loss of Namur; and the long list of battles and sieges in which these regiments took part during the latter part of the reign of William III. and Mary, those of Queen Anne, George I., and George II., and the early part of the reign of George III., including the battles of Steenkirk, Landen, Blenheim, Ramilies, Almanza, Oudenarde, Malplaquet, Dettingen, Fontenoy, Minden, Warburg, the American campaigns, and the battle of Valenciennes in 1793.

The First and Second Life Guards and the Royal Horse Guards all bear the words "Peninsula" and "Waterloo" on their guidons. The Grenadier Guards bear the memorable names of "Lincelles," "Corunna," "Barossa," "Peninsula," "Waterloo," "Alma," "Inkerman," and "Sevastopol" on their colours; and in addition to these, Corunna only being excepted, the Coldstream Guards and Scots Fusiliers have the words "Sphinx," "Egypt," and "Talavera."

To speak further of the achievements of the Household Troops in Belgium, Egypt, Spain, and Portugal, would be to write a military history of the reign of George III., or to tell again the oft-told but never tiring tale of the Peninsular War, the disastrous retreat on Corunna, the battle fought there on the eve of embarkation, the death and burial of Sir John Moore, the triumphs of Talavera, Vittoria, Salamanca, and Barossa, and the "crowning mercy" of Waterloo, in which battle the Household Cavalry and the First Dragoon Guards broke and utterly routed Napoleon's magnificent Cuirassiers, and won the right to bear the word "Waterloo" on their standards and appointments for ever.

From 1815 a long rest from war's alarm fell to the lot of the Household Troops until the outbreak of the Crimean war, in the hardships and glories of which the three regiments of Foot Guards participated. As the honour of the battle of Balaclava belongs peculiarly to the "six hundred," who were set face to face with sure and sudden death when they were launched against the Russian batteries, and rode, like heroes as they were, into the graves that yawned to receive them, so the glory of Inkerman adds especial lustre to the laurels of the British Foot Guards.

Amid the cold grey mists of that dark November morning they bore the brunt of an almost hopeless struggle, as line after line of Russian soldiers, maddened with drink, swarmed up the hill from the valley of the Tchernaya to recoil with broken ranks from the base of the little battery that the Guards held with desperate courage. It was the key of the position: to have been forced from it would have brought destruction on the entire British camp. They knew this, and officers and men would all have died there gladly, like Leonidas and his three hundred at the pass of Thermopylæ, rather than have quitted the earthwork alive, though not dishonoured. Tears trickled down the cheeks of their royal leader as he saw his men falling, like autumn leaves, before the fire of the infuriated foe. With bleeding heart he gasped, "My poor Guards! What will they say in England?" Ay! what, indeed? What, but honour to the men who esteemed life as nothing in comparison with England's reputation? What, but honour to the Duke who dared to sigh for his maimed and slaughtered men as a father would sorrow for his dying son? Even when ammunition failed them they did not abandon the post they had held so long, and at so great a cost. No! if they could no longer pour a shower of lead into the advancing masses of the Russians, they could at least rain stones upon them, and many a Russian soldier fell to the rear that day with loosened teeth and shattered jaws, smarting under the blows of the rough missiles that the Guards tore from the banks and mould around them. But succour was at hand: the red-breeched Zouaves of France came leaping to the rescue at the *pas de charge;* and, as they advanced, the Guards sprang, with a cheer, over the parapet of the earthwork, and drove the blades of Bayonne to the very muzzles of their muskets into the backs of the running foe, who left behind them more killed and wounded than the British numbered at the commencement of the battle.

It may have been noticed that all officers in the Guards are entitled to hold that rank in the army which is immediately above the rank which they hold in their own regiments: an ensign in the Guards being styled "ensign and lieutenant" in his commission, and so on. The privilege of holding the rank of lieutenant-colonels and captains in the army was granted to captains and lieutenants in the Guards in 1691, when the allied armies, under the command of William III., were encamped on the plain of Gerpynes, in the Netherlands, near the French frontier, a few weeks before the battle fought between the Allies and the French on the banks of the little rivulet near Catoir; but the rank of lieutenant in the army was not held by ensigns in the Guards until after the battle of Waterloo, when this privilege was conceded to them by the Prince Regent, in an order from the War Office, dated July 29, 1815.

The illustration that accompanies this chapter gives the present costume of the three regiments of Foot Guards—a scarlet tunic, lately introduced, with blue facings, white cross-belt and waist-belt, and black trousers, with a scarlet cord down the seams in winter, and white in summer. When in full dress, the whole wear bear-skin caps, but each regiment has distinctive ornaments on the collar of the tunic, etc.; and when in undress, the men belonging to each may be distinguished by the band round the cap—the Grenadier Guards wearing a red band, the Coldstream Guards a white band, and the Scots Fusiliers a band chequered with red and white.

The two regiments of Life Guards and the Royal Horse Guards all wear corselets—consisting of a breast-plate and back-piece—and helmets of polished steel, with breeches, sword-belts, cross-belts, and gauntlets of white leather. They are, however, to be distinguished by the colour of their coats, and the plume that they wear in their helmets—the Life Guards being clad in scarlet coats, and having white plumes, while the Horse Guards wear blue coats, and scarlet plumes. They are all armed alike, with sword and rifled carbine, and carry pistols in the holsters of their saddles, which are covered with white sheep-skin for the Life Guards, and black sheep-skin for the Horse Guards Blue. In undress the former wear a scarlet shell-jacket with blue facings, while the latter wear a blue shell-jacket with scarlet facings. The cap—black, with a scarlet band—is the same for each regiment.

Apropos of this subject, it may not be generally known that the First Royals, or First (Royal) Regiment of Foot, are a corps of Foot Guards by regimental tradition, if not by authority from the Horse Guards.

The writer of this chapter once knew an old Devonshire pensioner, John Sculley by name, who belonged to the "Fust Ry-uls," as he used to style his old regiment, who had fought in almost every one of the principal battles of the Peninsular war, and had escaped without a scratch.

"John," I would sometimes say to the old fellow, as he stood leaning on his spade, "what regiment did you belong to?"

"Why, Sponshus Pilut's Guards, to be sure," he would curtly reply. "I've told 'ee so often enough, I reckon."

"No, I think not. But Pontius Pilate's Guards—what a queer title! Why in the world were you called so?"

"Why, you see, the ridg'ment was raised in Sponshus Pilut's time, and that's how us got the name."

And this he implicitly believed.

CHAPTER III.

THE ENGINEERS.

GIBRALTAR is well named the Key of the Mediterranean. In peace it protects our commerce and our fleets, in war it affords equal facility for harassing our foes; by its position and its strength its possession is of the utmost importance to the English, and it has excited for the last century and a half the suspicion and the jealousy of other nations. The rock of Gibraltar projects into the sea about three miles. Its northern extremity, owing to its perpendicular altitude, is inaccessible; its southern extremity is known as Europa Point; and the southern and eastern sides are rugged and steep, affording natural defences of a very formidable character. It is only on the western side fronting the bay that the rock gradually declines to the sea; but the town of Gibraltar is so built that an attack upon it, however well planned, however strong or long continued, is almost certain of failure. The bay formed by the two points already named is more than four miles across. The depth of its waters, and the protection afforded by the headland, render the harbour remarkably secure, and it is well adapted for vessels of every description. The extreme depth of the water within the bay is a hundred and ten fathoms. The security of the harbour has been still further increased by two moles, one extending eleven hundred feet, and the other seven hundred feet into the bay. The bold outline of the rock is conspicuous and striking, as it lifts its colossal proportions into the sky, and against the intense blue of that sky every crag is sharply defined. From the water to the summit, from the land forts to Europa Point, the whole rock is lined with formidable batteries. Like a crouching lion it looks out to sea, and every foe is daunted by its aspect.

Gibraltar is essentially military. Sentinels, gateways, drawbridges, fortifications, guns pointing this way, that way, and the other, looking as if—supposing them to be fired—they would inevitably blow up one another; narrow streets of stairs which it is hard work in the hot sunshine to ascend; nothing to see when you reach the top but a line of ramparts, and another street of stairs in perspective. Excavated passages in the rock lead from point to point; every new position seems more impregnable than the last; awful heights rise above, terrific depths yawn below; guns peer—at the most unexpected points—from the sides of the rock, as if they were natural productions; tunnelled galleries open to the right and to the left, inviting or deterring the visitor. There is one huge chamber cut out of the solid rock, and serving as a battery or a banquet room as occasion may require; it is called St. George's Hall, and is the most formidable and singular cutting of Gibraltar. There is another excavation of the same character christened by the name of Cornwallis, but it is neither so spacious nor so elegant as that of St. George.

The people one meets in Gibraltar are a mixed multitude—the familiar English uniform is of course conspicuous, but for the rest it is only what we have read of, or heard of, or dreamed of in connexion with Gil Blas and Don Quixote. There is so much that is Spanish that you might fancy yourself in Barcelona; so much that is Moorish that you might fancy yourself in Morocco; so much that is English, Italian, Greek, Polish, Jewish, African, and Portuguese, that you might conceive yourself to be in the midst of an animated Ethnological museum on a large scale, opened at Gibraltar, regardless of expense.

The rock of Gibraltar, forming with Abyla in ancient times the far-famed pillars of Hercules, was captured from the Spaniards by Sir George Rooke in 1704. During the nine following years the Spaniards in vain tried to recover it, and in 1713 its possession was secured to the English by the treaty of the peace of Utrecht. But treaties are liable to be broken. When the men of the pen have finished their work the men of the sword may undo it. To hold the rock of Gibraltar by treaty was one thing, to hold it by strength was another. The fortifications required for its defence were necessarily on a gigantic scale, and the men of the pick and the shovel were in request. When we glance at the subterranean passages cut in the rock, the huge caverns scooped out of it, the long lines of rampart making the place impregnable, even though attacked by an enemy having the command of the sea, we may readily understand how important was the service rendered by the engineer and labourer. So important indeed was their work, that it added a new division to the British army—a division, that wherever our flag waves has done good service—namely, that of the Engineers.

Previous to the year 1772 all our great engineering works in connexion with military operations were mainly executed by civilians. The works at Gibraltar were entrusted to ordinary mechanics obtained from England and the Continent. These operatives were not engaged for any term of years, neither were they amenable to military discipline; they worked when they pleased, they idled when they pleased; they were wholly regardless of authority; received good wages; and their dismissal was in all instances more injurious to the Government than it was to the men.

The hindrance and inconvenience of this system led to the formation of a corps of *military artificers*. The idea was suggested to Lieutenant-Colonel Green by the useful result of the occasional occupation of soldiers who had learned mechanical trades previous to enlistment. He thought it possible that a sufficient number of these men might be banded together for the carrying on of all necessary engineering works, and that their employment would lessen the cost while it secured the completion of any engineering operation, and at the same time, that the men so employed would at any period be ready to participate in the defence of the place.

Lieutenant-Colonel Green submitted his suggestion to the Governor of Gibraltar. The governor approving the plan, it was recommended to the attention of the Secretary of State, and royal consent was given to the measure in a warrant dated March 6th, 1772: thus originated the corps of Royal Sappers and Miners.

The warrant authorised the raising and forming of a company of artificers, to consist of a sergeant-major, as adjutant, who was to receive 3*s*. a day; three sergeants, each of whom was to receive 1*s*. 6*d*. a day; three corporals, whose pay was 1*s*. 2*d*. a day; and sixty privates, and one drummer, each of whom was to receive 10*d*. a day.

The rank of adjutant attached to that of sergeant-major was not adopted, but it appears to have been taken by Thomas Bridger, who so describes himself on his wife's tombstone at Gibraltar, adding thereto a touching tribute to her charity, and a sneer at the end—like the sting in the tail of the serpent—at the parsimony of the Government.

"A more loving wife or friend sincere
Never will be buried here;
Charitable she was to all,
Altho' her income it was small."

Recruiting for this company was a service of but little difficulty, as permission was granted to fill it with men from the regiment then serving in the garrison. The whole of the civil mechanics were not discharged from the department on account of this measure; a few, on the score of their merit, were retained in the fortress; the foreign artificers were dismissed; most of the English "contracted artificers" sent home; permission, however, was given to any "good men" who chose to enlist; but not one availed himself of the privilege.

Before the close of the year 1772, the ranks of the company were almost full, and the system was found to work so well, that on the recommendation of the lieutenant-governor a fresh warrant was issued for the increase of the corps, and no sooner was it completed than the engineers proceeded with great spirit in the execution of the King's Bastion. On laying the foundation of this work, General Boyd, in his speech, desired that the bastion might be as gallantly defended as he knew it would be ably executed, and that he might live to see it resist the united efforts of France and Spain. His desire was fully realised. He not only lived to see what he wished, but materially to assist in the operations of the siege.*

In October, 1775, the company of Soldier Artificers was still further augmented, and consisted of one hundred and sixteen non-commissioned officers and men.

Gibraltar, ever since its capture by the English in 1704, had been a source of jealousy and uneasiness to Spain; as soon as ever an opportunity offered for the commencement of hostilities, Spain assumed an aggressive attitude, and in 1779 sat down before the place at St. Roque with a powerful camp, and sent out a fleet to cut off supplies. The gallant old General Elliot, and the no less gallant veteran Boyd, defended the rock nobly, and found their best help in the Soldier Artificers. The sufferings of the undaunted garrison were great—the price of mutton or beef being 3*s.* 0*d.* a pound, eggs sixpence each, and mouldy biscuit crumbs 1*s.* a pound; but the indomitable energy of the men never slackened; they laboured night and day, piercing the rock with subterranean passages, and forming vast receptacles for stores and ammunition in the solid stone. Failing in their efforts to reduce the garrison by

* A beautiful model of the King's Bastion is to be seen in the Rotunda, Woolwich.

famine, the French and Spaniards, after three years' beleaguering, began a terrific bombardment. Fire was opened with unexampled fury, and continued incessantly for days and weeks. The battering flotilla was warmly received by the "dwellers in the rock." But for a long period the battering ships seemed invulnerable. At length red-hot shot was employed by the garrison, and sheets of resistless flame burst in all directions from the flotilla: the whole of the batteries were burnt; the magazines blew up, one after another; and it was a miracle that the loss of the enemy by drowning did not exceed the number saved by the merciful efforts of the garrison.

The contest was still prolonged: the enemy were bent on reducing their invincible opponents at all cost. The British were in no mood to yield; red-hot shot was their grand specific; the Artificers were instantly employed in erecting kilns in various parts of the fortress, each kiln capable of heating a hundred shot in an hour.

The struggle continued for some time; from one thousand to two thousand rounds were poured into the garrison in the twenty-four hours, and this was kept up for months. During the cannonade, the Artificers under the engineers were constantly engaged in the diversified works of the fortress, and they began to rebuild the fortification known as the Orange Bastion, on the sea line, and in the face of a galling fire completed their work in three months. The number of the Artificers had been augmented by the arrival of one hundred and forty-one mechanics, under Lord Howe; but, even taking this into account, the erection of such a work in solid masonry, and under such circumstances, is unprecedented in any siege.

Failing to obtain the submission of the garrison either by famine or bombardment, the enemy attempted to mine a cave in the rock, by which to blow up the north front, and thus make a breach for their easy entrance into the fortress. The secret was revealed by a deserter; but very little attention was paid to his statement, until the discovery of the enemy's proceedings was made by Sergeant Thomas Jackson, who, making a perilous descent of the rock by the help of ropes and ladders, ascertained beyond all doubt the work in which the Spaniards were engaged. The ratification of peace put an end to all military operations, and terminated a siege which extended—with circumstances of unparalleled difficulty and danger —over a period of four years.

During the whole of this memorable defence, the Company of Artificers proved themselves to be good and brave soldiers, and no less conspicuous for their skill, usefulness, and zeal in the works—works, as the commander of the hostile forces [Duc de Crillon] remarked, "worthy of the Romans."

At the close of the siege, there were twenty-nine rank and file wanting to complete the number of Soldier Artificers. The deficiency was speedily supplied, and the company was never allowed to sink beneath its established number. A force of more than two hundred and twenty non-commissioned officers and artificers were employed in restoring the work which had suffered during the bombardment; and to expedite the labour, the Soldier Artisans were excused from all garrison routine, as well as from their own regimental guard and routine, and freed from all interference likely to interrupt them in the performance of their working duties. Still, to impress them with the recollection that their civil employments and privileges did not make them any the less soldiers, they were paraded, generally under arms, on Sundays; and to heighten the effect of their military appearance, wore accoutrements which had belonged to a disbanded Newfoundland regiment, purchased for them at the economical outlay of seven shillings a set. Perhaps no body of men subject to the articles of war were ever permitted to live and work under a milder surveillance; and it may be added, that none could have rendered service more in keeping with the indulgences bestowed.

In the summer of 1786 the company was divided into two, the chief engineer still continuing in command of both companies. About the same time, those men who were disqualified in any way for service were removed from the corps, and the enlistment of *labourers*, in addition to skilled hands, was authorized by the Government. Five batches of recruits were sent to the Rock in rapid succession. The second party of recruits, comprising fifty-eight men, twenty-eight women, and twelve children, were destroyed in a storm off Dunkirk. Only three persons escaped.

The valuable services rendered by the corps, and the hearty good-will with which they invariably laboured, led to a still further extension of their privileges. They were allowed to pass in and out of garrison on Sundays and holidays without a written pass, and to wear at pleasure whatever dress suited their inclination. It was not uncommon, therefore, for the non-commissioned officers and the respectable portion of the privates to stroll about garrison or ramble into Spain, dressed in black silk and satin breeches, white silk stockings, and silver knee or shoe buckles, drab beaver hats and scarlet jackets, tastefully trimmed with white kerseymere.

In 1787 the king's authority was granted "for establishing a corps of Royal Military Artificers." It was to consist of six companies, of a hundred men each. Officers of the Royal Engineers were appointed to command the corps; and when required to parade with other regiments the corps was directed to take post next on the left of the Royal Artillery. The companies were ordered to serve at Woolwich, Chatham, Portsmouth, Gosport, Plymouth, and one company was divided between Jersey and Guernsey. The companies at Gibraltar, although similarly constituted, remained a distinct and separate body until their incorporation with the corps in 1797. The recruiting was carried on by the captains of companies; there was no standard as to height fixed, but labourers were not enlisted over twenty-five years of age nor any artificer over thirty, unless he had been employed in the Ordnance Department and was known to be an expert workman of good character. The bounty given at first to each recruit was five guineas, but during time of peace it was reduced to three. Labourers promoted to the rank of artificers received a bonus of two guineas, an additional *3d.* a day, and were privileged to wear a gold-laced hat.

By the operative classes some opposition was offered to the enrolment of the Royal Artificers, and on more than one occasion a serious outbreak took place between the civilians and the military;

the jealousy, however, at last died out, and the old animosity was forgotten.

In 1791, a vessel bearing several recruits to Gibraltar encountered a terrific storm in the Bay of Biscay. The wreck and its circumstances gave rise to a song called "The Bay of Biscay O!"

The declaration of war with France, 1793, put an end to the comfortable and easy life which the Royal Artificers had been leading. They were, as soldiers, liable to be sent to any part of the world where the British Government might require their services. The idea of this liability ever being insisted upon seems to have been foreign to the minds of the corps. When it was known that their services would be required in the Low Countries and in the West Indies, many of them eluded service by providing substitutes, and some resorted to the very dishonourable alternative of desertion. Of the finest company sent out to the West Indies, not a man escaped the ravages of "yellow Jack." Those who served in Holland distinguished themselves by their bravery, especially at the famous siege of Valenciennes. The continuance of the war rendering it essential that the artizan companies should be kept in foreign stations, while the necessity for increased vigilance at home was each day becoming more urgent, led to the extension of the corps, and four new companies were enrolled—two to serve in Flanders, one in the West Indies, and one in Upper Canada.

The special company destined for service in the West Indies sailed from Spithead, November, 1793, and arrived at Barbadoes early in the following year. From thence they proceeded to Martinique, where their spirited conduct in the field commanded the admiration of the whole army. The companies which were sent both to Toulon and Flanders behaved also with much gallantry, proving that the Royal Artificers were not only skilled workmen but efficient soldiers.

In June, 1797, the Soldier Artificers Corps at Gibraltar were incorporated with the Royal Military Artificers; by this incorporation the latter corps were increased from 801 to 1075, of all ranks; but its numerical strength only reached 759 men. Detachments of the corps served with credit under Sir Ralph Abercrombie at Trinidad, and also in the unsuccessful attack on Porto Rico.

Among the measures suggested for reducing Porto Rico was one for taking the town by forcing the troops through the lagoon bounding the east side of the island. In order to ascertain whether the lagoon was fordable, David Sinclair, one of the Military Artificers, picked his way across at dead of night, reached the opposite shore in safety, and picked his way back again to report. He was rewarded for this daring act, but the fording of the lagoon presented so many difficulties as to be given up.

The memorable mutiny of the Fleet at Spithead was followed by the rising of some unprincipled men, who by every means endeavoured to shake the allegiance of the soldiery. The Plymouth Company of Artificers in an especial manner distinguished itself by its open and soldier-like activity against these disloyal exertions; in a printed document, bearing date May, 1797, they avowed at that momentous crisis their "firm loyalty, attachment, and fidelity to their most Gracious *Sovereign* and to their *Country*." The declaration was well timed, and had the desired effect.

Throughout the war in the Low Countries the Corps of Artificers rendered eminent service. One of their most important achievements was that of the total destruction of the Bruges canal.

About the same time a company of Artificers was sent to Turkey to operate with the troops of the Sultan against Napoleon, in Egypt. There also they distinguished themselves alike by their active service and good conduct. A Turk having attempted to stab one of the men, was sentenced by the Turkish governor to death; this punishment, at the earnest entreaty of the commanding officer, was mitigated, the culprit being sentenced to receive fifty strokes of the bastinado, to be imprisoned twenty years, and to *learn the Arabic language.*

In the West Indies the Artificers were exposed to worse than human foe. There the yellow fever decimated their ranks, but the conduct of the men throughout was both intrepid and humane, and in the despatches reference is frequently made to their exemplary conduct. When the mortality was at its height, three privates voluntarily devoted themselves to the burial of the dead, and worked on with unflinching ardour; surrounded by the pest in its worst form, inhaling the worst effluvia, never for a moment forsaking their frightful service, they laboured on inspiriting those about them by their example, until the necessity for their exertions no longer existed.

In 1806 a company of Military Artificers was established at Malta, and remained a distinct and separate body.

The necessity for an efficient body of trained artizan soldiers became, indeed, every day more obvious; and no expedition of any consequence was undertaken without a body of these men being included in the forces sent out. In America, in the Indies, East and West, on Mediterranean service, in the Peninsula, in the Low Countries, they were alike needed, and rendered excellent service. At home, also, they were continually employed in erecting new and strengthening the old fortifications, for it was anticipated that Bonaparte would visit our shores, and that stone walls as well as wooden walls would be required for our defence.

Throughout the Peninsular war the services of the corps were invaluable; in sap, battery, and trench work, in the making of fascines and gabions, in repairing broken batteries and damaged embrasures, in constructing flying bridges over the Guadiana, the Artificer vied with the regular engineers. Major Pasley, R.E., on his appointment to the Plymouth station, began regularly to practise his men in sapping and mining. He was one of those officers who took pains to improve the military appearance and efficiency of his men, and to make them useful, either for home or foreign employments. He is believed to have been the first officer who represented the advantage of training the corps in the construction of military field-work. After the failure at Badajoz (1811) the necessity of this measure was strongly advocated by the war officers. Then it was recommended to form a corps under the title of Royal Sappers and Miners, to be composed of six companies, chosen from the Royal Military Artificers, which, after receiving some instruction in the art, was to be sent to the Peninsula to aid the troops in their future siege operations.

In April, 1812, a warrant was issued for the formation of an establishment for instructing the corps in military field-work. Chatham was selected as the most suitable place for carrying out the royal orders, and Major Pasley was appointed director of the establishment. Uniting great zeal and unwearied perseverance with good talents and judgment, Major Pasley succeeded in extending the course of instructions far beyond the limits orginally assigned, and he not only filled the ranks of the corps with good scholars, good surveyors, and good draughtsmen, but enabled many, after quitting this service, to occupy, with ability and credit, situations of considerable importance in civil life.

At Ciudad Rodrigo and Badajoz, and other places made famous in the Peninsular war, the Military Artificers won the praise of Wellington, conducting themselves with the greatest gallantry and coolness.

On the 5th of March, 1813, the title of the corps was changed from that of Royal Military Artificers to that of Royal Sappers and Miners. A change of equipment was also introduced. In this respect many irregularities had crept in, the members of the corps in various parts of the world being variously armed, rather to suit their own fancy than to meet the exigencies of the work. Uniformity in the matter was of great importance, and this was gradually and effectually introduced.

When Napoleon, escaping from captivity in Elba, re-appeared in France, and the armies of the allies were again summoned to the field, at the instance of the Duke of Wellington the whole corps of Sappers and Miners was sent to Brussels to join his Grace's force, and were employed in constructing indispensable field-works, or improving the fortifications at Ostend, Ghent, Tournay, Oudenarde, Boom, Antwerp, Lille, Liepkenshock, and Hae. At the battle of Waterloo the Royal Sappers and Miners were not engaged, but three companies were brought conveniently near, to act in the event of their services being needed. After the battle, all the companies of the corps moved with the army towards Paris, and rendered valuable service in the construction of pontoon bridges. After the capitulation the men were encamped in the vicinity of Paris, until they could be removed to other stations or sent home. Two companies remained with the army of occupation; and in the naval victory of Algiers three of the companies worked at the guns with the seamen of the fleet, and gained equal credit with the navy and marines for their noble support.

In the Canadas the Sappers and Miners rendered themselves very useful, especially in the formation of a new citadel at Quebec; their efficiency also in pontoon work was universally acknowledged; of all the soldiers in the army no men more deserved well of their country—useful as they were alike in time of war and peace. "Indeed," says Sir John Jones, "justice requires it to be said, that these men, whether employed on brilliant martial services or engaged in the more humble duties of their calling, either under the vertical sun of the tropics or in the frozen regions of the north, invariably conducted themselves as good soldiers; and by their bravery, their industry, or their acquirements, amply repay the trouble and expense of their formation and instruction." In taking a bird's-eye view of the formation and growth of some of our military institutions, the Rev. G. R. Gleig thus speaks of the corps: "Besides the infantry, cavalry, and artillery, of which the army was composed, and the Corps of Engineers, coeval with the latter there sprang up during the period of the French Revolution other descriptions of force which proved eminently useful, each in its own department, and of the composition of which a few words will suffice to give an account. First, the Artificers, as they were called, that is to say, the body of men trained to the exercises of mechanical arts, such as carpentry, bricklaying, bridge-making, and so forth, which in all ages seem to have attended on a British army in the field, became the Royal Sappers and Miners, whose services on many trying occasions proved eminently useful, and who still do their duty cheerfully and satisfactorily in every quarter of the globe. During the late war they were commanded, under the officers of engineers, by a body of officers who took no higher rank than that of lieutenant, and consisted entirely of good men, for whom their merits had earned commissions. Their education, carried on at Woolwich and Chatham, trained them to act in the field as guides and directors to all working parties, whether the business in hand might be the construction of a bridge, the throwing up of field works, or the conduct of a siege. Whatever the engineer officers required the troops to do was explained to a party of Sappers, who, taking each his separate charge, showed the soldiers of the Line both the sort of work that was required of them and the best and readiest method of performing it. The regiment of Sappers was the growth of the latter years of the contest, after the British army had fairly thrown itself into the great arena of Continental warfare, and proved so useful, that while men wondered how an army could ever have been accounted complete without this appendage, the idea of dispensing with it in any time to come, seems never to have arisen in the minds of the most economical."

In the erection of the Great Industrial Exhibition of 1851 the Sappers and Miners afforded very valuable assistance, and won for themselves a warm eulogium from the Prince Consort. In the formation of the Camp at Chobham they were also very useful, and they were especially complimented for their exertions by Colonel Vicars and Lord Seaton; but it was during the war with Russia that they again figured most prominently before the public.

On the outbreak with Russia a detachment of the Sappers and Miners was sent out with the Baltic fleet, and a second company was despatched to the Aland Islands. They played an important part in the destruction of the forts and the capture of Bomarsund. Other detachments were sent to Turkey, and did good service at Gallipoli, Boulair, and Ibridgi, winning the "entire approbation" of Sir George Brown. At Scutari, Varna, Derno, and Rustchuk they were still further distinguished. Before Sebastopol, when shot and shell swept furiously into the trenches, the conduct of the men was everything that could be desired. "The country," wrote Lord Raglan, "was covered with water; the trenches extremely muddy, their condition adding greatly to the labours of the men employed in the batteries, chiefly sailors, artillerymen, and sappers. *They conducted their duties admirably.*" Everywhere in posts of danger were the Sappers; here piling up hides and fixing gabions; there fixing platforms, renewing sleepers, and fastening bolts; here crawling on the earth, more like a gnome than a man, but busy with pick and shovel, under a shower of rifle bullets; there black with gunpowder, blasting the rock to widen the trench; there the bright hammer of the Sapper plies on the newly-reared parapet, and affords a mark for the enemy; here the horn lantern of the Sapper gives feeble light to the busy workman, but a sure target to the foe; everywhere, in battery, trench, and mine, the Sapper is the centre of each party, toiling at his hazardous avocation through the long dark night.

While the French amused their leisure with private theatricals, getting up an impromptu theatre, the English Sappers built a church—built it entirely of siege apparatus, the materials so arranged that they were only in store, ready for use at a moment's notice: scaling ladders, gabions, fascines, timbers ready cut and shaped for gun platforms, a few planks and pieces of rope. Two scaling ladders locked into each other at the top, formed at certain intervals the columns which separated the aisles from the body of the church and bore up the roof. The framework of the outer wall was made of long upright timbers which leant against the summits of each set of ladders respectively, and were secured by cords. Across these a few joist beams were lashed, and the outer wall of gabions in a great degree rested on these horizontal supports. The roof was made by the platform timbers laid between the tops of the ladders on each side, and at right angles to these, fascines were laid in regular rows until a complete covering—but one admitting of free ventilation—was formed. There solemn service was often held, and good words spoken by good and brave men—with the Union Jack for a pulpit cloth.

Through the freezing winter and the wasting summer, for 337 days the Sappers carried on their work before Sebastopol. The trenches they made were nine miles long; twenty-two batteries were on the right, and twenty batteries on the left; in the formation of the works there were no less than 20,000 gabions, 4000 fascines, 340,000 sand bags, 7113 bread bags, and a hundred different extemporaneous expedients to give shape and solidity to the works.

They witnessed the triumphant end of their work; and they received no small share of honour and reward, for the work they had done was unsurpassed in ancient or in modern history.

During the Indian mutiny the services of the Engineers were of great advantage, and the bravery and determination of the men both in defence and attack were worthy of the highest commendation. In India there are, we believe, still employed in the engineering arm of our service no less than twelve companies of native Sappers and Miners.

We are all justly proud of our army, proud of its station among the armies of Europe; its appearance, discipline, drill; proud of the history of its achievements

> ——"of most disastrous chances;
> Of moving accidents by flood and field;
> Of hair-breadth 'scapes i' th' imminent deadly breach;"—

but there is no division of our army of which we should be more justly proud than of the Sappers and Miners. It toils for us wherever our flag is unfurled to the winds; it explores unknown regions; surveys and maps new and old regions; it makes roads where no roads were, and iron roads in place of common roads; it blasts rocks; heaves up drowned treasures from the deep; it serves as the pioneer of civilization abroad, and extends and consolidates civilization at home; it labours as hard in peace as in war—labour often unseen and unsuspected, but none the less worthy of the respect, honour, and admiration due to the brave sons of a brave people.

The Engineer corps of officers now consists of about four hundred of all grades, partly employed in building and repairing our defences, while the rest are more immediately attached to the Sappers and Miners, a body of some three or four thousand men, which now forms a constituent part of the Royal Engineers; indeed, the Sappers and Miners are now to be regarded as the main body of this arm of our service.

CHAPTER IV.

THE ROYAL WELSH.

NGLAND possesses many regiments that have a traditional as well as an individual existence. The memory of deeds of valour wrought by their predecessors is transmitted from generation to generation, and inspires the young soldier with the desire of equalling, if not surpassing, the heroism of those who have gone before. His regiment is the warrior's family, and each man feels, as the inheritor of a noble fame ought to feel, that he must do nothing unworthy of the past renown gained in older days. Thus it happens that there are certain regiments which may always be counted on in the hour of danger, and one of these is the 23rd Royal Welsh Fusiliers. The Prince of Wales's plume, with the motto "*Ich Dien*," betokens their nationality; and their claim to the proud words, "*Nec aspera terrent*," which they bear on their colours, has been justified by their gallant conduct in Egypt, and at Corunna, Martinique, Albuera, Badajoz, Salamanca, Vittoria, the Pyrenees, Nivelle, Orthès, Toulouse, Waterloo, Alma, Inkermann, and Sebastopol. All these names are emblazoned on their colours, and the successors of the heroes of the Peninsula and Waterloo proved in the Crimea that the regiment had not fallen from its high estate of honourable glory.

It will be interesting to our readers to glance briefly at the different engagements in which the Welsh Fusiliers distinguished themselves about the beginning of this century. They formed part of the expedition which sailed for Egypt in 1801, under the command of Sir Ralph Abercrombie, for the purpose of expelling the French from that country. The authorities at home knew as little about Egypt and the French forces there as the members of Lord Aberdeen's cabinet did about the Crimea and the strength of the Russian army. Our men had no other guide than an old map, which proved to be very incorrect, and Sir Sidney Smith, a gallant sailor but an indifferent geographer, who knew nothing of the interior of the country. Moreover, it was supposed that the enemy amounted to only 15,000 men, whereas they really numbered 35,000 veteran troops. The idea of sending 12,000 men, chiefly young soldiers, to expel such a body of veterans from a country where they were strongly intrenched, may excite some surprise, but British soldiers may do anything when properly led. On the 8th of March our men landed with such regularity and order that every brigade, every regiment, and even every company, drew up on the exact spot they were intended to occupy. The sea was as smooth as glass, and the bullets of the enemy fell as thick as hail-stones around the boats, but the landing force advanced and fell into their places with as much coolness as if they had been dressing for a review. The Welsh Fusiliers and three other regiments, including the gallant 42nd, landed in boats on the right, and were exposed to showers of grape and shell from the enemy's batteries; but, nothing daunted, they quietly disembarked, formed in line, and, without even stopping to load, rushed up the hill to charge the enemy with the bayonet. Half way up they were met with a volley from the enemy, but, pushing on, they reached the summit before they could reload, rushed furiously upon them, and drove them from their position. The general was proud of this first success, and thanked his men for having displayed "an intrepidity scarcely to be paralleled." On the 13th of March he was about to attack the right flank of the enemy, who anticipated his design, and descended from the heights to meet him; after considerable loss our men had to retire to their former position, where they remained till the 20th. On the evening of this day Sir Sidney Smith (the heroic defender of Acre) received a letter from an Arab chief, apprising him of the enemy's intention to fall upon the English with all their forces the following morning, but unfortunately the commander-in-chief paid no attention to this warning. Next morning he discovered his mistake; the French commenced the action by a feigned attack on the British left, but concentrated their most vigorous efforts against the right, where the Welsh Fusiliers were stationed. Their superiority in numbers procured them a temporary success. Our right flank was turned, and the 28th Regiment, who were most exposed to their impetuous attack, could with difficulty retain their position, though supported by the 58th and the Welsh Fusiliers, when the 42nd advanced to their aid, and proved that France's Invincibles were unworthy of their name by wrenching

——"the banner from her bravest host,
Baptised Invincible in Austria's gore."

Notwithstanding their superiority in numbers, the French were repulsed at every point; the English remained masters of the field; and this was the first of a series of successes which led to the evacuation of Egypt and the overthrow of all Napoleon's hopes of Eastern conquest.

In 1809 we find the Welsh Fusiliers at Corunna, in Spain. It would be foreign to our purpose to relate the events which preceded that battle; suffice it to say, that Sir John Moore, after a series of brilliant encounters with the enemy, was obliged to retreat. The Spaniards afforded no assistance to the retreating army, which was reduced to the greatest privations; officers and men suffered alike from hunger and fatigue; it was not unusual for the soldiers to point to some young aristocrat marching at the head of his company without shoes or stockings, and to say, with grim humour, "There goes ten thousand a year." On this, as almost every occasion, the officers bore up better than the men, so great is the influence which the mind has over the body. On reaching Corunna, where they were about to embark for England, our men were attacked by the French. Sir John Moore was prepared to receive them; the sick, the cavalry, and part of the artillery were already embarked; the remaining part of his forces were drawn up to meet the attack of the enemy. The Welsh Fusiliers formed part of General Fraser's division, which was stationed in the rear at a short distance from Corunna. The enemy charged again and again, but our men not only kept their ground and remained unbroken, but actually forced them to retire at the point of the bayonet. The battle began at mid-day, and at five o'clock in the afternoon the enemy were foiled at every point, and our army occupied a more advanced position than at first. The loss of the British was 800 killed and wounded, including their gallant leader, who was struck to the ground by a cannon-ball, and died in the hour of victory. His death has been commemorated in lines familiar to all our readers, and it is satisfactory to know that Soult, instead of insulting his ashes, caused a monument to be erected to his memory. It is by such generous acts that nations prove their manhood amid the fierce passions evoked by war.

The Welsh Fusiliers also took part in the reduction of Martinique, one of the French West Indian islands, which was compelled to surrender after a gallant resistance. In those stirring times a regiment seldom remained long in one place, and in 1812 we find them in Spain, where they were present at the battle of Albuera and the siege of Badajoz, which was defended by the French with obstinate valour. Many of our men perished in the breaches, and every species of missile was hurled upon them as they attempted to scale the walls. "Never, probably, since the invention of gunpowder," says Colonel Jones, "were men more exposed to its action than those assembled to assault the breaches." For two hours, shells, hand-grenades, and bags of gunpowder were hurled upon our men as they crowded into the ditch; when they rushed up the breach their passage was arrested by ponderous beams bristling with sword-blades, and loose planks studded with sharp iron points, which tilted up the moment they were trodden on, and precipitated the assailants into the ditch below. Again and again our men rushed against the glittering sword-blades and were shot down by the enemy from the walls above; the rear pressed on, and tried to make a bridge of the writhing bodies of their slaughtered comrades. About midnight 2000 men had fallen, and Wellington was about to give orders to retire, when he received notice that Picton had taken the castle by escalade. "Then the place is ours," he exultingly exclaimed, and sent word to Picton to retain the castle at all hazards. The attack was continued, and next morning Philippon, the French general, surrendered to Lord Fitzroy Somerset, better known to this generation as Lord Raglan. We must draw the veil of sorrow over the fearful scenes which were enacted by an infuriated soldiery when the devoted city fell into their hands; for three days all discipline was at an end, and the tumult only subsided when the rioters were exhausted with their excesses. We cannot give the exact loss of the Welsh Fusiliers, but, in common with all the other British regiments engaged in this siege, they suffered severely.

The next memorable event in the Peninsular War was the battle of Salamanca, which was fought on the 22nd of July, 1812. On the 16th of June, Wellington overtook the French near the right bank of the Tormes, the enemy retreating across the river. For several days both armies remained encamped on the opposite banks without molesting one another, and the most friendly intercourse sprang up between them. They were in the habit of conversing together and exchanging provisions, as if they had been on the best of terms. When the warfare was resumed, the French officers said, on parting, "We have met and been for some time friends; we are about to separate and may meet as enemies; as friends we have received each other warmly; as enemies we shall do the same." Warm indeed was the reception which they gave to one another on the blood-stained field of Salamanca. At first the French had the advantage, but an unguarded movement on the part of Marmont, their general, having caught the eagle eye of Wellington, he joyfully exclaimed, "At last I have them," and gave orders for a general charge. The French, remembering their former promise, presented a bold front to their assailants, who, pouring a destructive volley into the opposing columns, rushed upon them with the bayonet. Such was the impetus of the English attack that the close phalanx bent before it, swayed backward and forward like a ship struck upon a heavy sea, then broke and scattered over the plain. The French were completely routed, with the loss of 14,000 men. The victors behaved with great humanity to the vanquished; many of the fugitives, pursued by the cavalry, fled to the British lines for protection, which was readily granted. The infantry covered their retreat, and protected them from the sabres of the horsemen; once within their lines, they were safe from injury and insult; not a single man was bayoneted, plundered, or molested. It is pleasing to record such instances of humanity; it shows that the exchange of hospitalities on the banks of the Tormes was not forgotten in the hour of battle. The Royal Welsh and the other British regiments engaged in this battle were permitted to inscribe Salamanca on their colours in memory of their victory.

The next year, on the 20th of June, the 23rd saw the Peninsular campaign brought to a close by the battle of Vittoria. The French were commanded by Jourdan, and the English by Wellington. Our troops were completely victorious, and the expulsion of the French from Spain was one of the fruits of their victory. The French fought resolutely till Picton gave the word to charge, when our men bore down all opposition before them, and spread death and consternation through the ranks of the enemy, who fled with such precipitancy that they left all their artillery and baggage behind. Joseph Bonaparte, placed by his brother Napoleon on the throne of Spain, was present at the battle; he only escaped by leaving his carriage and mounting a swift horse. The royal calash fell into the hands of the 10th Hussars, who found in it all the portable valuables of his regalia. The whole of his equipage and treasures fell into the hands of the British. The booty was enormous; it comprised all that could minister to the appetites or pleasures of a sensual monarch. The most delicate wines and the rarest luxuries fell into the hands of our soldiers, who exchanged many a joke at the expense of the luxurious monarch as they regaled themselves with them; poodles, parrots, and monkeys were among the captives of war. Grim old Peninsulars amused themselves after the battle in getting up a sort of masquerade, in which they appeared in the uniforms of French generals, or displayed the most recent inventions of the Parisian mode on their somewhat ungainly persons, and Wellington allowed them to indulge their grotesque humour. And when it was reported to him that some of them had seized the French military chest and were loading themselves with money, "Let them have it," he said; "they deserve it, though it were ten times more." Among the other spoil was the bâton of Marshal Jourdan, which Wellington sent with his despatches to the Prince Regent: soon after this he received the bâton of an English field-marshal along with a very handsome letter. "The British army," said the prince, "will hail it with enthusiasm, while the whole universe will acknowledge those valorous efforts which have so imperiously called for it." While this victory made Wellington a field-marshal, it procured for the Welsh Fusiliers the honour of adding Vittoria to the other glorious names inscribed on their colours.

The battle of Vittoria was attended with the most important results. The scattered remains of the French army were driven through the rugged passes of the Pyrenees, and the British army advanced rapidly in the direction of France. The enemy sometimes endeavoured to rally in their retreat, but were successfully driven from the positions they occupied by the impetuosity of the Welshmen and Highlanders, whose early training specially fitted them to excel in this mountain warfare. The constant success of the British army led many to expect that France would yield, and allow Wellington to cross the frontier without further resistance; but Napoleon, elated with his recent successes in Germany, appointed

Soult to the command of the army of the Pyrenees, and that able general displayed such vigour and skill that there was some danger at first of the British losing all the fruits of the great victory of the 20th of June. On the 25th of July, 15,000 French troops attacked the British, about 3000 in number, at the pass of Maya, and for ten hours our men maintained the conflict, notwithstanding their inferiority in numbers. When their ammunition was exhausted they hurled stones at their assailants, who were arrested by the mass of dead and dying by which the pass was blocked, and were at length repulsed by the aid of some reinforcements. The pass of Maya will long be remembered in the annals of the British army; our soldiers fought as bravely there as the Greeks did at Thermopylæ.

We must omit the other stirring events of the Pyrenees, in all ot which the Royal Welsh acted a distinguished part, and enjoyed many advantages over others unaccustomed to a mountainous country. They had many extraordinary adventures, being sometimes enveloped in the mists that shrouded the summits of the mountains, and brought into fierce collision with the enemy, who were ignorant of their approach. After the two battles of Lauroren, the tide of success turned against Soult, who was almost taken prisoner at St. Estenau. Such were the skilful arrangements of the English general here, that the French army would have had to surrender had not three marauding British soldiers crossed the ridge which concealed their comrades, and thus warned the enemy of their danger. On such small causes do great events hinge! The cupidity of three Englishmen saved the whole French army. On the 1st of August Soult abandoned the Spanish territory, with the loss of 15,000 men; and on the 7th of September Wellington planted the victorious standard of Britain on the soil of France. Seven thousand of the allies were buried among the mountain passes of the Pyrenees, and the different regiments engaged were allowed to preserve the remembrance of this campaign on their colours.

The Royal Welsh next appear at the battle of the Nivelle, where the French, after obstinate resistance, were driven back, and the allies, profiting by this success, crossed the river, and established themselves between it and the sea. A succession of heavy rains rendered all movements impracticable for a time, and Soult did all he could to strengthen his position. Frost having set in, Wellington moved his forces on the 14th of February, 1814, and, in the course of sixteen days, constructed a bridge across the Adour, passed five large and several small rivers, traversed eighty miles of ground, drove the enemy from their strongest positions, was successful in one great battle and two combats, took many prisoners, and forced Soult to evacuate Bayonne. We can only enumerate his successes, and refer our readers to the history of those times for minuter details. The great battle was fought at Orthès on the 27th of February. At first, victory seemed to declare in favour of the French, but the English general bided his time with imperturbable calmness till a movement of the enemy placed them in his power. Every point was carried; the French retired at first in an orderly manner, till their left wing was attacked, when they were thrown into confusion, and ran off at full speed. The English pursued them for three miles till they reached Sault de Navailles, where scarcely any remains of Soult's army were to be seen. The loss of the enemy was estimated at 8000 men in killed, wounded, and prisoners, while that of the allies did not exceed 1600. Here, as usual, the Welsh Fusiliers were foremost in the fray, and their bravery was rewarded by the addition of Nivelle and Orthès to the other historic names on their colours.

Then followed the bloody and needless battle of Toulouse. We need not here stop to inquire who was the cause of that fearful carnage, or to refute the foolish assertion that the French gained a victory. Such a statement is inconsistent with the fact that Soult had to abandon Toulouse and all his lines of defence, while Wellington attained the object he had in view. It is said that Soult knew before the battle that Napoleon had abdicated, and that his only motive for fighting was a desire to retrieve his fame as a general; but we think no brave man—and Soult was brave—would sacrifice the lives of thousands for so unworthy a motive. After a furious contest the enemy were driven from the heights; again and again they returned to the attack with a gallantry which nothing but British valour could resist. At length they desisted from the attempt, and the field of battle remained in possession of the allies. That same evening Soult evacuated the city, and the following morning the allies took possession of it. In the course of the day they received official notice that Napoleon had abdicated. Then our soldiers began to think of home and all its endearments; they had done enough for fame, and a grateful country was waiting to welcome them to their native shores. The soft peace march, "Home, brothers, home," must have sounded sweetly in the ears of the Royal Welsh and the other veterans, who, under the command of their able leader, had liberated two kingdoms, fought eight pitched battles against the bravest soldiers and most skilful generals of France, reduced many fortresses by assault, and at length established themselves in the two principal cities in the South of France. Britain had issued from all her trials the most triumphant nation in the world, and had welcomed back with acclamation the wearied soldiers who had done so much to sustain her honour. Such men had a right to rest on their laurels. Their rest was brief. The caged eagle escaped from Elba. The veterans of the Peninsula had to buckle on their armour again. The Royal Welsh took part in that brief but glorious campaign which was brought to a close at Waterloo. Then for a period of forty years they had no opportunity of displaying their courage. Now followed the Crimean war, and deeds equalling "Greek and Roman fame," which earned for some of them the proud distinction of the Victoria Cross.

The gallant Welshmen gained their first Victoria Cross at the battle of the Alma. Russell's picturesque letters and Kinglake's bewitching pages have rendered many readers familiar with the chief incidents of that engagement; and it is here unnecessary for us to dwell upon them, for in future pages we shall relate the circumstances under which Colonel (then Captain) Bell gained at that first Crimean fight the honourable distinction of the reward "For Valour."

But the roll of brave men in the Royal Welsh is not exhausted by the mention of a single name. We are about to narrate the incident which forms the subject of the accompanying engraving, copied with no mean fidelity from that admirable collection of Mr. Desanges lately, in the Crystal Palace, known as the Victoria Cross Gallery. The incident here depicted occurred at the storming of the Redan on the 8th of September, 1855. Two hundred men of the Royal Welsh took part in that attack, and their loss in killed and wounded was very great. After the men of the 23rd had retired, it was found that Lieutenant and Adjutant Dyneley, an excellent young officer and a general favourite, was missing. It was reported that he had been struck down in the heat of the engagement, and some of the men described the spot where they had seen him fall. They would gladly have assisted him if they could have done so, but soldiers, while engaged, are expressly forbidden to leave their ranks for the purpose of carrying the wounded off the field.

The Highlanders, when first raised, were constantly in the habit of doing this; they could not stand by and see the sons of their chiefs dying on the field of battle without attempting to assist them. No man knew their character or habits better than the late Lord Clyde, and it was in allusion to this practice that he spoke these simple words while his men were still in column at the Alma with the enemy in front:—"Now, men, you are going into action. Remember this: whoever is wounded—I don't care what his rank is—whoever is wounded must lie where he falls till the bandsmen come to attend to him. No soldiers must go carrying off wounded men. If any soldier does such a thing, his name shall be stuck up in his parish church."* The perfection of discipline is to make every unit in a regiment or an army act in unison with the whole like a piece of machinery, and it is evident that if every soldier were to follow out his own will the result would be inextricable confusion. It is hard for a man to see officer or comrade struck down by his side on the field of battle without being allowed to

* When the Highland regiments were first formed, it was customary to stick up the name of any man who had misconducted himself in his parish church, and this was deemed the severest of all punishments. This has now become an obsolete custom.

Corporal Robert Shields, 23rd Regiment (Royal Welsh Fusiliers), finding the Body of his wounded Adjutant, Lieut. Dyneley.

assist him; but on such an occasion he has no choice—the pleadings of humanity must yield to the voice of duty; he may turn aside his head in sorrow, but he must still advance. It was so with the Royal Welsh as they advanced against the Redan; they saw their gallant young adjutant fall, but there was the dark parapet in front, and their first duty was to gain that. And when our men were hurled from the ramparts into the ditch, where they were slaughtered without being able to offer any resistance, it was only natural that all their thoughts should be concentrated on themselves, and that the fate of young Dyneley should be forgotten. But it was different when the attack was over: there was a general feeling of regret for one whom all had loved. While they were lamenting his fate, it occurred to some of the officers that he might not yet be dead, and, while they were deliberating what should be done, Corporal Robert Shields volunteered to go out to the front from the fifth parallel and bring the body in. It was a daring act of courage, all the more deserving of admiration that it was dictated solely by a feeling of humanity without any expectation of reward. The difference of rank does not always prevent friendships from springing up between officers and men, and young Dyneley had found the way to the hearts of all who knew him. Corporal Shields was not blind to the danger he incurred; he knew that he carried his life, as it were, in his hand, but he was prepared to risk everything to save his officer. In the Homeric age it would have been said that some invisible goddess watched over him and turned aside every hostile blow. He groped his way over the field, covered with the slain, till he reached the spot where poor Dyneley lay. Our engraving represents the discovery of the body. The poor lieutenant is lying on his back, still alive, but with the tide of life ebbing fast away; the corporal, with sorrow and sympathy depicted in every feature of his manly, bearded face, is bending over him, with one hand outstretched and the other grasping his rifle. He would willingly have raised the boyish figure in his arms and borne him back to his comrades, but it was too late; all that he could do was to hurry back in search of medical assistance. He passed through a heavy fire of musketry unhurt, and reached the trenches, where he found

Dr. Sylvester, the assistant-surgeon of the regiment, who at once consented to return to the spot where Dyneley lay. He was still alive, but human skill could avail him nothing; all that the tenderest friendship could do was done by Sylvester, who dressed his wounds and supported him with stimulants. Shields returned to the trenches and persuaded some of his comrades to accompany him and to assist in carrying off the body of the dying adjutant. The Emperor of the French, on hearing of this heroic action, conferred on Corporal Shields the Cross of the Legion of Honour, and our Queen bestowed on him the Cross which bears her own name. No one will grudge it to him or to Dr. Sylvester. Mere bravery may often border on bloodthirstiness; but valour combined with humanity is the most godlike of all virtues. Such a man as Corporal Shields is an honour to the British army, and he deserves to receive honourable mention amongst the most fearless of England's soldiery.

An officer who is just, kind, and considerate will never find his men ungrateful. Instances are on record where soldiers have laid down their own lives to save those of officers they loved, and have thus sealed their affection with their blood. On one occasion, when Lord Cornwallis was giving orders to charge the French in Canada, a Highland soldier rushed forward and placed himself in front of his officer, who asked him what he meant. "You know," said the Highlander, "that when I enlisted to be a soldier, I promised to be faithful to the king and to you. The French are coming, and while I stand here neither bullet nor bayonet shall touch you, except through my body." It was with difficulty that he could be persuaded to resume his place in the ranks. An equally striking proof of faithful attachment was exhibited at the siege of Bergen-op-Zoom by the servant of an officer of the name of Fraser. The latter had directed his servant to remain in the garrison while he conducted his men to attack a battery belonging to the enemy. The night was pitch dark, and the party had such difficulty in proceeding that they were obliged to halt for a time. As they moved forward, Captain Fraser felt his path impeded, and putting down his hand, seized hold of a plaid, the wearer of which was grovelling at his feet. Imagining that it was one of his own men trying to escape, he drew his dirk and tightened his grasp, when he heard the voice of his servant imploring for mercy. "Why, what brought you here?" "It was just my love for you," said poor Donald. "But why encumber yourself with a plaid?" "Alas! how could I ever show my face to my mother," she was Fraser's foster-mother, "had you been killed or wounded, and I not there to carry you to the surgeon or to Christian burial? And how could I do either without a plaid to wrap you in?"

Our soldiers have not degenerated, and there are still in the ranks of the British army men who want only an opportunity to show the same courage which has already entitled their comrades to wear Victoria's Cross.

CHAPTER V.

OUR HIGHLAND REGIMENTS.

BOUT a century ago the Highlanders were regarded as little better than a race of savages. Their dress, their language, and their manners were the subject of ridicule among their Southern neighbours, and their well-known attachment to the house of Stuart excited the suspicion and the distrust of the government of the day. "When the English thought of the Highlander at all," says Macaulay—"and it was seldom that they did so—they considered him as a filthy, abject savage, a slave, a papist, a cut-throat, and a thief." The great historian then proceeds to show that this estimate bordered very closely on the truth, and that the Highlanders were little better than they were represented to be. He seems to feel a cruel pleasure in exposing the weaknesses of those whose blood flowed in his own veins, and he, doubtless, meant to display in his picture of Highland manners a proof of his own impartiality. He gives implicit credence to all that he finds in "Burt's Letters," without reflecting that the author, from his very position, must have felt and written like a partisan. Burt was an officer of Engineers employed under General Wade in constructing those roads which opened up the Highlands to the advance of the English forces. He remained in the North from 1726 to 1737, and amused his friends in the South with those letters, in which he professed to describe the manners of the alien race among whom he was placed. There is no reason to believe that he was wilfully untruthful, but the work in which he was engaged rendered him hateful to the Highlanders, and he hated them cordially in return. He was probably unconscious of this feeling himself, but it is perceptible in almost every line he wrote. Johnson carried with him to the Highlands all the prejudices of his countrymen, and a good many others peculiar to himself; but his rugged nature was softened by the hospitality he everywhere met with, and he occasionally gives forth a grunt of approval. The reaction produced by the publication of his "Tour to the Hebrides" was increased by the appearance of the poems and novels of Scott, which created a sort of *furore* in favour of everything Highland, and rendered the land of the mountain and the flood almost classical. Royalty itself condescended to listen to the songs which it would once have been treason to sing aloud; the garb of old Gaul was assumed by many who had no right to wear it; the tartan became a favourite article of dress with both sexes; every nook and corner of the North was explored; the land of Ossian became the land of romance, and its inhabitants were invested with every possible virtue.

The gallant deeds of the Highland regiments in every quarter of the globe added to the general enthusiasm for Caledonians. It was long, indeed, before the English government would believe that they could be trusted. To have armed the Highlanders about the beginning of the last century, would have been deemed as much an act of insanity as to arm at the present hour the New Zealand Maoris. Scottish men were known to be under the control of their chiefs, and their chiefs, almost to a man, were devoted to the Pretender. No wonder, then, that the government hesitated before accepting their services; it was not till 1730—only one hundred and thirty years ago—that the first experiment was made. Six companies of Highlanders were then raised, each company being independent of the other. They were known as the *Il Reicudan Dhu*, or Black Watch, to distinguish them from the *Seideran Dearag*, or Red Soldiers. They derived their names from the colour of their clothes; the regular soldiers wore scarlet, as they do now, while the Highland companies retained their sombre tartan. There was no lack of men: gentlemen of good family were proud to serve as privates under their native officers; for the whole country had been disarmed, and this indignity was deeply felt by a race who, even in times of peace, never went forth without dirk or claymore. The cadets of good families were proud to serve, if only in the ranks, because they were thus entitled to bear arms; and to carry a weapon was regarded as a proof that the bearer was a gentleman. The pay privates received was small to a degree, yet poverty was so universal that the pittance they took from government was not to be despised. They were stationed in small parties over the country, and seem to have discharged the same duties as are intrusted to the rural police at the present day. In 1739 four additional companies were raised, and the whole were formed into a regiment of the line. Such was the origin of the first Highland regiment in the service—the gallant 42nd, still known as the Black Watch.

It would be foreign to our purpose to trace the origin and history of all the Highland regiments. That task has already been ably performed by General Stewart, of Garth, who served for many years in the 78th Highlanders, and was appointed governor of the island of Tobago, in the West Indies, where he died. It is somewhat singular that Macaulay appears to have been ignorant of this work, which contains far more valuable information regarding the Highlands than is to be found in "Burt's Letters." General Stewart's book is now almost forgotten; it is rarely to be met with, save in the libraries of country gentlemen in the North, whose forefathers figure in its pages. But it deserves a better fate. No writer has ever possessed a keener insight into the manners and customs of the warlike race whom he was proud to hail as his countrymen, or has described them in peace and in war with a more graphic pen. By birth a Highlander, by profession a soldier, he mingled freely with his clansmen, spoke their language, and had ample opportunities of witnessing their courage in every quarter of the globe. His "Military Annals" read like a romance; they have all the charm of novelty, because they present us with a picture of manners and feelings that have now died out.

"The simple system of primeval life—
Simple but stately—hath been broken down;
The clans are scattered, and the chieftain power
Is dead."

It may be said with equal truth that our Highland regiments are dead; they live only in name. We have regiments composed chiefly of Scotchmen, but there are few Highland soldiers of pure Celtic origin. The Highlands must have been far more populous than they now are, or they never could have raised eighty-six regiments, including local corps, in the course of the four wars in which this country was engaged after 1740. Most of these regiments were formed between 1778 and 1809, and altogether they must have included in their ranks, from first to last, as many as 70,000 or 80,000 men. Some of them were raised before the American rebellion, and Lord Chatham takes credit to himself for having been the first to recognise their invaluable qualities in war:—"I sought for merit wherever it was to be found. It is my boast that I was the first minister who looked for it and found it in the mountains of the North. I called it forth, and drew into your service a hardy and intrepid race of men, who, when left by your jealousy, became a prey to the artifice of your enemies, and had gone nigh to have overturned the state in the war before the last. These men in the last war were brought to combat on your side; they served with fidelity, and they fought with valour, and conquered for you in every part of the world."

There is no exaggeration in this, and the minister is entitled to all the credit he claims. He knew that a race so warlike and restless would prove a source of constant danger, unless those qualities were turned to some profitable account, and it was a wise and liberal policy to employ them in defence of that throne which they had recently almost overturned. The old feeling of clanship was retained; the chiefs and their kinsmen received commissions, and their clansmen were proud to rally around them. Every gentleman of good birth who could raise a hundred men was appointed captain; those who could bring only twenty or thirty ranked as subalterns. Sometimes a little pressure was used by the chiefs, but generally the men were ready to serve. The regiments thus raised were composed almost exclusively of Highlanders. Gaelic was spoken alike by officers and men, and chaplains familiar with the mountain tongue were appointed to every regiment. Gentlemen who could not obtain commissions at once were content to serve in the ranks till vacancies occurred. Two men of gentle birth, privates in the Black Watch, were presented to George II. in 1743. "They performed," says the *Westminster Journal*, "the broadsword exercise, and that of the Lochaber axe or lance, before his Majesty, the Duke of Cumberland, Marshal Wade, and a number of general officers assembled for the purpose in the great gallery of St. James's. They displayed so much dexterity and skill in the management of their weapons as to give perfect satisfaction to his Majesty. Each got a gratuity of one guinea, which they gave to the porter at the palace gate as they went out," and this, not that they were dissatisfied with the gift, or that their purses were over-well plenished, but they could not have accepted money without forfeiting their own respect and their position as gentlemen.

Now it did sometimes happen that men not of the Highland race were smuggled into these Highland regiments. For example, two gentlemen, anxious to obtain commissions in the Black Watch, and unable to find the requisite number of men among their own countrymen, enlisted eighteen Irishmen at Glasgow. Some of them were O'Donnels, O'Lachlans, and O'Briens, and as such would have been at once rejected by Lord John Murray, the colonel, who would accept none but Highland recruits. The two ingenious gentlemen got over the difficulty by changing Patrick O'Donnel, O'Lachlan, and O'Brien into Donald Macdonnel, Maclachlan, and Macbriar, under which names they were enrolled in the regiment without any suspicion of their nationality. The Lowland Scotch seldom thought of entering these regiments. When the battle of Fontenoy was fought, there was not a soldier in the Black Watch born south of the Grampians, and only two of the Milesian Highlanders were alive. So high was the reputation of the regiment that it could always obtain more Highland recruits than were required. The bounty was a guinea and a crown; but not gold attracted the young mountaineers: they were led to enlist by the thirst of glory and the honour of belonging to a regiment which had already covered itselt with fame on many a hard-fought field. So late as 1776, when the Black Watch embarked for service in America, it still retained its strictly national character: all the officers but two were Highlanders, while among the privates we find 931 Highlanders, 74 Lowland Scotch, 5 Englishmen (in the band), 1 Welshman, and 2 Irishmen. This distinctive formation held till 1779, when an attempt was made to destroy the exclusively Highland character of the regiment by drafting into it a body of 150 recruits, the sweepings of the gaols of London and Dublin. The 42nd had hitherto borne a high reputation; the conduct of the men had been exemplary; corporal punishment almost unknown. The commanding officer remonstrated against the admission of these recruits, of whom 16 died during the voyage to America, and 75 others found their way to hospital on landing. The government yielded to his remonstrances: the recruits were drafted into the 26th Regiment in exchange for the same number of Scotchmen. The introduction of the representatives of Richard Cameron into the Black Watch was attended with the worst consequences: flogging and like punishments became more frequent; and the men, accustomed to these degrading spectacles, lost that fine sense of honour which had hitherto distinguished them.

When, in 1793, the 78th Regiment was raised, we find that the strength of the corps was 1113 men, of whom 970 were Highlanders, 129 Lowland Scotch, and 14 English and Irish. Several of the officers belonged to Lowland families, and brought a certain number of their retainers with them: the Englishmen probably belonged to the band, as in the case of the 42nd. In 1805 the proportion of men in the regiment, which was now stationed in India, was pretty much the same: it contained 835 Highlanders, 184 Lowlanders, 8 English, and 9 Irish. The Highlanders must have been taller then than they are now. After the tallest men were selected for the Grenadier company, there still remained a hundred considerably above the standard of height in light infantry regiments.

The Celtic element predominated equally in the 93rd, or Sutherland Highlanders, which was raised in 1800, and consisted of 631 Highlanders, 460 of whom belonged to the county of Sutherland. Eleven years later the numerical strength of the regiment was 1049: with the exception of 17 Irish and 18 English, all of these men belonged to Scotland.

The 92nd, or Gordon Highlanders, was raised in 1794 by the last Duke of Gordon, then Marquis of Huntly, and by his mother, the beautiful and witty Duchess Jane. The duchess used to frequent the country fairs, and when she saw a likely youth she would try every persuasion to induce him to enlist. When all other arguments failed, she would place a guinea between her lips, and no young Highlander, however pacific, could refuse the bounty thus proffered. One kiss of that beautiful mouth was worth dying for.

Three-fourths of Duchess Jane's regiment were Highlanders; all the rest were Lowlanders, except 35 Irishmen, whom one of the officers was obliged to accept, *faute de mieux*, to make up his complement. In 1825 the numbers were 716 Scots, 51 English, and 111 Irish; in 1857, 1043 Scots, 7 English, and 40 Irish.

The only other regiment which retains the garb of old Gaul is the 79th, or Cameron Highlanders, raised in 1793 by Allan Cameron, of Errach, in the northern counties. About four-fifths of the men were Highlanders; the rest were English or Irish. In 1857 the regiment consisted of 895 Scots, 37 English, and 39 Irish.

The 71st, 72nd, and the 74th are also ranked as Highland regiments, and recruit chiefly in the North; but for many years they have substituted the trews for the kilt, and are composed chiefly of Lowland Scotch. The same may be said of the regiments that retain the kilt; most of the men are Lowland Scotch, natives chiefly of the large manufacturing towns. The Highlands at present scarcely supply sufficient recruits to keep up the strength of two regiments; whereas we find that during the first forty years of this century the Isle of Skye, only 45 miles long and 15 broad, gave us 21 lieutenant and major-generals, 45 lieutenant-colonels, 600 majors, captains, and subalterns, 10,000 privates, and 120 pipers. The recruiting parties stationed in that island meet now with indifferent success; but it is the same everywhere in the Highlands.

Many of the men in these old Highland regiments bore the same

Bounty offered to the Highlanders by Jane, Duchess of Gordon.

name. We find, for example, in one regiment of 800 men no less than 700 who have the word Mac prefixed to their names. In another we find no less than nine John Roses; and as for Donald Macdonalds, their name was legion. The drill-sergeant showed his ingenuity in distinguishing the bearers of the same cognomen by jocular allusions to their personal appearance, which must occasionally have been not altogether gratifying to the nick-named. In the same company there would be Donald Macdonald with the red hair, Donald with the big feet, Donald with the long legs, Donald of Skye, Donald of Harris, and so forth. When all other means of distinguishing his recruits failed him, the drill-sergeant had recourse to figures, and ranked them as Donald Macdonald No. 1, No. 2, No. 3. No wonder he occasionally got confused amongst so many Donalds, and lost his temper.

About the close of the last century the citizens of Edinburgh found much amusement in listening to the calling of the muster-rolls of one of the newly-raised Highland regiments stationed there, and studying the ingenuity of the sergeants in distinguishing the countless Macs and Donalds in their different companies. The ludicrous effect of such scenes was enhanced by the guttural accent and imperfect English of the speakers, who, if we may judge by the following specimen, seem occasionally to have had peculiar ideas of military duty:—

"Tonald Mactonald No. 5," cried the sergeant, going over the muster-roll of his company.

"Here!" cried a voice so shrill and abrupt that it excited a general titter in the ranks, and the unbounded indignation of the sergeant.

"Here, ye tamm'd rogue! Is that the way she speaks to a shentleman? But we a' ken Tonald's a liar, sae pit her down absent, and tak' her to the guard-room."

"Tonald Mactonald No. 6," continued the sergeant.

There was no answer. The sergeant broke forth into a sort of soliloquy—

"Tonald Mactonald No. 6; that's my sister's son frae Achallatus. Ay, ay, Tonald; she was aye a modest lad, that never spak' till she was spoken to, so we'll put her down present."

And thus the sergeant went over the whole roll, accompanying each name with some remark which showed the estimation in which he held the bearer.

The soldiers of all these regiments wore the scarlet jacket and waistcoat, with a tartan plaid, the lower part of which was wrapped round the body, and the upper thrown loosely over the left shoulder. The plaid served a double purpose: it guarded the soldier's shoulders and firelock from rain by day, and was used as a blanket by night. It was attached to his middle by a belt, from which his pistol and dirk, or small dagger, were suspended. On his head was worn the blue bonnet with a border of tartan as at the present day, and a small tuft of feathers or a piece of bearskin; the kilt was of different colours to distinguish the regiments. The arms were supplied by government, and consisted of a musket, a bayonet, and a large basket-hilted broadsword. In 1769 some alteration was made in the dress of the 42nd; the men were provided with white cloth waistcoats, and goatskin and buff leather purses; the officers began to wear light hangers instead of the heavy broadsword, which was used only in full dress; and the sergeants were provided with carbines, and laid aside the ponderous Lochaber axes they had hitherto carried. In 1776 the broadswords and pistols were laid aside. The regiment was then serving in America, and it was objected that the broadswords impeded their movements by getting entangled in the brushwood. An attempt was subsequently made to induce them to dispense with the kilt, and to adopt the garb of the Saxon. It was objected to it then, as now, that it was too hot in summer and too cold in winter; but the Highlanders stood out stoutly against the proposed innovation, and the notion of changing the kilt was abandoned. "We were allowed," writes a veteran son of the Gael, "to wear the garb of our fathers, and, in the course of six winters, showed the doctors that they did not understand our constitution; for in the coldest winters our men were more healthy than those regiments who wore breeches and warm clothing." But now that the kilt is no longer worn in the Highlands, and few Highlanders enlist in the kilted regiments, it seems an anomaly to retain an article of dress which, we venture to say, was never worn by

nineteen-twentieths of our present soldiers till they entered the army. A large proportion of the officers are English, and it is rather hard that they should have to adopt a dress which must strike them at first as barbarous, if not indecent. It is singular, however, that Englishmen serving in Highland regiments are usually as fond of the kilt as the Highlanders themselves, and would be quite as ready to protest against the adoption of a less peculiar costume.

As to the Highlander's mode of fighting, it was the simplest thing in the world. He discharged his musket, threw it aside, drew his bonnet over his brow, and rushed upon the foe, leaving all the rest to God and his own good broadsword. It was so that he conquered at Prestonpans and elsewhere, but it would be difficult to assert that his undisciplined valour rendered him superior to troops thoroughly drilled, or that the broadsword is more formidable than the bayonet. General Stewart, nevertheless, is of a different opinion:—"From the battle of Culloden, where a body of undisciplined Highlanders, shepherds and herdsmen, with their broadswords cut their way through some of the best disciplined and most approved regiments in the British army (drawn up, too, on a field extremely favourable for regular troops), down to the time when the swords were taken from the Highlanders, the bayonet was in every instance overcome by the sword."

In one of the skirmishes with the French in Egypt, a young sergeant of the 78th killed six of the enemy with the broadsword; the weapon was the same as that still used by sergeants in Highland regiments. The half-dozen Frenchmen were not cut down while retreating, but in fighting with the bayonet, hand to hand, against the broadsword. The gallant sergeant met his death-blow from a sabre-stroke from behind as he was returning to his company, after cutting down the last of his six foes. Many other proofs of the efficacy of the basket-hilted weapon might be given, but we question whether its warmest admirers would prefer it to the bayonet in a close attack.

CHAPTER VI.

OUR HIGHLAND REGIMENTS—*continued.*

THE Highlanders possessed naturally a great aptitude for war. It has been said that hunting is the nearest approach to war in times of peace; and the Highlander, when not engaged in war, devoted himself to hunting, fishing, and the practice of athletic sports and manly exercises. He was a deer-stalker before deer-parks were invented, when deer-stalking was something different from the easy slaughter now known by that name; he was accustomed to bear hunger, thirst, and fatigue without complaint; to sleep in the snow with no other covering than his plaid; to encounter the members of a hostile clan with no other weapon than his broadsword. He possessed the virtues and physical qualities that fit men for war. He was impetuous in attack and cool under fire. In the hour of danger he exhibited such courage and presence of mind as nothing could daunt. At Fontenoy and elsewhere he has thrown himself on the ground as the enemy began their fire; when their bullets had whistled harmlessly over his head, he would rush forward till his musket almost touched their breasts, and pour in the deadly discharge; he would then retreat, receive their fire as before, and advance in the same manner. If he had not been possessed of the greatest coolness and self-possession, such a mode of fighting could only have led to inextricable confusion.

From an old pamphlet, published in 1745, we learn that a Highlander of the 42nd Regiment killed nine Frenchmen with his broadsword at Fontenoy, and would probably have added to the number of the slain if he had not lost his arm. In a skirmish with the Americans in 1776, Major Murray, of the same regiment, being separated from his men, was attacked by three of the enemy. His dirk had slipped behind his back, and, being very corpulent, he could not reach it: he defended himself as well as he could with his fusil, and, watching his opportunity, seized the sword of one of his assailants, and put the three to flight. It was natural that he should ever retain that sword as a trophy of victory. In another skirmish during the same war, a young recruit belonging to Fraser's Highlanders slew seven of the enemy with his own hand. At the close of the engagement his bayonet, once perfectly straight, was twisted like a corkscrew. At the affair of Castlebar, in Ireland, when men of other regiments retreated, a Highland sentinel refused to leave his post without orders. It was in vain that they tried to persuade him to retire—he stood there alone against a host. Five times he loaded and fired; a Frenchman fell at every shot. Before he could put his musket to his shoulder a sixth time the enemy were upon him, and many a bayonet passed through his body. The power of discipline could scarcely carry a man farther than this. The soldier who could meet a host without flinching must have had the soul of a hero. Highlanders have been equally patient and enduring in meeting the onsets of hunger and famine. The 1st Battalion of the 78th Regiment was wrecked during the passage from Java to Calcutta in 1816. The days and nights from the 9th of November to the 6th of December were spent on the rocky isle of Preparis, without shelter and almost without food. One ounce of bread and half a glassful of rice was the daily allowance of each person for nearly a month. At length even this miserable supply failed, and the shell-fish picked up at low water became their only means of support. At such a juncture the most generous of men might have become selfish; but such was the effect of discipline among these half-famished Highlanders, that with death staring them in the face they could resist the cravings of hunger, and bring all their gatherings to one common stock, which was equally divided among them all. Their fortitude was rewarded by the arrival of a ship which carried them in safety to Calcutta.

Numerous proofs of their cunning and address in war might be cited. On the day before the battle of Fontenoy the Earl of Craufurd advanced with the Highlanders to examine the enemy's outposts. A Highland soldier, stationed in dangerous proximity to the enemy, was annoyed by one of their sharpshooters firing at his post, and had recourse to an ingenious expedient to rid himself of this annoyance. He crept stealthily forward and placed his bonnet on the top of a stick near the verge of a hollow road. While the Frenchman's attention was fixed on his supposed antagonist, Donald advanced unperceived to a spot where he could take sure aim, and brought down the unfortunate marksman. In a skirmish with the American rebels in 1777, Sergeant Macgregor, of the 42nd, was severely wounded, and remained insensible on the ground. Unlike Captain Crawley, who put on his old uniform before Waterloo, the sergeant, who seems to have been something of a dandy, had attired himself in his best, as if he had been going to a ball, and not to a battle. He wore a new jacket with silver lace, large silver buckles in his shoes, and a watch of some value. This display of wealth attracted the notice of an American soldier, who, actuated by no feeling of humanity, but by the sordid desire of stripping the sergeant at leisure, took him on his back and began to carry him off the field. It is probable that the American did not handle him very tenderly, and the motion soon restored him to consciousness. He saw at once the state of matters, and proved himself master of the occasion. With one hand he drew his dirk, and, grasping the American's throat with the other, he swore that he would stab him to the heart if he did not retrace his steps, and bear him back in safety to the British camp. The *argumentum ad hominem* in the shape of a glittering dagger before his eyes was too much for the American. On the way to the camp he met Lord Cornwallis, who thanked him for his humanity, but he had the candour to admit the truth. His lordship, who was much amused at the incident, gave the American his liberty, and, on Macgregor retiring from the service, procured for him a situation in the Customs at Leith. He probably thought that the man who could entrap a Yankee would be more than a match for any smuggler. In a war with the Cherokees in 1760, Allen Macpherson, a private in Montgomery's Highlanders, fell into the hands of the enemy. Anxious to escape from the cruel torture that awaited him, he signified that he had something of importance to communicate. An interpreter was introduced, and the Indians stood by in solemn silence. He informed them that he was a medicine-man, and knew of certain herbs, which, if applied to the skin, would enable it to resist the sword or the tomahawk, though wielded by the strongest arm; if they would conduct him to the woods, and allow him to collect these herbs, he would use them so as that their bravest warrior might strike at his neck without injuring him. Such an assertion found ready credence with superstitious Indians, and they complied with his request. Macpherson was as cool and confident in his bearing as if he had nothing to dread: he rubbed his neck with the juice of the first herbs he had picked up, laid his head calmly on a block of wood, and invited the ordeal. An Indian raised his tomahawk and struck at his neck with such force that his head flew several yards from his body. The Cherokees, far from resenting the trick which had been played upon their credulity, expressed their admiration of his address and courage by refraining from torturing the other captives. We could give many proofs of the Highlander's ingenuity in attacking others or defending himself, but we confine ourselves to a single incident which tends to prove his dexterity in imposing on the enemy. During the siege of Quebec, the French had planted sentries along the river to challenge all who approached. During the night attack which ended in the capture of the town, the first boat with English troops was observed and challenged. "*Qui vive?*" A moment's hesitation, and all would have been lost. An officer of Fraser's Highlanders who had served in Holland, and knew the watchword, at once replied, "*La France.*" The second part of the challenge was given and satisfactorily answered. The sentinel became troublesomely inquisitive. "*A quel régiment appartenez-vous?*" "*Au régiment de la Reine.*" It was fortunate that the captain knew that a regiment of that name was serving in Quebec. The soldier, satisfied with these replies, allowed all the boats to pass without further challenge: he thought it was an expected convoy with provisions, and no time was lost when the magic word "*passe*" was heard. The other sentries took it for granted that all was right; there was only one who had some suspicion. Struck with the silence on board the boats, he rushed down to the water's edge, and called, "*Pourquoi est-ce que vous ne parlez pas haut?*" The suspicion implied in this question was at once disarmed by the officer replying in a subdued tone, "*Tais-tois, ou nous serons entendus.*" That cunning Highlander had not studied French for nothing—it gained for the British: Quebec.

A striking trait in the character of the Highlanders was their devoted attachment to their own regiments and officers. When clanship had all but died out in the North, it was found lingering among the Highland soldiers. The Highlander's regiment was his clan, and his colonel his chief; and to his corps and commander he did the same fealty as in the days of yore to clansmen and their head. This feeling was peculiarly prominent in those regiments which were under the command of cadets of ancient Northern families, who felt in themselves and tried to revive in their men the old ties of clanship. Cameron, of the 92nd, who fought and fell at Quatre Bras, was less the colonel than the chief of that gallant regiment, which was raised partly in Lochaber, his native district. He knew every man in his regiment, and watched over their interests as if they had been his brothers or his sons. An angry look or a stern word from him was dreaded more than the lash. He was their father, and when he fell there rose from his mountain children that wild wail of sorrow which once heard can never be forgotten. Brave, impetuous, and headstrong, jealous of his own honour and that of his regiment, Cameron has always struck us as the *beau idéal* of a Highland officer of the better class; while Captain MacTurk, that admirable creation of Scott, may be safely accepted as the faithful representative of a once numerous class, the all but countless subalterns who had risen from the ranks, and who puzzled the post-office and confused the directory by the similarity of their names. The old clannish feeling is perceptible in the language used by Highland veterans in alluding to their past services. They do not say that they served in the 42nd, the 78th, the 79th, the 92nd, or the 93rd regiment; but, when inspired by usquebaugh or ancient reminiscences, they begin to fight their battles o'er, they preface their narrative with, "When I was in the Black Watch, the Ross, the Cameron, the Gordon, or the Sutherland regiment." The name to them is everything: the number by which the regiment is known at the Horse Guards is a number, and nothing more. This attachment of the Highlanders to their own regiments was so well-known during the last century that it was sometimes taken advantage of by the recruiting sergeants, who assumed the Highland dress, and persuaded the recruits they were about to join a Highland regiment. When such was not the case, the rage of the Highlanders on discovering the imposture was unbounded; they appealed to the military authorities, and on their obtaining their discharge re-enlisted at once in one of their own regiments. These regiments, when first raised, could always command a larger number of men than they actually required. When the Fraser Highlanders embarked for foreign service in 1776, it was found that more men had joined than the strength of the different companies admitted, and several were dismissed. Such, however, was their anxiety to serve, that they concealed themselves in the ship, and were not discovered till the fleet was at sea. An incident occurred on this occasion which proves that the *esprit de clan*, if we may so speak, was even stronger than the *esprit de corps*. A hundred and twenty men had been raised on the forfeited estate of Cameron of Lochiel, so as to entitle him to a company: detained by sickness in London, he was unable to join his regiment in Glasgow. The Camerons, unwilling to serve any one but their chief, hesitated to embark, till young Fassiefern, one of their clansmen, and a near relative of Lochiel, was appointed to the command of the company, when all their scruples were removed. Lochiel, on hearing of the conduct of his men, hurried down from London; but the fatigue of the journey brought on a fresh attack of disease, to which he fell a victim in a few weeks. The regiment was under the command of General Fraser, a son of Lord Lovat. He addressed the Camerons in Gaelic, and his eloquence had much effect in winning them back to obedience. While he was speaking, a venerable Highlander was seen leaning on his staff and listening with rapt attention. When he had finished, the old man stepped up to him, and seizing his hand with an easy familiarity which marked the intercourse of all classes in the North, said, "Simon, you are a good soldier, and speak like a man; as long as you live, Simon of Lovat will never die." The general, doubtless, appreciated this double compliment; his father was a favourite among the Highlanders, and it was implied that the son was worthy of the sire. The young recruits always wished to serve under officers of their own clan, and felt it a hardship to be separated from them. It was not enough that they served in the same regiment; they wished to belong to the same company. Young Fassiefern brought a hundred Lochaber men to join the 92nd at Aberdeen. When it was proposed to draft them into different companies, they refused to be separated, or to serve under any officer save their young chief. It was only by pledging his honour that he would watch equally over the interests of all that he could persuade them to submit; his letters to his father prove that he never forgot his promise. They were true to one another to the end; when a Lochaber man died, Cameron followed him to the grave, reminded his sorrowing comrades of his soldierly virtues, and told them to "give him the smoothest bed, and to cover him with the greenest sod." To understand the delicacy of this order, one must have witnessed a Highland funeral, or seen the smooth, level, turf-covered graves in a Highland churchyard. There was no sacrifice which they were not prepared to make for officers who thus studied their interests and feelings. They were as jealous of their honour as of their own; cowardice in the chief brought disgrace on his clan. There was a singular display of this feeling in one of the Crimean battles: a young Highland officer left his place in front of his company and began to retreat, when a sergeant seized him by the throat, and swore he would run him through the body if he did not turn. He chose rather to meet the fire of the Russians than the glare of the sergeant's angry eye. This jealousy of their officers' honour gave rise to an amusing incident during the attack on Fort Washington in 1777. The hill on which the fort stood was almost perpendicular, but the Highlanders rushed up the steep ascent

Major Murray and the Highlanders at Fort Washington

like mountain cats. When half-way up the heights they heard a melancholy voice exclaim, "Oh, soldiers, will you leave me?" On looking down, they saw Major Murray, their commanding officer, at the foot of the precipice; his extreme obesity prevented him from following them. They were not deaf to this appeal: it would never do to leave their corpulent commander behind. A party leaped down at once, seized him in their arms, and bore him from ledge to ledge of the rock till they reached the summit, where they drove the enemy before them and made two hundred prisoners. Major Murray was not the only corpulent warrior among those Highland soldiers. Sir Robert Munroe of Fowlis, who commanded them at Fontenoy, was so fat that his own men had to haul him from the trenches by the legs and arms; he advised them to fall flat on the ground when the enemy fired, but remained erect himself, remarking that it was easy for a man of his weight to lie down, but not so easy to rise. Some of the men seem to have been as remarkable for height as their officers were for breadth. Thus we read of Samuel Macdonald, or "Big Sam," of the Sutherland Fencibles, who was seven feet four inches in height, and stout in proportion. As the other men would have looked like pigmies beside such a giant, he stood on the right of the regiment when in line, and marched at its head when in column, followed by an immense mountain deer, between which and him there were certain physical, if not spiritual, affinities. He was an excellent drill, and, like most giants, extremely good-natured. Ordinary rations would not have sufficed to sustain such a corpus; he was therefore allowed half-a-crown a day of extra pay. Attracting the attention of the Prince of Wales, he made him one of the porters at Carlton House. But Macdonald soon tired of this inactive life, and longed to be with his old comrades of the 93rd. He rejoined the regiment, and died at Guernsey in 1802. Sam's regiment seems to have been remarkable for the size and muscular strength of the men. It had no light company, and as more than 200 men were upwards of five feet eleven inches in height, they were formed into two grenadier companies, one on each flank of the battalion.

The retirement or the removal of one of their favourite officers to another regiment called forth the strongest feelings of sorrow, and sometimes almost led to open resistance. It occasionally happened that these officers were Englishmen, who with the garb of the mountains had adopted all the feelings of the mountaineers. Cadogan, who commanded the 71st in the Peninsula, was a Saxon, and yet no Celt was ever dearer to his men. The Pretender would never have been so popular in the North if he had not worn the tartan; the same may be said of Montrose and Dundee, neither of whom was a Highlander by birth. If English officers failed to gain the affections and respect of their men, it was because they failed to make themselves acquainted with their character, and inadvertently wounded their feelings. Such cases, however, were rare. English officers serving in Highland regiments possessed the *esprit de corps* as much as the Highlanders themselves. At first, as we have shown, all the officers belonged to the North, and it was a point of honour with the men either to protect them in battle or to avenge them if slain. We might cite many cases where Highland soldiers sacrificed their own lives to save those of their officers, stepping before them and receiving in their own bodies the bullet or the bayonet-thrust aimed at their officers' breasts. When a favourite fell, woe betide the enemy at the next charge: every Highlander fought as if his arm alone were the instrument of vengeance. When Cameron fell at Quatre Bras, by a shot fired from the upper storey of the farm-house, his men rushed with a wild shout on the building, burst their way in, and avenged by the slaughter of all its occupants, the death of their leader.

While the duty of avenging the death of a beloved officer was incumbent upon all, it devolved with peculiar stringency on his foster-brother, who always kept near his person in battle. This duty is frequently alluded to in the proverbial expressions of the North. "Kindred to twenty (degrees), fosterage to a hundred," was a received maxim in the code of Celtic ethics. "Woe to the father of the foster-son who is unfaithful to his trust," is another old saying which proves that this tie was regarded as sacred. Scott has described this singular relationship among the Highlanders in "Waverley," and many illustrations might be given of the deeds of unselfish devotion to which it gave rise. Often the foster-brother thrust himself before his officer, and shielded him from danger by the sacrifice of his own life. If he had failed to do so, his own mother would have been the first to reproach him for his cowardice—ay, and to disown him as her son. There was much of the old Spartan feeling among these Celtic mothers. The wives of those Northern chiefs seem to have had no great liking for the primary duties of domestic life; instead of rearing their own children, they distributed them among their tenantry, who considered themselves honoured by the confidence thus reposed in them. This singular custom tended to render the tie between the chief and his clan closely intimate: they felt themselves to be members of one great family. Cameron of Fassiefern, with whose portrait our readers are familiar, was followed wherever he went by his faithful henchman and foster-brother, Ewen M'Millan. His devotion to his chief was unbounded; it absorbed every other feeling, and became the master-passion of his life. At the battle of St. Pierre, Ewen gave an amusing proof of his regard, not only for his master, but also for his master's property. Cameron's horse, being wounded, fell, and nearly crushed him. A Frenchman rushed forward to bayonet him while thus disabled; but, before the blow had reached, Ewen came up and pierced the Frenchman to the heart. Ewen then raised his master from his dangerous position and conducted him to a place of safety, after which he returned and carried off the saddle on which Cameron had sat. All this was done with the greatest coolness, though the battle was at its height, and the bullets of the enemy were flying on every side. When Ewen rejoined his company, he displayed his trophy to his comrades, and exultingly exclaimed, "We must leave them the carcass, but they sha'n't get the saddle where Fassiefern sat." It was evidently a seat of honour, and too sacred an object in Ewen's eyes to be left in possession of the French; and to save the saddle the disgrace of receiving part of another's person, he was ready to risk his life. When Cameron fell at Quatre Bras, his devoted foster-brother was in a moment at his side, and, raising him in his arms, he bore him from the field of battle till he found a cart, on which he laid him. Seating himself by his side, he propped the head of his dying chief on his own faithful breast, and tried in vain to stanch the life-blood fast ebbing away. It was all in vain: the bullet had done its deadly work, and Ewen could only weep over the grave of one for whom he would have gladly died. Such faithful attachment deserved to be rewarded, and Cameron's father provided Ewen with a farm on his own estate when he obtained his discharge after the battle of Waterloo.

It may amuse our readers to learn the opinion of the Highlanders formed by those who have encountered them in the field of battle. Their strange dress, their lofty stature, their unknown tongue, and their singular mode of fighting, all naturally produced a deep impression on the minds of their enemies, who regarded them almost with a feeling of superstition. A French writer, alluding to the battle of Fontenoy, says, "The British behaved well, and could be exceeded in ardour by none but our officers, who animated the troops by their example, *when the Highland furies rushed in upon us with more violence than ever did a sea driven by a tempest.*" The Highlanders took part in the capture of Guadaloupe; and it appears from letters written from that island that the French had formed the wildest notions regarding the *sauvages d'Ecosse* (Scotch savages), as they were pleased to term them. They believed that they would neither take nor give quarter, and that they were so nimble that, as no one could catch them, nobody could escape them; that no man had a chance against their broadswords; and that, with a ferocity natural to savages, they made no prisoners, and spared neither man, woman, nor child. As the Highlanders were always in the front during the attack on the island, we need not be surprised that the good people of Guadaloupe quailed at the sight of such a redoubtable foe, and offered but little resistance. Such was the activity of the Highlanders in attacking them at different points, that they believed that they amounted to several thousands, whereas their real strength was only 800. A French general, in reference to the gallantry of the Highlanders at Toulouse, said, "Ah, these are brave soldiers. If they had good officers, I should not like to meet them unless I were well supported." As their officers had never received much training for war, their bravery was often more conspicuous than their knowledge of the military art.

Keith's Highlanders particularly distinguished themselves in the German wars which were carried on about the middle of the eighteenth century. Macaulay has shown that the English at one time did not hold their Northern neighbours in high estimation; but it appears that the Germans entertained still more erroneous ideas regarding them. "The Scotch Highlanders," says a writer in the *Vienna Gazette* of 1762, "are a people totally different in their dress, manners, and temper from the other inhabitants of Britain. *They are caught in the mountains when young*, and still run with a surprising degree of swiftness. As they are strangers to fear, they make very good soldiers when disciplined." The writer proceeds to admit that they are not without some amiable qualities, and charitably concludes his article by expressing a hope "that their king's laudable, though late, endeavours to civilize and instruct them in the principles of Christianity will meet with success." The French and Germans, along with Englishmen, have during the last hundred years learned to know the Highlanders better.

We happened the other day to find ourselves in the society of a number of officers, some of whom had seen service in every quarter of the globe. Allusion was made to Highland soldiers, when an English colonel exclaimed, "They are the most troublesome fellows in the service. I have seven of them in my regiment, and they have given me more annoyance about their rights and grievances than all my other men."

"The reason is very simple," rejoined an officer, who hailed from the land of the Gael; "you don't know how to manage them."

In these simple words may be found the secret cause of the mutinies which so frequently broke out among the Highland regiments when first organized. The government of the day did not know how to manage them: hence insubordination, discontent, and frequent mutiny. The 42nd, or Old Black Watch, was, as we have shown, the first body of Highlanders formed into a regular regiment. Many of the privates were men of good family and liberal education, who were drawn into the service by their natural love of arms. It was distinctly understood that the sphere of their services was not to extend beyond their native country, to which they were warmly attached; and when in March, 1743, they were ordered to proceed to England, many of the leading men of the North, including Lord President Forbes, ventured to remonstrate. Their remonstrances were vain; the government persisted in their resolution, but the suspicions of the Highlanders were disarmed by appealing to their vanity. They were assured that the king was anxious to see so gallant a regiment, and that after being reviewed by royalty they would be allowed to return to their native land. The men were treated with the greatest kindness in the different English towns through which they passed; their warlike bearing and correctness of conduct secured for them the admiration and esteem of all with whom they were brought into contact. On the 14th of May they were reviewed on Finchley Common by Marshal Wade, in the presence of vast crowds who had hurried from London to see *les sauvages Ecossais*. It was unfortunate the king was not present at this review; his absence induced the Highlanders to lend a ready ear to the insidious report circulated among them by the adherents of the Stuarts that they were about to be transported to the American plantations. The Highlanders were stung to madness by the supposed treachery; but, with characteristic caution, they concealed their intentions till their plans were matured. They whispered to one another that, "after being used as rods to scourge their own countrymen, they were now to be thrown into the fire." They resolved to die rather than submit to such a fate.

On the night between Tuesday and Wednesday after the review they assembled on a common near Highgate, and commenced their march to the land of their birth. They had friends and sympathisers in the city who supplied them with provisions. Their march was conducted with such secrecy that for a week nothing was known of their route. They had reached Lady Wood, between Brigstock and Deanthorp, about four miles from Oundle, when Captain Ball, an officer of Wade's regiment of horse, was sent to treat with them. He requested them to lay down their arms and surrender at discretion, but they declared with one voice that they would be cut to pieces rather than submit, unless they were allowed to retain their arms and received a free pardon. All that Captain Ball could promise was to recommend them to mercy; but the pride of the Highlanders revolted at such a proposal.

"Hitherto," then exclaimed the captain, "I have been your friend; but if you continue obstinate an hour longer not a man of you shall be left alive; and for my part, I assure you, I shall give quarter to none."

The Highlanders, who had too much generosity to resent this bold language, sent two of their number to escort him out of the wood. The guides were won over by his eloquence: one of them remained with him, while the other returned and tried to persuade his comrades to submit. Surrounded as they were by superior numbers, they were, after some negotiation, induced to surrender. They received a free pardon, and soon after embarked for Flanders, where their deeds of bravery atoned for their temporary disaffection.

A similar incident occurred in the case of a Highland regiment in the service of William III. It was the ardent love of country that led them to refuse to embark for Holland, and their devotion to King James that led them to drink his health while there in preference to that of their own prince. Some one reported this to William.

"Do they fight well, these Highlanders?" asked the king.

"None better," was the reply.

"Then," said the king, "if they fight so well for me, let them drink my father's health as often as they choose."

There was much magnanimity in these words. The Highlanders soon learned to drink William's health as heartily as they had done his father-in-law's.

In the year 1779 a circumstance occurred which proves in the most striking manner the attachment which the Highlanders have ever cherished for their own regiments. In the month of April two strong detachments belonging to the 42nd and 71st regiments arrived at Leith from Stirling Castle, *en route* to North America to join their respective regiments. On learning that they were about to be drafted into the 80th and 82nd, both Lowland regiments, the men firmly refused to obey this order, or to serve in any regiments save those for which they had been enlisted. A little friendly remonstrance might have won them over, but the authorities unfortunately adopted the idea of reducing them by force, and troops were sent to Leith for the purpose of subduing the mutineers and conveying them to Edinburgh Castle. This was no easy task, as the event proved. The Highlanders offered an obstinate resistance, and in the conflict which ensued, Captain Mansfield, of the South Fencible regiment, and nine men were killed, and thirty-one soldiers wounded. At length, overpowered by numbers, the Highlanders were compelled to surrender, and were shut up in Edinburgh Castle. In the month of May three of the prisoners, Charles Williamson and Archibald Mac Ivor, of the 42nd, and Robert Budge, of the 71st, were tried by court-martial for having been guilty of mutiny and inciting others to the same crime. The line of defence they adopted gives us considerable insight into the state of the Highlanders at this period. Mac Ivor and Williamson stated that they enlisted in the 42nd, a regiment composed exclusively of Highlanders, and wearing the Highland dress. Their native tongue was Gaelic, and they knew no other, having been born in counties where English was almost unknown. They had never worn breeches in their lives, and the only garb they could wear with comfort was the garb of old Gael. This dress had indeed been prohibited by Act of Parliament; but the government had connived at the use of it, provided that it was made of plain cloth and not of tartan. For these reasons they could neither understand the language nor use the arms, or march in the dress of any other than a Highland regiment. Budge's defence was substantially the same. They submitted to the court that, on reaching Leith, the officer who had conducted them there informed them that they were now to consider themselves soldiers of the 82nd, a regiment wearing the Lowland dress and speaking the English tongue. No order from the commander-in-chief was shown to them, nor had they any opportunity of submitting their grievances to him. They had no intention to

resist lawful authority; they only wished to remonstrate against an act of flagrant injustice. They would have gone willingly to the castle if the order had been explained to them; but the officer sent for that purpose told them that they were to join the Hamilton regiment immediately, and they considered themselves justified in repelling force by force. Every reader will feel his blood boil with indignation on learning that these three poor Highlanders were all found guilty and sentenced to be shot. The spirit of clanship, however, was too strong in the Highland regiments to admit of this sentence being carried into effect, and the king was pleased to grant them a free pardon, "in full confidence that they would endeavour, by a prompt obedience and orderly behaviour, to atone for their atrocious offence." Without passing an opinion on the atrocity of the offence, we have much pleasure in adding that all the prisoners proved themselves worthy of the royal clemency. They were drafted into the second battalion of the 42nd, and were uniformly distinguished for their steadiness and good conduct.

It may be safely affirmed that the Highland regiments never displayed a spirit of insubordination, except on those occasions when the government of the day attempted to treat them with injustice by transferring them to Lowland regiments, or ordering them to embark for foreign service when they had enlisted to serve for a limited period at home. The 77th regiment, or Athole Highlanders, was raised in 1778 by the young Duke of Athole. The Murrays have always been a warlike race, and their young chief, the present Duke of Athole, the possessor of princely estates, is serving in Canada with the 2nd battalion of the Scots Fusilier Guards. The Athole Highlanders embarked for Ireland in June, 1778, and did garrison duty there till the war was over. The part they had to play was somewhat difficult; the Irish were disaffected, and hated the troops sent to control them; but the conduct of the Highlanders was so exemplary as to secure for them the respect of their enemies. Mr. Eden, afterwards Lord Auckland, Secretary for Ireland, bears honourable testimony to this fact. After alluding to the gentlemanly bearing of the officers, and the excellent conduct of the men, he says—"Once, upon the sudden alarm of invasion, I sent an order for the immediate march of this regiment to Cork, when they showed their alacrity by marching at an hour's notice, and completed their march with a despatch beyond any instance in modern times, and this, too, without leaving a single soldier behind."

There are few regiments at the present day that could undertake the same march at an hour's notice, and complete it without leaving a single man behind; such a fact says much for the discipline, strength, and pluck of the Athole Highlanders. The government showed their appreciation of these services by attempting to break faith with them. The Highlanders had enlisted for three years. Their period of service had now expired, and they naturally expected to be disbanded. Instead of this, they were sent to Portsmouth to embark for foreign service. At first they offered no resistance; when they caught the first view of the fleet at Spithead as they crossed Portsdown Hill, they pulled off their bonnets and gave three cheers at the prospect of a brush with Hyder Ali. If the government had been wise enough to tempt them to re-enlist by the offer of a fresh bounty, a gallant regiment might have been preserved to the British army; but, unfortunately, they had no sooner reached Portsmouth than emissaries from London began to poison their minds by pointing out to them the injustice of the authorities in sending them abroad when they ought to have been disbanded. It was even insinuated that they had been sold to the East India Company at so much a head, and that their officers had shared in the purchase-money. These representations had the desired effect. The Highlanders, suspicious of their officers, and brooding over their wrongs, refused to embark. For several days they remained in a state of mutiny, during which they attempted to gain possession of the main guard and garrison parade, when one of the invalids who opposed them was accidentally killed. No sooner was it known that the poor man had left a widow than the Highlanders expressed the deepest regret, and raised a considerable sum for her relief.

The greatest anxiety was caused at Portsmouth by the presence of a thousand men free from all restraint; but the lives and property of the citizens were respected, and no complaints were ever made against the Highlanders. Though they had reason to suspect their officers of treachery, they almost invariably continued to treat them with deference and respect. On hearing, however, that two or three regiments were approaching to force them on board, they flew to arms and marched out to offer them battle. On finding that it was a false report, they quietly returned to their quarters. The Duke of Athole, his uncle, Major-General Murray, and Lord George Lennox, hurried down to Portsmouth in the hope that their presence and influence would induce the men to embark; but the minds of the latter were too much embittered by a sense of injustice to be swayed by the counsels of their hereditary chiefs. The discipline of the regiment was as strict as if they had been still under the command of their officers. Their arms and ammunition were placed in one of the magazines, and a strong guard placed over them while the rest of the regiment slept or partook of their meals. Twice a day they appeared at the grand parade, along with the adjutant and other officers. They were as careful of their dress and personal appearance as before. The government were at a loss what to do with the dreaded Highlanders. One day it was proposed to turn the great guns on the ramparts against them; but, fortunately, this proposal was overruled; the bloodshed would have been great, the result doubtful. At other times it was suggested to send some regiments stationed in the neighbourhood against them. On hearing this the Highlanders flew to arms, drew up the drawbridges, placed sentinels on them, and prepared to offer an obstinate resistance.

At length the question of the mutiny was brought under the consideration of Parliament, and the just claims of the Highlanders were admitted. The regiment was disbanded, and the men spread through the Highlands the report of the injustice with which they had been treated, and thus prevented many of their countrymen from entering the army. When treating of this affair, General Stewart observed that "If government had offered a small bounty when the Athole Highlanders were required to embark, there can be little doubt they would have obeyed their orders, and embarked

6

as cheerfully as they marched into Portsmouth." This untoward event will remind our readers of what occurred in India when the attempt was recently made to transfer the European troops from the service of the East India Company to that of the imperial government. Through the niggardly policy then adopted, thousands of men inured to service in that trying climate were roused into a state of mutiny, and compelled the authorities to grant them their discharge. In this case, as in that of the Athole Highlanders, a small bounty would have settled the difficulty and satisfied every claim.

There are old people still alive in Scotland who remember the sensation created in the days of their boyhood among all classes by "the affair of the wild Macraes." The Macraes never rose to the dignity of a clan; they were a small sept that lived under the protection of the Mackenzies of Seaforth. The Earl of Seaforth had forfeited his title and estates in consequence of the part he took in the rebellion of 1715, when many of the Northern gentry rose in favour of the Pretender. Kenneth Mackenzie, the grandson of this earl, bought the family property from the crown, and was created Viscount Fortrose in the Irish peerage. In 1771 the family title was restored to him, and the Earl of Seaforth, anxious to prove his gratitude to the government of the day for the favours he had received, offered in 1778 to raise a regiment among his own clan for general service. The Highlanders had already acquired a distinguished name on many a battle-field, and his offer was at once accepted. All the gentlemen of the clan Mackenzie came to the aid of their chief, and a corps of 1130 men was soon raised: 500 Highlanders belonged to Seaforth's estates; 400 to the Mackenzies of Scatwell, Kilcoy, Applecross, and Redcastle; about 200 were Lowland Scotch; 43 were English and Irish. It is interesting to mark the constitutional elements of this and other Highland regiments. The fact is undeniable that the Highlands of Scotland were far more populous a century ago than they are now. The poorer inhabitants have been driven to Canada and other colonies; their small farms have been changed into deer-parks or sheep-walks; the landlords have increased their rentals, but the country has lost an important class and reaped no adequate advantage in return. The regiment thus embodied was known as the 78th, or Seaforth Highlanders. It is not to be confounded, however, with the present 78th, or Ross-shire Buffs; it is now represented by the 72nd, or Duke of Albany's Own Highlanders. Almost all the officers were Mackenzies, and the sons and brothers of the different lairds vied with one another in selecting the best men that could be found on their estates. The results of this care on their part were apparent when the regiment was inspected at Elgin in May, 1778: of those 1130 men not one was rejected—an astounding fact when we consider that nearly one-fourth of our recruits are now pronounced unfit for service in consequence of some physical defect. In the month of August they embarked for Leith, where "the affair of the wild Macraes occurred.

CHAPTER VII.

OUR HIGHLAND REGIMENTS—*continued.*

THE Macraes, as we have already said, had never attained to the dignity of a clan; they were a sort of *caterans* or pilfering tinkers, who had found it convenient to place themselves under the protection of the chief of the Mackenzies. It appears that Seaforth had no particular liking for his pilfering *protégés*, and deemed this a favourable opportunity for getting quit of them. It is a fact not generally known that our Highland regiments have often obtained their best recruits from the fraternity of *cairds* or *caterans*. About half a century ago the whole of the North of Scotland was infested with these marauders, who, under the guise of mendicancy, levied contributions on the inhabitants of the rural districts, and lived a jovial, careless life. They were present at every marriage feast and merry-making, where the broken meat became their perquisite; sometimes they devoured the feast itself, and left the guests to shift for themselves. There was no rural constabulary in those days to keep them in check, and these Ishmaelites did very much whatever they chose. They were unrivalled in wrestling, single-stick, and every athletic sport; they were the best dancers on the village green; they could do everything but work or settle down to any fixed employment. They were essentially a nomadic race, ever on the move, sleeping by night in country barns, starting with the earliest dawn, and levying their contributions from door to door. We remember a gang of *caterans* or *cairds* who frequented the county of Aberdeen more years ago than we should like to tell. They all bore the family name of Young, and belonged to the same sept. One of them—Peter Young—was a great thief, and made himself almost as notorious as Jack Sheppard by breaking out of every gaol in Scotland. These *caterans* came to a singular end, and disappeared from the country. This is how it happened.

The 92nd or Gordon Highlanders had suffered much in the Peninsular War, so that constant drafts had to be sent out from home to recruit their strength. When all other resources failed, the country gentlemen bethought themselves of an ingenious plan by which they could at once fill up the vacant ranks in the 92nd, and get quit of some unpleasant neighbours. They caused all the able-bodied *cairds* to be seized and conveyed to the neighbouring seaport, where they were shipped off to join the 92nd. Such a thing, of course, could not be done at the present day, but strange things were done half a century ago in Scotland as elsewhere. Many a man who had no desire to be a sailor or a soldier was impressed or forced to serve in the army or navy against his will. This impressment of the Youngs proved the death-blow of the race. Not one of them ever returned from the Peninsula, but we have heard old pensioners of the 92nd declare that they were at once the greatest thieves and the smartest soldiers in the regiment.

The wild Macraes seem to have been men of much the same stamp as the Youngs, and Seaforth doubtless had his own reasons for wishing to get quit of them. These *caterans* were as much attached to their native land as if they had been the possessors of countless acres; they were their own masters, and had tasted the sweets of liberty. Seaforth knew that he could never persuade such men to enlist for foreign service, but he had sufficient influence to induce them to serve for a limited period at home, or rather to join the 78th on that understanding. It was only on reaching Leith that they discovered that they were intended for service in the East Indies, when symptoms of disaffection appeared among them. The report spread that Seaforth had sold them to the government. Loud complaints were heard that they had been cheated of their pay and bounty money. The wild Macraes were not the men tamely to submit to such injuries, and the stinging sense of wrong was intensified by the representations of certain parties hostile to the government of the day. Their slumbering discontent broke forth into open mutiny on receiving orders to embark; they absolutely refused to do so, and marched out of Leith with pipes playing, and two plaids fixed on poles instead of colours. On reaching Arthur's Seat—the beautiful hill which overlooks Edinburgh, and is familiar to every tourist who has visited the North—they encamped on its summit, and remained there for several days. Though in a state of open mutiny, they respected the property of the citizens, and conducted themselves with so much propriety that public sympathy was excited in their favour, especially among the lower classes, who supplied them abundantly with provisions. The authorities deemed it more prudent to inquire into their grievances than to attempt to reduce them by force. After much negotiation they professed themselves satisfied, and marched back to their quarters at Leith with pipes playing and Seaforth at their head.

After serving for some time in the Channel Islands, they embarked in March, 1781, for the East Indies. Seaforth died during the voyage, before he reached St. Helena, and his death had such a depressing effect upon the men, that no less than 230 of them died before they reached India. They took part in all the different battles which were fought till the conclusion of peace in 1783, when, in terms of their agreement with government, they had a right to return home. Few of the Macraes lived to revisit their native land; most of them had died during the voyage, or succumbed to the fatal effects of the enervating climate. Only 300 of the men remained in India; but these, reinforced by volunteers from other regiments returning home, and by a detachment of 200 recruits from the North, were formed into a new regiment, which has ever since been known as the 72nd, or Duke of Albany's Own Highlanders.

A similar mutiny, proceeding from the same causes, broke out in the 81st, or Aberdeenshire Highland Regiment, in 1783. This regiment was raised in 1778 by the Hon. Colonel William Gordon, of Fyvie, a son of the Earl of Aberdeen by his third wife, a

daughter of the Duke of Gordon. She was a sister of that Lord Lewis Gordon who took part in the rebellion of 1745, and whose absence from home is lamented in a charming Jacobite song which is still popular in the North. It is related of her that she took her stand close to the road by which the Duke of Cumberland and his army were marching south after the victory of Culloden, holding her infant son in her arms. Judging by her portrait, which we have seen, she must have been a very beautiful woman; and the duke, struck by her appearance, said, with his usual coarse bluntness, "Who are you?" The countess drew herself up to her full height, and looking him steadily in the face, boldly answered, "I am the sister of Lord Lewis Gordon." Cumberland turned aside his head and passed on. The Earl of Aberdeen was well advanced in years when he married her, and it was agreed that the property of Fyvie should be settled on her or her offspring after his death. The Hon. William Gordon, who was the eldest son by this marriage, succeeded to the property, and rose to the rank of colonel in the service. In March, 1777, he received letters of service to raise a Highland regiment in his native county, and it was embodied in 1778 under the name of the 81st, or Aberdeenshire Highland Regiment. Its strength when first raised was 980 men, 650 of whom belonged to the Highlands of Aberdeenshire; a very large proportion were members of the clan Ross, the chief of which is James Ross Farquharson of Invercauld, a lieutenant-colonel in the Scots Fusilier Guards. The regiment marched to Stirling, and soon after embarked for Ireland, where it spent three years. In 1782 it was removed to Portsmouth, and received orders to embark for the East Indies. These orders were in direct violation of their terms of enlistment, which were the same as those of the Athole Highlanders, and the men, having agreed to serve till the conclusion of peace, the preliminaries of which were now settled, refused to embark, and claimed their discharge. They were, doubtless, encouraged to take this step by the example of the Athole Highlanders, and the success which had attended their assertion of their rights. The government, deeming it useless to attempt to reduce them by force, yielded to their demands, and sent them to Edinburgh, where they were disbanded in 1783. There is a tradition in the county that this mutiny was owing more to the cruelty of their colonel than the injustice of government. Few of them belonged to his own clan, and he treated them with a harshness to which the proud spirit of the Highlanders would not tamely submit. We have met with old veterans who could tell many stories of "Whipping Willie Gordon," the sobriquet he obtained in the regiment through his fondness for the lash. He left the service with the rank of general, and spent his latter days at Fyvie Castle, where he professed himself a misogynist, and ended by marrying his cook.

An insurrection, attended with still more disastrous results, occurred in the Grant or Strathspey Fencibles in 1795. This regiment was raised by Sir James Grant of Grant in 1793, and about two months after the declaration of war by France, and, with the exception of three Englishmen and two Irishmen, was composed entirely of natives of the North. After being embodied at Forres, and inspected by General Leslie, the Grant Fencibles were stationed in most of the towns in the South of Scotland till 1795, when we find them at Dumfries. As a general rule, the best understanding has always subsisted between the Highlanders and their officers, and there is no sacrifice they are not prepared to make for those who have secured their confidence; but their proud, unbending spirit rebels at once against treachery or injustice. Enough has been already written to justify this assertion, and what we are about to relate tends only to confirm it. In 1794, when the regiment was stationed at Linlithgow, an attempt was made by the officers to persuade the men to extend their service, which, in terms of their enlistment, was confined to Scotland. It is probable that this attempt on the part of the officers originated merely from a desire to secure their own position in the army for a longer period, and it would probably have succeeded if they had won the confidence of the men by a frank avowal of their motives. As it was, they disclosed only enough to excite their suspicions, and the report spread that they had been sold to government. Nothing further was done in the matter at the time, but the officers were eyed with distrust, and a bad spirit sprang up in the regiment.

An incident occurred at Dumfries the following year which brought matters to a crisis, and caused an open mutiny. The greatest freedom of intercourse was permitted between officers and men when both belonged to the same clan. This familiarity did not interfere with the strictness of discipline any more than it does in the French army, in which it has survived till the present day. An amusing illustration of this familiarity occurred in the 93rd Highlanders when they were stationed in Canada. There belonged to the regiment a young lieutenant—who, in virtue of his being the inheritor of an illustrious Scottish name and twenty thousand a year, deemed it the correct thing to remain ignorant of even the simplest military duty—and a private named Jock Muir, an excellent soldier, but an inveterate drunkard. There was a mutual understanding between the lieutenant and Jock that they should stand by one another in every emergency, or, in other words, that Jock should stand by the lieutenant when on duty, and whisper into his ear the word of command, and that the lieutenant should screen Jock when he got drunk. This system of reciprocity answered admirably for a time, but at length the lieutenant, from inadvertency or some other cause, allowed Jock to be punished, and Jock determined to have his revenge. An opportunity soon offered. The regiment was on parade, and the lieutenant, as the officer of the day, had to give the word of command. Turning to Jock, he said, "What is it? What must I say?" But Jock remained stiff and erect — no answer proceeded from his lips. "What am I to do, you fool?" said the poor lieutenant, losing his temper. "Run hame, mon! run hame!" roared Jock, in a stentorian voice which was heard over all the lines, and caused a general titter in the ranks. The lieutenant, acting on Jock's advice, sold out and returned home, where he was much respected as a kind-hearted country gentleman.

Now it was a somewhat similar incident that rekindled the flame of discontent and caused an open mutiny among the Strathspey Fencibles at Dumfries in 1795. Militia officers are doubtless a highly-respectable class of men, and deserve well of their country in every respect, but they cannot be expected to possess the efficiency and skill of those who have devoted themselves to the profession of arms. The officers of the Strathspey Fencibles were men of good family, but as they had never seen any service they knew little about the management of troops, and sometimes exposed their ignorance in the presence of their own soldiers. On one occasion a contradictory order given by an officer called forth a jocular remark from one of the men, which was evidently much relished by his comrades. The officer lost his temper, put the offending parties in the guard-room, and threatened them with punishment—an indignity to which the proud spirit of the Highlanders refused to submit. They considered themselves disgraced by the threat, rushed to arms, and released their comrades by force. Soon after this the regiment was marched to Musselburgh, where Corporal James Macdonald and Privates Charles and Alexander Macintosh, Alexander Fraser, and Duncan Macdougall were tried for mutiny, found guilty, and condemned to be shot. In the case of Macdonald the sentence was commuted to corporal punishment —one of the first instances of a Highland soldier having been flogged. They were marched out to Gullane Links, East Lothian, on the 16th of July, and on reaching the ground were informed that only two would have to suffer the penalty of death. The two Macintoshes were called upon to draw lots, and the fatal one fell upon Charles. He and Fraser were immediately shot in the presence of the Scotch Brigade and other regiments assembled to witness this melancholy spectacle. The other men who had taken part in the mutiny were drafted into regiments serving abroad, and nothing further is known of their fate. No subsequent act of insubordination is recorded against this regiment, which was disbanded in 1798. It is singular to learn that less than seventy years ago in this civilised country the life or death of a human being depended on his drawing a lucky or unlucky number.

About the same period a mutiny broke out in the Breadalbane regiment, which gave rise to an incident that will remind our readers of the classical story of Damon and Pythias, and serve to illustrate the high spirit of honour which then prevailed among the Highlanders. This regiment was raised by the Earl of Breadalbane in 1793, and consisted of three battalions, whose united strength amounted to 2300 men. Some idea may be formed of the population of the Highlands at this period from the fact that 1600 men were obtained from the Breadalbane estates alone. We question whether one-fourth of that number could be raised there at the present day. Soon after the regiment had embodied it removed to Glasgow, and remained there till 1795, when a mutiny, similar in character and results to the one mentioned above, broke out among the men, who accused their officers of having sold them to the government for foreign service. The mutiny was soon suppressed, but when orders were given to apprehend the ringleaders it was found that so many of the men were equally implicated in the affair as to render it difficult to make a distinction. This difficulty was obviated by some of the men coming forward, taking all the blame upon themselves, and offering to suffer in the place of their less guilty comrades. Such an instance of generous self-sacrifice is unparalleled in the history of the British army, if not of the whole human race. The prisoners were sent to Edinburgh Castle to await their trial, and a singular incident occurred soon after they left Glasgow. The party was under command of Major Colin Campbell, one of their own officers, and one of the prisoners expressed a wish to speak to him in private. This man, Macmartin, belonged to the same part of the country as Major Campbell, and had always borne an excellent character, so that he had no difficulty in obtaining the desired interview. He stated frankly that he had given up all hope of escape, and was prepared to meet death. There was only one matter which weighed on his conscience and caused him much trouble: he had had some dealings with a friend in Glasgow which could only be settled by a personal interview; if this were denied, his friend would suffer much loss and inconvenience. If he were permitted to return to Glasgow he gave his solemn promise to rejoin the party before they reached Edinburgh.

"Major Campbell," he added, "you have known me since I was a child; you know my country and kindred, and you believe I shall never bring you to any blame by a breach of the promise I now make to be with you in full time to be delivered up in the castle."

At the present day a soldier would no more think of making such a proposal than an officer would dream of entertaining it. But

Major Campbell was a kind-hearted man. He had known the prisoner from childhood, and had the fullest confidence in his honesty and good faith. Though aware that the non-appearance of the prisoner would entail the most serious consequences to himself, he unhesitatingly complied with his request, and Macmartin returned to Glasgow, had an interview with his friend, transacted his business, and started before daylight for Edinburgh to redeem his pledge. Being dressed in the uniform of his regiment, he was afraid to travel by the main road lest he should be apprehended as a deserter, and took a circuitous route through the woods; the result was that, though he escaped detection, he failed to reach Edinburgh at the appointed hour.

As Major Campbell approached the city his anxiety increased. He caused the party to march slowly, in the hope that he might still appear; but, finding no pretext for further delay, he was at length obliged to march the remaining prisoners to the Castle. Just as he was in the act of handing them over to the governor of the prison, and before the latter had time to examine whether the number of prisoners tallied with the report, poor Macmartin rushed up, pale with anxiety and fatigue, and trembling with apprehension lest his generous benefactor should suffer through his absence. A few moments later, and all would have been discovered; as it was, he was able to join his fellow-prisoners without attracting the notice of the governor, and to explain the cause of his temporary absence to Major Campbell, who used often to allude to the incident in after-life as a proof of the high spirit of honour which prevailed among his men.

It is satisfactory to add that Macmartin's life was spared. All the prisoners were tried, and four of their number condemned to be shot; but only one of them underwent this punishment. From the narrative of these mutinies the inference is undeniable that they were caused not so much by the insubordinate spirit of the Highlanders as by the injustice with which they were treated by the military authorities. During the present century our Highland regiments have served in every quarter of the globe, and have been as distinguished for their subjection to discipline as for their valour in the field.

CHAPTER VIII.

OUR HIGHLAND REGIMENTS—*continued.*

THE Highland regiments have always been distinguished for their attachment to their native land. This feeling prevails more or less among the inhabitants of all mountainous countries, where the grand and the sublime in nature is so deeply imprinted on the mind in childhood as, in all after years, to exercise a powerful influence upon the imagination. It was for this reason that the national air of the Swiss, the "*Ranz des vaches*," was prohibited in armies composed partly o. natives of Switzerland, its familiar notes bringing back their snow-clad mountains and deep glens so vividly to their remembrance that they could no longer resist the temptation to desert in order to revisit the scenes of their infancy. The same deeply-rooted feeling, as we have seen, led the Highlanders at first to confine their services to the land of their birth, and to break forth into mutiny when an unscrupulous government attempted to break faith with them. Once embarked, however, for foreign service, much as they longed for "the land of the mountain and the flood," a high principle of honour prevented them from deserting their colours. Patiently they waited till permitted to return, when the love of country sometimes displayed itself in a way that reminds the classical reader of Ulysses' return to his beloved Ithaca. Thus, when the 42nd Highlanders landed at Port Patrick in 1775, after an absence from Scotland of thirty-two years, many of the old soldiers leaped on shore with enthusiasm and kissed the earth, which they grasped in handfuls. This occurrence would be appreciated by the writers of *Punch*, who, among other quips at the expense of the Scotch and their erratic tendencies, inform us that the North British railway is the only one which yields no returns. As a matter of fact, the exodus from the North is only temporary, and side by side with the love of adventure and gain, an ardent feeling of patriotism is to be found in the heart of every Scotchman. This feeling it is that induces him to toil beneath the burning sun of the tropics, and to visit the most distant parts of the globe in search of that wealth which, once acquired, enables him to "go back" to his native land and enjoy the fruits of his industry.

The warm desire to revisit the land of his birth enables the Highlander to submit to the most trying privations without a murmur, and to resist the strongest temptations to desert to the enemy. During the war carried on by the English against Hyder Ali in India, more than a hundred men of Macleod's Highlanders fell into the hands of that bloodthirsty despot, who tried in every way to induce them to enter his service. Finding that his most liberal offers had no effect, he tried to break their spirit by acts of cruelty. They were treated with every indignity; their only food was unwholesome rice, doled out to them in quantities barely sufficient to sustain life. They were exposed to the burning heat of the sun by day, and to the unhealthy dews that descend by night. Daily their numbers were reduced by disease; death stared them in the face. They had but to renounce their religion and their country to obtain the amplest rewards from the tyrant into whose hands they had fallen, but they preferred death to dishonour. Such a fact is creditable to the Highlanders; more—it is honourable to humanity itself. There is no spectacle so noble, says an ancient writer, as that of a good man struggling against adversity; these Highland prisoners had to engage in that struggle with little or no hope of deliverance in their time of trouble.

This same regiment took part in the unfortunate expedition under General Whitelock, which, in 1806, attempted to seize Buenos Ayres. It was owing to no lack of bravery on the part of our soldiers that their efforts were not crowned with success, but no amount of courage could compensate for the incapacity or treachery of the officer in command. Our army had to capitulate to the Spaniards, and remained in their power till peace was concluded. During this interval the Spaniards began to tamper with the Highlanders, and to hold out inducements to them to desert. These allurements were not without their effect upon those of them who happened to belong to the same religion. No less than thirty-five were induced to go over to the enemy. An incident occurred on this occasion which proves in the most striking manner the influence that home associations still continue to exercise over the minds of the Highlanders. A soldier named Donald Macdonald had almost yielded to the solicitations of the Spaniards to remain at Buenos Ayres, and while he was still wavering a comrade attempted to dissuade him from his purpose. Using no argument, he appealed to his heart by singing that touching Highland melody, "Lochaber no more." The song awoke a thousand memories of home and country. The tears started into poor Donald's eyes, and as he wiped them away he exclaimed, "Na, na! I canna stay! I'd maybe return to Lochaber nae mair."

We know that a considerable mind has given forth his decision that if he had the making of a people's songs, he cared not who made their laws; and the case of this Highlander, brought back to a sense of duty by one of the songs of his infancy, proves that in certain natures an appeal to the feelings is far more powerful than any appeal to the intellect. Nor has "Lochaber no more" lost its magic power over the Highland heart. We have seen many proofs of the contrary, one of which may be given. There is—or at least there was recently—in the Scots Fusilier Guards a soldier of the name of Roderick Ross, a native of Inverness-shire. Roderick had the build of a giant, but the heart of a child; he stood six feet four inches in his stockings, but was as soft and tender-hearted as a young maiden. He was respected as a brave soldier who had done his duty well all through the Crimea, but his friends the pipers of the regiment could not always resist the temptation to amuse themselves by reviving, or rather eliciting, his ardent love of country. The bagpipes begin to utter the wailing notes of "Lochaber no more," Roderick's huge frame is agitated like a mountain ash in a storm; tears spring to his eyes, and, unable to control his emotion, he rushes from the room exclaiming, "I canna stand 'Lochaber no more;' it aye gars (makes) me think o' deserting."

To get back to Macleod's Highlanders at Buenos Ayres. While a few went over to the Spaniards, the regiment as a whole remained faithful to their colours, and their fidelity called forth the warm approval of the authorities. On their return home they were stationed at Cork, where General Floyd, a veteran officer who had often witnessed their gallantry in India, presented them with new colours, and referred in his address to the temptations they had overcome. "You now stand on this parade," he said, "in defiance of the allurements held out to base desertion. You are endeared to the army and to your country. You insure the esteem of all true soldiers and good men." The 42nd Highlanders were still more distinguished for their attachment to their colours. Many of the privates were gentlemen of birth and education, who preferred the profession of arms to every other, and were possessed of as fine a sense of honour as the officers under whom they served. In the war of American Independence they were brought frequently into contact with the insurgents, and exposed to those temptations to desert which many of our soldiers formerly belonging to regiments now stationed in Canada have not been able to resist. The 42nd passed through five campaigns with their honour pure and unsullied; they had to endure many privations; their ranks were thinned by the bullets of the enemy; they had no prospect of promotion in the British service; they might have risen to the highest rank in that of the insurgents. And yet not one of their number deserted; the regiment remained free from this stain till it received a draft of an inferior class of men from the 26th Regiment, a few of whom went over to the enemy. These men, however, did not strictly belong to the 42nd, and never possessed that *esprit de corps* by which the Highlanders were animated. We question whether it can be said of any other regiment at the present day that it has passed through five campaigns without losing a single man by desertion. Macdonald's Highlanders, then known as the 76th Regiment, could lay claim to the same honourable distinction; they passed through the whole of the American campaign, and, though often tempted by the insurgents to renounce their allegiance, they all remained true to their colours. The same might be said of the Royal Highland Emigrant Regiment, which was raised among the sons of the Gael in Canada in 1778, and took an active part in the defence of Quebec against General Arnold. Even in cases where a Highlander was tempted to desert his colours there seems often to have remained a feeling of remorse which we should look for in vain at the present day among those *bounty-lifters* who live by defrauding their country, and esteem perjury to be the most venial of offences. This feeling of remorse manifested its presence and its power in an effort to atone for the past offence such as can leave no doubt regarding its sincerity, for their worst enemies will admit that when a Highlander consents to part with his money, it may be taken for granted that he is thoroughly in earnest. A soldier of the 91st or Argyleshire Highlanders was tempted to desert. He embarked for America, and became a settler there. Fortune smiled upon him in the land of his adoption, but there was a weight upon his conscience he could not shake off. In the midst of all his prosperity he never ceased to remember that he was a perjured man, a deserter from the British army. He had not the moral courage to return to his duty, and to submit to the punishment which his offence merited, but some years after his desertion he sent home a letter with a considerable sum of money to procure one or two men to enlist in his former regiment, "as the only recompense he could make for breaking his oath to his God and his allegiance to his king, which preyed on his conscience in such a way that he had no rest night nor day."

This anecdote leads us to notice another trait in the character of our Highland soldiers; they were emphatically religious men, and they were prepared to make any sacrifice for their faith. They were little versed in theology, but, like Cromwell's Ironsides at Dunbar, they put their trust in God and kept their powder dry. The great mass of them were Presbyterians, and in foreign and far-distant lands they continued to worship as their fathers had worshipped. Soldiers at that period were the most irreligious of men; they "swore terribly in Flanders" and elsewhere. We may form some idea of their morals from Hogarth's well-known "March to Finchley." Any display of religious feeling on the part of a soldier excited such surprise as to prove its extreme rarity, especially in the case of the Highlanders, who were esteemed at first to be little better than savages. When the 42nd Regiment first visited the metropolis, the Londoners were surprised to observe that officers and men never sat down to table without first saying grace—a religious observance which should be honoured, but which has become obsolete in our mess-rooms at the present day. An English historian shows how surprised his countrymen were "to see these savages, from the officer to the commonest man, first stand up and pull off their bonnets, and then lift up their eyes in the most solemn and devout manner, and mutter something in their own gibberish, by way, I suppose, of saying grace, as if they had been so many Christians." Of course, in the eyes of this wiseacre, they could not have been Christians, because they expressed their devotion in a gibberish which, as he charitably implies, was as unintelligible to the Deity as it was to himself; but we know how to judge these things by a different standard, and we condemn the man who could write so narrowly. At first a chaplain was attached to every regiment, and Dr. Carlisle, of Inveresk, mentions in his memoirs, that one of these chaplains, during an engagement in America, freely exposed himself to the fire of the enemy, in order to encourage the young soldiers by his example. We question whether such a display of clerical courage would meet with the approval of the authorities at the War Office at the present day; certain facts have come under our notice that would tend rather to an opposite conclusion. These regimental chaplains had to mess with the officers, and it was imagined that the presence of a clergyman would have an elevating influence upon the latter; experience, however, soon proved that the chaplains, instead of elevating the officers, were, through daily contact, brought down to the same moral level, and it is a significant fact that Burns, although his national spirit was great, considered them fair game for his satire. About the commencement of the present century chaplains were attached to brigades and not to regiments, and this continued to be the case during the Peninsular war. It thus occasionally happened that certain of our Highland regiments, when serving at remote stations, had no provision made for their religious wants, and were left entirely to their own resources. Some idea of their attachment to their faith may be formed from the efforts they made to secure the services of ministers of their own creed. "The Sutherland men, or 93rd Highlanders," says General Stewart, "were so well grounded in moral duties and religious principles, that, when stationed at the Cape of Good Hope, and anxious to enjoy the advantages of religious instruction agreeably to the tenets of their national Church, and there being no religious service in the garrison, except the customary one of reading prayers to the soldiers on parade, the men of the 93rd formed themselves into a congregation, engaged and paid a stipend (collected from the soldiers) to a clergyman of the Church of Scotland (who had gone out with the intention of teaching and preaching to the Caffres), and had divine service performed conformably to the ritual of the Established Church. Their expenses were so well regulated that, while contributing to the support of their clergyman from the savings of their pay, they were enabled to promote that social cheerfulness which is the true attribute of pure religion and of a well-spent life." There are few regiments in the service now that would be prepared to make the same sacrifice, and if our chaplains were dependent entirely on voluntary contributions they would soon be reduced to a state of starvation, as church parade is usually the most distasteful of all duties to a soldier. It deserves to be mentioned to the honour of the 93rd Highlanders that they have always displayed the same religious fervour and readiness to contribute to the support of a clergyman of their own church. About twenty years ago the regiment was stationed in a remote part of Canada, where they had no opportunity of enjoying the instruction of one of their own ministers. To meet this want they formed themselves into a congregation, and contributed a sum sufficient for the support of a minister, who continued to labour among them till they were ordered home. Many of our Highland regiments are at present stationed in India, and it is satisfactory to add that acting-chaplains, who are liberally paid by the Indian government, are attached to each of them.

The advantages of religious instruction were manifest in the absence of crime and of most of those vices which have now become deeply rooted in the British army. These gallant veterans devoted to religious purposes the money which is now too often spent in dissipation, and the advantages of the course were evident in the high moral tone which existed among them. They knew the value of money, but they would not retain a sixpence they did not consider to be their own. We find, for example, in the case of a Highland regiment, that on landing in Ireland they marched to Waterford the same day, where they received billet-money on their entrance into the town. The same evening they received orders to proceed at once to New Ross. Any other soldiers would have retained their billet-money as their perquisite, but the Highlanders, with a simple honesty which most men would be more disposed to admire than to imitate, returned it to the billet-master. So correct was the conduct of the men that in some regiments corporal punishment was almost unknown. In the Royal Highland Emigrant Regiment only one man was brought to the halberts during the time they were embodied. For the lengthened period of forty years there were few courts-martial and no cases of flogging in the 42nd Regiment. The value of this fact will be appreciated by all who are familiar with the statistics of punishment in the British army during the prevalence of war. It was only when a foreign element was introduced in the shape of a draft from another regiment that crime and its consequences became more frequent. The old soldiers refused to associate with those who had been brought to the halberts; they looked upon the latter as disgraced, whereas at the present day a soldier suffers nothing in the estimation of his comrades though he may have been guilty of almost every crime. *Would that one could revive that high moral tone among our soldiers which led the 42nd Highlanders to raise money sufficient to purchase the discharge of those ruffians whom they esteemed to be a disgrace to the regiment.* The presence of such men carried contamination with it, and soldiers who were proud of their regiment and jealous of its honour were ready to make any sacrifice to get quit of them. The remedy, as might have been expected, proved insufficient. The infusion of the criminal element was too powerful to be eliminated by any such means. The offering of a premium for vice tended only to increase the evil which it was intended to remove, but such a fact places in the most favourable light the high sense of honour by which the men of the 42nd were influenced.

When punishment was inflicted upon the Highlanders themselves, it was usually for insubordination. While devotedly attached to those officers who treated them with justice and kindness, they were ever ready, as we have shown, to resist any attempt to deprive them of their rights. It unfortunately happened that they were sometimes placed under the command of officers ignorant of their character and feelings, who tried to carry matters with a high hand and to rule them by terror more than by affection. In such cases the most lamentable consequences followed: a spirit of insubordination sprang up, which the severest punishment failed to repress. We find, for example, that the 75th Regiment, on landing in India in 1780, was placed under the command of an officer whose great ambition it was to introduce the Prussian system of discipline, the nature of which may be learned from Carlyle's "Life of Frederick the Great." Such a system may have been well adapted to the gigantic foot-soldiers whom Frederick William delighted to see around him, but it was subversive of all discipline when applied to a Highland regiment. The proud spirit of the mountaineers refused to be smothered with pipeclay or be shackled with red tape, and a mutiny would probably have ensued if the martinet had not been removed to make place for another officer, who, uniting firmness with due regard to the feelings of the men, soon regained for the regiment its former high character. A striking contrast to the temporary demoralisation produced in the 75th by the folly of the commanding officer was presented by the 78th or Ross-shire Highlanders, who were stationed in India about the same time under the command of Colonel Mackenzie of Suddie, one of their clansmen. During six years spent in different parts of the Bengal Presidency their conduct was so exemplary as to call forth the warm approval of the authorities and to produce a desire to imitate in other regiments the system which had produced such excellent results.

What more striking proof can there be of the hallowing influence of home associations on the mind of the Highlander? When serving in foreign lands he never forgets his native village, his father's home, and the good name bequeathed to him as his only inheritance. His great ambition is to do nothing to disgrace that name or to forfeit the good opinion of the little community to which he expects some day to return. "What will they say at home?" is the first thought that occurs to him after a hard-fought field; and a feeling of honest pride springs up in his heart as he thinks that the deeds of himself and his comrades will be talked of in the circle he lived in before he became a soldier. Lord Clyde and other generals knew how to turn this feeling to the best account, and no man will ever make a good soldier who has no social ties and no regard for public opinion. It is pleasing to add that the same honourable feeling still subsists in the 78th, and that such men as Havelock and Outram have borne testimony to the good effects produced by it. It deterred the regiment, when first raised, from the commission of crime, and thus saved them from the disgrace of corporal punishment. For many years flogging was unknown; it was not till 1799 that an offence meriting this punishment occurred. The miserable offender was at once tabooed by his comrades, who felt themselves disgraced by his conduct, and avoided him as if he had the plague-spot; so that, driven to despair, he might have been tempted to lay violent hands on himself if the colonel had not interposed in his behalf. Knowing that no change could be effected in the feelings of the men, he deemed it best to send him home to England, where his crime would be unknown, and he might thus have an opportunity of retrieving his character. It happened as he expected: the man justified the colonel's decision and turned out an excellent soldier, whereas if he had been allowed to remain in the regiment he would have been lost. Thus justice tempered with mercy was the saving of this soldier, as it had been of many others. Would that all commanding officers displayed the same humane and considerate spirit in the treatment of those under their command! The entries in the defaulters' book would be fewer in number, and the *morale* of the British army higher than it is at the present day.

We have already alluded to the excellent character of the 93rd Highlanders, who enjoyed the same immunity from punishment as the 78th. While other regiments became partially demoralised through the admixture of improper characters, the Sutherland Highlanders remained uncontaminated, and preserved a uniform line of good conduct. Punishment is usually more frequent in the light infantry companies, because the men are selected on account of their physical appearance without reference to moral character. For a period of nineteen years no case of punishment occurred in this or any other company of the 93rd, and this regiment still retains that *esprit de corps* which has been handed down in the ranks, and is as powerful for good as the inheritance of a noble name or the pride of ancestry. The Sutherland men, instead of spending their leisure hours in drunkenness and debauchery, have devoted them to those athletic sports which muscular Christianity has revived among other classes. Every one will admit that it is better to brace the physical frame by running, leaping, dancing, and tossing the kaber (manly exercises in which the 93rd are still proficient), than to weaken it by vicious indulgence. Wherever they have been stationed, at home or abroad, their exemplary conduct has earned for them the confidence of those among whom they lived, and procured for them admission into circles from which the majority of soldiers are excluded. Colonel Cameron of Fassiefern bears honourable testimony to the good conduct of the 92nd Highlanders. In writing to his father during the Peninsular war he thus alludes to his own clansmen who had followed him to the field:—"Not one of the poor fellows who came with me has ever behaved ill; none of them is even a questionable character."

The exemplary conduct of the Highlanders is to be attributed partly to the admirable arrangements connected with the internal economy of the different regiments. Their messes were managed by the non-commissioned officers, or old soldiers who had charge of the barrack-room; it was so arranged that those who belonged to the same glen or district, or were connected by the ties of friendship or blood, should occupy the same room and be seated at the same table. Such distinctions are ignored at the present day, so that the man of education and refinement who has been forced into the army by poverty or misconduct is obliged to associate by day and by night with the vilest of his species, and to have his sense of propriety outraged by their conduct and conversation. Need we wonder that he should soon be brought down to the moral level of those around him? In the Highland regiments this evil was avoided; every barrack-room was like a large family establishment, the occupants of which spoke the same language, wore the same dress, belonged to the same clan, and cherished the hope of returning to the same glen. Public opinion was as powerful for good in such a community as in civil life; all had an equal interest in sustaining the good fame of the mess to which they belonged. After defraying all the necessary expenses for breakfast, dinner, and other necessaries during the week, the surplus pay was placed in a stock purse and carefully guarded. When it reached a certain amount it was lent out at interest; the system of savings-banks had not yet been introduced into the army. When a soldier left the regiment he had usually sufficient money to establish himself in some kind of business, the profits of which, added to his pension, enabled him to spend the remainder of his days in comfort. So long as he remained in the regiment he had always enough to procure the usual necessaries, and to remit something to his friends in the old country, when they stood in need of such assistance. Large sums of money thus reached the North, and must have been acceptable in every way to those who received them. We have already shown how the Sutherland men, while stationed at the Cape of Good Hope, supported a minister of their own religion from their limited pay. While attentive to the duties of religion, they were not deaf to the voice of nature. They remembered those who had first taught them to respect religion, and acknowledged the obligation by ministering to their wants. All remitted something to the old folks at home—in several cases individual soldiers sent as much as £20 each. When the regiment landed at Plymouth in 1814, after eight years' service at the Cape, upwards of £500 were deposited in one bank to be remitted to Sutherlandshire; this was exclusive of sums forwarded through the post-office and through officers proceeding to the North. Before the Poor Law was introduced into Scotland, it was the great ambition of the poorest of the peasantry to accept no public relief; this feeling was common to all, and the greatest sacrifices were made by sons and daughters to prevent parents from *coming on the board*—*i.e.*, from accepting assistance from the offertories made at the different churches for the benefit of the indigent. This feeling accompanied the Highland soldier to distant lands, and led him to submit to many privations in order to save money for the support of his parents, who were thus enabled to retain their self-esteem and to enjoy the respect of the community in which they lived.

On examining the papers of the late Sir Ewen Cameron of Fassiefern, the father of Colonel Cameron of the 92nd Highlanders, it was found that large sums of money had been remitted from different parts of the world by soldiers for the support of their parents. Writing from Alexandria, 24th August, 1801, to his father, Colonel Cameron thus alludes to this trait in the character of his men:—"I wrote you before leaving Newport, inclosing a bill on Charles Erskine for money belonging to *Ewen dubh Taillear* (black Hugh the Tailor), and from Marmorice Bay, a letter with money for *Ewen dubh Coul* (black Hugh of Coul); also money for the two Macphies." Writing on the 14th December, 1809, after his return from the disastrous expedition to Walcheren, Colonel Cameron says—"The Bo-man's (cattle-herd's) son has begged of me to forward you (inclosed) one half of ten-pound note to assist his father's family. The other half he will forward to his brother by next post. He is a very *siccer* (steady) lad."

It is a pleasing duty to commemorate the filial affection of those gallant old soldiers who have now gone the way of all flesh, and to testify from our own experience that in the ranks of our Highland regiments there are still men possessed of the same frugal habits and the same dutiful attachment to their parents as the Bo-man's son. If the number has diminished of late years, it is because the feeling of honest pride which led the children to provide for their parents has been weakened through the operation of that Poor Law which has effected so many important changes in the social condition of the lowly.

CHAPTER IX.

OUR HIGHLAND REGIMENTS—*continued.*

THE health of the British army both at home and abroad has improved very much of late years. The British soldier is better fed, better clothed, and better lodged now than he ever was before; hence in India the mortality has been reduced by one-half, and a corresponding change has been effected in the number of admissions to our military hospitals. Still the fact cannot be overlooked that a larger amount of sickness prevails among soldiers than among civilians of the same age and rank in life, whose physical wants are less carefully attended to; and while other causes may intervene, this difference is to be attributed mainly to the habits of the men themselves. The surest test of the moral character of a regiment is the number of admissions to hospital. When a regiment is demoralised, the wards will be crowded; when a healthy moral tone prevails in the ranks, they will be comparatively empty. Drunkenness and immorality have done more to thin the ranks of the British army, and to crowd our unions with discharged soldiers, than the bullets of the enemy, the scorching sun of the tropics, the fatigues of actual warfare, or the malaria of unhealthy stations.

On consulting the statistics of mortality connected with the Highland regiments when first raised, we are surprised at the small number of casualties which occurred among them. They were always first in the field of danger, and yet there were fewer deaths among them than in many regiments in time of peace. We find, for example, that the 42nd Regiment embarked for Flanders on the

18th of June, 1794, and landed at Ostend on the 26th of the same month. They shared in all the hardships of that unfortunate expedition, and took part in the disastrous retreat to Deventer, the miseries of which have been compared to the sufferings of the French after the burning of Moscow. Disease, the result of the severity of the weather and the want of food and proper clothing, thinned the ranks of the British army; many of our best soldiers sank under the accumulated hardships which beset them. The Dutch, on whose gratitude they had the strongest claims, inhospitably closed their doors against the sufferers, and refused to render them any assistance. The result was that some of the newly-raised regiments lost more than three hundred men by disease alone, while the 42nd, which had three hundred young recruits in its ranks, lost only twenty-five men, including those killed in battle, from their disembarkation at Ostend till their embarkation at Bremen on the 14th of April, 1795. This immunity from disease is to be attributed to their temperate habits as much as to their natural strength of constitution and power of enduring fatigue and privation. An amusing incident occurred while the regiment was stationed at Alost in the month of July. A party of 400 of the French cavalry entered the town, and being mistaken for Hessians, met with no resistance till they reached the market-place, where one of them attempted to cut down a 42nd Highlander of the name of MacDonald, who was walking along, unsuspicious of danger, with his basket on his head. He was severely wounded in the hand which held the basket, but promptly drawing his bayonet with the hand which was disengaged, he attacked the dragoon with such fury that he was compelled to retreat. Donald then continued his course, muttering his regret that he had not his father's good broadsword to cut the rascal down. The enemy were soon recognised and driven from the town. It is worthy of remark that the practice of enticing mere boys into the service was then unknown in the Highland regiments. The profession of arms was so popular in the North, that they could always find a sufficient supply of able-bodied men. Their average age on enlistment was twenty-two years, a period of life not too young to render them incapable of enduring the hardships and sufferings of military service, nor too old to unfit them for learning that discipline without which an army would soon degenerate into an armed mob. In short, they were picked men, and the advantage of this carefulness of selection was manifest in their exemption from disease, and their power of enduring privations under which others less robust would have succumbed. The Ross-shire Fusiliers when reduced were as strong and efficient as when embodied. Not one man had died during the period of service, a case unparalleled, we believe, in the annals of the British army. The money which is too often spent in the canteen or in still worse places was remitted to their friends, and this generous self-denial was not without its reward.

Another characteristic trait in the character of these men was their quiet, orderly, and kind deportment to the inhabitants of the different countries in which they were stationed. Soldiers are apt to look upon themselves as a distinct class, and to assume a certain haughty bearing in their dealings with civilians, who, of course, are prone to retaliate. The Highlanders seem never to have forgotten that they were only civilians in arms, bound by the laws of courtesy as well as by the rules of military discipline. During the years 1743-44 the 42nd Regiment was stationed in different parts of Flanders, under the command of Field-Marshal the Earl of Stair, where, if they had been so disposed, they might have levied contributions on the powerless inhabitants. The latter, however, had such confidence in their honesty and integrity, that they specially requested to have them appointed the guardians of their property, and bore willing testimony to the faithfulness with which they had discharged this duty. Few of them, we are told, were ever drunk, and they as rarely swore. They retained in Flanders the simple habits of their own native glens, and when they left, the Elector-Palatine wrote to his envoy in London, desiring him to thank the King of Great Britain for the excellent behaviour of the regiment while in his territory, "for whose sake," he adds, "I will always pay a respect and regard to a Scotchman in future."

In the month of May, 1815, the intelligence reached England that Napoleon had escaped from Elba, and the three Highland regiments which had been stationed in Ireland at once embarked for Flanders, and took up their quarters at Brussels, where they became very popular among the inhabitants. They were billeted among the citizens, who, instead of regarding this as a hardship, rejoiced in their presence, and had such confidence in their honesty, that they often committed their shops to their care when they had occasion to go out. It was not unusual to see a stalwart Highlander nursing a Flemish baby, and handling it as tenderly as if he had been "to the manner born." But, in truth, our Highland soldiers have always been remarkable for their fondness for children. When the 78th Highlanders forced their fiery way to the Residency at Lucknow, and were welcomed by the starving women whom they had saved from a fate worse than death, they seized the children from their arms, pressed their bearded faces against their tender cheeks, and shed tears of generous pity over them. Those tears did not unman them or unfit them for their duty, as all who are familiar with the annals of the Indian campaign will at once admit. No wonder that the kind-hearted Highlanders at Brussels made a favourable impression on the hearts of the Flemish maidens with whom they were brought in contact. A soldier of the 42nd had gained the affections of the daughter of a wealthy tradesman in whose house he was quartered at Brussels, and though he had never told his love, a mutual understanding had sprung up between them. When the British forces advanced to Waterloo, the Flemish maiden trembled for the fate of her lover. The power of Napoleon was shattered on that hard-contested field, but the Highlanders returned not to Brussels. The 42nd embarked for England, and arrived in the vicinity of Edinburgh on the 18th of March, 1816, where they were welcomed by the inhabitants with acclamations of joy, and entertained at a public dinner. The postal arrangements were not so perfect in those days as at present. Long weary months passed away, and the Flemish maiden heard nothing of her lover. One day a party of Highlanders were carousing together in Edinburgh, and toasting their sweethearts, as was the custom at that period. It was observed that one of them was silent, and refused to toast his mistress. "Leave him alone," the others said;

"we all know that he left his heart at Brussels." The remark had scarcely been made when it was announced that a person had called to see him. On entering another room, he found there a young lady dressed in the deepest mourning, who rushed forward and welcomed him with a cry of joy. It was the Flemish maiden. In broken English, and with many tears, she told him of all the anguish she had suffered from his absence and silence. She had borne it all till the death of her father left her mistress of her actions, when she resolved to visit England in order to ascertain his fate. On reaching London, she learned that the 42nd had been sent north to Edinburgh, and followed the regiment there. She only knew her lover's name, but a soldier, touched with pity by her romantic tale, searched the town till he discovered where he was. The rest may be left to the imagination of our readers. The war was now over, and she had no difficulty in purchasing the discharge of her lover. The officers of the regiment took an interest in the young couple, and were present at their marriage, after which the Highlander and his bride returned to Brussels, where they established themselves in business, and were as prosperous as they deserved to be.

Often, indeed, in the history of the Highland regiments—

> "Shine martial Faith and Courtesy's bright star
> Through all the wreckful storms that cloud the brow of War."

We could multiply instances of their kindness and forbearance to the helpless inhabitants of foreign lands, whom they might have plundered with impunity, and of the proofs of gratitude shown by the latter to their benefactors.

Alluding to the services of Keith's and Campbell's Highlanders with the allied army in Germany in 1759, the *Vienna Gazette* of 1762 says—"From the goodness of their disposition in everything, the boors are much better treated by these savages than by the polished French and English."

When these two regiments were ordered home, such was the character they had established for themselves during three campaigns that the inhabitants of Holland welcomed them with acclamations on their march through that country, and the women crowded around them and presented them with laurel-leaves. This display of friendly feeling may have been owing partly to the long services of the Scotch Brigade in the Dutch service, and the frequent intercourse between the two countries; but it was elicited in a great measure by the excellent conduct of the Highlanders themselves. After landing at Tilbury Fort, they marched for Scotland, and were treated with the most marked attention by the citizens of the different towns where they halted, especially by those of Derby, who presented the men with gratuities in money. This unusual liberality is said to have sprung from a grateful remembrance of the respect shown for their persons and property by the Highlanders when they visited the town in 1745, under the command of Charles Edward, the Young Pretender.

Some of these Highlanders had given a remarkable proof of the high spirit of honour which prevailed among them before leaving Scotland. Every one is familiar with the massacre of Glencoe, that detestable deed of butchery the details of which, after the lapse of more than a century, cannot be read without a shudder of horror. Part of the Mac Ians had escaped, and when Charles Edward landed in the North, their young chief joined his standard with a hundred and fifty men, and accompanied him in his march to the South. At first success attended his arms, and the Highland army passed near a beautiful mansion, the property of the Earl of Stair, whose forefather of the same name, from motives of private revenge, had caused the unfortunate Mac Ians to be murdered in cold blood by those whom they had welcomed as friends. It was part of the policy of Prince Charles to conciliate the Lowland proprietors who still kept aloof from his cause, and a guard was posted for the protection of Lord Stair's house, which was believed to be in some danger of being attacked by the Mac Ians in revenge for the massacre of their forefathers. No sooner had the chief of Glencoe heard of this precaution than he deemed his honour insulted, and demanded an interview with the prince.

"If a guard must be posted here," he said, "let the Mac Ians, who have most reason to hate the name of Dalrymple, supply that guard. If you refuse this request it must be from want of confidence in the MacIans, who, finding themselves distrusted, can no longer follow your standard. They are willing to die for you, but they will not submit to the insult of being watched by others."

It was fortunate that the prince understood the character of the

Glencoe.

young MacIan, and granted his request. The guard was duly posted, and the mansion of the Dalrymples received no injury. When we consider that old Lord Stair was the author of the massacre of Glencoe, and that revenge among the Highlanders was almost a sacred duty, we cannot withhold our admiration from the chief who could restrain his men on such an occasion, and from the men who voluntarily submitted to such restraint. The name of young MacIan of Glencoe is worthy of being ranked with those of Scipio and other heroes of antiquity, who knew how to practise, under the pressure of strong temptation, the difficult duty of self-denial.

> "This murderous chief, this ruthless man,
> This head of a rebellious clan,"

spared the mansion of his hereditary foe.

Such were the elements of which our Highland regiments were formed. When the mountaineers transferred their services to the House of Hanover, they did not lose their distinctive character; they shrank from no duty, however dangerous, but they never inflicted unnecessary suffering on the unprotected. The latter were always prepared to express their sense of their forbearance, and to lament their removal to another station. After the battle of Waterloo the 78th Regiment did garrison duty at Brussels till 1816, when they received orders to return home. The inhabitants had come to regard them as a part of themselves, and requested the mayor to try to prevent their removal. This could not be done, but the mayor expressed the feeling of his fellow-citizens by issuing the following document:—"As Mayor of Brussels, I have pleasure in declaring that the Scotch Highlanders who were garrisoned in this city during the years 1814 and 1815 called forth the attachment and esteem of all by the mildness and suavity of their manners and excellent conduct, insomuch that a representation was made to me by the inhabitants, requesting me to endeavour to detain the 78th Regiment of Scotchmen in the town, and to prevent their being replaced by other troops." The mayor's eulogium applies to all the Highland regiments stationed at Brussels, but the 78th were the best known because they had been longest there. *Les braves Flamands* witnessed their departure with the liveliest feelings of regret. "They are kind as well as brave;" "they are part of ourselves" (*enfans de famille*); "they are lions in the field, lambs in the house." Such were the expressions that greeted the plumed warriors of the North as they marched for the last time through the streets of Brussels.

Nor was it in foreign lands alone that the Highlanders secured the confidence and esteem of the inhabitants by their good conduct. The 92nd, or Gordon Highlanders, who were embodied in 1794, and derived their name from having been raised chiefly on the estates of the Duke of Gordon, in the counties of Aberdeen, Banff, and Inverness, were ordered to Ireland in 1798, to assist in quelling the insurrection which had broken out in that unfortunate country. Nothing could be more trying to the temper of the men than the duties they had to perform. They were constantly moved from place to place in the midst of a hostile population. On one occasion they had to march ninety-six Irish miles in three successive days, with arms, ammunition, and knapsacks. Notwithstanding their arduous duties, and the avowed hostility of the population to the red-coats, the Gordon Highlanders conducted themselves with such forbearance, that, on their being removed elsewhere, public testimony was borne to the fact that they had been "exemplary in all duties; sober, orderly, and regular in quarters." They had earned the same good character when stationed in the island of Corsica in 1795, and such was the estimation in which they were held in Ireland, that a parting address was presented to the Marquis of Huntly, the colonel of the regiment, in which it is said that "peace and order were re-established, rapine had disappeared, confidence in the government was restored, and the happiest cordiality subsisted since his regiment came among them." Many of the privates in this regiment belonged to a different class from those who usually enter the army; they were the sons of respectable farmers, who had been induced to enlist by the personal influence and blandishments of the beautiful Duchess of Gordon, the mother of their colonel.

In the Peninsula the conduct of the 92nd was as exemplary as in Ireland. Unmoved by hunger and the example of others, they respected the lives and property of those who could offer no resistance. Napier has rendered his readers familiar with the horrors which followed the capture of St. Sebastian in Spain. A more pleasing picture is presented by the conduct of the Gordon Highlanders and the old "fighting 50th" when they drove the French from the town of Aire on the 2nd of March, 1814. Places thus captured were almost invariably given up to pillage and destruction, and the miserable inhabitants deemed themselves fortunate if they escaped with their lives. On this occasion there was not a single act of plunder or violence; the Highlanders took quiet possession of the town, and paid for every article they required. Their generous forbearance produced such an impression on the inhabitants of Aire, that they presented an address to Colonel Cameron expressive of their gratitude for exemption from plunder and rapine, the usual fate of the defenceless in times of war. The Highlanders have always been popular in Ireland; they are sprung from the same Celtic stock, and speak a dialect of the same language. Though they had no sympathy with the Irish during the rebellion of 1798, and took an active part in quelling it, they were guilty of no unnecessary cruelty, and discharged their duty in such a way as to conciliate the esteem of those who were opposed to them. It was said of them that "their conduct and manners softened the horrors of war, and they were not a week in a fresh quarter or cantonment that they did not conciliate and become intimate with the people."

At this period duelling was an established custom in the British army, and some of the Highland officers were as ready to take offence as Sir Lucius O'Trigger in *The Rivals*, or the redoubtable Captain MacTurk in *St. Ronan's Well.* They were jealous of their personal honour, and as ready to challenge one another as those of a different race. We read of a Captain Campbell who fought a duel in a dark room without seconds, and killed his opponent. The absence of witnesses led the jury to give a verdict of murder, and the unfortunate man was hanged. A duel was fought at Gibraltar, in 1795, between Captain, afterwards Colonel Cameron, and Lieutenant, afterwards Sir John Maclean, in consequence of some disputed point of precedency. Both escaped without any serious injury. The Marquis of Huntly, the colonel of the 92nd, to which Cameron and Maclean belonged, took them to task for their conduct, and warned his officers against the practice of duelling. "I have the more right to insist upon this," he said, "as I believe you are all, more or less, connected with my father's estates." The hot-blooded Cameron started to his feet. "I," he exclaimed, "have no connexion with your father's estates or your father's clan; such an argument, therefore, cannot apply to me." The marquis knew how to soothe his wounded feelings, and this was his first and last duel. Nothing more readily rouses a Highlander's ire than any insult offered to his country, his language, or his dress, and strangers, ignorant of this peculiarity, were sometimes involved in quarrels without any intention of giving offence. We remember the case of an English officer, the nephew of an archbishop, who happened to be seated at a mess-room table opposite to a Highlander who wore the national costume, the uniform of his regiment. They were strangers to one another, and it was their first and last meeting in this world. The English officer made some bantering remark on the Highlander's dress, which was regarded by the latter as an insult, and led to an immediate challenge. They agreed to settle their difference at once, and on the first exchange of shots poor Mr. ——, the English officer, fell. Highland soldiers have now learned to bear any amount of "chaff" on their national peculiarities without taking offence, but national feeling was stronger and more sensitive in former days, and the barbarous custom of duelling often led to death in cases where an apology would now be deemed ample atonement. It is somewhat remarkable that the horror excited by the death of an Indian officer, slain in mortal combat by his own brother-in-law, an officer of the Life Guards, and a Highlander by birth, produced such a reaction, that the custom of duelling—that barbarous relic of a barbarous age—may now be regarded as obsolete.

An interesting work might be written on the female warriors of all nations, including the standing army of the King of Dahomey. In every country and in every age there have been men who, in point of valour, were women; and women who, in point of valour, were men. The Amazons of antiquity, the *vivandières* of France, and the camp followers of the British army, would all be entitled to some passing notice; but more attractive still would be the personal history of those women who, instigated by the promptings of valour or love, have entered the army and served for years without their sex being discovered. The wives of soldiers who have followed their husbands to the field, sharing their dangers and ministering to the wants of the wounded, might also find place in such a work, to which we willingly present the following contribution. Towards the close of last century, a stalwart, buxom Scottish lass became the wife of a private in the 42nd Highlanders, and was permitted to accompany the regiment when it embarked, in 1795, to take part in the expedition to the West Indies. She soon learned to share in all the hardships and dangers of a soldier's life, was frequently under fire, and became as skilful in dressing wounds as the most experienced surgeon. She was known to every one in the regiment, and was equally a favourite with officers and men. She was present at, and took part in, the attack on the island of St. Vincent, then occupied by the French and the insurgent natives. In one of the skirmishes between the 42nd and the enemy, Lieutenant-Colonel Graham was severely wounded, and left insensible on the field. After a time his own men returned and, believing him to be dead, dragged his body across the rough channel of the river to the sea-beach. The motion elicited some signs of life, and they hastened in search of a surgeon; meanwhile the body was borne along in a blanket for about four miles till they reached a post occupied by the 42nd. Colonel Graham still continued insensible, and no surgeon could be found to dress his wounds or restore him to consciousness. It was plain then, unless something were done at once he could not long survive, as a bullet had entered his side, come out beneath his breast, and shattered two of his fingers. He was already exhausted with the loss of blood. Fortunately for him our Highland Amazon was at this post, and at once proceeded to act the part of the good Samaritan. She washed his wounds, and bound them up with such skill that the surgeons, on their arrival, did not find it necessary to unloose the dressing. The colonel remained in a dangerous state for three weeks, when he was removed to England, where he gradually recovered and rose to the rank of Lieutenant-General and Governor of Stirling Castle. It is to be hoped that he did not forget the kind-hearted woman to whom he owed his life.

Be that as it may, she accompanied the 42nd in their different expeditions, and proved herself a skilful nurse in hospital, a fearless leader on the field of battle. Wherever her husband went she followed, watching over his safety, and threatening to avenge him if he fell. There is reason to believe that, like other veterans, she came at length to love fighting for its own sake, and that anxiety for the safety of her husband was only a cloak to justify her presence amid the wild excitement of the battle-field. On one occasion, before the commencement of an attack, the officer in command, being anxious to expose her husband to as little danger as possible, left him in charge of the men's knapsacks, which they had thrown aside before rushing up the hill. He remained at his post, but his wife, borne along by an irresistible impulse, rushed forward at the head of the attacking columns, and cheered them on to victory. No man could refuse to follow where a woman led the way. Three redoubts were carried in rapid succession, and just as the officer was giving orders to charge the fourth and last, he was suddenly tapped on the shoulder. On turning round he beheld his friend, the female warrior, with her clothes tucked up to her knees, and the proud expression of victory in her face. Seizing his hand, and shaking it heartily, she exclaimed, "Well done, my Highland lad! See how the brigands scamper, like so many deer! Come," she continued, "let us drive them from yonder hill." Her advice was acted on, and the success of the Highlanders was complete. When the fighting was over, friend and foe shared alike in her sympathies. Her skilful hand, like the spear of Achilles, could heal the wounds it had made.

About forty years ago, in almost every village in Scotland might be seen tall, erect, gray-headed old men, retired veterans, who, after fighting the battles of their country in every quarter of the globe, had returned to the place of their birth, the memory of which had haunted them during long years of absence and exile. They were the leaders of public opinion in the small community in which they lived—the village Nestors, from whose lips dropped words of wisdom, tales of strange adventure, and dangers encountered by sea and land. They feared God and honoured the king; they had only one failing—an overweening love of the bottle; they were the oracles of every tap-room, where, amid the applause of their boon companions, they fought their battles o'er again, even to the thrice routing of all their foes and the thrice slaying of the slain. It was not the mere love of drink that led them there; mingled with this weakness was the pleasure of recalling scenes in which they had borne a part, battles in which they had fought and conquered. Often the schoolboys on the village green would cease from their sports and gather round one of these veterans in an admiring circle, as, seated beneath a shady tree and leaning on his crutch, he told of the gallant deeds of the Gordon Highlanders or the Old Black Watch. His rude eloquence never failed to awaken the enthusiasm of his audience, and many a Scottish soldier was first led to think of the profession of arms, and to long, like Norval, to follow some brave chieftain to the field, from listening to these veterans. They have now gone the way of all living; we know of only one veteran survivor of Waterloo in the North, but we can recal many who lived and flourished a quarter of a century ago. Old Hyderabad stands before us at this very moment. There he is, with all the towering majesty of six feet and some additional inches, with shaggy eyebrows and straggling hair as white as snow, with a rough, stern, but not unkindly face, rendered still more stern by a sabre-cut on the brow, with his formidable pike-staff in one hand, and his ram's-horn "sneeshin'-mull," or snuff-box, in the other. His real name was James Bruce, but he was universally known as Hyderabad, from the interminable stories he told of the capture of that Indian city, at which he assisted. His stories occasionally exceeded the bounds of credence; for example, he used to relate that any eccentricity of manner observable in his conduct arose from a singular accident which happened to him at Hyderabad. He was fighting his way through the streets, when a bullet-wound in the leg laid him prostrate; one of his assailants rushed upon him and laid open his skull with a cut of his sabre. "I put up my hand to my head," said James, "to feel what was the matter; it so happened that I had just been takin' a pinch and forgot to put up my mull. Aweel, you see, I was so startled at the size of the hole in my head that I lost hold of my sneeshin'-mull, and it dropped inside my skull. Up came the doctor, and, without thinking of the mull, he clapped the skull together and trepanned it; the wound soon healed, but sometimes I feel a little queer in the head." No wonder that he did, considering that he believed that there was a ram's-horn in the place where his brains should have been. The delusion had originated from a sunstroke which he received in India, and which would have killed any other man than Hyderabad. It is worthy of remark that, though he was universally known as Hyderabad, few ever ventured to address him by that sobriquet; it was dangerous to take liberties with one whose pikestaff was ever ready to punish any impertinence. We can only recal one occasion when James was thus addressed. He was walking with stately gait through a country fair, when a young urchin, set on by his older companions, walked up to him, and said in his most winning way, "How d'ye do, Old Hyderabad?" Had the earth yawned beneath James's feet he could not have looked more surprised than he did on hearing these ominous words; here was an urchin who barely reached his knee addressing him familiarly by that name which the boldest never ventured to mention in his presence. It was like a mouse insulting a lion, but what could he do? He was too tender-hearted to touch a child, but such liberties must be repressed, so he flourished his pikestaff in the air and gave a yell such as a savage gives when he despatches his foe. Years have elapsed since James uttered that yell; his voice is now among the voices of the night; but it is still ringing in the ears of him who evoked it, and who fled in terror from the redoubtable presence, and equally redoubtable pikestaff, of Old Hyderabad.

Nor have we forgotten Old Corunna, the one-eyed veteran, who fought with Abercrombie in Egypt, and helped to lay the green turf on the grave of Sir John Moore in Spain. Many were the stories he used to recount of that disastrous retreat, of that fatal embarkation. We have seen his one eye dimmed with a tear as he spoke of Moore, that gallant leader who was dear to his men amid all their sufferings; we have seen it lighted up with genuine humour as he told of wealthy officers marching at the head of their men without shoes or stockings, and the latter whispering to one another, "There goes ten thousand a year." Unlike Hyderabad, Corunna was of small stature, but wiry as a terrier, retaining his vigour to the last, and ready to meet all comers. The fame of one of his encounters still lives in his native parish, and has long survived him. At the period when he flourished, it was not unusual for professional prizefighters to visit country fairs and to challenge the rustics to a friendly combat. If the challenge was not accepted, they claimed, and usually received, a certain sum of money; if they fought and failed to win, the money belonged to the victor. It so happened that Corunna was refreshing himself in a booth or tent at one of these country fairs when a noted pugilist appeared and gave the usual challenge. No one seemed disposed to take it up, till Old Corunna, over-brimming with whisky and valour, rushed from the tent, divested himself of his great-coat, and went at the bully with such thorough good will and masterly science that victory soon declared in his favour. That was, perhaps, the proudest day in poor Corunna's existence. During the fight a thief had stolen his great-coat, but this loss was very soon made up, and Corunna remained to his death the champion of the parish. He has several sons now serving in the British army.

CHAPTER X.

THE PIPERS OF OUR HIGHLAND REGIMENTS.

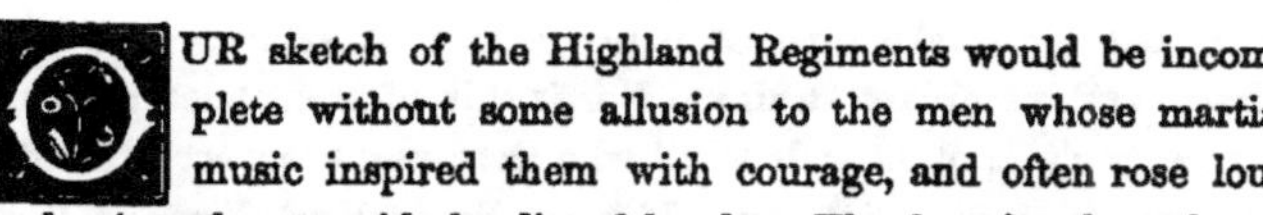

UR sketch of the Highland Regiments would be incomplete without some allusion to the men whose martial music inspired them with courage, and often rose loud and triumphant amid the din of battle. The bagpipe has always been a favourite instrument of music among the Celtic race. There is reason to believe that its invention is almost coeval with the origin of the human race; traces of it, at least, are to be found in the bas-reliefs of those ancient cities which have been brought to light by modern explorers. It was known to the Hindoos, the Chinese, and the Assyrians; it is still valued and appreciated by the natives of Ireland and Brittany. It may be justly regarded as the national instrument of Scotland, inasmuch as all our Scottish regiments are provided with pipers; and our Highland soldiers have always preferred their inspiring strains to every other kind of music. This feeling of preference has been well expressed by the poet:—

> "Then wild and high the Cameron's gathering rose,
> The war-note of Lochiel, which Albyn's hills
> Have heard, and heard, too, have her Saxon foes.
> How in the noon of night that pibroch thrills,
> Savage and shrill! But with the breath which fills
> Their mountain pipe, so fill the mountaineers
> With the fierce daring which instils
> The stirring memory of a thousand years;
> And Evan's, Donald's fame rings in each clansman's ears."

The influence of music depends very much upon association. The *Marseillaise*, for example, is to most men simply a warlike air, inferior to many others with which they have been familiar from infancy, while to the Frenchman it is the sacred chant of liberty, presaging the downfall of tyrants, and the destruction of all that stand in the way of human progress; the *Ranz des Vaches* awakens no unusual emotion in the breast of him who hears it for the first time, while to the Swiss, wandering in foreign lands, it brings back the snow-capped mountains, the wooden chalets, the tinkling of the cow-bells in the deep valleys, and all the other reminiscences of his native land. The sound of the bagpipe may be to the Saxon the least or the most disagreeable of all sounds; it revives no past associations; it awakens no patriotic feeling; it rather repels by its harsh and discordant strains. Nor is this effect confined to any one race or class; it extends to all who have not been accustomed to the war-pipe from infancy. If you ask an Englishman, "Do you like the bagpipes?" he answers with a significant smile, "Yes; but I like them best at a distance." Habit, however, is all-powerful in modifying this feeling of dislike; we have known English officers and soldiers serving in Highland regiments who came to prefer the pibroch to every other kind of music, and became, in this respect, more Scottish than the Scotch themselves. But we question whether a Frenchman, with all his acknowledged politeness, was ever betrayed into any expression bordering on admiration of Highland music. We have a lively remembrance of the expressive shrug which a Frenchman gave, when we asked him how he liked the bagpipes, and of the comical way in which he stopped his ears, as if still haunted with the horrible sound. A genuine Celt would attribute such symptoms of aversion to prejudice, affectation, or even to some worse motive; you could never convince him that the shrill notes of his favourite war-pipe could cause an unpleasant sensation on your tympanum.

An amusing illustration of this Celtic obtuseness of perception may be given. About half a century ago an accomplished young French nobleman, who recently held an appointment of importance at the Court of St. James's, was fortunate enough to secure the hand of a Scottish lady, who was heiress to a title in her own right, and to extensive estates in the north. After his marriage, which was celebrated in England, the happy couple went to spend the honeymoon at an ancient castle belonging to the lady in a remote part of the Highlands. This was, perhaps, rather a mistake, as the French do not understand our English institution of the honeymoon, and consider that throwing two young people together for a month tends rather to make them tired of one another's society. Be that as it may, they reached the Highlands in safety, and spent the first night in the ancient castle. The excitement and fatigue of the journey kept the Frenchman awake the greater part of the night, and he had just dropped quietly asleep at an early hour in the morning, when all at once he was roused to consciousness by a loud discordant noise beneath his window. Springing to his feet, he drew aside the curtains to ascertain the cause of this disturbance. It was a charming morning, the grass on the lawn was glistening with dew-drops, and the heath-clad mountains were tipped with the golden rays of the rising sun. But he had no eye for the beauties of nature; every other feeling was absorbed in indignation at being roused from his pleasant slumber by an old fellow in the Highland garb, who was strutting backwards and forwards on the lawn and playing ' Hey, Johnnie Cope, are ye waukin' yet," to his own intense satisfaction. If the indignant Frenchman had stopped to inquire, he would have found this was old Donald, the family piper, who had been in the habit of waking the family by this morning serenade ever since he entered on his office; but his only thought was how to get rid of this nuisance, so he shouted, "*Allez, allez-vous en, tout de suite!*" "Sir!" said Donald, surprised at hearing himself addressed in a language which he did not understand. "Go, go away," said the Frenchman. "Your music is execrable; it is murderous; it will kill me." If the earth had yawned before him, Donald could not have stood more aghast than he did on hearing these words. The sound of the bagpipes was to him the most delightful of all music, and he could not understand how it could be otherwise than pleasing to everyone else. But here was a man who actually ordered *him*, the family piper, away; who pronounced his music murderous, and declared it would kill him. There must be some mystery in this, some secret cause for this unaccountable dislike. The bagpipes were silent; but Donald walked backwards and forwards on the lawn, holding his head erect, distending his nostrils, and sniffing with indignation at the insult offered to him. "Maybe the carl (fellow) does na like music," he at length burst forth; "or maybe he does na like *me*. What ails him at the bagpipes? By my faith, I have it now; he heard a little too much of them at Waterloo!"

While our Scottish regiments have ceased to be composed exclusively of Scotchmen, they have still retained their pipers. They are not the only musicians attached to these regiments, for there are the brass bands besides; but the national music is always most appreciated by those who belong to the north. When the drum and the fife cease, and the bagpipes strike up some well-known pibroch or march, you can tell by their heightened colour and beaming eyes who are the Scotchmen in the ranks; cheered on by that music, they will rush on to danger or to death without dismay. It was a mistake to deprive these regiments of their pipers, as was done in some cases; and Scotland ought to cherish the memory of William IV. for restoring them to the Scots Fusilier Guards.

The number attached to each regiment was originally twelve, but it has now, in some instances, been reduced to six. While the pipers may be regarded as non-combatants, they have contributed largely to every victory gained by their countrymen, not only by the animating strains of their music, but by their coolness and self-possession in the hour of danger. Many instances of this might be given; in truth, the pipers imagined that the result of the day depended in no small measure on the unceasing shrillness of their war notes and their constant presence in the thickest of the battle. The 42nd Highlanders formed part of the attacking party which captured Fort Washington in 1777. Determined to have their own share of glory, they scrambled up the precipice, holding on by the brushwood and shrubs which grew out of the crevices of the rocks. The first to reach the summit was one of the pipers, who, as soon as he had made good his footing, began to play; he knew that he was thus concentrating all the fire of the enemy on himself; but what was death to him so long as his comrades secured the victory? His body, riddled with bullets, fell from point to point till it reached the bottom of the rock, mangled and disfigured; but the Highlanders went on with a ringing cheer, and carried everything before them. The piper had the soul of a hero, and who will say that he died in vain?

At the battle of Porto Novo, which was fought in 1780, Macleod's Highlanders, now known as the 71st, or Glasgow Light Infantry, was the only British regiment on our side. The whole army under Sir Eyre Coote did not exceed eight thousand men, while the force under Hyder Ali consisted of twenty-five battalions of infantry, four hundred Europeans, between forty and fifty thousand horse, and above one hundred thousand matchlock men and peons, with forty-seven pieces of cannon. Notwithstanding their superiority of numbers, the enemy were driven from all their entrenchments, and compelled to retire. The 71st, or 73rd as it was then called, was on the right of the first line, and led all the attacks. Their unbending firmness and daring courage called forth the warm approval of General Coote, who acknowledged that he was mainly indebted to them for his victory. During the battle his attention was particularly attracted to one of the pipers, who never ceased to play, and gave forth his loudest and most warlike notes when the fire became hottest. This music was more eloquent than any words; it told them they must conquer, as their fathers had conquered before them. "Well done, my brave fellow," cried the General, "you shall have a pair of silver pipes for this!" There was no Victoria Cross in those days, or he would have had it. When the battle was over Sir Eyre did not forget his promise; a handsome pair of pipes was presented to the regiment, with an inscription bearing witness to the General's appreciation of their high character. Need we add that this gift has been sacredly preserved?

At the battle of Assaye, where the Duke of Wellington, then known as General Wellesley, established his character as one of the first leaders of the day, the 78th Highlanders acted a distinguished part. The British army was drawn up in a line of fifteen battalions, with the 78th on the right and the 74th on their immediate left. In the advance, the 78th had to attack a battery of nine guns which supported the enemy's left; before they reached it a body of eight hundred infantry rushed forward with the apparent intention of forcing their way between the 78th and the 74th, and thus breaking the line of attack. In order to intercept them these two regiments obliqued their march, and moved forward with ported arms. On observing this movement, the enemy drew up on the other side of a muddy ditch and kept firing till their last man fell. They were impelled by religious fanaticism, and next morning upwards of five hundred bodies were found lying near the ditch. The loss of the British was trifling; the 78th, who were exposed to the hottest fire of the enemy, had only nine men killed and twenty-one wounded. At the commencement of the battle, the musicians of the 78th had received orders to attend to the wounded and to carry them to the surgeons in the rear. This office was usually entrusted to the members of the band, but the orders were not intended to include the pipers, who were expected to accompany the regiment and to animate the men by their war notes. One young piper, who had never taken part in a battle before, from a mistaken sense of duty, laid aside his instrument and devoted himself to the wounded. His conduct was regarded as a dereliction of duty by his comrades, and exposed him to their reproaches and ridicule. It was all very well for the flutes and hautboys to cease their music; they could well be spared; but who ever heard of a piper sinking himself to the same level, and doing work which specially belonged to them? It was his duty to be in front of the battle, in the hottest of the fight; to go to the rear with the *whistlers*, as the bandsmen were derisively termed, was contrary to all the proprieties of Highland etiquette. The poor fellow, who had erred from ignorance and was not deficient in courage, felt these reproaches very deeply, and longed for an opportunity to retrieve his character. He had not to wait long; the battle of Argaum soon followed that of Assaye; in the advance the young piper played with such animation and evoked such soul-stirring notes from his instrument, that the Highlanders could

scarcely be restrained from breaking the line and rushing upon the enemy before the preparations were completed. The Colonel, in fact, could only restrain his men by silencing the musician, who thus recovered his good name, and led on his comrades in many a future fight.

The colonels of Highland regiments, knowing the influence exercised over the men by the pipers, have usually treated them with a consideration due rather to that influence than to their mere rank. This has been specially the case when the colonels happened to be Highlanders themselves. Every mountaineer is passionately fond of the mountain pipe; it awakens a thousand associations of the past; it inflames the glow of patriotism; it speaks to his heart at once. It tells him of scenes of joy and sorrow where it has enlivened or soothed him in the far north; it recals the coronach that was played at his father's grave, the pibroch to which his clansmen have ever marched to victory; it reminds him of the strains that shall welcome his return when the sword has been restored to its scabbard. In foreign lands, after years of exile, the rude sound of the mountain pipe rouses in the soberest Highlander a species of enthusiasm; his foot involuntarily beats time to the music; he can scarcely restrain himself from dancing as he used to dance in the days of his youth; often he throws aside his bonnet, and dances as if he were still a youth. He looks rather ashamed when the performance is over, and his grandchildren begin to congratulate him on his agility, but he cannot help it; the sound of the bagpipe, like the sting of the tarantula, sets him a whirling at once. An amusing proof of this recently occurred within our knowledge at a semi-religious fête which was held in the open air, in one of our most distant colonies, for the purpose of clearing off the debt on a Scotch church. The Scotchman, like Froissart's Englishman, takes his pleasure sadly; everything was as grave and decorous as possible, till all at once a venerable piper, an old pensioner of the 42nd resident in the colony, produced his bagpipe, and struck up a lively Scottish air. The thing was wholly unpremeditated; but in a moment every one, young or old, selected his partner, took his place on the green sward, and danced as if he had been possessed. The piper played his best, and the reels only ceased when the sun went down. In the enthusiasm of the moment, the people forgot the object of the meeting; the piper was the master of the occasion, to whom even the minister had to give place; his music blew away the load of cares and years, and made them all young again. We remember another instance: Some years ago we were residing in a certain town in the east where there were a good many Scotchmen. In truth, there are few towns, east or west, north or south, where Scotchmen are not to be found. The sound of the bagpipe had probably never been heard there before; but one night, at a late hour, the pibroch of Donuil Dhu was heard in the streets. It had the same effect on the Highlanders as the sound of the trumpet on the war-horse; it roused them from their midnight slumbers, and brought them into the street, where they formed an admiring circle around the performer, an eccentric wanderer, who had travelled over the greater part of India and China. Goldsmith's flute enabled him to visit France and Italy; the Highlander's bagpipe had carried him over the greater part of the continent of Asia. Those who did not like his music bribed him to go away, so that in either case he found the means of subsistence. Need we add that every house was thrown open to him; that parties were got up to do him honour; that he was fêted and feasted for months, and at length dismissed with the means of continuing his travels without the aid of his bagpipe.

The Highlander will admit at once that the bagpipe is not the gentlest of instruments, nor the one best adapted to a drawing-room; but there is no affectation in the assertion that its effect upon him is different from that of any other music. The feelings which other instruments awaken are general and undefined; but the bagpipe speaks to his heart at once, and reminds him of his own romantic land. The colonels of our Highland regiments do well to encourage the pipers, for they have contributed by their music to almost every success which their comrades have won. In almost every field of danger, in many an hour of victory, the proud warlike strains of the pibroch have been heard; and often, when every other instrument has been silenced amid the din of battle, the war-pipe has been carried by its devoted bearer into the very thickest of the fray, where it was hushed at length by the hand of death.

We have always looked upon Colonel Cameron, of the 92nd Highlanders, who fell at Quatre Bras, as the beau idéal of a Highland officer; no one entered more warmly into the feelings of his men, or was more successful in gaining their confidence. They looked up to him as their natural chief and protector; they appealed to him when they had any grievance, and they never appealed in vain. They delighted to observe that he had all the tastes and feelings of a Highlander; that he was familiar with the accents of the mountain tongue, and was passionately fond of Highland music. He was proud of the pipers of his regiment, whom he always treated with the greatest kindness and consideration. When marching at the head of his regiment, it was his delight to see them around him, and to listen to their martial music. He thus acquired an influence over his men, which no officer, ignorant of their language, music, and most cherished associations, could ever have obtained. They were ready to follow him anywhere, and when he fell, they wept for him as a father. At the battle of Vittoria, he was ordered to seize the heights, and to hold them while he had a man left. No order could have been more welcome; he ordered the pipers to play the "Cameron's Gathering," and inspired by the war-notes of this favourite pibroch, the 92nd rushed up the steep declivity and carried all before them. They made good their position, and retained it, though exposed to a most destructive fire, which thinned their ranks, but failed to shake their courage or to silence the shrill notes of their favourite instrument.

At the battle of Maya, which was fought soon after, the Highlanders had to maintain the conflict for ten hours against five times their number. Napier, the historian of the Peninsular war, thus alludes to their conduct and that of their leader on this occasion: "That officer (Cameron) still holding the pass with the left wings of the 71st and 92nd, then brought their right wings and the Portuguese guns into action, and thus maintained the fight; but so dreadful was the slaughter, especially of the 92nd, that it is said the advancing enemy were actually stopped by the heaped mass or dead and dying; and then the left wing of that regiment coming down from the higher ground smote wounded friends and exulting foes alike, as mingled together they stood or crawled before its wasting fire. Never did soldiers fight better—seldom so well. The stern valour of the 92nd would have graced Thermopylæ." They held their ground till their ammunition was almost expended, and some of them began to hurl stones at the enemy, when General Burnes despatched a considerable body of troops to their assistance. Their strength was so reduced that they were forbidden to charge; but seized with a warlike enthusiasm, they rushed upon the enemy and drove them from the ground they had lost. The pipers contributed in no small degree to produce this enthusiasm; they headed the charge, and struck up the favourite war-tune, "The Haughs of Crowdale," composed centuries ago to commemorate a celebrated battle in which the Highlanders took part. Their warlike music inspired their comrades with a fury which nothing could resist; but the loss was fearful. The strength of the regiment was about 750 men; nearly half that number fell, and nineteen officers were killed or wounded. Well might the poet exclaim, on hearing of such deeds of heroism—

"And oh! loved warriors of the minstrel's land,
Yonder your bonnets nod, your tartans wave;
The rugged form may mark the mountain band,
And harsher features and a mien more grave.
But ne'er in battle throbbed a heart so brave,
As that which beats beneath the Scottish plaid;
And when the pibroch bids the battle rave,
And level for the charge your arms are laid,
Where lives the desperate foe that for such onset stayed?"

These redoubtable musicians exhibited occasionally a sort of grim humour in the tunes which they selected. When the 92nd and 71st surprised General Gérard with three thousand of the finest French troops in Spain, at the village of Aroys des Molinos, and took or destroyed more than two-thirds of them, the first intimation of their presence was given by the pipers playing, "Hey,

Johnnie Cope, are you waukin' yet?" a highly appropriate tune, composed originally on the occasion of the defeat of Sir John Cope by the followers of the Pretender at the battle of Prestonpans. There is an old song sung to the same air, of which we remember only one verse—

> "Charlie wrote a letter from Dunbar,
> Saying Johnnie meet me if ye daur,
> And I'll teach you the art of war,
> So early in the morning."

After the defeat of the French, the Highlanders amused themselves by composing a song to the air of "Johnnie Cope," with the refrain, "Hey, Monsieur Gérard, are you waukin' yet?" which is more remarkable for patriotic feeling than poetical power. One verse may be given.

> "Go and tell Napoleon, go,
> While Freedom's laws he tramples low,
> That Highland boys will be his foe,
> And meet them all in the morning."

No wonder that Cameron appreciated and respected a class of men who did more by their music than mere valour could have effected, and animated their comrades by the strains familiar to them from infancy. A characteristic anecdote is related by General Gordon, of Lochdhu, who served during the Peninsular war in the 50th regiment, and had frequent opportunities of witnessing the gallantry of the 92nd. He and Cameron were fording the river Nive, at Cambo; the French opposed their passage, and a hostile bullet struck down Cameron's favourite piper, who was marching by his side. If his own brother had fallen, he could not have exhibited deeper feeling or anxiety. He stopped to render assistance, and, on finding that the poor piper was beyond the reach of all human aid, exclaimed, in a tone of deep emotion, that he had rather have lost twenty men of his regiment.

At the battle of St. Pierre, which was fought a few days after the passage of the Nive, the 92nd charged early in the day against two French regiments, which yielded and broke; but Soult brought such a storm of artillery to bear on them, that they in their turn were forced to retire. The 50th and the Portuguese held their ground and fought desperately till the 92nd had time to reform. Then Cameron gave the word to advance; the pipers sounded the charge, and the Highlanders rushed forward with colours flying and music playing. They were but a small force compared to the enemy, but nothing could resist their impetuosity; and they drove the French across the valley, remaining in possession of the field. Napier thus alludes to their conduct on this occasion: "How gloriously did that regiment come forth again to charge, with their colours flying, and their national music playing as if going to a review. This was to understand war. The man who in that moment, and immediately after a repulse, thought of such military pomp, was by nature a soldier."

No one will question the justice of this remark; but some praise is also due to the pipers, who were as jealous of the honour of the regiment as Cameron himself. His last hours were soothed by the music he loved so well. He was present on the evening of the 15th of June, at the celebrated ball given by the Duchess of Richmond, and was requested by the Duke of Wellington to withdraw privately from the room, and to march with all speed to Quatre Bras. He lost no time in executing this order; animated by the martial strains of the Cameron's Gathering, the 92nd were in front of the enemy by 2 P.M. Deserted by the Belgian horse, and assailed by fearful odds led on by the fiery Ney, the Highlanders and the Black Brunswickers repelled the attacks of the enemy again and again; many gallant officers and about three hundred privates were struck down, but they never dreamed of retiring. At length Cameron asked permission of the Duke, who was stationed among them, to charge the enemy. "Have patience," said the Duke, "and you will have plenty of work by-and-by." The French advanced, and took possession of the farm-house; the Duke waited till they began to push on to the Charleroi road, when, turning to the Colonel, he exclaimed, "Now, Cameron, is your time—take care of that road." On hearing these words, the 92nd cleared the ditch at a bound, rushed upon the enemy, and drove them back;

but, in the moment of victory, a shot fired from the upper story of the farm-house, passed through the body of their gallant leader, and his horse, pierced by several bullets, sunk to the earth. A wild wail of sorrow rose from his devoted followers, as they rushed madly on the house to avenge the death of one whom they loved as a father. Ewen Macmillan, his faithful foster-brother, aided by another private, bore him beyond the reach of the enemy's fire, to a deserted house near the village of Waterloo, where they stretched him on the floor. His first inquiry was for his beloved Highlanders; on hearing that they had fought with their usual gallantry and success, he said: "I die happy, and I trust my dear country will believe that I have served her faithfully." None ever served her better, or shed his blood more willingly in her defence.

His remains were hastily interred in the *Allé Nerte*, on the Ghent road. Next year they were conveyed in a man-of-war to Scotland, and buried in the aisle of the old church of Kilmallie, in Lochaber, where so many of his forefathers sleep. No less than three thousand Highlanders accompanied the funeral cortége, and the wailing notes of the coronach were echoed back from the heath-clad mountains, as they conveyed him to his last home. A monument was erected to his memory; the inscription was written by Sir Walter Scott, who tells us in his "Field of Waterloo" how

"Cameron in the shock of steel,
Died like the offspring of Lochiel;"

and thus alludes to him in his "Dance of Death"—

Apart from Aleyn's war array,
'Twas there Grey Allen sleepless lay—
Grey Allen, who for many a day,
  Had followed stout and stern,
Where, through battle, rout, and reel,
Through storm of shot and hedge of steel,
Led the grandson of Lochiel,
  The valiant Fassiefern.
Through steel and shot he leads no more;
Low laid 'mid friends' and foemen's gore;
But long his native lake's wild shore,
And Sunard rough, and wild Ardgour,

And Morven long shall tell;
And proud Ben-Nevis hear with awe,
How, at the bloody Quatre Bras,
Brave Cameron heard the wild hurrah
Of conquest as he fell."

It is a characteristic fact that his last prayers were offered up in his own mountain tongue, and that his last hours were soothed by that mountain music which was blended with his earliest associations and his proudest reminiscences. Other Highlanders have shown on their death-beds the same predilection for that music which, however harsh and unmeaning it may sound in the ears of a stranger, is dear to the heart of every mountaineer, animating him in the hour of danger, and soothing him in sorrow. A singular anecdote is related of Rob Roy, the celebrated freebooter, whose name is familiar to all the readers of Scott's well-known story. The bold outlaw was often threatened with the gallows, but his cunning and daring enabled him to escape that fate. He died in his own house at an advanced old age. As his end was approaching he learned that a friend who had once been his foe, and was still regarded by him with suspicion, was about to pay him a visit; he roused himself at once, and prepared to meet him. No sign of weakness or approaching dissolution must be witnessed by his former rival; attired in full Highland costume, he seated himself in his arm-chair and ordered his piper to play his favourite tune. When the visit was over, he lay quietly down and died.

At the storming of Ciudad Rodrigo, which was captured on the 6th of April, 1812, after a desperate resistance on the part of the French, Lieutenant Alexander Grant, of the 74th Highlanders, leading the advance, was the first to enter the castle, but fell in the moment of victory. John M'Lauchlan, the regimental piper, particularly distinguished himself on this occasion. He was the foremost in the escalade, and on mounting the castle wall, began to play the regimental quick step, "The Campbells are coming." Animating his comrades by the lively strains of this favourite air, he marched along the ramparts at the head of the advance, with as much coolness as if he had been on the parade ground. A shot from the enemy pierced the bag of his instrument, and stopped his music for a time, but John realized the importance of the occasion, and proved himself equal to it. If the music ceased, the courage of his comrades might flag, and the victory, already half won, might be lost: it should never be said that he failed in his duty; so he quietly seated himself on a gun carriage, and amid a hurricane of shot and shell, began to repair his instrument, which was speedily done. In a few minutes "The Campbells are coming" was heard again amid the roar of battle, and John had the satisfaction of witnessing the surrender of the fortress. If he attributed the success of the day partly to his own almost superhuman efforts, we must not be too hard upon him. "As proud as a piper" has become a proverbial expression in the north, and whoever has witnessed a contest of some score of pipers, and seen them strutting backward and forward on a raised platform, with inflated cheeks and waving tartans, will at once perceive its accuracy.

Much more might be said of our friends, the pipers, and we are almost loth to part with them. We might have told how one who was attacked by a French cuirassier at Waterloo took deliberate aim at him with his pipe, when the Frenchman, believing it to be some infernal machine, turned his horse and rode off at full speed, and how another, assailed by a tiger in India, blew such a blast on his instrument that the animal rushed into the thickest depths of the jungle to escape from the fearful sound.

But space fails us. The golden age of the pipers is gone for ever; the college of Skye has ceased to issue its diplomas, and the wail of the pibroch may be heard more frequently in Canada and Australia than in the Highlands of Scotland. The warlike race who fought our battles and shed their blood so profusely in our defence, has removed to other lands, and the bleating of sheep may be heard in the valleys they once occupied. Lowland lairds, without the shadow of a claim to rank as chiefs, without a drop of Celtic blood in their veins, have gratified their vanity and striven to enhance their importance by surrounding themselves with pipers, and have thus incurred the sarcasm of Bon Gaultier in one of his witty poems:—

"Fhairshon swore a feud
Against the clan M'Tavish,
Marched into their land
To plunder and to ravish.

"For he did resolve
To extirpate ta vipers,
With four-and-twenty men
And five-and-thirty pipers."

It is easy to find players on the bagpipes; performers whose accent proves that they belong to the Highlands of Highgate or Holborn Hill, may be heard in any street of London; but the genuine race of pipers, with their chivalrous spirit, and their undying devotion to their own regiments, has died out. The pipers even of our Scottish regiments are rarely Highlanders by birth: they have generally been instructed in the use of the instrument after entering the army. Such men may play tolerably well, but they cannot be expected to have the old *esprit de corps*.

A favourable exception is to be found in Ewen Henderson, the pipe-major of the 1st battalion of the Scots Fusilier Guards, who is at once a good piper and a genuine Highlander. He is a son of Angus Henderson of Annat, who joined the 92nd when first raised, served with it till the battle of Waterloo, rose to the rank of colour-sergeant, and lived till a few years ago to enjoy his well-earned pension. Ewen is a worthy son of a worthy sire: a living representative of what the pipers once were; a favourable specimen of the Celtic race. He feels the dignity of his position as pipe-major of a gallant regiment, and the sound of his war-pipe has been heard at Alma and Inkerman. It has also sounded in more peaceful scenes. He had the honour of performing before the Princess of Wales at Buckingham Palace a few weeks after her arrival, and was rewarded with some kind words and a golden Napoleon, which he wears at his watch chain and will not part with till his dying hour. "Will you take five pounds for it, Henderson?" said an officer to whom he showed it. "No, sir, not five hundred!" said Ewen, with the chivalrous feeling of an old paladin. The intrinsic value of the coin was less than a pound, but who shall estimate its value in Ewen's eyes? Long may he be spared to wear it!

CHAPTER XI.

COLONEL BELL AND THE VICTORIA CROSS.

IN a previous chapter we traced the history of the Royal Welsh Fusiliers (23rd Regiment). We showed how they won their laurels in Egypt, in Spain, in the West Indies, in the Pyrenees, and at Waterloo. We described the act of humanity by which Corporal Shields and Dr. Sylvester earned the Victoria Cross, and the gallant deed by which Sergeant (now Captain) Luke O'Connor attained the same honourable distinction. But the roll of heroes among the Royal Welsh is not yet exhausted, and we are now about to show how Colonel (then Captain) Bell conducted himself with such gallantry as to justify his sovereign in bestowing on him the Cross of Valour. Mr. Desanges' picture No. IX., which has been faithfully copied by our artist, introduces Captain Bell in the act of capturing one of the enemy's guns at the battle of the Alma. In order to understand this event, it is necessary to glance briefly at the position which the Royal Welsh occupied during the battle. The soldiers of No. 1 company, under the command of Major Lysons, had the honour of being the first British troops that landed in the Crimea. As soon as they had disembarked, Brigadier Airey sent them to attack some arabas, or Russian waggons, which were seen in the distance; on coming up to the Cossack escort, they fired upon them and put them to flight. This was the commencement of the campaign. Fourteen arabas, full of firewood and fruit, with their drivers and bullocks, remained in the possession of the Royal Welsh, and were the first waggons used in the Land Transport of the army.

From the period of disembarkation till the battle of the Alma, the Royal Welsh had no opportunity of distinguishing themselves. In this engagement they formed part of Sir George Brown's right brigade, which was under the command of General Codrington, an officer of the Guards, who, having visited the East from motives of curiosity, was induced to accept this important charge. The only orders he had received from Sir George were to advance with his brigade till he had passed the river which flowed through the valley at the foot of the heights where the Russians were drawn up. When a general has confidence in his subordinates, he does well to allow them a certain freedom of action, as it is impossible to anticipate all the eventualities which may occur on the day of battle. The left brigade of the Light Division was under the command of General Buller, who is said to have received the same instructions as Codrington. The two brigades advanced steadily in the direction of the river, the bank of which, on the Russian side, varied from eight to fifteen feet in height, but was not so steep as to prevent our men from obtaining a footing on it. The river itself was of no great depth, but the bank on the side of the allies was covered with gardens and vineyards, which our men could not cross without getting into disorder. As they advanced they became exposed to the fire of the enemy, who had erected on the opposite heights two batteries mounted with brass guns which swept the plain. When the Welsh Fusiliers and their companions of the right were brought within long range, they deployed and halted. It was a bright, sunny day—not a cloud in the sky, nor a breath of air stirring—and our men, suffering from thirst and fatigue, helped themselves to clusters of grapes, and lay down leisurely on the ground, careless of the balls which were whizzing past them and occasionally thinning their ranks. The vineyards afforded them a scant shelter from the fire of the enemy; but when the final order was given to advance, our men were thrown into some confusion, owing to the broken ground, overgrown with the tendrils of the vines, on which they had to form. Codrington's brigade was the first to advance, carrying with them the 19th Regiment, who were only too glad to place themselves under the guidance of such an impetuous leader.

The Russians poured on them the fire of all their batteries, and many fell before they could find cover beneath the steep bank on the opposite side. There they halted to reform, and at this moment three Russian regiments advanced, and poured down a vertical fire upon them from the summit of the bank. A leader less resolute than Codrington might have given orders to retreat; but it was his first battle, and the gallant guardsman was bent on winning his spurs. He rode his small Arab charger round to a spot where the bank was less precipitous, and with some difficulty contrived to reach the summit. It was unfortunate that, instead of the plumed hat of a general, he wore an officer's foraging cap, and, being recently appointed to the command of the brigade, few of his men recognised him. Still, the sight of an officer forcing his way almost alone up the heights was enough to inspire his men with the desire of following, and Colonel Yea, of the 7th Fusiliers, rode his cob up the steep bank, encouraging the soldiers, by his voice and example, to come on.

It was impossible for the regiments to form on the broken ground which they occupied, but the whole of Codrington's Light Division cleared the bank, carrying with them the 19th and 95th Regiments, who were only too eager for the fray. These brave fellows were the first to begin the battle of the Alma. If the Russians had had the courage to charge them as they appeared on the summit of the bank, broken and breathless, they might have rolled them back into the river below; and the fate of battles often depends on a first success. A column of the enemy descended the hill with this intention, and advanced towards the ground occupied by the 19th Regiment and some of the left companies of the 23rd, who opened such a smart fire upon them that they retreated, and found shelter in a hollow near the Great Redoubt. Having thus got quit of their assailants, they joined their comrades, who were pressing on towards the Great Redoubt in broken columns and much disorder. As yet the Russian battery was silent, but when our men had reached some three hundred yards from it, first one gun and then another began to fire upon them with round shot, grape, and canister. They were crowded so closely together that every round shot which pierced their ranks cut its way through, leaving a long furrow of dead behind. But the open space thus left was at once filled up, and our men pressed forward as gallantly as before in the direction of the Great Redoubt. The slaughter was fearful, and none suffered more than the 23rd, who had twelve of their officers and half of their rank and file smitten down before they reached the guns which were dealing death amongst them. Their gallant leader with the foraging cap and the eye-glass was still in front, and wherever he went they were prepared to follow. A sort of half-cry rose from their lips as his horse fell and a cloud of dust concealed him for a moment from their view; but it was only for a moment. Mounting his horse, he turned gaily to his followers, and said, "I am all right, lads. Twenty-third, be sure I'll remember this day."

It was such a day as can never fade from the memory of those who took part in it; but the Welsh Fusiliers have special reason to remember it. Their ranks were thinned, but they still pressed forward, and followed their gallant leader as he leaped his horse into the midst of the enemy's works to show his men there was no danger. The Russians were seized with a sort of panic; the artillerymen began to limber up their guns and to fall back upon their reserves, which were posted in the rear. A sort of cry of disappointment rose from our men at the thought that there was no more fighting to be done—"The Russians are retreating; they are limbering up. Stole away! stole away!"

But the fighting was not over; there was still bloody work to be done on the heights of the Alma. The enemy's artillery continued their fire as they retreated, and many of our men were struck down as they approached the empty embrasures. The first to mount them was young Anstruther, who carried the colours of the Royal Welsh. Though an officer of that regiment, he was a Scotchman by birth, and his conduct that day will invest a name already distinguished in the annals of the North with a halo of glory. He was a mere boy, fresh from school, but he was determined to do some deathless deed on this the morning of his first battle. Leaping and running are favourite pastimes in Fife, as in every Scottish county, and none could run better than the light, boyish figure that held aloft the colours of the Royal Welsh, and pressed forward before all the others. He was the first who gained the redoubt, and, planting the butt-end of the colours in the centre of the parapet, he stood for a moment clutching it in his arms, breathless and silent, as if surprised at his own audacity. There were hundreds of hearts beating high with admiration as they saw the slim figure of the Scottish youth on the summit of the parapet. Alas! it was seen there only for a moment. A bullet passed through his body, and he fell, dragging with him the flag-staff, as if he would not part with it even in death. The crimson folds of the colours, which covered his body like a pall, were stained with a deeper dye as his heart's blood ebbed away. The soul of the young hero was gone. But it was no time for tears; the colours were in danger, and the colours must be saved. Butler, the other colour-officer, was slain; but William Evans, a swift-footed Welshman, mounted the parapet, drew the flag-staff gently from the hands of the dying boy, and held it aloft, to show that the Royal Welsh were the first to mount the Great Redoubt. He then, in accordance with military etiquette, handed the colours to Corporal Luby, his superior officer, who, in turn, delivered them up to Sergeant Luke O'Connor, with whom they remained during the rest of the day. No wonder that young Anstruther fell: no less than seventy-five bullets passed through the colours, and the pole of one of them was shot in two, and had to be spliced with a cord.

It was on this occasion that Colonel E. W. D. Bell, of the 2nd Battalion of the Royal Welsh, gained the Victoria Cross. This decoration, so coveted and prized, was devised by her whose name it bears in 1856, and was intended to be a reward of valour for all who distinguished themselves, whatever their rank might be. Its value is enhanced by the fact that Victoria confers this Cross with her own hand whenever this is practicable—an honour which cannot fail to be appreciated by the happy recipient. Our readers have a good idea of its form from the initial letter to our first chapter, but a brief description may not be out of place. It is a Maltese cross of bronze, with the royal crest in the centre, beneath which is an escroll bearing the words, "For Valour;" the date of the act of bravery is inscribed on the centre of the reverse, and the name and corps of the recipient are engraved on the bar to which the ribbon is attached. A sprig of laurel is embossed on this bar, which is attached to the cross by the letter V suspended on a red ribbon or a blue one, as he who gains it happens to be a soldier or a sailor. This decoration, however, is not confined to the army and the navy; civilians who have distinguished themselves by their bravery have as good a claim to it as those who belong to the profession of arms, and several of this class nobly earned it during the Indian Mutiny. Every private or non-commissioned officer thus decorated is entitled to a pension of 10*l.* a year; every fresh act of bravery equal to the first procures for him an additional bar and a further pension of 5*l.* There is no danger, therefore, of the wearers of the Victoria Cross being tempted to rest on their laurels; they have an intelligible motive for striving to increase them. Their names are published in the *London Gazette*, along with the record of the deeds of bravery by which they earned the distinction.

> "A king may make a belted knight,
> A marquis, duke, and a' that,"

but distinguished bravery alone can make a Victoria Cross man. A marquis or a duke may have attained his rank by means that would not bear too close inspection, but the Victoria Cross invites your inspection; its wearer must always be *sans peur*, if not *sans reproche*.

No one will grudge Colonel Bell the distinction which he earned at the Great Redoubt on the heights of the Alma. He was charging at the head of his company at the moment when the Russians were retreating with those guns which had dealt such havoc among our men. All had been drawn away by the artillery horses except a brass 24-pound howitzer, which still remained in position, and gave rise to a singular contest among our soldiery. Each was anxious to claim it as his own, so as to point to it afterwards as a proof of his prowess, and an officer of the 33rd, named Donovan, is said to have been the first who scratched his name upon it. Bell, however, took no part in this contest; his thoughts were elsewhere. Farther

Captain Bell, Royal Welsh Fusiliers, capturing a Russian Gun at the Battle of the Alma.

on, in the rear of the redoubt, he saw a Russian driver urging on with whip and spur three horses which were dragging a brass 16-pounder gun; in a moment he was alongside the driver, and held a revolver to his head. The latter understood the significance of such an act, and, slipping from his horse, took to his heels. Bell seized the bridle of one of the horses, and, aided by a soldier of the 7th Fusiliers, named Pyle, led them round the shoulder of the parapet to the rear of our line, where he met Sir George Brown, the general in command of the Light Division. Now, it is the duty of a captain to be at the head of his company, and the general is said to have reminded him of this fact in language of considerable emphasis. There was no help for it; Bell had to relinquish his prize, and to return to his company, but the gun was safe; the horses drew it down the hill, where it remained till after the battle. The gun is now to be seen at Woolwich, and the horses were put into our "Black Battery." At the close of the war, Captain Bell's heroism was not forgotten; he was decorated with the Victoria Cross, and is now a colonel.

We have already alluded to Lieutenant Anstruther's heroic death, after he had planted the flag-staff of the Royal Welsh on the summit of the parapet. When he fell, the Queen's colour was picked up by a private, who gave it to Corporal Luby; it was afterwards carried till the end of the battle by Sergeant Luke O'Connor. The gallant sergeant was shot in the breach, and fell at the same time as young Anstruther; but his wound was not mortal; he soon recovered himself, and refused to go to the rear, though urged to do so by Lieutenant Granville. He received the highest praise from Major-General Codrington on the field, and was rewarded with a commission in his own gallant regiment, in which he now holds the rank of captain. He was also present at the assault on the Redan, on the 8th of September, 1855, where he behaved with great gallantry, and was shot through both thighs. At the close of the war he received the Victoria Cross and the Sardinian war medal. The latter decoration was also bestowed upon Corporal Luby, who was instrumental in saving the Queen's colour at the battle of the Alma.

The British casualties in this battle were 25 officers killed, and 81 wounded; 337 non-commissioned officers and men were killed, 1550 wounded, and 19 missing. No regiment suffered more than the Royal Welsh Fusiliers. Eight of their officers were killed, and 5 wounded (one of them mortally); 3 sergeants and 40 rank and file were killed, or died of their wounds; 9 sergeants and 143 rank and file were wounded; 2 were missing. The slaughter among the senior officers was so great that the command of the regiment devolved on Captain Bell, who brought it out of action. The regimental colour was carried by Sergeant Honey Smith after Lieutenant Butler fell; it was intrusted to him by Major-General Codrington, as no officer could be spared from his company. In a letter written from the seat of war, Corporal Harwood gave a graphic description of the circumstances under which the Royal Welsh were so fearfully cut up:—"The 23rd was in the Light Division, and on we went, covered by two companies of the Rifle Brigade. We crossed a vineyard, and were led by Colonel Chester through the river, the opposite bank of which was very steep. The colonel went through with us—we all shared alike—and, as we clambered out, the enemy gave us a fierce fire, the cannons belching forth murderous volleys of grape and round shot, and musket-balls fell as thick as hail. The men fell dead and wounded before me and at my side. They fell in every direction, and mechanically I still pressed on, untouched. Up the hill we went with the Rifle Brigade, and half-way up the heights we reached the cannons' mouths which were planted on the embankments. Our regiment was about to cross the stockade in the enemy's position, when the word was given, 'Cease firing, and retire!' because we were in danger of firing on the French. Our colonel rushed in front of us, shouting, 'No, no; on, lads!' He fell with the word on his lips; he never spoke or raised his head again. We *did* retire then, and an unfortunate mistake it was; for the enemy returned to the guns we had once silenced, and gave us some terrific volleys; but we soon rallied, and, supported by the 7th, 33rd, a portion of the Guards, and the Highlanders, we rushed up the hill again, and the enemy fled in every direction." This and other letters written by our soldiers during the Crimean War took the nation by surprise; they proved that there were men, unknown to fame, in the ranks of the British Army who could use the pen or the sword with equal skill.

There are certain acts of courage which compel our admiration without obtaining the unqualified approval of our cooler judgment. Colonel Bell's daring in capturing the Russian gun must be placed in this category. No one will question his courage, or dispute his right to the Cross of Valour; no one will wish his deed undone, or desire that he had acted otherwise. And yet it must be admitted that in leaving his own men he was guilty of a breach of discipline which is more worthy of admiration than imitation. It was his duty to have remained with his company; and if every officer were to yield in battle to the same impulsive bravery, all discipline would be at end and the results would be most disastrous. The first duty of all soldiers is implicit obedience to the commands of superior authority; to this rule there is no exception, save in the case of officers of high rank, who on the field of battle must always be guided partly by circumstances in executing the orders they have received. We are not, therefore, to condemn Sir George Brown for expressing his emphatic disapproval of Captain Bell's conduct in leaving his company to seize the Russian gun. Sir George, doubtless, admired his courage, but he must have felt that courage ought in every case to be subordinate to discipline. Such was the opinion of Sir Colin Campbell at the storming of the Secunder Bagh at Lucknow. We shall described in a future chapter the fearful scene of carnage which took place there in consequence of the massacre at Cawnpore. The tumult was at its height when a Highland officer rushed up to the spot where Sir Colin, mounted on his grey horse, stood in the centre of his staff. The Highlander was wild with excitement, and bore on his person traces of the bloody work in which he had taken part. One word of praise from those stern lips was the richest reward his heart could covet. Extending the red banner which he held in his hand towards the general, he joyfully exclaimed, "I have killed the last four of the enemy with my own hand, and here, sir, are their colours." A Highlander himself,

Sir Colin could appreciate the impetuous courage of his countryman, but his duty as a general was imperative; he could not applaud an act which was a violation of discipline. "Confound the colours, sir! where's your regiment? Go back to your regiment, sir! I thank you for your zeal and gallantry, but go back to your regiment." The excited and impulsive Highlander obeyed this command, and, doubtless, felt at the moment that the reproof, though grave, was not unmerited. Such also must have been the feelings of Captain Bell when he received the stern command to return to his company and relinquish the Russian gun. If that gun had not remained in our possession after the battle, we doubt whether Colonel Bell's undisciplined valour would have met with the same recognition from his grateful country. Success may sometimes justify such a step, but we repeat that such deeds of impulsive bravery are more to be admired than imitated. It must be borne in mind, however, that Colonel Bell received the Victoria Cross, not only for capturing the Russian gun at the Alma, but also for bringing the regiment out of action when his superior officers had fallen, and exhibiting the same daring spirit on many subsequent occasions. It is a pleasure to see his manly figure among the other heroes in the Victoria Cross Gallery, and we hope he will long continue to wear the badge of distinction which his sovereign conferred upon him.

CHAPTER XII.

COMMANDER (NOW CAPTAIN) FIOTT DAY, R.N., AND THE VICTORIA CROSS.

OUR sailors do not occupy a very prominent place in Mr. Desanges' Victoria Cross Gallery. We find that only four of his paintings have been devoted to the gallant deeds of our naval heroes, but we must not infer from this that British sailors are inferior to British soldiers, or that blue jackets have deteriorated since the days of Nelson. This is far from being the case, as we all know. But two conditions are necessary to constitute a hero: it is not enough that a man be brave, he must also have an opportunity of displaying his bravery. There are, doubtless, many Hampdens sleeping in our village churchyards, and many Nelsons serving on board our ships; all that has been wanting is the opportunity of displaying their patriotism or their courage. We are all more or less the creatures of circumstances; the race is not always to the swift, nor the battle to the strong, because the swift and the strong are often debarred by fate from either running or fighting. Time and chance, as the wise man tells us, happen to all. Nelson would never have been a hero if he had not robbed an orchard, and Fiott Day might have been known only as a very intelligent commander in the British navy if it had not been for the Crimean war.

It was one of the oratorical or conversational hits of Lord Palmerston, that if the Crimean war had no other advantage, it at least extended our knowledge of geography. Some hard-headed people may imagine that we paid dear for the lesson, but not one will deny that the long-protracted contest *did* increase our knowledge of those semi-barbarous regions, the names of which, we fear, were little familiar even to those schoolboys who had gained the first prizes in geography. Knowledge thus acquired, however, is seldom permanent; when the war ceased, our interest in the localities where the great battles were fought became less vivid. It is well that the rising generation, in whom all the hopes of England are centred, should be familiar with the courage, the endurance, and the heroic deeds of those who took part in that disastrous war; such knowledge excites their sympathy, stimulates their ambition, and elicits that spirit of adventure which has made Britain the mistress of an empire far more extended than that of ancient Rome.

Mr. Desanges has trusted more to his pencil than his pen in depicting the gallant deed by which Captain Day obtained the Victoria Cross. We read that "with great gallantry this officer landed and twice successfully carried out a reconnoissance within the enemy's lines at Genitchi, advancing to within about 200 yards of the enemy's gun-vessels." Most readers will exclaim, "Where is Genitchi?" Few even professed geographers would be able to answer such a question, and as our interest in paintings depends much on our intimacy with the scenes they represent, we invite our young readers to do as we have done—to open their atlases at Russia in Europe, and to examine the map. It may save time to state at once that this incident occurred during the Crimean war, and that Captain Day commanded one of the vessels engaged in the expedition. Now, on examining the southern extremity of Russia in Europe, it will be seen the only entrance from the Sea of Azov into the Senish or Putrid Sea is through the Straits of Genitchi. These straits are very narrow in most maps—in fact, so narrow that we have to strain the eye a little before we can perceive them. On the right-hand side of these straits stands the town of Genitchi, from which they derive their name. It is situated on the slope of a lofty eminence, and is a place of considerable strength.

During the Crimean war it was strongly garrisoned with nearly twenty thousand Russian troops, to protect it from the attacks of the allies. To the left is the Spit of Arabat, which was occupied by strong bodies of Cossack horse artillery and cavalry, which formed a continuous line of pickets all the way to Arabat. It is about seventy miles in length, and of an average breadth of half a mile, though in some places it is not more than two hundred yards. Its broadest part is opposite the town of Genitchi, where it is between three and four miles across. At this particular point it is covered with numerous lagoons and strips of water, varying in size, all of which are covered with thick rushes and weeds, and are a favourite resort of different kinds of water-fowl. We have mentioned that pickets of Cossacks were stationed along the whole of the Spit of Arabat, and there were constant skirmishes between them and our sailors. Such slight exchanges of civility tended to vary the monotony of naval life, but the adventure in which Captain Day distinguished himself was of a far more dangerous character.

It is said that he advanced within two hundred yards of the enemy's gunboats; but to understand the exact nature of this heroic deed we must enter more into detail. On the inner side of the Spit of Arabat, opposite the town of Genitchi, were several guard-houses, in front of which four gunboats were moored, in such a position as to cover the entrance of the straits, and to bring under their fire any vessel that attempted to force its way. Setting aside these gunboats, it would have been a most hazardous undertaking for any boat to have attempted to pass the town so as to reach the Sivash, as the passage is not more than three hundred yards broad, and the whole of the heights which command it were lined with troops and field-pieces. Any boat that attempted to run the passage would have been within range of the fire of all these field-pieces, and exposed to almost certain destruction. Still it was of the last importance that the passage should be made, as it was only in this way that the supplies which were poured into the Crimea and enabled the Russians to prolong the contest could be cut off. These supplies were conveyed from the mainland by the Chingan bridge, and the great object of the naval expedition was to destroy this bridge. Still the undertaking, as we have said, was most hazardous, and another plan had been attempted. To Captain S. Osborne belongs the honour of having first discovered the position of this bridge. Captain Osborne is, doubtless, known to all our readers as a charming writer as well as a brave sailor, and he had recourse to an ingenious expedient to obtain the desired information. He caused two light boats, which he had transported across the narrowest part of the Arabat spit at night, to be launched on the Sivash, and approached near enough to the bridge to ascertain its exact position. It was a work of great difficulty to get even these light boats pushed through the mud, and Osborne narrowly escaped being captured. It would have been impossible, of course, to navigate heavily-armed boats on the muddy straits, supposing that our sailors had succeeded in getting them across the spit. Several experiments were made, but the attempt was given up as impracticable.

Soon after the fall of the south part of Sebastopol, Captain Day was stationed in the *Recruit*, which was under his command, off the Straits of Genitchi. While cruising along the coast, he had his attention directed to the fact that the enemy's forces appeared to be less numerous than usual, more especially in the vicinity of the town and on the opposite spit. He at once despatched two gunboats to explore; on their return they reported that few of the enemy were to be seen. A brilliant idea occurred to Captain Day; it struck him that now was the time to make his way across the spit, and to capture the gunboats which covered the passage. He at once proceeded to act upon it. At this time, the writers of leaders in the daily press were very critical in regard to our navy, and easily proved upon paper that it was practicable to force a passage through the Genitchi Straits. There was a feeling among our sailors that if the thing could be done it would be acceptable, not only to the admiral in command, but also to the public at home. Good people at home, who carelessly criticise the exploits of our soldiers and sailors by their comfortable firesides, little imagine what daring deeds are done to secure their applause. "What will they say at home?" was the exclamation of Nelson after one of his great victories; and the man who does not value the good opinion of his fellow-citizens is not likely ever to do a heroic deed, or to occupy a niche in the temple of Fame.

Captain Day was not ignorant of the danger of attempting this

Commander George Fiott Day, R.N., reconnoitring within the Enemy's Lines at Genitchi

reconnoissance. About a month before, Captain L'Allemand, of the French steam-vessel *Mouette*, had done so, and failed. He not only lost his own life, but several of the sailors who accompanied him were killed. Captain Day had the sagacity to perceive that this disaster was the result of the Frenchman's imprudence. He had taken with him some twenty of his men—a force too small to offer any effectual resistance in the event of discovery, and too numerous to be able to escape detection. It occurred to him that one man might succeed where twenty had failed; but where was that man to be found? No one could hope to succeed, unless he had the step of an Indian and the eye of a hawk. In his earlier days, Captain Day had learned to stalk the red-deer on the mountains of the North, and the acuteness of vision and stealthiness of tread he had thus acquired were now employed for the benefit of his country. It is not to be supposed that self is altogether forgotten in the hour of heroic self-devotion; promotion, the world's applause, and Westminster Abbey are dimly present to the mind of the most unselfish of men when undertaking some daring enterprise. To secure the applause of his admiral and a step in the service may have weighed a little with Captain Day; but we are sure that the danger itself had a certain irresistible attraction to his mind. He waited anxiously for a night suitable for the attempt, and on the 19th of September he was enabled to take the bearings of the Russian gunboats from the mast-head of his ship; he was enabled at the same time to mark the exact position of the guard-houses on the spit. He then resolved to land as soon as it was dark, and to try to make his way across without being observed. Accordingly, as soon as evening set in, he put a couple of sailors in his smallest boat, and, taking a small pocket-compass, some matches, his double glasses, and revolver, he at once landed. He took the precaution to put his commission in his pocket, so that his rank might be recognised if he were taken prisoner. He landed on the beach abreast his own ship, and told the sailors to remain in the boat at a sufficient distance from land to be beyond the reach of the enemy's fire, in the event of a surprise; they were to remain there and not to make any noise, whatever might happen, unless he hailed them to pull in.

It would be impossible to relate all the adventures of that night; suffice it to say that our hero *did* make his way across, after a long and wearisome journey, without being detected. He passed through many of the enemy's pickets, which, as he had anticipated, were few, and widely scattered. He was thus enabled to have a good view of the Russian gunboats, which he found were moored close to the shore, and likely to remain in that position. The idea occurred to him that they could easily be surprised, as they were very slightly armed, and no attack was expected by the enemy. Nothing, however, could be done without the sanction of Captain Osborne, and our hero had reluctantly to retrace his steps. He reached the beach about two o'clock in the morning, after tramping about among bogs and morasses for more than seven hours, and found his boat all safe. He was in constant danger of detection, in consequence of the numerous water-fowl with which the lagoons abounded being disturbed by his approach, and thus putting the sentries on the alert; but his old deer-stalking habits stood him in good stead: he was not discovered.

On the following day Captain Osborne arrived, and Commander Day communicated to him all that he had witnessed during the previous night. It was fortunate that in Osborne he had a leader quite as bold and daring as himself, who entered warmly into his plans, and admitted that the attempt might be crowned with success. He received from him the promise that, if an expedition were sent, he should take part in it—an assurance which afforded him much satisfaction. On the following day Captain Osborne was obliged to leave, and Commander Day, on cruising along the coast, observed that the enemy appeared to be as numerous as ever. It occurred to him, as he anchored for the night off his old anchorage, that it would never do to allow the expedition to be undertaken with so many of the enemy scattered about, as it would only end in disaster and the capture or slaughter of all who took part in it. To prevent such a calamity, he resolved to make another reconnoissance. After the statement he had given to Osborne about the number of the enemy, he felt that a great responsibility rested upon himself, and that it was far better to expose his own life to danger a second time than involuntarily to cause the loss of many valuable lives. None but a gallant and good man would have reasoned thus, or incurred so great a danger. He determined, therefore, to land at once, in order to ascertain the real strength of the enemy, and thus be enabled to report to Captain Osborne whether it would be advisable to undertake the expedition. He felt it to be his duty to do this, as he had led him to believe that the enemy's forces were far less numerous than they now appeared to be.

Accordingly, employing the same tactics as before, he landed at sunset. The night was bitterly cold, and so intensely dark that he had to grope his way at every step. He soon discovered that he was off the right track, and more deeply involved among the Russian sentries than was at all pleasant or desirable; but he never for a moment lost his presence of mind, and it was to this cause that he owed his safety. He crept along with all the stealthiness of a Red Indian, stopping every moment, and feeling his way at every step. He soon saw enough to satisfy him that the enemy's forces were far too numerous to admit of the possibility of their being captured or surprised. There was no help for it; the expedition must be abandoned, and he must try to reach his vessel in safety. This was no easy undertaking; if it was difficult to advance, it was still more difficult to retreat. The place was full of quagmires and pits, into which he repeatedly fell, and, to add to other delightful sensations, more than one ball came whizzing past his ears in such close proximity as to be far from pleasant. It was his impression at the moment that the sentries had discovered him and were firing at him; but he was satisfied afterwards that this was not the case. They were only firing in accordance with their usual custom, to show that they were on the alert, and thus avert the attack they dreaded.

After nine hours' wandering he reached the beach, and the sight of the blue waves must have been as grateful to him as the first glimpse of the ocean to the Ten Thousand Greeks in their retreat. But his dangers were not yet at an end: he looked everywhere for his boat, but it could not be seen; he waded up to the waist in the water, and, putting his mouth close to its surface, so as to veil the sound, he shouted to them to come in. There was no answer. In his desperation he drew his pistol from his belt, and, placing it close to the water, fired. It did not strike him at first that this act was more likely to attract the attention of the enemy than that of the men in the boat; but as soon as he heard the report of the pistol he was alive to the extent of the danger which he had incurred through his imprudence. His safety lay in the proximity of his own vessel, which was so close to the beach that the Cossacks could not approach the shore without being under range of her guns. It was a fearful position to be placed in. He was shivering with cold, his feet were benumbed, and his clothes saturated with wet. Overpowered with fatigue and half-dead with exposure, he threw himself down on the beach and prayed earnestly for the dawn. It was one of those hours which may concentrate in themselves more than the agony of a whole lifetime. Such hours are never forgotten in after-life, and are often the starting-point of a new existence. But we need not dwell upon those weary hours that preceded the dawn. A little before daylight, Mr. W. H. Parker, an officer of Commander Day's vessel, pulled in along shore to see if he could see anything of one who, it was feared, was either dead or in the hands of the enemy. He found him prostrate on the beach, and nearly frozen to death. But such men have a wonderful tenacity of life. He soon recovered sufficiently to inquire why his men had not pulled in when he hailed them. It appeared that they had heard the report and seen the flash of his pistol, but thought it might have been some of the sentries near the beach. They imagined that they heard him approach the shore, but thought that they were carrying out his instructions in not approaching nearer to the land, as he had told them that in the event of his being chased he would swim out to the boat. They listened and watched, but as they heard nothing more they imagined that he had not come down. The following morning he was too ill to move. A less powerful frame would have succumbed under the physical suffering of that night. Captain Osborne, who had returned, visited him the same day on board his ship, and persuaded Captain Day to address to him that despatch which elicited a letter of approval from the Admiralty and earned for him the Victoria Cross.

Captain Day was, undoubtedly, the only man in England who felt any surprise when his sovereign conferred on him this proof of her favour. It has been cynically remarked that no man is a hero in the eyes of his valet. It is certain that no true hero is ever esteemed to be so by himself. There is a glorious absence of all self-consciousness in true genius and heroism. The man whom the whole world admires is often the least conscious of his own merits.

CHAPTER XIII.

LIEUTENANTS MOORE AND MALCOLMSON, AND THE VICTORIA CROSS.

HO among our readers has not been interested about Persia—that mysterious land in which such wonders have been said to exist? So many of the tales in the "Thousand and One Nights" refer to Persia, that most boys, at least, are well acquainted with some of the peculiarities of the people.

Although it is difficult to pronounce any decided judgment as regards the actual antiquity of any Eastern nation, yet there seems to be but little doubt that before England had even emerged from a condition of semi-barbarism, civilization had made considerable progress in Persia; and although that nation is principally famous to us on account of its tales of winged monsters, dragons, enchanters, and genii, yet this peculiarity may be in consequence of early travellers bringing to us that which was at the time the most acceptable; and as we in England can scarcely assume to have been lovers of science and truth during more than three hundred years, it is possible that any profound or philosophical truths brought from the East would have been formerly as little appreciated as a book of algebra would be in a nursery. The laws of the Medes and Persians are referred to in the Bible, and in the book of Esther reference is made to a King Ahasuerus, who it is said ruled over one hundred and twenty-seven provinces, which then constituted the kingdom of Persia.

It is stated by some of the earliest writers that the Persians were a nation of shepherds, hardy and warlike, that they gradually increased in numbers and power, and conquered and brought under their rule less powerful nations, until they became almost the greatest people of the East.

The most celebrated of the ancient kings of Persia was Cyrus, who organized the Persians, gave them special laws for their guidance, political institutions, and established a well-disciplined army. This Cyrus not only became King of Babylon, Media, and Persia, but at length, by the right of conquest, obtained absolute dominion over the greater part of Asia.

Cyrus was succeeded by his son Cambyses, who was a man that delighted in war. He died in consequence of a hurt which he received while mounting his horse.

Following Cambyses was Artaxerxes; and we then come to Darius, who loved conquest better than had any of his predecessors. This king was desirous of obtaining the homage even of Greece, and sent heralds to claim it, but without success. He then raised a large army and invaded Greece, but the Athenians under Miltiades met him, and gained a great victory, known as the battle of Marathon, and fought two thousand three hundred and fifty-two years ago.

Xerxes succeeded Darius, and continued the attack on Greece. It was during this war that Leonidas, with his band of Spartans, defended the pass of Thermopylæ against such overwhelming odds —a deed which would certainly have gained him the Victoria Cross in modern times.

Darius III. had reached the dangerous condition of a very rich but not a warlike king; when then, he, by means of his wealth, incited other nations to make war upon Alexander, King of Macedonia, this great conqueror determined to attack Persia—a feat which he accomplished with so much success that he everywhere defeated the Persians, who for upwards of a hundred years were, in a great measure, under the yoke of Greece.

In more modern times Persia has been invaded by the Tartars, a vagrant race of hunters and shepherds who were warlike and organized enough to subjugate Persia.

With the exception of the early wars with the Greeks already referred to, the Persians, up to the year 1700, had not met in battle any of the armies of Europe. Peter the Great of Russia had, however, for a long time been desirous of extending his territory to the banks of the Caspian Sea, and had merely waited for a pretext to wage war with Persia. He did not seek an opportunity in vain, for a Russian caravan returning from China was plundered by the Persians, and this offence so irritated the Russian autocrat that he put himself at the head of his army, sailed from the Volga, and landed at Daghestan. Shortly after hostilities ceased, and Russia obtained from the Persians the towns of Baku, Derbund, and several provinces. During this period the Persians were also at war with the Afghans, who had invaded Persia and had been the cause of much misery.

The late Czar Nicholas of Russia had no sooner ascended the throne than he commenced war with Persia, and at length, in 1828, concluded a treaty by which he gained several provinces.

About the years 1836, 1837, a collision took place between the Persians and the Afghans. It was the object of the Persians to gain possession of the district of Herat. Now this district lies on the north-west of India, and may be called one of the barriers to our Eastern Empire, and as such it is essential to be preserved as an independent state. In July, 1837, the Persians marched an army against the Afghans, and, after a siege of ten days, succeeded in capturing Ghorian, and in December commenced the siege of Herat.

Various remonstrances had been made to the Persians by the British authorities in connexion with the attack upon Herat, but without avail, and they merely had the effect of making the English unpopular. At this time a confidential messenger bearing despatches for the British minister was insulted and detained by the Persians. This and one or two other similar proceedings on the part of the Persians, in addition to their attack upon our then allies the Afghans, rendered amicable communications with them out of place, so that in June, 1838, our minister quitted the Persian court and ceased any friendly communication with the Persians.

During March, 1839, Sir Frederick Maitland, commander-in-chief of the naval forces in India, landed some men from the *Wellesley* at Bushire. It appears that there was only one locality at which a landing or embarkation ought to have taken place, and in the present instance this custom was not paid attention to, and it was nearly leading to unfortunate results, as the Resident was threatened by a large party of armed men. Fifty marines and about thirty sepoys were provided with sixty rounds of ball cartridge each, and, under the command of Captain (now Lieutenant-General Sir S.) Ellis, approached the shore. Upon coming within range a heavy fire was opened on this small party, wounding several men, but fortunately killing none. A rapid pull, a leap on shore, and steady advance towards the position occupied by the Persians, had the effect of driving the enemy away, and the small body of Europeans effected an entrance into the Residency and commenced preparations for carrying off the Resident to the ships.

At this time, however, a heavy gale of wind sprang up, which lasted three days, and entirely prevented communication by boats between the vessels and the shore. The Persians, knowing this, rather anticipated the capture or massacre of the small party left on shore, but so decided were the proceedings of the officer in command and so judiciously were his arrangements made, that his enemy, although numbering ten to one, thought it more prudent to leave him alone.

During each evening of these three days the Persians used to assemble to the number of several hundreds and make demonstrations as though they purposed attacking our men, but no sooner did they appear than the little garrison was turned out and kept under arms, ready and willing for a fight should the Persians feel so disposed. This bold proceeding seemed to have the effect of awing them, for no attack was made, and even a field-work that was being constructed in front of the Residency was not continued, upon Captain Ellis's intimation that he would fire upon the working party the instant a spade was put into the ground.

On the fourth day after landing, a reinforcement was sent from the ships, and the whole party, including the Resident, safely passed through the armed throngs and embarked in the boats.

Each of these, provided with a gun, pulled out, showing a muzzle directed on the rabble and ready to discharge its iron hail should a shot be fired at the boats.

Towards the end of 1855 it was evident that the Persian Government did not intend to keep faith with England, for in December Prince Sultan Moorad Meerza set out from Tehran in command of an army that was to act against Herat. Whilst our Government was remonstrating with that of Persia on this proceeding, several insults were offered to the British officials at Tehran, and the right of asylum accorded to the residence of the British mission was violated. After various futile attempts to obtain redress, war was at length decided upon, and an expedition was despatched to the Persian Gulf from India.

In January, 1857, the expedition embarked, and reached its destination at the end of the month, and shortly after was landed at Bushire. The Arabian and Persian coasts on either side of the entrance to the Gulf are desolate in the extreme; steep cliffs without any sign of vegetation rise from the water's edge, whilst inland there seems no sign of a habitation; several barren islands stud the coast on both sides, and are the residence of a few sea-birds only.

The village of Bushire, which was captured with scarcely any opposition, is a place of some importance. It is imperfectly defended by a wall, with towers at intervals to afford a flank defence. The town itself is composed of narrow streets or alleys, whilst the buildings are square and solid-looking. The places of interest in the town are the church, the bazaar, and a reservoir. In the background is a range of mountains which is usually covered with snow.

The troops forming the Persian expedition were very soon actively employed. On the 3rd of February the entire force was assembled and drawn up in order of march. This force consisted of the 64th Regiment, 78th Highlanders, 20th and 26th Regiments of Native Infantry, the 2nd Light Infantry, and 4th Bombay Rifles, 3rd Light Cavalry, some horse artillery, and field batteries—a somewhat diminutive army with which to invade a kingdom, but one which was found efficient enough for the work it was called upon to perform.

During the first two days' march this little army encountered two of the most disagreeable incidents of a tropical climate. First a gale of wind sprang up, carrying with it a huge cloud of sand, which penetrated not only the eyes, nose, mouth, and ears, but seemed actually to force its way into the pores of the skin. When the army halted, and were bivouacked in order of march, a tremendous thunderstorm burst upon them, rain and hail coming down in torrents, when both officers and men were drenched to the skin, for they had no cover such as tents or trees. A piercing cold wind blew upon them, and rendered their condition more trying than can easily be imagined except by those who have experienced similar inconveniences. But many examples have shown that nothing can daunt the courage or decrease the ardour of the British soldier, especially when led, as he was in this instance, by such a man as Outram.

It was known that the Persians were in order of battle at about eight or nine miles from the spot on which the troops had bivouacked on the night of the 4th of February; therefore, before proceeding on the march on the morning of the 5th, the loaded arms were discharged and reloaded, in order to avoid the damaging effects of the night's rain.

Shortly after mid-day the Persian army was discovered in an intrenched position. A short halt took place, in order to get the regiments into their proper positions, when, to the annoyance of our men, the enemy were seen in full retreat, which they continued at such a pace as to prevent their being overtaken, except by a few of our cavalry who attacked their rear-guard.

Our troops immediately took possession of their intrenched camp, in which were large quantities of ammunition, grain, and camp equipage. The intrenched position was found very weak, and would easily have been taken by our little army, whereas a village near, termed Brás-Joon, had it been but slightly fortified, would have become a most formidable position.

During the 6th and 7th of February the troops were occupied in destroying military stores and searching for hidden guns, treasure, &c. On the night of the 6th an alarm occurred in the camp, and the whole force stood to their arms. Fortunately, the moon shone brilliantly, and thus a probable disaster was avoided, for one of the corps mistook a patrol of the Poonah Horse for a party of the enemy, and skirmished up to it, but fortunately discovered the mistake before a shot was fired.

These night alarms — especially with soldiers not thoroughly trained — are invariably dangerous, the probability being that friends are mistaken for enemies, and shots not unusually exchanged. We were once witness to a scene which, although ludicrous afterwards and to the lookers-on, was certainly unpleasant to the principal performer. It happened that a soldier in his shirt and trousers had wandered some distance from our camp during the night, when an alarm arose that the enemy were upon us. Men scarcely awake rose to their feet, rifle in hand, and seeing a white object in the distance rushing towards them opened fire on it. The more the unfortunate man shouted (for he was within the white object, which was his shirt) the more rapid was the firing at him, until he came sufficiently close to be recognised. Fortunately the darkness of the night and the hurried manner in which the men fired saved him from being hit.

On the evening of the 7th of February the return march of the army commenced towards Bushire, the enemy having been observed retreating amidst the fastnesses of the mountains far away. Until midnight all was quiet, and no enemy was expected, when suddenly the discharge of musketry in the rear caused the forces to be on the alert, and it was then found that the rear-guard was attacked. In less than half an hour the whole army was surrounded by skirmishers and galloping horsemen, who yelled and trumpeted, making as much noise as possible. One of the Persian buglers, who was acquainted with the English calls, sounded the "Cease firing" repeatedly, close to the Highlanders.

Our troops, although surprised in a great measure, were as steady as though on parade, and received the charges of the enemy's cavalry with a fire which emptied many saddles. This exhibition of courage and discipline was the more commendable,

Lieutenant John Grant Malcolmson, 3rd Bombay Light Cavalry, rescuing his brother officer, Lieutenant and Adjutant Arthur Moore, at the battle of Kooshab.

considering very few of the men had ever previously been under fire.

During the greater part of the night the Persians kept up a desultory fire, which, however, produced but little damage, and when at daybreak the fire slackened it was feared that there would not, after all, be any real battle; but as the morning fogs dispersed the enemy were seen in position, their right resting on a village called Khoosh-aub. Several dry watercourses were in their front, and these were lined with skirmishers. There were also large bodies of cavalry on both flanks, and altogether a force of about 8000 (one-fourth of which was cavalry) was assembled to oppose us.

As soon as there was light enough a rapid cannonade commenced on both sides, whilst a change of front was made by our own commander, immediately after which the advance was made with but little loss, considering the heavy firing brought against us.

The fire from the Persian guns was soon almost silenced by that from our own, which was carried on at a tolerably close range.

Our cavalry, consisting of some irregulars and the 3rd Bombay, finding some of the enemy's horsemen opposed to them, made a brilliant charge, fairly sweeping the enemy before them. There were only two or three of the regular battalions of the Persians that stood their ground at all or retired in regular order. The 3rd Cavalry charged through these men, who received them with tolerable steadiness. It was on this occasion that Lieutenant A. Moore gained the Victoria Cross.

Lieutenant Moore was first within the square at which his regiment charged. His horse fell dead beneath him, and he would soon have fallen a victim had not a brother officer (Lieutenant Malcolmson) fought his way back and assisted him with difficulty out of the crowd of the enemy. Both Lieutenants Moore and Malcolmson gained the Victoria Cross for their conduct on this occasion.

The result of this battle was the entire rout of the enemy, who were defeated at every point, and in the retreat were cut up by the artillery and cavalry. A couple of brass guns were captured, a standard, and a large number of muskets. The Enfield rifle, which was used in this affair, cast terror on the Persians. On one occasion a horseman, who was making threatening demonstrations at a distance of 800 yards, was neatly picked off by a good shot, an officer in the 2nd European Light Infantry. About 700 dead were found on the field, and a vast number of wounded were carried away.

The troops, after the battle, moved off a short distance and bivouacked, but were very shortly disturbed by heavy rain, which continued without interruption during several days. The roads became almost impassable, the soil—a mixture of clay and sand—being ankle-deep in mud. The troops at length were forced to halt, and without complaining stretched themselves in the mud, and took that rest which all so much required. Although the distance from the field of battle to the lines at Bushire was over forty miles, yet it was passed by the troops, under all the disadvantages named, in thirty hours. The loss on our part during these proceedings consisted in one officer and eighteen men killed, four officers and sixty men wounded.

Shortly after these events another expedition was undertaken by our troops, and with complete success, the Persians, although brave men, lacking that essential to make them good soldiers—viz., discipline. There are several nations of the East—the Chinaman, Hindoo, and others—who have scarcely any fear of death, and who would rather cast themselves on their own swords and thus perish than fall into the hands of an enemy, and yet when these men meet in battle our own soldiers they invariably suffer an almost ignominious defeat, in consequence of their want of discipline and of steadiness under fire.

The soil and climate of Persia do not appear to be very favourable: during the day it is intensely hot, and during the night equally cold. In summer, likewise, the heat is intense. Vast deserts of sand occur in many places, and long ranges of sterile mountains cross the country in various parts. Vegetation is not very abundant, and cultivation is carried on but scantily. Game, however, abounds in many places, deer, antelopes, partridges, and wild-fowl being found, and the lion is also said to be occasionally seen.

Whether we consider the Persians as soldiers, their country as a paradise, or their cities as noble works of art, we find ourselves disappointed; for the first are little better than a half-trained rabble, their country is not fertile, and their cities are badly constructed and dirty. So that after contemplating these items we can candidly exclaim, "There's no place like home."

Bushire

CHAPTER XIV.

CAPTAIN W. A. KERR, SOUTH MAHRATTA HORSE, AND THE VICTORIA CROSS.

ON the evening of the 8th of July, 1857, a party of officers belonging to different regiments in the Indian service were seated round the mess-room table in the barracks of Sattara, in the Bombay Presidency. An expression of anxiety was depicted on all their faces, and they spoke in that hushed subdued tone which men usually assume in moments of great peril. And they had reason to look anxious. The Indian Mutiny had already broken out, and recent events showed that its limits were not to be confined to the Bengal Presidency. The seeds of disaffection had been sown among their own men, and they knew not at what hour they might be called upon to meet them in open mutiny. The Orientals can veil the most treacherous designs under the deepest secrecy, and every officer felt, as it were, that he was carrying his life in his hands. At any hour the men, outwardly so respectful and obedient, might enter the very room where they sat and shoot them down at the mess-table. They had done so in other cases, and what guarantee had these that their lives were more secure? The inhabitants of Sattara were at no pains to conceal their rebellious tendencies, and their men were only restrained by that discipline which soldiers find it so difficult to shake off from openly expressing their sympathies with them. In truth, the whole country was in a state of slumbering rebellion, and no one could tell when the embers of disaffection might burst forth into an open flame. They felt as Prometheus might have felt if he had been bound to the sides of Mount Etna, in hourly expectation of an eruption. Escape there was none. If it came to the worst, they could meet their fate like brave men, and die sword in hand.

One young officer, whose stalwart frame and slight accent betokened his Northern origin, took a more hopeful view of the subject. This was Lieutenant William Alexander Kerr, of the South Mahratta Horse, an officer who had already secured the confidence and respect of the wild troopers under his command. He expressed his conviction that, however treacherous the other native troops might prove, he could always count on the loyalty of the South Mahratta Horse, and if any emergency should occur it would be seen that their courage was equal to their loyalty. The words had scarcely passed his lips, when an orderly entered the room and delivered a slip of paper to the officer in command. The door was carefully closed to prevent the servants from hearing, for at that trying period almost every native was suspected to be a rebel in disguise. The paper was then read aloud. It proved to be a telegraphic message from Kolapore, a town about seventy-five miles distant from Sattara. Its contents were such as might well appal the bravest heart. The 27th Regiment of Bombay Native Infantry had suddenly mutinied and murdered all the officers on whom they could lay their hands. Those who escaped had taken shelter in the Residency, where they were guarded by a troop of the South Mahratta Horse and the Kolapore Light Infantry. The mutineers, from carelessness or ignorance, had neglected to cut the telegraph wires, and the beleaguered party had thus been enabled to communicate with their countrymen at Sattara, to whom they made an urgent appeal for assistance. Almost destitute of provisions, and surrounded by a merciless foe thirsting for their blood, they could not hold out long, and if they yielded their fate was certain. In this the hour of their need they turned to their countrymen for assistance.

A momentary silence ensued. It was not that they were unwilling to incur any risk in order to aid those whose case was so desperate; the only question was whether they could trust their men in such an undertaking. Kerr was not the man to unsay the words he had just spoken. He had expressed the confidence he reposed in the loyalty and courage of his men; he was now prepared to prove that that confidence was not misplaced.

His position as adjutant of the regiment afforded him the best opportunities of becoming acquainted with the personal character of the men. He was brought into daily contact with them; had to listen to all their grievances; had to receive the complaints made against defaulters; and, in minor cases, to decide the punishments to be awarded. Unswerving firmness and impartial justice are the two qualities most requisite to enable one to obtain a powerful hold on the Oriental mind, and these two qualities Lieutenant Kerr possessed in the highest perfection. He knew his men, and his men knew him; they could, therefore, trust one another in the hour of danger. He at once volunteered to lead a party of the South Mahratta Horse to the rescue; all the assistance that could be spared was fifty men. Small as that number was for such an undertaking, he did not hesitate to take the command. No time was consumed in needless preparation; in half an hour he was in the saddle and on the road. We use the expression "road" in a figurative sense; literally speaking, there was no road at all, merely a rough path leading through the cotton-fields, where the horses sank to the fetlocks, often to the knees, in the mud. The distance to be travelled was only seventy-five miles: a short distance to those accustomed to railways and steamers, but those familiar with the roads in India will appreciate the difficulties which Kerr and his gallant little party had to surmount. It was the middle of the monsoon season; the rain descended in torrents; the country was half flooded; the smallest streams were converted into dangerous rivers. But the gallant band went on; swam their horses over three large and two smaller rivers, besides seven nullahs, all swollen with the heavy rains, and reached Kolapore within twenty-six hours. We have all heard of Dick Turpin's ride to York; but the rapid advance of Lieutenant Kerr and his party, in such a country, and at such a season, was scarcely less wonderful.

They did not arrive a moment too soon. The mutineers, elated by a temporary success, were ready to offer them battle. They had already encountered the Kolapore Light Infantry, and defeated them with considerable loss. After this they had taken up their position in a pagah, or fortified square with circular bastions, situated near the town. This pagah was a place of considerable strength, and the attacking party had no artillery to effect a breach in the walls. Recourse was had to the rajah, who lent them a couple of old guns, which, on trial, were found to be useless. Night was at hand, and Kerr knew well the danger of delay; if he waited till morning, his men, worn out and discouraged, might refuse to follow him. All his hopes of success depended on an immediate attack; so he resolved at once to carry the place by storm. His men had already witnessed his courage; he had headed the party which occupied the brushwood outside the pagah; he had laid the guns at thirty yards' range from the western bastion under a heavy fire; he had passed through all this unhurt. The Orientals, fatalists by creed and by constitution, have the greatest faith in the luck that attends certain leaders; they recognised in Kerr one of the favourites of Allah, and were prepared to follow him wherever he chose to lead.

He did not give them long to wait. Causing the sowars to dismount from their horses, he placed himself at their head and led them on to the attack. On approaching the walls they found that the task they had undertaken was one of no ordinary difficulty. The only entrance to the place was by small doors of thick teakwood, from five and a half to six feet in height, which the mutineers had taken the precaution to block up with large stones, so as to render them almost as solid as the walls. If they had been provided with guns this obstacle might easily have been removed; but, as the event proved, the two lent by the rajah were evidently intended more for ornament than use.

But Kerr was not a man to be easily discouraged. His conduct proved the truth of the good old adage, that "where there's a will there's a way." Among the dismounted sowars there was, fortunately, one who entered readily into his plans, and volunteered to share with him the danger. This was Gumpunt Row Deo Ker, a gallant trooper, worthy to be known and admired by all who can appreciate valour in the field, though the singularity of his name will, we fear, prevent it from ever becoming familiar to our readers as a household word. Kerr and Gumpunt armed themselves with crowbars and marched through the heavy fire of the enemy till they reached one of the small doors. Both plied their instruments so well that they soon made an aperture sufficiently wide to admit a man in a stooping attitude. It seems almost miraculous that no hostile bullet should have reached them while thus engaged, but they escaped unhurt. The opening was made, but who would have the courage to be the first to enter? To do so was almost certain death: the rebels were waiting and watching to shoot down the first man who appeared inside the walls, and yet there was not a moment's hesitation. Kerr rushed through the opening, followed by Gumpunt Row and others whose courage was inspired by the example of their daring leader. As soon as he appeared within the pagah, twenty of the mutineers took deliberate aim and fired a volley at him. He had the presence of mind to retain his stooping position, and all the bullets passed harmlessly over his head. He did not give them time to reload, but rushed at them sword in hand. They fought with bayonets, and kept their ground for a time, till several of them were killed and wounded. Nothing could resist the impetuous onset of the stormers: the rebels were driven back till they found refuge in a house which covered the other entrance. It so happened that this house was loopholed, and the rebels were thus enabled to continue their resistance. They fired heavy volleys upon the attacking party as they advanced, and did everything they could to make good their position; but it was all in vain. Kerr, followed by his brave sowars, got round the flanks, set fire to the building, and burnt the enemy out. The other mutineers retreated through the door already alluded to, and began to barricade it. This spot now became the central point of attack and defence; the mutineers quitted the other bastions which they had been defending, and joined the party who had formed the barricade. Knowing the fate that awaited them if they yielded, they fought with all the fury of despair.

The great point was to effect an entrance. This could only be done by removing the barricade. This was a task of no ordinary

Captain William Alexander Kerr, South Mahratta Horse, at Kolapoor.

danger; whoever undertook it had to count on concentrating on himself the whole fire of the enemy. Here again Lieutenant Kerr boldly exposed his life to almost certain destruction by rushing forward, crowbar in hand, and emulating the vigour of the Black Knight in "Ivanhoe" in the ponderous blows he struck. It seemed that day as if he bore a charmed life; the bullets of the rebels whistled around him in every direction, but still he plied his crowbar till the barricade began to yield. At length, as on the former occasion, he made an opening wide enough to admit a person in a stooping position. As soon as this was done he rushed through, followed by his faithful attendant, Gumpunt Row, who was resolved to share his leader's fate. The rebels were waiting their approach, and no sooner had they appeared within the walls than they were met by a volley, from which they fortunately escaped unhurt. Without giving them time to reload they rushed upon the mutineers, and a desperate hand-to-hand combat ensued. The rebels were far superior in numbers, but that was their only advantage. The storming party, animated by the example of their gallant leader, already counted on victory. For a time the event seemed doubtful; the enemy, driven to their last corner, offered an obstinate resistance. A ball cut the chain of Lieutenant Kerr's helmet, another hit his sword-blade with such force that it turned the edge. The faithful Gumpunt Row, though wounded in the foot, never quitted his master's side; at one moment, when his life was exposed to imminent danger, he shot the assailant dead. Another mutineer rushed up and discharged his musket so close to Lieutenant Kerr's face that for an instant he was blinded by the powder. It was only for a moment, and as soon as he recovered his sight he ran his sword through the body of his adversary with such force that it required a violent effort to withdraw it. While he was struggling to do so, one of the enemy, watching his opportunity, rushed up and struck him a violent blow with the butt-end of a musket. Such a blow would have placed a less powerful man *hors de combat;* as it was, Lieutenant Kerr staggered beneath it and almost lost his consciousness. Another rebel, observing his helpless condition, ran forward to dispatch him, but Gumpunt Row, watching over his master's safety, was ready to receive him. A bullet from his musket stretched him lifeless on the ground. Lieutenant Kerr, instantly recovering himself, killed a second. Assailants and defendants were now enveloped in such a cloud of smoke that it was difficult to distinguish one another or to mark the various incidents of the contest, which raged with the greatest fury. Lieutenant Kerr, though severely wounded, pressed the advantage he had gained by driving the enemy before him; he knew that all depended upon his example and courage; if he had fallen or hesitated for a moment the sowars would have retreated and the enemy escaped. As it was, they followed him wherever he went, and showed by their conduct that the natives of India, when properly led, are capable of the most heroic deeds.

The mutineers were pressed so hard that they at length gave way, and took refuge in the inner keep. This building had been used as a temple, and was a place of considerable strength. The rebels barricaded the door and began to fire through an opening on the storming party. The latter had consisted originally of seventeen sowars; of these only six or seven continued to follow their gallant leader; all the rest had been killed or disabled. Lieutenant Kerr advanced with this handful of men to attack the rebels in their last refuge. On approaching the door, it was found that the crowbars made no impression upon it, and that some other means of forcing an entrance must be adopted. Lieutenant Kerr proved himself as ingenious in resources as he was gallant in attack. Observing a quantity of hay close at hand, he seized some of it and carried it to the door of the temple. He was closely followed by Gumpunt Row, who set fire to the hay. The door was gradually consumed, and the stormers, who during this interval had been exposed to a heavy fire, rushed in. None of the mutineers escaped; all of them were either captured or slain.

This brilliant affair, in which Lieutenant Kerr bore such a distinguished part, was attended with the most important consequences: it checked the rising spirit of revolt in the province where it occurred, and revived the confidence of the officers in the native regiments under their command.

The loss sustained by the storming party was very severe. Their leader was seriously wounded. Of his seventeen followers eight were killed on the spot, and four subsequently died of their wounds. Not one of them escaped unhurt. If we take into account the obstinate resistance of the enemy, the smallness of Kerr's troop, and the heavy fire to which they were exposed, the only ground for surprise is that any of them should have escaped at all. It was impossible that such gallant conduct should have passed unnoticed or unrewarded. The press of India was loud in expressing the admiration which was felt by all, and Colonel Maugan, the officer commanding at Kolapore, brought Lieutenant Kerr's distinguished conduct under the notice of the Adjutant-General of the Bombay army, in the following terms:—

"Lieutenant William A. Kerr, of the Southern Mahratta Irregular Horse, took a prominent share in the attack of the position, and at the moment when the capture was of great public importance, he made a dash at the gateway with some dismounted horsemen, and forced an entrance by breaking down the gate. This attack was completely successful; and the defenders (to the number of thirty-four, all armed with muskets and bayonets) were either killed, wounded, or captured—a result which may with perfect justice be attributed to Lieutenant Kerr's dashing and devoted bravery. I would therefore beg to be permitted to recommend Lieutenant Kerr for the highly honourable distinction of the Victoria Cross."

Our readers, after reading the above narrative of Lieutenant Kerr's exploits at Kolapore, will agree with us that he deserved this honourable distinction, so dear to every soldier's heart. Soon after these events he returned to England, where he was invested with the Victoria Cross, and afforded Mr. Desanges an opportunity of perpetuating the remembrance of his gallantry. He has now returned to Bombay, and holds the rank of captain in the South Mahratta Horse. If circumstances should ever arise demanding such displays of valour, it will be found that his arm is as strong and his heart as brave as when he stormed the pagah at Kolapore and repressed the mutiny of the 27th Bombay Native Infantry.

CHAPTER XV.

PRIVATE HENRY WARD, V.C., 78TH HIGHLANDERS.

T is a remarkable fact that Private Henry Ward and Sir H. M. Havelock, Bart., the officer whose life he saved, have both been decorated with the Cross of Valour. The career of Havelock, the avenger of Cawnpore, the deliverer of Lucknow, is matter of history; but the important services and distinguished bravery of his son, who owes his life to Private Ward, ought to be recorded for the admiration and imitation of all who wish to deserve well of their country. He was born at Chinsurah, in the Bengal Presidency, in the year 1830; his father, then a lieutenant in the 13th Regiment, had formed the acquaintance of the Baptist missionaries at Serampore, and was married on the 9th of February, 1829, to Hannah Shepherd, the youngest daughter of the Rev. Dr. Marshman, a distinguished member of that body. Henry Marshman Havelock was the first fruit of this marriage, and had to share from his earliest infancy in all the vicissitudes and dangers of a soldier's child in India. While still an infant under twelve months of age, he had to accompany his parents on a voyage up the Ganges and was seized with a sudden attack of illness. On this occasion his father exhibited the same calm courage and presence of mind which he afterwards displayed on many a battle field. "To render the case more disheartening," he wrote, "we were entirely destitute of the only remedies which we believed likely to be effectual. We had no calomel, and no lancet, and no skilful hand to use it; and the young sufferer grew worse every hour. The danger seemed imminent, and our distress was not trifling. I therefore determined myself to try my skill as an operator, and with a very indifferent substitute for a lancet, and, I fear, not a very steady hand, succeeded in giving relief to my first patient. I should think this a very tedious story to write to one who did *not* know how the human heart, even the heart of one who has passed through many scenes of suffering and danger, attaches itself to these little ones in their years of helplessness. My clumsy attempts were certainly blessed beyond our hope, for the little sufferer soon became calmer and calmer, and his fever sensibly diminished." We record this incident, because it proves that tenderness of heart is not incompatible with the sternest courage: the two qualities may, and often do co-exist.

It is unnecessary to dwell on the education or boyhood of young Havelock: from the earliest period he had expressed a desire to adopt his father's profession, though, judging from his subordinate rank in the army, he had little reason to expect rapid promotion. He obtained his commission in 1847, and at the commencement of the Indian Mutiny held the rank of lieutenant in the 10th Regiment. When his father received the command of the moveable column which was to be formed at Allahabad, and to consist of the 64th Regiment and 78th Highlanders, he was appointed Deputy-Assistant Adjutant-General of this force, and accompanied them in their advance to Cawnpore. He had already held the appointment of adjutant in his own regiment, and acted for a time as aide-de-camp to his father on this his first campaign. He was present at the battle of Futtehpore, where his gallantry attracted the notice and excited the admiration of his father, who, in the original draft of the despatch he had written, thus alludes to his services:—"I shall incur risk of suspected partiality when I further record that the boldness, and activity, and quick perception of Lieutenant Havelock, 10th Foot, my son, and aide-de-camp, on this his first action on shore, inspired me with the hope that he will do his country good service long after I am in the grave." No one can read these words without emotion, or fail to sympathize with the father of such a son, and yet such was the tenderness of Havelock's conscience, the almost morbid dread that paternal partiality might have led him to exaggerate the merits of his aide-de-camp, that the passage was omitted in the revised copy of the despatch. We question whether there be many officers in the service who would exhibit the same reticence, or practise the same self-denial under similar circumstances; but Havelock was one of a thousand. Though he had the Spartan self-denial to omit his son's name in his published despatch, he speaks of "the boy H." in admiring terms in his private letters, and circumstances soon occurred which led him to believe it to be his duty to recommend him for the distinction of the Victoria Cross.

A brief statement of these circumstances may not be out of place. On the 16th of July, 1857, Havelock was close upon Cawnpore, and after allowing his exhausted troops a few hours' rest in a mango grove, until the fierce heat of the midday sun had abated, prepared for action. Nana Sahib having completed his work of butchery in the town, had marched forth with his army, and taken up a strong position at Atherwas, the point where the road leading to the cantonment branches out from the main trunk-road to Cawnpore. He there commanded five villages, with numerous intrenchments, armed with seven guns; his infantry was stationed in the rear. Havelock perceived at once that the guns could not be silenced, or the intrenchments carried without sacrificing many valuable lives, and with his small army he had none to spare. He therefore quietly wheeled his force round to the left of the enemy's position, behind a screen of clumps of mango. When the rebels detected this manœuvre, they endeavoured to strengthen their left flank by bringing up their cavalry, and opening fire in that direction with all their artillery. Then followed a series of operations which proved, in the most striking manner, the superiority of the British infantry to the recreant foe opposed to them; though inferior in numbers, and exhausted by their long march, they advanced under a heavy fire with as much coolness as if they had been on parade; and when the word was given, "Charge," they rushed forward with a ringing cheer, and drove the enemy before them at the point of the bayonet. Four villages were thus taken in rapid succession, and seven guns fell into our hands. As a last effort the enemy planted a 24-pounder on the cantonment road, by which our men had to advance, and inflicted severe loss on the gallant little band. Our artillery cattle were so exhausted with heat and fatigue, that the guns could not be dragged forward to silence the 24-pounder, and the enemy, encouraged by their temporary success, began to rally with the evident intention of renewing the engagement. The moment was critical: all depended upon the capture of the enemy's gun. This task was assigned to the 64th Regiment, who advanced along the road amid a shower of grape, under the command of Major Stirling. An officer commanding a regiment ought always to be mounted, especially in action: he is thus a conspicuous object to his men, and his presence inspires them with fresh courage. Unfortunately, Major Stirling's horse had been wounded by the bursting of a shell, and he was obliged to lead on his men on foot. It does not appear that there was any hesitation or irresolution on the part of the 64th, anything, in short, to justify another officer in attempting to supersede the one already in command; on the contrary, their conduct throughout the day was rewarded with the highest praise in a public despatch. While they were in the act of advancing, young Havelock, perceiving no officer at their head, and knowing how much depended on the capture of the gun, yielded to an almost irresistible impulse by riding forward, and placing himself at the head of the regiment. Gallantly he advanced in front of them, amid a storm of grape, cheering them on by his voice and example, till he rode his horse to the very mouth of the cannon which had arrested our progress. It was seized by the 64th, and the enemy losing all heart fell back on Cawnpore, where they blew up the magazine, and then went on to Bithoor.

General Havelock, who had witnessed the gallantry of his son, resolved to recommend him for the Victoria Cross. We have already seen how on a previous occasion he had omitted his name from a public despatch lest he should be suspected of partiality: this circumstance, perhaps, rendered him more anxious to do justice to him now. There was no reason in the world why he should be debarred from this honour if he had fairly earned it, because his father happened to be the officer in command. It appears, however, that he himself wished the affair to be overlooked. It is not for us to specify the motive by which he was actuated: it may have been a tender regard for his father's character of impartiality, or an apprehension of the storm of hostility which the bestowal of this honour would excite, or the consciousness that he was not justly entitled to it. Be this as it may, the fact is certain that he persuaded his father to suppress the telegram which he had prepared for the Commander-in-Chief. He was more anxious that his own merits should be overlooked than that his father's good name should be impugned: he was willing to wait. On the return of the troops to Cawnpore after the battle of Bithoor, General Havelock having occasion to recommend another officer for the Victoria Cross, no longer felt himself justified in overlooking the claim of his own son. "I also recommend for the same decoration Lieutenant Havelock, 10th Foot. In the combat at Cawnpore he was my aide-de-camp. The 64th Regiment had been much under artillery fire, from which it had suffered severely. The whole of the infantry were lying down in line, when perceiving that the enemy had brought out their last reserved gun—a 24-pounder—and were rallying around it, I called up the regiment to rise and advance. Without any other word from me, Lieutenant Havelock placed himself on his horse in front of the centre of the 64th, opposite the muzzle of the gun. Major Stirling, commanding the regiment, was in front, dismounted; but the lieutenant continued to move steadily on in front of the regiment, at a foot pace, on his horse. The gun discharged shot till the troops were within a short distance, when they fired grape. In went the corps, led by the lieutenant, who steadily steered on to the gun's muzzle, until it was mastered by a rush of the 64th."

It is worthy of remark, that this recommendation was concealed from his son, and only communicated to him after his father's death by Lieutenant Hargood, General Havelock's aide-de-camp. This circumstance is to be regretted on many grounds: if the telegram had been submitted to young Havelock before it was forwarded to the Commander-in-Chief, we are certain, from our personal knowledge of his character, that he would have so modified certain expressions it contains as to have avoided wounding the tender sensibilities of those who felt aggrieved by them. Without doing any injustice to himself he might have done more justice to Major Stirling, and the officers of the 64th; but the responsibility rests not with him but with his father, who, before the storm excited by the publication of this telegram had burst forth, had already gone the way of all living, and was indifferent to popular praise or blame. The Cross of Valour was awarded to Lieutenant Havelock in March, 1858, and on reading it in the *Gazette*, the officers of the 64th Regiment, considering that they had just cause of complaint against both father and son, addressed a letter of expostulation to Sir Colin Campbell, the Commander-in-Chief in India. There is no reason to believe that the gallant old chief was actuated by any personal feeling in the matter, but he felt it to be his duty to forward the letter of expostulation to His Royal Highness the Duke of Cambridge, accompanying it with certain strictures implying grave censure on father and son.

Men who have spent so many years in the service as Lord Clyde are naturally opposed to innovations. There is a certain period in life when we all become conservative in principle. Old men, since the days of Homer, have ever been prone to exalt the past at the expense of the present; and Lord Clyde was no exception to this rule. He regarded the Victoria Cross with the same distrust with which he regarded every other innovation. In his own hot youth he had exhibited the most daring courage at Badajoz, and elsewhere, when there was no Victoria Cross to be earned; and he held that courage, like virtue, was its own reward. Devotion to duty, without regard to after consequences, was the principle by which he himself was guided during his long career; the soldier who was animated by a sense of duty required no outward stimulus. The promise or expectation of some badge of distinction as a reward for heroism or gallantry in the field was sufficient, in his opinion, to incite young officers ambitious of honour and reckless of their own lives to rush into rash enterprises without consulting their superiors. Discipline, or, in other words, subjection to lawful authority, he esteemed the highest ornament in every young soldier;

no heroic action could atone for any violation of this primary duty.

It is not necessary here to expose the fallacy of such reasoning. Our soldiers were quite as brave when there was no Victoria Cross at all as they are at the present moment: that Cross was intended not to *create*, but to *reward* valour. The British soldier requires no outward stimulus, no promised reward, to incite him to do his duty: a true hero will prove himself to be a hero, because it is his nature to be so, and he cannot help it. Nelson never thought of ribbons or peerages when he was fighting our battles at sea; his only ambition was to conquer or to die. The soldier or sailor who distinguishes himself in action never dreams of reward: he is a hero, and he does heroic deeds almost without knowing it. Of all the men who wear the Victoria Cross upon their breasts, there is not one, we believe, who ever thought of that badge of distinction at the moment he earned it. It was innate heroism or tender humanity that placed him at the head of the forlorn hope, or led him to risk his own life to rescue a wounded comrade. The man who would do such deeds from such a purely mercenary motive as the love of applause, would be unworthy of the name of soldier; his selfishness would be even more remarkable than his courage. The Queen's own Cross was not intended to encourage such selfishness, or to reward such courage; nor has it ever done so. Many of those who wear it were surprised at its being awarded to them, so humble was their estimate of the value of the deeds by which they obtained it; no one ever performed those deeds for the purpose of being awarded the Victoria Cross. It is the expression of our national admiration for deeds which demand some public recognition, and cannot be adequately rewarded in any other way.

These remarks have been elicited by the strictures with which Sir Colin Campbell accompanied the letter of expostulation from the officers of the 64th Regiment, which he forwarded to His Royal Highness the Duke of Cambridge. In that letter they complained, with much appearance of reason, that their own honour and that of the regiment had been compromised by an officer of the staff usurping the place of Major Stirling, the officer in command, when there was nothing to justify him in doing so. Major Stirling was at the head of his regiment, and the 64th were discharging the duty assigned to them. If he was not mounted, there was a sufficient reason for this: his horse had been wounded by the bursting of a shell, and was unable to carry him. If the regiment had betrayed any irresolution, or hesitated to advance, the occasion might have justified young Havelock's interference; but they positively denied that such was the case, and requested that some steps might be taken to vindicate their honour, which had been impugned by awarding the Victoria Cross to one whose conduct was more deserving of censure than of praise.

It is difficult to take a cool, dispassionate view of this affair; our sympathies are naturally with the young lieutenant, but we must endeavour to be just. No one can find fault with the officers of the 64th for writing such a letter: to a soldier reputation is everything; and the fair fame of a regiment, like that of a woman, if once lost can never be regained. Every regiment in the service has its distinctive character, as much as every soldier who belongs to it; it was clearly, therefore, the duty of the officers of the 64th to protest against a measure which reflected on them and the soldiers under their command. Their silence would have been a tacit admission that there was ground for such reflections; their protest was a natural appeal against them.

We have the sincerest respect for the memory of General Havelock: no one can read his life, or trace his career, without being convinced that he was a good man and a gallant soldier. This conviction, however, does not imply that he was perfect, or exempt from those weaknesses to which the very best men are subject. A father is always liable to the charge of partiality when judging of the merits of his own son, and is often blinded by paternal affection to the actual merits of the case. It would be improper for him to form one of a jury while his son was being tried, much more so to sit upon the bench as the presiding judge. This was the position which General Havelock occupied on this occasion, and we must not blame him too much if, in his anxious desire to do justice to his son, he inadvertently failed to do justice to Major

Stirling, and the officers and men of the 64th Regiment. He acknowledges that Lieutenant Havelock placed himself on his horse in front of the centre of the 64th, and that he did so without any orders from him. He admits the fact: the only question is, was he justified in doing so? If the regiment had been repulsed, or had hesitated to carry out the orders they had received, any officer of the staff would have been justified in taking the command, and in leading them on to victory. It has never been attempted to be shown that such was the case. The 64th were steadily advancing under the command of Major Stirling, when Lieutenant Havelock, acting on the impulse of the moment, rushed forward and placed himself at their head. The general, in his telegram, contrasts the position occupied by Major Stirling with that occupied by his son:—"Major Stirling, commanding the regiment, was in front, dismounted; but the lieutenant continued to move steadily on in front of the regiment, at a foot pace, on his horse." It is unfortunate that he should have omitted to state that Major Stirling was dismounted because his horse had been wounded by the bursting of a shell; there would thus have been no ground for the suspicion that he was dismounted from choice, and not from necessity. It may be that the general was ignorant of this fact; but he ought to have ascertained why Major Stirling was dismounted before he mentioned it in a telegram, which must, sooner or later, become public. The indignation of the officers and men of the 64th was only natural, and Sir Colin Campbell truly expresses their feeling when he says, "By such despatches as the one alluded to it is made to appear to the world that a regiment would have proved wanting in courage, except for an accidental circumstance; such a reflection is most galling to British soldiers, indeed, is almost intolerable, and the fact is remembered against it by all the other corps in Her Majesty's service. Soldiers feel such things most keenly. I would, therefore, beg leave to dwell on the injustice sometimes done by general officers when they give a public preference to those attached to them, over old officers who are charged with the most difficult and responsible duties."

No one will accuse Sir Colin of having ever been influenced by this undue preference; his desire ever was to do justice to all, and he saw no merit in any action which was not strictly connected with the discharge of duty. He had no sympathy with impulsive acts of bravery, because he considered them to be subversive of discipline, and often injurious to others. At the battle of the Alma he threatened the 42nd with a punishment which they all dreaded, if they left the ranks to succour the wounded; at the relief of Lucknow he publicly reprimanded a Highland officer, his personal friend, who had left his regiment to show him a flag which he had just taken from the enemy. He was actuated by no personal feeling, he was only expressing his own inward conviction when he thus alluded to Lieutenant Havelock's impulsive act. "This instance is one of many in which, since the institution of the Victoria Cross, advantage has been taken by young aides-de-camp and other staff-officers to place themselves in prominent situations for the purpose of attracting attention. To them life is of little value, as compared with the gain of public honour; but they do not reflect, and the generals to whom they belong do not reflect, on the cruel injustice thus done to gallant officers, who, beside the excitement of the moment of action, have all the responsibility attendant on this situation."

Sir Colin's judgment, in estimating the motives by which Lieutenant Havelock was actuated in placing himself at the head of the 64th Regiment, was evidently biassed by the prejudices he entertained against the Victoria Cross. There is no reason to believe that the love of public honour, or any such selfish feeling, induced that gallant officer to expose his life; his own anxious desire that his conduct should be overlooked proves the contrary. If his object had been to obtain the Victoria Cross, he would certainly never have persuaded his father to suppress the telegram in which he recommended him for that honour. His father's good fame was dearer to him than any honour which his country could confer, and he knew that his father could not allude to him as he had done without raising a storm of opposition. He wished, therefore, that the matter should be overlooked and forgotten. He had acted on the impulse of the moment; all depended on the steadiness with which the 64th advanced; he saw them without a mounted leader, and, without stopping to inquire the cause, he rushed forward and placed himself at their head. When he discovered afterwards that Major Stirling's horse was wounded, and that he had supplanted that officer in the command of his regiment while faithfully discharging his duty, he must have felt that he had inadvertently treated him with injustice, and that the public recognition of his conduct as desiring reward would increase the wrong. He owed Major Stirling an apology for having usurped his place, but he had done nothing to earn the Victoria Cross, which was never intended to be an incentive to impulsive acts of undisciplined valour. It must have been with feelings of surprise and regret that he read his father's telegram, which was not published in India till after his death, and learned that the Victoria Cross had been awarded to him for this particular deed. In the interval he had done other deeds of valour which fully merited this honour, and excited the admiration of every British soldier in India; it was unfortunate that the father, in his anxious desire to do justice to the son, should not have waited a little longer.

The remonstrance on the part of the officers of the 64th Regiment was only natural and just; it was their duty to vindicate their own honour now that Major Stirling was no longer able to answer for himself and for them. That unfortunate officer died soon after he was promoted to the rank of lieutenant-colonel, on the special recommendation of General Havelock, for the part he acted at the battle of Cawnpore. This fact is sufficient to prove that he had not failed in his duty, and that there was nothing in his conduct to justify another in usurping his place. The general, also, bestowed the highest praise upon the regiment. In his despatch, after the battle, he says: "Nor was the gallant 64th behind; charging with equal bravery another village on the left, and firing four volleys as they rapidly advanced up the rising ground, they soon made the place their own, and captured its three guns. . . . . But the 64th, led by Major Stirling and my aide-de-camp, who had placed himself at their front, were not to be denied. Their rear showed the ground strewed with wounded, but on they silently and steadily came; then, with a cheer, charged and captured the unwieldy trophy of their valour." In the general order, which appeared on the morning after the battle, he says: "64th, you have put to silence the jibes of your enemies throughout India. Your fire was reserved till you saw the colour of your enemies' moustaches—this gave us the victory." It is unfortunate that the general should have revived those jibes, by making it appear to the world that the 64th would have failed in the hour of danger, had it not been that his own son placed himself at their head.

These remarks, we trust, will not be misunderstood. We willingly acquit the present Sir H. Havelock of all blame in the matter. He did not wish to obtain the Victoria Cross for this particular act; it was, in a measure, forced upon him without his knowledge or consent. But having once obtained it, he was determined to show that none could be more worthy to wear it. He acted as deputy-assistant adjutant-general to the army which advanced under the command of his father and Sir J. Outram for the relief of Lucknow, and greatly distinguished himself at the passage of the Charbagh bridge, where the enemy offered an obstinate resistance to our entrance. From this bridge to the Residency was a distance of about two miles; and this interval was intersected by trenches, traversed by palisades, and commanded by loopholed houses. Between eight and nine o'clock on the morning of the 25th of September, 1857, the army of rescue received the order to advance; as soon as the first brigade, under the command of Sir J. Outram, had passed the advanced picket, they were assailed by a heavy fire in front, and Captain Maude, R.A., pushed bravely forward with the loss of one-third of his men. His coolness and courage opened a passage for our army till they reached the Charbagh bridge, which crosses the canal. This bridge was defended by six guns—one of them a 24-pounder—which swept the passage and threatened destruction to all who approached. Here the enemy had resolved to make their stand, and no position could have been better chosen. The houses on either side were loopholed and flat-roofed, each one forming a separate fortress, from which the enemy could fire upon our men with comparative safety. So severe was the enemy's fire that our troops were obliged to halt for a time, and to lie down wherever they could find shelter. Owing to the narrowness of the road, only two of Maude's guns could be brought forward, and the men who worked them, being without cover, were killed or wounded, so that they had to be replaced by volunteers from the infantry. General Neile, who commanded the first brigade in the absence of Sir James Outram, ordered the Madras Fusiliers to advance and to storm the enemy's battery. The words had scarcely passed the general's lips when young Arnold, of the Fusiliers, who was ever first when danger was to be faced, dashed across the bridge followed by a few of his men. Two mounted staff-officers, Colonel Tytler and Lieutenant Havelock, swept across the bridge with this little band of heroes, who were assailed by a storm of grape from the enemy's battery. Arnold was shot through both legs; Colonel Tytler's horse was killed; few of the little band survived that fatal fire. Lieutenant Havelock was the only one who appeared on the bridge when the smoke cleared away; seated calmly on his horse, the mark for a hundred bullets, he waved his sword in the air, and encouraged the Fusiliers, by voice and gesture, to advance. Wherever an officer leads the way the British soldier will not hesitate to follow; officers and men dashed forward over the prostrate bodies of their comrades amidst a storm of grape, seized the enemy's guns, and bayoneted all who dared to resist their onset. It would be difficult to overestimate the value of Lieutenant Havelock's gallant conduct on this occasion. He seemed to bear a charmed life, and his gallant stand on the Charbagh bridge, when all around him had fallen or been put *hors de combat*, ought never to be forgotten. In the days of chivalry such a deed would have won him his spurs; no one will attempt to deny that it fully entitled him to the Victoria Cross. Sir James Outram, who came up in time to witness the rush of the Fusiliers and the capture of the enemy's battery, thus alludes to his conduct in a letter addressed to his father: "Throughout the tremendous fire of guns and musketry which the enemy directed across the Charbagh bridge, Lieutenant Havelock, with the Madras Fusiliers, stormed the bridge, took the guns, and cleared the streets sufficiently to allow of the troops in the rear closing up. I cannot conceive a more daring act than thus forcing the bridge; and the officers who led the Fusiliers on that occasion, in my opinion, most richly deserve promotion. But hazardous as was their position, they being on foot, and, therefore, not readily distinguished from their men, risked little comparatively with Lieutenant Havelock, the only officer on horseback, who cheered the men on at their head, and became the target of the enemy's musketry. I shall feel truly delighted to learn that you accept my recommendation of this brave officer, and I shall deeply regret having divested myself of the command during the advance on Lucknow, if, from what I regard as a morbidly sensitive delicacy, you withhold from Lieutenant Havelock, because he is your relative, the reward to which, as a soldier, he has so unmistakably established a first claim."

General Havelock, being ignorant of the result of his first recommendation, cordially adopted the suggestion of "one whose proved gallantry and devotion to the service peculiarly fitted him to judge of these qualities in another," and recommended Captain Maude, R.A., and Lieutenant Havelock for the Victoria Cross. Intermediately, before his despatch could reach England, the Cross had been awarded to Lieutenant Havelock for his services at the battle of Cawnpore, and no additional honour was conferred upon him. In terms of the Royal Warrant of the 29th of January, 1856, those who, after receiving the Cross, perform a second act of distinguished bravery, may be rewarded with an additional clasp or bar, and Sir James Outram was much disappointed that this reward was not conferred upon Lieutenant Havelock. That he had fairly earned it at the Charbagh bridge, cannot be denied even by those who dispute his claims at the battle of Cawnpore; it is easy to conceive, but unnecessary to specify, the reasons why it was withheld from him. It is sometimes good for young soldiers "to learn to labour and to wait:" the son would have lost nothing if this truth had been present to the father's mind after the action at Cawnpore.

We come now to the particular incident which afforded Private Henry Ward, 78th Highlanders, an opportunity of gaining that Cross which was also to be worn by him whose life he saved. After cheering on the Fusiliers to victory, Lieutenant Havelock received orders to look to the safety of the convoy, as the baggage, the wounded, and the followers defiled over the bridge. The heroic bravery of the 78th, who performed the convoy, repelled every attack of the enemy, and, after a sanguinary struggle of three hours, the last waggon crossed the bridge. Lieutenant Havelock had just given orders for the Highlanders to be withdrawn, when he was shot by a musket-ball through the left elbow joint, and fell down insensible. No time was to be lost; he was raised from the ground, placed in a doolie, and carried forward with the other wounded. In the chapter on Dr. Home and the Victoria Cross we will tell how it fared with our wounded on that fearful night, and the gallant Havelock would have been butchered with those who fell into the hands of the enemy, if Henry Ward had not stood by him as his guardian angel. When the convoy of litters containing the wounded, guided by Mr. Thornhill, of the Civil Service, who had mistaken the way, entered a large open square they were enveloped in the enemy's fire, and the escort, consulting their own safety, rushed across, leaving the litters behind. A little band of heroes still stood by the wounded, and braved that murderous fire; among these was Henry Ward, who had charge of Lieutenant Havelock's doolie. When the native doolie bearers threw down their burdens and fled, Henry Ward encouraged his to remain, and to press forward through that fearful fire. One of his comrades, Private Pilkington, who belonged to the escort, was wounded, and knowing the fate that awaited him if left behind, threw himself into the doolie where Havelock lay. The bearers were about to drop their double load and to make their escape, when Ward, who was too generous to leave a comrade behind, compelled them to press on, and never left the doolie till it reached the Residency. The wounded in the other doolies were murdered by the enemy to the number of thirty or forty, and Lieutenant Havelock's escape is almost miraculous. He owes his life to Henry Ward, who for this act of intrepid gallantry was rewarded with the Victoria Cross.

Lieutenant Havelock succeeded his father in the baronetcy, and the pension of 1000*l.* per annum which had been awarded to him by Government. Before he left India, in 1859, he had attained the brevet rank of lieutenant-colonel, and obtained his company in the 18th Royal Irish. We have already mentioned that the Victoria Cross was conferred upon him in March, 1858, and on his return to England it was affixed to his breast by the hands of our gracious Sovereign, and the memory of the father was thus honoured in the person of the son. Amid the honours and acclamations which awaited his return, he did not forget the gallant Highlander who saved his life. Henry Ward accompanied him to Aldershot, where he was employed on the staff as his servant, but occupied rather the place of a humble friend. Master and servant were both decorated with the Victoria Cross, and bound together by closer ties than that relation usually implies. Ward was proud of his master, and, we need scarcely add, that his master was proud of Ward. A feeling of justice compels us to mention that Henry Ward, though he has served his time in a Highland regiment, is not a Highlander by birth; he is a native of Norfolk, but, like many other Englishmen who have assumed the tartan, he has the *esprit de corps* quite as strong as if he were a genuine son of the Gael.

When, in 1863, the 2nd battalion of the 18th Royal Irish were ordered to New Zealand, to aid in repressing the Maori rebellion, Lieutenant-Colonel Sir H. M. Havelock proved his devotion to his country by at once resigning his staff appointment, and hastening to rejoin his regiment. If the rules of the service had permitted it, Henry Ward would have accompanied him, and shared in the dangers of Maori warfare; as it was he had to return to his regiment, the gallant 78th. The military career of Lieutenant-Colonel Havelock in New Zealand has been as distinguished as in India. Soon after his arrival he was appointed to the staff in the Quarter Master General's department, and continued to hold that appointment till he left for England, in the beginning of 1865. In February, 1864, he exhibited great gallantry during a skirmish with the enemy at Mangapiko, in the Waikato; the rebels had attacked a party of our men, who were imprudently bathing in the river, and would have cut them off, if Lieutenant-Colonel Havelock had not hastily collected a small band of imperial and colonial forces, and hurried to their assistance. After a smart engagement the rebels were dispersed, and the colonial officer, who co-operated with Lieutenant-Colonel Havelock, was recommended for the Victoria Cross, though he occupied a subordinate place, and acted a less distinguished part. His leader had already obtained this honour, but we mention this circumstance to show that he has earned it again and again. At the capture of the pa, at Orakau, on the 1st of April, 1864, he exposed his life with a boldness almost bordering on recklessness, and contributed much to the success of the day by the promptitude with which he brought up the mortars from Awamutu, when every other expedient had failed. A gallant soldier, a good Christian, he is worthy of the name he bears and of the honours he has received, while his conduct to Henry Ward proves that he can appreciate bravery in others, and that he is not ungrateful to the man who saved his life.

CHAPTER XVI.

LIEUTENANT ANDREW CATHCART BOGLE, V.C., 78TH HIGHLANDERS (NOW CAPTAIN 10TH FOOT).

ALL our readers are more or less familiar with the distinguished part which the 78th Highlanders acted in the suppression of the Indian Mutiny. In our last chapter we showed how Henry Ward, a gallant private of this regiment, won the Victoria Cross by saving the life of the present Sir H. M. Havelock, then a lieutenant in the 10th Regiment, when he was severely wounded at the relief of Lucknow. The high opinion which the elder Havelock had formed of the Highlanders, when they were serving under him on the Euphrates during the Persian war, led him to rejoice when he found that they formed part of the moveable column with which he was to advance for the relief of Cawnpore. He thus alludes to them in one of his confidential reports:—"There is a fine spirit in the ranks of this regiment. I am given to understand that it behaved remarkably well at the affair of Rhooshab, near Bushire, which took place before I reached the army; and during the naval action on the Euphrates, and its landing here (in Persia); its steadiness, zeal, and activity under my own observation were conspicuous. The men have been subjected in this service to a good deal of exposure, to extremes of climate, and have had heavy work to execute with their entrenching tools, in constructing redoubts and making roads. They have been, while I had the opportunity of watching them, most cheerful, and have never seemed to regret or complain of anything but that they had no farther chance of meeting the enemy.

I am convinced the regiment would be second to none in the service if its high military qualities were drawn forth. It is proud of its colours, its tartan, and its former achievements."

The battle of Cawnpore, fought on the 16th of July, 1857, justified the opinion thus expressed, and proved that the wearers of the tartan were worthy of their predecessors who conquered at Maida and Assaye. Our victory was complete; but it failed to save the lives of the helpless women and children who had fallen into the hands of that bloodthirsty monster Nana Sahib, whose name will ever live in the annals of the Indian mutiny as the impersonation of all that is perfidious and cruel. He was the adopted son of Bajee Row, the Peishwa, or head of the ancient Mahratta confederacy, and proved himself worthy of such a father. Bajee Row, in 1818, endeavoured in the most treacherous manner to destroy Mr. Mountstuart Elphinstone, the British resident at his court; but, having failed in this attempt, he was driven from Poona, his capital, and, after being chased through the country for several months, was defeated at the battle of Kirkee. His power was thoroughly crushed, so that he might have been forced to surrender at discretion; but he was admitted to terms, and endowed with an annuity of 90,000*l.*, which he lived to enjoy for thirty-two years. After his death his immense wealth was inherited by his adopted son, who had established himself at Bithoor, about sixteen miles from Cawnpore, and lived on terms of intimacy with the officers of the garrison, who never suspected his loyalty or good faith. For years he had contrived to dissemble the bitter spirit of hostility to the English which was rankling at his heart, and which sprang from no other cause than the withdrawal of the pension enjoyed by his father. When the native troops at Cawnpore began to exhibit symptoms of disaffection, he volunteered to aid Sir H. Wheeler in protecting the treasury from their rapacity, and his offer was accepted. It was only when the Sepoys broke into open mutiny that he threw off the mask, placed himself at their head, and ruthlessly butchered all the European and native Christians who had not been able to escape to the entrenchment. With his thirst for blood whetted rather than allayed by this carnage, he now closed round the entrenchment, the last refuge of the Europeans, and directed all his efforts to compel the gallant little garrison to surrender. Their heroic defence, protracted from day to day and from week to week, in the vain hope of relief, amid exposure, privation, and the incessant fire of the enemy's artillery, is one of the most touching episodes in the history of British India, and cannot be read without a feeling of deep emotion. The men would rather have died sword in hand than negotiate with the murderer of the fugitives from Futtyghur; but their hearts were melted by the sufferings of the helpless women and children crouching in holes dug out beneath the walls of the entrenchment; and for their sakes, on the very day when Havelock assumed command of the column intended for their relief, they began to think of capitulating.

The cannonade had continued for more than three weeks, and of the 870 persons who survived, 330 were women and children. While they were still hesitating, a message was brought from Nana Sahib, offering the garrison a safe conduct to Allahabad, with permission to take their arms, baggage, and ammunition with them, on condition that they surrendered at once. Sir H. Wheeler, anxious if possible to save the women and children from that death which was already staring them in the face, reluctantly agreed to accept this offer: he seems to have done so contrary to his better reason, and almost with a presentiment of the calamity that was about to overtake them. But it seemed their only chance of safety, and a fearful responsibility would devolve upon him if he neglected or rejected it. The Nana took an oath on the waters of the Ganges, which to a Hindoo and a Brahmin is the most sacred and binding of all oaths, that he would carry out the terms of capitulation to the very letter; and it was scarcely conceivable that he could prove faithless to his engagement, and perjure himself. They knew nothing of his deep-rooted hatred of the English race, his long-cherished scheme of revenge, his burning thirst for human blood; they remembered only his pleasant parties at Bithoor, and imagined that from such a man they had nothing to dread. At first all seemed to be well: when they left the entrenchment, they found boats prepared to convey them to Allahabad, and the women and children were greeted with expressions of sympathy and solicitude, which were as sincere as the caresses the tiger bestows on its victims. No sooner were the whole party seated in the boats than three signal guns were fired, and a destructive fire was opened on the helpless fugitives from guns concealed along the bank, and the pieces with which the rebels were armed. The shrieks of despairing mothers, clasping their infant offspring to their breasts, and striving to shield them from the murderous fire, were heard amid the booming of the guns, the rattle of musketry, and the maddening yells of the inhuman fiends to whom the work of destruction was entrusted. It was a preconcerted massacre: bands of native infantry and cavalry had been stationed on either bank of the river to cut off the retreat of those who tried to escape from the boats by swimming; only one or two contrived to elude their vigilance, and to reach a place of safety. Two hundred women and children were taken back to the town: with solemn hands and beating heart we draw the veil of silence over their fate. The well at Cawnpore can never be forgotten, and the feeling of confidence which we once reposed in the natives of India may not be restored for centuries.

After his victory of the 16th of July, Havelock allowed his exhausted troops to rest for the night on the field of battle, and entered the town the following morning. No language can describe the scenes of horror which greeted them on every side when they reached the entrenchment, and learned the hideous revelations of the slaughter-house and the well. It was enough to melt a heart of adamant; and we know that men, usually callous and indifferent to human suffering, cannot allude to what they witnessed on that day without a startled expression, as if the scene were still before them. Some will tell you, that for nights after they woke up in an agony of terror, so powerful was the impression left on their minds by that fearful spectacle. The floor of the slaughter-house was covered with blood; the lower part of the walls was marked with sword-cuts aimed at the helpless creatures crouching together on the ground; tresses of long hair were still adhering to the walls and pillars; articles of female attire were scattered about saturated with the blood of those who once had worn them; leaves of the Bible, of the Prayer Book, and of a work entitled "Preparation for Death," were picked up on every side by the horror-struck soldiers. One man picked up a piece of paper with the words "Ned's hair, with love," written on it; on opening it he found a lock of boy's hair; his mother had not parted with it till she parted with life. On the walls, written in pencil, or scratched in the plaster, were such inscriptions as these:—"Think of us;" "Avenge us;" "Your wives and families are here in misery, and at the disposal of savages;" "Oh, oh! my child, my child!" The last words are the most touching of all; there was no thirst for vengeance, no solicitude for self, in that mother's breast; her only thought was of her child, and its impending fate. Well might one of the officers exclaim—"Oh! how thankful I am that I have no wife, no sisters out here!" One sickens and shudders at the very thought of such scenes: what effect must they have produced on those who actually witnessed them, who saw the blood-stained floor, and the limbs of murdered babes and women protruding from the well into which they had been thrown? The deepest emotions are those which can find no expression: few words were spoken; but as the Highlanders looked into one another's faces, a strange expression came over them: the rugged brows were knit, the quivering lips were sternly compressed, and the fierce glare of the eye told of the conflicting passions within. There was unspeakable pity for those tender babes and women so cruelly murdered; but stronger and more overwhelming was the thirst for vengeance which found expression on many a battle-field, in the shout "Remember Cawnpore!" and in the deadly bayonet thrust. The deepest emotion was excited by the discovery of the body of Sir Hugh Wheeler's daughter, for it was already whispered among the soldiers that this heroic woman had displayed the spirit of a Judith in avenging her insulted honour. The exact circumstances attendant on her death will never be known; but it is certain that by her example she taught her countrywomen to prefer death to dishonour. In one version of the story, she shot five Sepoys in succession with a revolver, and then threw herself into a well to escape from the others; in another version, she is said to have cut off the heads of no less than five men with a sword; while Mr. Shepherd, one of the survivors of the massacre, relates that, having been forced by a trooper of the 2nd Native Cavalry to accompany him to his hut, she rose in the night, seized his sword, killed him and three other men, and then threw herself into a well. It is certain that she behaved like a high-souled English gentlewoman, and there was something in the story of her fate that touched the heart of every soldier that entered Cawnpore. It has been related, that the Highlanders with reverent and loving hands committed her body to the dust; but, before doing so, removed the hair from her head, sent part of it to her relations, and divided the rest among themselves; counted every hair, and swore a solemn oath, that for every one a mutineer should die. We can understand the feeling which might have dictated such an oath; but the expression of it in the manner related, is too sensational and melodramatic for the stern, rugged nature of the Highlanders; it had no foundation in truth, and, like the story of Jessie Brown at Lucknow, was evidently got up for stage effect.

But we must hurry on from these maddening scenes to the battle of Oude, where Captain Boyle, then a lieutenant in the 78th Highlanders, gained the Victoria Cross. The victory of Cawnpore failed to produce that feeling of elation among our soldiers which usually accompanies such an event. The following day a deep silence reigned throughout the encampment, broken at intervals by the melancholy wail of some Highland dirge as the dead were conveyed to their last home; for cholera had begun to decimate our little army, and proved a more formidable foe than the mutineers in arms against us.

As the Nana had still a considerable army under his command, it was considered probable that an attempt would be made to regain Cawnpore, and General Havelock marched his troops on the morning of the 18th of July to a position west of the town, where he was safe from attack, and could intercept the enemy if they tried to advance from Bithoor. By selecting volunteers from the infantry he was enabled to increase his irregular horse from nineteen to sixty, and this small troop rendered important services during the remaining part of the campaign. Dreading that his men might give way to intemperance, he caused the commissariat to buy up all the intoxicating liquors that were to be found in the town, and to give out only such quantities as might be taken with safety. On the morning of the 19th, he learned from the spies who had been sent out to watch the movements of the enemy, that their army was broken up; the Sepoys, seized with a sudden panic, had deserted their ranks, and sought for safety on the other side of the river; the Nana himself had fled from the field on a swift elephant, accompanied by a few of his followers, and never halted in his flight till he reached the kingdom of Oude. On receiving this intelligence, General Havelock despatched a party of his men to take possession of Bithoor; no resistance was offered by the enemy, and the greater part of the plunder which had been carried off from Cawnpore was recovered. That town was not left defenceless; a field-work was constructed, and a small garrison of 300 men was left to occupy it. Having completed his arrangements, he prepared, on the morning of the 21st of July, to advance to the relief of Lucknow. The passage of the Ganges was a most difficult undertaking; the river, swollen by the heavy rains, was more than 1600 yards wide; the bridge of boats had been destroyed by the rebels; the boatmen had disappeared, and it would have been dangerous to entrust the transit of the men to inexperienced hands. After some delay and difficulty, a number of the old boatmen were tempted to return by the promise of pardon for their past misconduct, and additional pay; and in four days the whole of our troops found themselves on the Oude bank of the Ganges, where the general, who had superintended the embarkation in person, joined them. The gallant Neil was left to hold Cawnpore during his absence, and displayed an energy which inspired the minds of the disaffected with terror; he had only three hundred men under his command, but with this little force he restored the *prestige* of our army throughout the surrounding districts by capturing many rebels, and recovering public property, and by organizing a body of irregular cavalry, which kept the road open between Cawnpore and Allahabad. In addition to this, he had charge of all the sick and wounded who had been left behind; but this heroic man, whose career was soon to be cut short at Lucknow, was indefatigable in the discharge of his numerous duties. It is the characteristic of such men as Havelock, that they can impart to others something of that dauntless courage and unflagging energy by which they themselves are animated.

On the 28th of July, Havelock's army reached Mungulwar, a village situated six miles from the Ganges, on a ridge elevated about two hundred feet above the surrounding country, where they might have held their ground against all the rebels in Oude. But their only desire was to push on to Lucknow; they might still be in time to rescue the beleaguered garrison from the rebels, who were hemming them in on every side. This desire was strengthened by the arrival of a messenger, who contrived to elude the vigilance of the rebel army at Lucknow, and reached our camp in safety, bringing with him a plan of the town, and a valuable report from Brigadier Inglis, written partly in Greek characters as a measure of precaution. Havelock saw all the danger of the undertaking. "If the worst come to the worst," he said to his son, "we can only die sword in hand." Death to him had no terrors: the only question was whether he could fight his way to the Residency with 1500 men, and ten badly-equipped guns. The enemy were closing in upon him in front and rear; he must cross the bridge across the Sye at Bunnee, which the rebels had entrenched and covered with their guns; he must be prepared to repel the 3000 men which the Nana had collected to intercept his retreat. With their minds fresh from the horrors of Cawnpore, there was only one desire among our men—to go on, to conquer or to die. Havelock expressed the feeling of all, when writing to the Government, on the 28th July, he said, "The communications convince me of the extreme delicacy and difficulty of any operation to relieve Inglis; it shall be attempted, however, at every risk." There spoke the spirit of a true soldier, of one in whose mind every other consideration was subordinate to a sense of duty.

The little army started at daybreak on the morning of the 29th of July, and, after advancing about three miles, reached the town of Oude, which was occupied by the enemy. Their position is thus described by the general, in the despatch which he wrote after the battle:—"The enemy's right was protected by a swamp, which could neither be forced nor turned; his advance was drawn up in a garden enclosure, which, in this warlike district, had, purposely or accidentally, assumed the form of a bastion. The rest of his (advance) force was posted in and behind a village, the houses of which were loopholed. The passage between the village and the town of Oude is narrow. The town itself extended three quarters of a mile to our right. The flooded state of the country precluded the possibility of turning in this direction. The swamp shut us in on the left. Thus an attack in front became unavoidable."

The general perceived that the enemy enjoyed every advantage of position, but he lost no time in commencing the attack. The passage between the village and the town of Oude was very narrow, but it was along this passage that our troops had to advance, as they were hemmed in by the swamp on one flank, and on the other by the floods which had swept over the adjoining country. There were two regiments in whose courage and steadiness under fire the general had the fullest confidence; to them was assigned the post of honour. On the 29th of July, about six o'clock in the morning, the 78th Highlanders and the 1st Madras Fusiliers advanced along the passage, supported by two guns, and met with a determined resistance. The bastioned enclosure was carried at the point of the bayonet, and the enemy fell back on the village, where they opened a destructive fire upon our men from the loopholed houses. On this the general ordered the 64th and 84th Regiments to attack a gateway on the left, and the 78th Highlanders to force an entrance by a narrow passage on the right. Private Patrick Cavanagh, of the 64th Regiment, was the first to clear the wall behind which the enemy were sheltered; he stood there alone, confronted by at least a dozen of troopers, but the intrepid Irishman never dreamed of turning his back on the foe. He stood there immovable as a rock, till he was literally cut to pieces before his comrades could come to his aid; by his side lay three of the enemy, whom he had killed with his own hand. Havelock was ever ready to distinguish merit wherever it appeared, and after the battle he thus alluded to this incident: "There were men among you whom I must laud to the skies. Private Patrick Cavanagh, of the 64th, died gloriously, hacked to pieces by the enemy, when setting a brilliant example to his comrades. Had he survived, he should have worn the Victoria Cross, which never could have glittered on a braver breast. But his name will be remembered as long as Ireland produces and loves gallant soldiers."

Another gallant soldier, who equally distinguished himself on this occasion, met with a better fate. When the 78th Highlanders advanced along the narrow passage to the right, they found the end of it barricaded by a wall breast high, with the houses loopholed on either side. The enemy were thus enabled to bring a cross fire to bear upon our men as they approached the wall, and it was necessary to dislodge them. This task was assigned to the Light Company of the 78th Highlanders, who swarmed around the gateway, and strove in vain to effect an entrance. Crowded together in a narrow space, the men were exposed to the enemy's cross fire without being able to retaliate, and several of them were struck down. They tried the wall on every side, like bees rushing against a hive the door of which has been closed, but it resisted all their efforts. A gun was sent for to enlarge the opening and break down the barricade, but the gunners, being exposed to the enemy's fire, were soon either killed or wounded. Little impression can be made on a mud wall by artillery, and the enemy, emboldened by their temporary success, began to believe their position to be impregnable. But the sequel proved that it was not so. Andrew Cathcart Bogle, a young lieutenant of the 78th, saw before him an opportunity of distinction, by which he did not fail to profit; he knew that by forcing that gateway he was holding his life in his hand, but he was prepared for such a sacrifice if his country required it. Collecting a few men of his own regiment, whom he knew and could trust, he gave the word of command, and charged in at their head through the narrow opening in the gateway. A shower of bullets descended on the devoted little band, but on they went, driving the enemy before them and clearing the way for their comrades, who could not refuse to follow such an example. The gallant leader of this forlorn hope was struck down with the cheer of victory on his lips, but strong arms raised him gently from the ground, and bore him to a place of safety. He was severely wounded, but he thought little of his wounds when, on the following day, he received a visit from the general, who esteemed it his duty to thank him personally for the daring courage he had displayed, and the noble example he had set before his men. Nor did Havelock's appreciation of his conduct end here; he was resolved that his courage should meet with a more signal and permanent form of reward than any language, however complimentary, could convey, and drew up a special report of his gallantry, which was forwarded to His Royal Highness the Commander-in-Chief. In consequence of this report, the young lieutenant, who soon recovered from his wounds, and has done good service to his country elsewhere, was decorated with the Victoria Cross, which he still continues to wear on his manly breast. Over the gateway at Oude might well have been inscribed the words which Dante read over another gateway, and has bequeathed to us in his "Inferno"—

"Lasciate ogni speranza, voi ch' entrate"—

but true courage rises superior to every difficulty, and the gleaming sword can arrest hope in her flight.

The greatest results often bring on the smallest events, and it is the work of the historian to trace the connexion between effects and their causes. The charge through the gateway at Oude was not an isolated act of bravery, important only to the immediate actors; it was one of those daring deeds which tell upon armies, and inspire them with confidence in their own courage. The smallest reverse may lead to a panic, and strip a regiment or an army of that *prestige* which it has already acquired; while one daring deed thrills with electric force through officers and men, and produces the conviction that they are invincible. Such a conviction was a needful element of power in such an army as Havelock's, where every man had to confront ten of the enemy, and to fight as if the rescue of Lucknow depended on his single arm. Regarded in this light, the entrance through the gateway at Oude may be regarded as one of the most important events in the Indian campaign, and the young Highlander who led the forlorn hope on that occasion was well entitled to the Cross of Valour, and deserves to live in the annals of the Indian campaign. He now belongs to a different regiment, but his heart still warms at the sight of the tartan, and he is not likely ever to forget how his trusty Highlanders stood by him on that day.

The rebels fought on this occasion with a courage worthy of a better cause; when the village was set on fire, they continued to occupy the loopholed houses, and offered the most determined resistance. But nothing could withstand the ardour of our troops; they forced their way through the village, drove the enemy before them, and captured their guns. At length our little army was enabled to debouch between the village and the town of Oude, where they saw the rebels drawn up in great strength in an open plain—infantry, cavalry, and artillery. Havelock perceived at once that their object was to obtain possession of the town, and thus arrest him on his first day's march. Without a moment's hesitation he pushed forward his troops, already elated with success, till they reached a patch of dry ground, about half-a-mile in extent, surrounded on every side by swamps. Having thus obtained a position between Oude and Lucknow, he drew up his force in line, with four guns in the centre and two on each wing, all bearing on the high road in front, along which the enemy were rapidly advancing. The latter were vastly superior in numbers, but Havelock, unencumbered with native troops, could count on the fidelity and courage of his men, and calmly awaited the approach of the rebels, till they halted in front of our line, and commenced the action. Our artillery then opened fire upon them, and tore through their dense columns massed together on the narrow highway; every discharge left an open passage in their ranks, and told how well our gunners had done their work. In vain they attempted to deploy their force and escape our murderous fire; their guns were engulphed in the swamp; the bullets from our Enfield rifles emptied the saddles of their cavalry; all discipline was at an end; the enemy fled before us in confusion. Then arose the cry, "Remember Cawnpore!" and hundreds of our soldiers, thirsting for vengeance, leaped into the swamp, wading up to the knee and sometimes to the waist, in pursuit of the fugitives, who met with all the mercy they deserved. As the high road was crowded with them, two guns were rapidly moved forward, and their heavy fire prevented them from rallying, and completed their discomfiture. The enemy's artillerymen fought with desperate courage; when their companions in guilt thought only of consulting their safety by flight, they stood by their guns to the last, and scorned to retreat. If all the rebels had fought with the same spirit the result might have been different; as it was, our victory was complete; fifteen guns fell into our hands; the high road was covered with heaps of dead and wounded; and the enemy's loss would have been still greater, if we had had cavalry to follow up the pursuit.

Thus ended the action at Oude, with a loss of 300 men to the enemy. Havelock, acting on the principle of the ancient Roman, who thought that nothing was done so long as anything remained to be done, took immediate steps for following up his success; after a halt of three hours for refreshment, the bugle sounded, the men fell into their ranks, and marched forward to Busherutgunge. This was a walled town, intersected by the Lucknow road, with wet ditches and a gate defended by a round tower, four pieces of cannon, and loopholed buildings within the walls; on the other side was a deep broad pond, or sheet of water, crossed by a causeway. It was a position of such strength, that a few brave men might have defended it for days against a whole army; but the rebels, discouraged by their recent reverses, were unable to withstand the impetuosity of our attack. To the Highlanders and Fusiliers, in whom he could always trust, Havelock gave orders to advance, under cover of the guns, to capture the earthworks and enter the town, while the 64th Regiment made a flank movement to the left, so as to cut off all communication with the town by the chaussée which crossed the lake. The attacking party, being exposed to a heavy fire, were ordered to lie down for a little, till our artillery had weakened the enemy's defences, and caused their fire to slacken; then, on receiving the order to advance, they sprung to their feet, rushed to the trench, cleared it at a bound, and passed through the gate with that wild cheer at which the enemy had already learned to tremble. At the same time the 64th appeared in their rear, and the discomfiture of the enemy was complete; abandoning their guns, they fled in confusion through the town and over the causeway, pursued by the victors. If the 64th had executed the orders they received, and taken possession of the causeway, the whole body of the rebels, intercepted in their flight, might have been put to the sword or taken prisoners; but that regiment for some unknown reason lagged behind, and failed to reach their destination in sufficient time to cut off the enemy's retreat. In vain the general despatched his aide-de-camp, and urged them to advance; it was too late; the golden moment was past, and night closed in on our weary soldiers, who had been on the move from sunrise to sunset. The general rode on some distance, and then returned by the causeway, which was crowded by the Highlanders and Fusiliers leaning on their arms. All were glad to see the brave old man who had twice led them to victory in one day, and from the ranks rose the enthusiastic cry, "Clear the way for the general!" "My lads," he replied, with that ready wit which wins the hearts of soldiers, "you have done *that* to-day already." Such praise was neither unmerited nor unappreciated by those on whom it was bestowed. "God bless the general!" burst from a hundred lips; they were but a handful of men, but under such a leader they were prepared to withstand a host, and already counted on victory.

Thus, on the 29th of July, 1857, Andrew Cathcart Bogle won the Victoria Cross, and General Havelock two battles. Our loss amounted to twelve killed and seventy-six wounded, while the enemy are supposed to have lost half as many men as our whole army. The value of such actions is not to be calculated by their immediate results so much as by the moral influence they exercise; they did not enable Havelock to advance at once to the relief of Lucknow, but they inspired the men with confidence in their general themselves, and produced the conviction that they would yet subdue the flames of rebellion which were burning so fiercely around them.

CHAPTER XVII.

DR. J. JEE, C.B., V.C., SURGEON; ASSISTANT-SURGEON V. M. M'MASTER, V.C.; AND LIEUTENANT AND ADJUTANT HERBERT T. MACPHERSON, V.C.

NO less than six Victoria Crosses were awarded to the 78th Highlanders, for distinguished conduct in the field during their heroic march to relieve the beleaguered garrison at Lucknow. We have already shown how this honourable distinction was attained by Private Henry Ward, and Lieutenant Bogle: it now remains for us briefly to relate the circumstances under which four other officers of the same regiment—one of whom does not occupy a place in Mr. Desange's Gallery—earned for themselves the Cross of Valour.

On the 29th of July, 1857, General Havelock fought two battles and gained two victories. The mutinous Sepoys, who had taken up a strong position in the town of Oude, which is intersected by the great road from Cawnpore to Lucknow, endeavoured to intercept the army of rescue in their advance, but were driven from their position with considerable loss. They then fell back upon Busherutgunge, another fortified town, but Havelock gave them little time to rest; in a few hours he was upon them: the 78th Highlanders and the Madras Fusiliers rushed forward with their usual impetuosity, and carried everything before them. The loss of the enemy in these two battles amounted to more than a thousand men; it would have been still greater if Havelock had been provided with cavalry to follow up his victory. The road to Lucknow was now open to him. Many a prayer was offered up for his speedy arrival by the half-famished garrison, whose only hope of deliverance was in him. But was he in a position to advance? Cholera, that insidious foe which almost invariably follows in the track of an army in the field in India, had struck down one-fourth of his gallant band; men who had charged with irresistible fury in the morning, found themselves at night writhing with agony in the deadly grasp of their invisible enemy. In the two battles he had lost nearly a hundred men in killed and wounded; the number was small, but a few more such victories would leave him without an army. He had yet to advance thirty-six miles through a country occupied by the enemy, before he could reach Lucknow, and he had not more than twelve hundred men able to march. This number might be diminished by one-fourth, as he would require a convoy of three hundred men to escort the sick and wounded. It was a severe struggle, but the conclusion was irresistible: the garrison at Lucknow could not be rescued from the fifty thousand rebels that environed them on every side by Havelock's available force, which fell short of the full complement of a single regiment.

There was no help for it; he must retrace his steps to Cawnpore, and wait there for reinforcements. He was not the man to hesitate in the path of duty; the order was given to fall back on Oude, where his army spent the night. The Highlanders and Fusiliers, flushed with their recent successes, and confident in their own courage, listened to this order with dismay. The road to Lucknow was before them, and why should the general refuse them permission to advance? Did he distrust their courage? They had stood by him in seven battles, and won him as many victories. In such moments of enthusiasm, men's feelings are strung to the highest pitch; rough-bearded soldiers were seen to wipe the tears from their eyes when, for the first time, they turned their backs upon the enemy. No doubt Havelock felt it as much as any soldier under his command; but he was a man who never allowed feeling to interfere with duty, and when he had once made up his mind nothing could swerve him from his purpose.

The beginning of the month of August was gloomy in the extreme; the garrison at Lucknow, with the massacre of Cawnpore fresh in their memories to remind them of the fate that awaited them if they fell into the hands of the bloodthirsty wretches who hemmed them in on every side, fought as the Greeks fought at Thermopylæ, and chose rather to bury themselves beneath the ruins than surrender. It may be that Havelock suffered more than they did: his heart bled for them; he was prepared to make any sacrifice to save them; but their safety depended on his having a sufficient army to effect their rescue. Neile behaved like a gallant soldier: every man who could be spared from Cawnpore was sent to his aid, and every man who came was welcomed as a treasure. Gradually the little army swelled in numbers till it reached an efficient strength of 1400 men, which it never exceeded; but there were no cowardly, treacherous natives in the ranks, and the general and his soldiers had the fullest confidence in one another.

Again the faces of the men were turned towards Lucknow, and their former enthusiasm revived. On the 4th of August the army was on the march, and the small body of volunteer cavalry was sent forward to reconnoitre. They dashed through Oude without interruption; but on reaching the scene of Havelock's second victory, they found the enemy had taken possession of a series of hamlets between the town and the lake, with the evident intention of blocking up our line of communication. On the same evening they galloped back to Oude, and informed Havelock that the rebels were waiting his approach. After a night's bivouac, the army resumed their march, and soon joined issue with the enemy on the scene of their former victory. The result was not long doubtful: shelled from the town by our guns, the rebels were chased through the hamlets by the Highlanders and Fusiliers, and pursued to an open plain beyond. The day was ours, but the victory led to nothing; the enemy again awaited our advance, and Havelock was obliged to retire to his former quarters.

The letters which the gallant old man wrote at this juncture to his family and friends, prove that this was one of the most trying periods of his life. His conduct was liable to misconstruction even among his own men; but he was sustained by a sense of duty, and the inward consciousness of right. If he had ever entertained

14

any doubts about the necessity of falling back upon Cawnpore, they were removed by the position of things in that town. On his arrival, Nana Sahib, the butcher of Bithoor, had collected a body of troops, and was threatening our army on every side; his cavalry swept through the suburbs, and even attempted to force their way through the town. Our communications with Allahabad were threatened, and an immediate blow must be struck. While Havelock was preparing to recross the Ganges, on the morning of the 11th of August, a succession of spies brought him information that four thousand rebels had advanced from Nawabgunge to Busherut, the scene of his former victory, with the evident intention of hanging on his rear, and attacking his column during the passage. To have crossed the river under such circumstances would have been fraught with difficulty, if not with danger, and the rebels would have boasted that they had driven the British forces from the province of Oude by their superior valour. Havelock, knowing that an apparent success on the part of the enemy would destroy the prestige of his former victories, and spread the flame of rebellion through the province, turned round like a lion at bay, and advanced for the third time to encounter the rebel army. On the afternoon of the 11th, his column was in motion, and his advanced guard drove the enemy from the town of Oude. On reaching Busherut, he found their army spread out to a great distance to the right and left, and strongly entrenched in the centre. Their numbers have been estimated at 20,000 men, and their position had been chosen with great skill: their right rested on a village on the main road, where they had established a battery among the gardens; their left, on a rising ground, protected by three guns. Their line is said to have extended five miles, and Havelock saw the necessity of postponing his attack till the following day. His wearied troops returned to Oude, where they bivouacked on the wet ground, and spent the night without shelter amid a deluge of rain. But nothing could daunt their ardour. They rose on the morning of the 12th ready to follow their leader to victory. Our right wing, which consisted of the 78th Highlanders, the Fusiliers, the Sikhs, and part of the Volunteer Cavalry, began the attack, and steadily advanced, till their progress was arrested by a swamp, which in the distance presented the appearance of dry land. As soon as they were within range, the enemy unmasked their battery, which poured forth a deadly shower of round shot, shell, canister, grape, and shrapnel; but, fortunately, their guns were pointed too high, and our men were withdrawn without suffering much loss. The Highlanders moved on to the main road, while the Fusiliers, supported by four guns, diverged to the right. It was no time for manœuvring; an effort must at once be made to silence the enemy's fire—the most severe we had yet encountered. A flanking fire was opened on the enemy's line, which threw them into confusion, and at the same moment the Highlanders, now reduced to about a hundred, steadily advanced till they were within a short distance of the enemy's guns, when they dashed forward with a shout, rushed upon the principal redoubt, and carried it at the point of the bayonet, without firing a shot. The honour of being the first to enter the redoubt was equally divided between two of their officers; and when the officers lead the way, the men will never refuse to follow. The enemy's infantry broke and fled, and the Highlanders, seizing two of their guns, turned them against them, and drove them through the hamlets to an open plain beyond. Our loss amounted to thirty-two men, while the rebels lost upwards of three hundred; and the general having attained the object he had in view, slowly retraced his steps to Cawnpore, with the two guns he had captured. On reaching that town, the gallantry of the Highlanders in carrying the enemy's redoubt was recognised in the order of the day; and the general promised to recommend for the Victoria Cross the officer, non-commissioned officer, or soldier who had been the first to enter this work. The Highlanders had charged with such impetuosity, that Colonel Hamilton, their commanding officer, had some difficulty in ascertaining to whom the honour belonged: in such cases, it is best to leave the matter to the decision of the men themselves, and this was done in the present instance. It appeared that two young officers, Lieutenant Campbell and Lieutenant Crowe, cleared the wall of the redoubt at the same moment; the honour was equally divided between them, and both would doubtless have been decorated with the Cross of Valour if they had survived the campaign: but poor Campbell was cut off by cholera the following day, and the distinction was awarded to Lieutenant Crowe, who still continues to enjoy it. This was the second Victoria Cross bestowed upon the 78th Highlanders since Havelock assumed the command of that gallant regiment.

But the fighting was not yet over; other opportunities of distinction awaited those who knew how to profit by them. No sooner had Havelock brought his column across the Ganges, on the 13th of August, than he began to concert his plans for striking a blow at Nana Sahib, who had resumed his former position at Bithoor. On the 14th, the men enjoyed a day's repose; on the 15th, the gallant Neile left his entrenchment with a mere handful of soldiers, surprised the enemy's left wing, and drove them, with considerable loss, from the vicinity of Cawnpore. On the 16th, Havelock advanced in the direction of Bithoor with a body of 1300 men, nearly all the available forces that could be collected in the town. After a fatiguing march of eight hours beneath the fierce rays of a tropical sun, they came upon the enemy, who had taken up a strong position in front of Bithoor. They had two guns, and an earthen redoubt in and near a plantation of sugar-canes and castor-oil trees, which reached above the heads of the men, while their batteries, effectually masked, were defended by thick ramparts flanked by entrenched quadrangles. Their position was also flanked by two villages, with loopholed houses and walls: in the hands of a braver foe it would have been almost impregnable; but the Highlanders and Fusiliers, mindful of their past victories, advanced with the certainty of success. After a brief exchange of artillery-fire, those two regiments received the order to charge: the Fusiliers soon cleared the entrenched quadrangles of the enemy, and drove them before them at the point of the bayonet; while the Highlanders rushed upon the battery which was immediately in front of them. On they went, alternately lying down and starting up again, so as to escape the fierce discharges of grape and canister with which the rebels strove to arrest their progress. Now they are in front of the battery, and the foremost of them have cleared the parapet; for a moment the rebels dared to cross bayonets with them, but it was only for a moment; they quailed beneath the stern gaze of the mountaineers, turned, and fled. They were driven through the town of Bithoor, which fell into our hands; it was impossible to pursue them farther, and our troops bivouacked on the ground they had so bravely won. Here, as on every other occasion when victory crowned our arms, the want of cavalry was severely felt: we reaped all the honours, but few of the solid advantages which attend success.

The battle of Bithoor was the conclusion of Havelock's first brief, but brilliant campaign for the relief of Lucknow. In a few weeks with a single column he had defeated the enemy, who were vastly superior to him in numbers, in five pitched battles; thrice he had advanced in the direction of Lucknow, and thrice he had been compelled to rètire, not by the rebels, but by the ravages of disease, and the want of transport for his sick and wounded. Every victory he gained weakened his numbers, and might almost have justified the exclamation of Pyrrhus—"Another such victory, and I am undone." Every urgent appeal for reinforcements remained unheeded, and his little army required repose. It was not that the authòrities were unwilling to reinforce him, but they had really no troops to spare, so fiercely had the tide of rebellion set in on every side. When he returned to Cawnpore on the 19th of August, he had seventeen officers and four hundred and sixty-six men cn the sick list; or, in other words, about one-fourth of his army was unfit for service, and the rest were so exhausted that they could scarcely take the field. Havelock and Neile thirsted to encourage their handful of men by leading them against the enemy; but they knew that personal feeling must be subordinate to the one great object of the campaign—the relief of Lucknow. It would have defeated that object to have frittered away their forces in gaining victories which ended in nothing; all that could be done was to recruit the exhausted energies of their men, and to wait for reinforcements.

The rebels, encouraged by their apparent inactivity, and mistaking its cause, asembled in great force on the Oude side of the river, and threatened to cross at two different places; while, on the other bank, the small British force from Calpee was exposed to the attacks of the Gwalior Contingent. This compulsory delay was equally trying to all; but what could be done with an "army" of seven hundred men, when opposed to thirty-seven thousand armed and disciplined soldiers? Every day the general's telegrams became more urgent and importunate. He was prepared "to fight anything and at any odds;" but he knew that it would be madness to advance to Lucknow with the mere handful of men under his command. There were twenty thousand rebels between him and that town; and though the fact was well established, that the Asiatics were unable to withstand the fierce onset of the smallest number of British troops, yet no victory was gained without a certain amount of loss on our part; and this loss, added to the ravages of disease, would have caused his little army to melt away before he reached Lucknow. On the 21st of August, he announced that, if he were not speedily reinforced, he would abandon the enterprize as hopeless, and return to Allahabad, from which he had begun his career of victory about two months before. Meanwhile, he continued to strengthen his position at Cawnpore, and to send his sick and wounded to Allahabad, so that all who remained might be able to take the field.

It would be difficult to say which of the two—Havelock or Inglis—was most to be pitied. The former, after he was compelled to retreat, wrote a note, which the messenger contrived to convey to Inglis in safety. Nothing was concealed; his failure was freely admitted, and he concluded by saying, "You must aid us in every way, even to cutting your way out; if we can't force our way in. We have only a small force." Inglis received this note on the 15th, and on the 23rd the messenger, who was seven days on the way, and had many narrow escapes, brought back his reply. The garrison at Lucknow was reduced to the last extremity: within the walls of the Residency were 120 sick and wounded men; 220 women, and 230 children; their stock of provisions was almost exhausted; officers and civilians had to toil from morning to night like common labourers; cholera and the bullets of the enemy were gradually thinning their numbers: but amid all their privations and sufferings they never dreamed of surrendering. It was better to die within their entrenchments than to be massacred in cold blood by the ruthless foe without; so they continued to hold out till the end of the month, when hope again began to dawn upon the little army of rescue at Cawnpore. Two thousand men belonging to different regiments were on their way from Calcutta to join them; and the Naval Brigade, which was composed of five hundred "blue jackets," under Captain Peel, who had already distinguished himself in the Crimea, had left by steamer on the 20th. There was a quarter of a million of public money in the Residency at Lucknow; but the Governor-General wrote to Havelock to leave it behind, or to use it in any way that might best contribute to the deliverance of the garrison.

A new actor now appears upon the scene. The gallant Outram, the Bayard of India, "sans peur et sans reproche," having brought the Persian war to a successful conclusion, hurried back to Calcutta, and was appointed to the chief command in the Cawnpore district. He entered on his command at Cawnpore on the 18th of August, two days after Havelock had gained his tenth victory over the rebels. On the 1st of September he reached Allahabad, where he found himself at the head of nearly 1700 men of different regiments. Leaving 300 to garrison the town, he hurried on with the rest to reinforce Havelock. Officers and men were equally anxious to have a brush with the "Pandies," and to prevent the horrors of Cawnpore from being repeated at Lucknow. After cutting off a body of 300 insurgents who were about to cross the Ganges into Doab, Outram joined Havelock on the 15th of September, and in the exercise of a noble self-denial which will endear his name to posterity more than all his brilliant achievements, offered to serve as a volunteer in that army which he had a right to command. In the spirit of true charity, he sacrificed personal feeling to a higher sense of justice, and insisted that Havelock should complete the work he had so well begun. He admired Havelock with that sincere, unselfish admiration which none but such generous souls can feel, and scorned the idea of robbing him of his laurels. On the 16th he issued an order, announcing that Havelock was promoted to the rank of major-general, and would continue to hold the command of the army until the relief of Lucknow had been achieved; he himself would accompany it as a volunteer, proud to serve in any capacity under such a leader. Havelock's heart was touched by this "characteristic generosity of feeling," which had the best effect upon the men, and infused into them something of that chivalrous feeling of which Outram had given such a noble display.

Before leaving Cawnpore, the two generals telegraphed to the Governor-General to inquire whether, if Lucknow were recaptured, they should hold it at all hazards, so as to maintain the *prestige* of the British arms, and received the following sensible reply:—"Save the garrison; never mind our *prestige* just now, provided you liberate Inglis: we will recover *prestige* afterwards. I cannot just now send you any more troops. Save the British in the Residency, and act afterwards as your strength will permit." Better advice could not have been given, and the two generals proceeded at once to act upon it. Two months had elapsed since Havelock entered Cawnpore as a conqueror; his noble spirit chafed at the thought that his victories had contributed nothing to the rescue of the garrison; but now a brighter prospect opened up before him; his army was reinforced, and he and Outram marched forth from Cawnpore with the stern resolve to save the half-famished women and children at Lucknow, or perish in the attempt. All ranks were animated by the same feeling; they had confidence in their generals and in themselves, and they already counted on success.

On the 19th of September they crossed the Ganges into Oude by a bridge of boats which had been constructed by Captain Crommelin, and the enemy assembled on the banks offered only a feeble resistance. The rapid advances of our men enabled them to overtake them on the 21st, when they rushed upon them, turned their right flank, drove them from their position, and captured four of their guns. No wonder that success attended an army in which

Outram was serving as a volunteer: during the day he headed one of the charges, and the men, inspired by his example, carried everything before them. The enemy were pursued with such rapidity that they had not time to destroy the Bunnee bridge over the Sye, and on the 23rd Havelock again overtook them. They had now taken up a strong position, and were resolved to make a desperate stand: their left was posted in the enclosure of the Alum Bagh, and their centre and right on low hills. This position was so close to Lucknow that the firing could be distinctly heard in the Residency; and when Havelock discharged his biggest guns, to tell them that help was at hand, the garrison thought it the grandest *feu de joie* they had ever heard. The dying seemed to receive new life; some wept, others prayed; all prepared to welcome their deliverers. But though they were now only two miles from Lucknow, they had still many difficulties to encounter, and Havelock saw the necessity of giving his wearied troops, who had been marching three days under a deluge of rain, a little repose before entering on the final struggle. On the 24th he pitched his camp, and allowed his men to rest till the morning of the 25th, when, leaving his baggage and tents under the charge of an escort in the Alum Bagh, he resumed his march.

It is unnecessary here to describe the heroic advance of our little army, the fierce resistance they encountered, the losses they sustained, and the decisive victory they at length obtained; all this is matter of history, and can never be forgotten. If we confine our attention to the Highlanders, and the part they acted in the rescue of Lucknow, we do so from no desire to depreciate the courage of others who shared in the dangers of the day; our only object is to show in what way three brave men earned for themselves the Cross of Valour and a place in Mr. Desanges's gallery. The Highlanders, the 90th Light Infantry, and the Sikh Regiment of Ferozpore formed the second infantry brigade, under the command of Colonel Hamilton, who held the temporary rank of brigadier. After the desperate resistance of the rebels at the Char Bagh bridge had been overcome by the gallant charge of the Madras Fusiliers, the Highlanders received orders to advance by the Cawnpore road to the Residency, so as to cover the passage of the troops and baggage, and protect them while the heavy guns captured from the enemy were being thrown into the canal. While the rest of the troops defiled to the right, and began to thread their way through the narrow lane which led to the Residency, the Highlanders maintained their position at the head of the street till the camp followers, with the baggage and wounded, had crossed the bridge. For three hours they remained there, immovable as a rock, unshaken by the menaces of the insurgents; again and again the rebels dashed themselves against them in overwhelming numbers, and were driven back at the point of the bayonet; their supply of ammunition had repeatedly to be renewed; their ranks were gradually thinned by the murderous fire to which they were exposed; but they only drew the closer together, and fought on as before. This, the post of danger, had been assigned to them; they were determined to guard it to the last.

Maddened by their own losses and the continued resistance of the Highlanders, the rebels had recourse to another mode of attack. Two brass 9-pounders were dragged forward, and brought to bear on the Highlanders; not a moment was to be lost; the first discharge would leave furrows of dead and wounded in their ranks. Herbert Macpherson, the adjutant of the regiment, proved himself equal to the occasion. This brave young officer was endeared to the men from family connexion and personal character; he was a son of that Colonel Macpherson who commanded the regiment for many years, and shared their dangers in almost every part of the globe. He was almost a son of the regiment, and the feeling of attachment which the men cherished toward him on his father's account, was increased by the considerate kindness with which he discharged the duties of adjutant. He had only to lead the way, and they would follow him anywhere. There were the guns drawn up in front of them, ready to pour forth their murderous fire; Macpherson leaped forward, waving his sword; he was not left alone; others were soon by his side; then came a rush, a cheer, a brief conflict, and all was over. The two guns were seized by brawny arms, and hurled into the canal: after this the Highlanders calmly resumed their former position, and continued to act on the defensive. The impetuosity of their attack was only equalled by their firmness under fire, and these two qualities are rarely united in the same men. The non-combatant officers were animated by the same spirit, and proved themselves worthy of the regiment to which they belonged. Numbers of wounded Highlanders were scattered along the streets of Lucknow in the course of that bloody conflict, and the two surgeons of the regiment frequently risked their own lives in ministering to their wants and superintending their removal. Ten officers and one-fourth of the men were killed or wounded; the skill, the courage, and the energy of the surgeons were taxed to the utmost. Soldiers are not ungrateful, and the Highlanders proved on this occasion that they could appreciate the calm courage of M'Master, who bound up their wounds while the bullets of the enemy were whistling around his head, as well as the dashing bravery of Macpherson, who led them on when they seized the two guns and hurled them into the canal. Two Victoria Crosses were awarded to the regiment, and it was left to the corps to decide who were the men most worthy to wear them. One was assigned to Lieutenant and Adjutant (now Major) Macpherson, for the deed of distinguished courage which we have already described; the other was bestowed, by the universal acclamation of the soldiers, on Assistant-Surgeon Valentine M'Master, for the devoted gallantry with which he risked his life in binding up the wounds and securing the retreat of the men under his charge disabled by the bullets of the enemy. The same honour was afterwards conferred on Dr. J. Jee, the surgeon of the regiment, who had displayed the greatest courage and humanity in bringing in and attending to the wounded.

In two months the Highlanders had fought twelve battles; in four days they had lost *one-third* of their number; their march through the streets was like a march through a sea of fire; but onward they went, dauntless, though not unscathed. And now they are within the walls of the Residency, where the ladies are pressing around them, and rendering thanks to heaven for their deliverance, and yielding their babes to the fond caresses of those stern warriors whose eyes, still glaring with the fury of battle, are soon suffused with tears, as they restore them to their mothers and turn aside to talk of comrades who have fallen, or of the dear ones they have left behind. The Rachels of Lucknow had no occasion that night to weep for their children because they were not; a strong hand and a mighty arm had brought them deliverance; and many a lip trembled with the grateful prayer of the Hebrew warrior: "Not unto us, not unto us, O Lord! but unto Thy name do we give glory."

CHAPTER XVIII.

"LUCKNOW" KAVANAGH AND THE VICTORIA CROSS.

THE Siege of Lucknow forms one of the most interesting episodes in the history of the Indian Mutiny. No event connected with the war excited a deeper interest in this country, and it is impossible, even after the lapse of nine years, to reflect on the gallant defence of a small body of soldiers and civilians shut up within the Residency, the patient endurance of the women, and the heroic efforts to effect their deliverance, without a certain thrill of emotion. Among the many who distinguished themselves at this critical period, a prominent place is held by T. Henry Kavanagh, an Irish gentleman belonging to the uncovenanted service, who happened to be stationed at Lucknow with his wife and children. The report of the massacres at other stations induced the Kavanaghs to remove from their own house to two rooms in the Post Office near the Residency, and these they continued to occupy during all the privations and miseries of the subsequent siege, and until the final rescue. As soon as the native regiments mutinied, the small garrison of Europeans at Lucknow, under the command of Sir Henry Lawrence, prepared to defend themselves to the last: provisions were collected, the fortifications strengthened, and the civilians enrolled into companies of combatants. Before the middle of June, 1857, the whole province of Oude had cast off its allegiance to the British Crown; the English residents had perished or betaken themselves to flight; Lucknow alone remained, like a mighty rock, with the British flag displayed on its summit, dashing back the waves of insurrection and mutiny. All the rage of the rebels was concentrated against it: again and again they advanced to the attack; but the gallant band of defenders, though weakened by suffering and thinned by the bullets of the enemy, proved to their recreant assailants that they would sooner bury themselves beneath the ruins than surrender; and India, in truth, could not have been retained as an appendage of our Crown if it had not been defended by men equal in courage to those who first reduced it to subjection.

The garrison, not satisfied with maintaining the defence, sent small bodies of cavalry to rescue their countrymen at the neighbouring stations, and occasionally made sorties against the enemy. In one of these affairs they were overpowered by numbers at a place called Chinut, and obliged to retire within their entrenchments with considerable loss. This disaster, coupled with the massacre of Cawnpore, of which they had just heard, had a depressing effect upon the garrison at first; but the thought that a similar fate awaited their wives and children if they fell into the hands of the enemy, inspired the men with the courage of despair. Their numbers were reduced, but still they held out. Every mine of their assailants was countermined; every rent in their walls was repaired almost as soon as made. In the obstinacy of their defence they equalled the inhabitants of Saragossa; and there was many a fair maid who lauded their courage, tended the sick, and prayed with the dying. During the first part of the siege, Kavanagh was so prostrated by illness that he could render no assistance; he lay chafing in his bed, like the wounded knight in "Ivanhoe," listening to the din of battle and bemoaning his hard fate. The report of gallant deeds done by others filled his heart with such rapture, that, he tells us, it would have burst if a friend had not leaned on his chest to keep down its emotions. There is no instance, perhaps, on record where strong mental emotion exercised a more powerful influence over the physical frame than in Kavanagh's case. On the 20th of July he was able to leave his bed, and from that day to the final rescue he proved himself brave amongst the brave. He tells us that from the years of his boyhood he had longed to do some deed to immortalise his name, and his youthful aspirations met with so little sympathy that his uncle assured him he was born to be hanged. But Kavanagh is not the first who has been misunderstood in early life. When he returned from India, the admired of all admirers, his friends were better able to appreciate his character.

Towards the end of July, cholera, fever, and small-pox joined their ravages to those of war, and cut off many of the garrison. On the 7th of August, Kavanagh had a narrow escape from death. He had left his house to report himself to his superior officer, and unwittingly exposed himself to the fire of the enemy, from which he was rescued by two of his friends who saw his danger. His courage was not of a calculating character, and his warlike enthusiasm having led him to fire without orders, he was placed under arrest. He was soon released, and, taught by experience, was content for the future to check his undisciplined ardour and to obey the directions of his superiors. August passed drearily away. The defenders, when there was a lull in the attack, climbed to the roofs of their houses and looked out, like sister Anne, for assistance which never came. Hope and despair alternately gained the mastery over them. They rejoiced as they thought of the serried ranks of their countrymen advancing; they shuddered as they thought of their wives, and sisters, and children, exposed to the same fate as the victims of Cawnpore. At one time they amused themselves with reckless gaiety in writing lampoons upon one another; now they gave way to unreasoning despondency, and cursed the heartlessness of their countrymen in leaving them thus to perish amid the ruins. In this, as in similar straits, the women were far more hopeful and unselfish than the men: they concealed their own fears, and often starved themselves that their husbands and children might eat. The ministering angels of that beleaguered fort, their presence exercised a wholesome power which gave hope to the despairing and courage to the feeble. Had there been none of the gentler and weaker sex in Lucknow, it is doubtful whether its garrison of strong men would have stood out so long.

September passed slowly away without bringing the expected aid. The enemy changed their tactics, and tried to reduce the garrison by hunger. Our countrymen, no longer roused to exertion by the fierce excitement of fighting, sank into a sort of stupor, and bewailed the dull monotony of their existence, which was occasionally relieved by the bands of the mutineers playing familiar airs, and more especially the National Anthem. Meanwhile Havelock, with his gallant little force, was fast advancing to their help. The Highlanders were on the march to Lucknow, though the shrill music of the war-pipe was not yet heard within its walls. Our readers are all, doubtless, familiar with the story of Jessie Brown, the Scottish servant-maid, whose watchful ear drank in the slogan and pibroch of her advancing countrymen when others could hear nothing. It is always an invidious task to dispel a pleasing illusion, but a sacred regard for truth compels us to state that Jessie is a purely mythical being—a creature of the imagination as much as Mrs. Harris. The story of Jessie is one of those *canards* with which French journals delight to entertain their readers; it first appeared in the *Pays*, was dramatised and introduced on the stage, and Jessie's paternity, we understand, has been the subject of litigation. Notwithstanding our protests, she will doubtless live in the future history of Lucknow till a second myth-destroying Niebuhr appear to vindicate the truth. On the afternoon of the 25th of September the garrison could hear, not the sound of the bagpipe, but the boom of Havelock's artillery, and all who could walk hurried to the roofs of the houses and strained their eyes to catch the first glimpse of their countrymen. On they came, a small but resolute body, driving the enemy before them at the point of the bayonet, and pressing them into the river, where many of them perished. Little resistance was offered till the advance column began to force their way through the Red Gate, where the enemy opened a murderous fire of small arms upon them. There was no time to pick up the wounded or rescue the bodies of the slain. A rush was made, and Havelock's band was within the walls. The enthusiasm of the garrison knew no bounds: they cheered, they waved their hats, they wept with irrepressible joy, they embraced and implored blessings upon their deliverers. Poor Kavanagh, with true Milesian hospitality, offered his last three bottles of liquor to the exhausted soldiers, who required no pressing to induce them to empty them.

For a time all was joy within the garrison, but there was still much work to be done, much suffering to be endured. The Red Gate was still in the possession of the enemy: Kavanagh undertook to conduct a party to a spot where they could seize it by surprise. At the moment of danger the two young officers in command lost courage, and treated their guide as a drunken madman. An unsuccessful attempt was made to reach the Alum Bagh, where there was a small garrison of our men. On this occasion Kavanagh was one of the first to advance, the last to retreat; he often spent whole nights in the mines, worked his way into those of the enemy, and brought his revolver to bear upon them with deadly effect. A master of Hindustani, he could scold as well as shoot, and it was difficult to say whether his tongue or his rifle was more galling to the enemy. Havelock's men brought no provisions with them, and, as there were now more mouths to be fed, the rations were reduced in quantity. We have heard many a soldier say that he would rather go without his dinner than his pipe, and the poor smokers had to use dried tea and bitter herbs as a substitute for tobacco. But the sufferers bore up manfully, and their sufferings were all but forgotten when, on the 9th of November, a spy arrived with a despatch from Sir Colin Campbell, announcing that help was at hand. Plans had been previously drawn up for the guidance of the Commander-in-Chief in effecting his entrance into the Residency, but it was felt that they could be of little use unless some one familiar with the locality could reach his camp for the purpose of explaining them.

Here was an undertaking of no ordinary danger. The guide would have to pass through the hostile ranks of the mutineers in disguise; if detected, he would have to submit to a death of torture.

15

No wonder, then, that the bravest heart quailed before such an adventure. But the moment was urgent; the provisions were nearly exhausted; if the relieving army met with a check the whole garrison might perish. In this emergency Kavanagh came forward and offered his services. Not from mere recklessness. He knew the extent of the danger. He had counted the cost, and was prepared for success or failure. In Sir James Outram, the Chief Commissioner, he found a kindred spirit who could appreciate such an act of self-devotion: Outram entered readily into all his plans, and undertook to afford him every assistance. At first the native spy refused to encounter the risk of passing through the ranks of the enemy in company with a European in disguise, but his scruples were overcome. Kavanagh borrowed from the natives the different articles of clothing he required to complete his disguise, and when, arrayed in Oriental costume, he entered Outram's quarters, his appearance was so altered that his most familiar friends failed to recognise him. The painter of the pictures composing the Victoria Cross Gallery, Mr. Desanges, has chosen this meeting as a subject for his canvas. The dignified Oriental is Kavanagh; the short, thick-set figure, who, cigar in mouth, is holding a plan of Lucknow in one hand, and giving the last touch to Kavanagh's beard with the other, is the late Sir James Outram, and he is surrounded by officers of the garrison; in the background are Kunoujee Lal, the native spy, and some servants. At half-past eight o'clock on the evening of the 9th of November Kavanagh started on his arduous mission, followed by the prayers and best wishes of all who were intrusted with the secret. His most anxious thoughts were of his wife and children, who believed that he was to spend the night in the mines. The darkness of the hour was favourable to the enterprise. On reaching the river Goompty they had to strip and wade across. After crossing the river they crept up a trench for about three hundred yards, till they came to a grove of trees, where they stopped to dress. A man came down to the river to wash, but, fortunately, he did not observe them; they regained their confidence, and advanced towards the huts of the enemy in front. Kavanagh exchanged greetings with a matchlock-

man, taking care to be the first to speak. On proceeding about seven hundred yards farther they reached the iron bridge across the Goompty, and were challenged by a native officer. Kavanagh remained a little in the shade: the officer, satisfied with the answers of the guide, allowed them to pass. They continued to advance along the left bank of the river, where they were met by numbers of sepoys, till they reached the stone bridge, where they glided past the sentry, and found themselves in the principal street of Lucknow. As it was part of their policy to court rather than avoid observation, they advanced along the main street, where no one challenged them, till they reached the open country, when a watchman inquired who they were. The answer was satisfactory, and they passed on cheerfully for four or five miles through the fragrant groves and beautiful woods which surround Lucknow, when they discovered that they had taken the wrong road and were close to the pickets of the enemy. The native guide was alarmed lest Kavanagh should suspect his honesty; but, reassured on this point, he endeavoured to find the right path. In wandering through the fields they met with singular adventures: they tumbled into ditches, and were nearly drowned; they alarmed the dogs of the native villages, and had to conceal themselves in a canal; they entered a wretched hut, and persuaded the female inmates to point out the way. About one o'clock in the morning they came upon an advanced picket of the enemy. Kavanagh marched up to them boldly, and, after answering their challenge, was allowed to pass. They were now close to the Alum Bagh, which was garrisoned by the English, but the native guide dissuaded Kavanagh from attempting to pass through the numerous rifle-pits and detachments of the enemy by which it was surrounded. At three o'clock they reached a mango grove, where a native sentinel, hearing their approach, gave the alarm, and the guard was called out. Startled by this unexpected danger, the native guide lost courage, and threw away the despatch for Sir Colin Campbell. It was a trying moment, but Kavanagh retained his presence of mind, and disarmed their suspicions by his confident bearing and ready answers. The guide had the politeness to show them the way to Umroula, a village on the route to the English camp, which, they said, they wished to reach; and, after walking on for some distance, they tumbled into a jheel, or swamp, and were once more nearly drowned. They continued to advance with the water often as high as their necks: Kavanagh, being the taller of the two, had often to hold up Kunoujee Lal by the neck to keep him from sinking. Their clothes were torn from their bodies by the tall reeds, and, worse than this, the paint was washed from Kavanagh's hands by the muddy water: it was fortunate that it did not reach his face. After floundering in the swamp for two hours, they reached the land in such a state of exhaustion that they had to rest for a quarter of an hour.

Resuming their route, they entered the village, and found several men sleeping near the *chubootra*, or native office. Rousing one of the sleepers, they informed him that they were spies sent to discover the strength of the enemy, and requested him to direct them to the English camp. The sleeper, enraged at being disturbed, gave them a surly answer; and, advancing, they passed to the other guards about three hundred yards apart. It was fortunate for them that the enemy had thrown out no sentries, and were seated in a half-drowsy state around their watch-fires. They passed between the two fires without being challenged, and soon after met some villagers, who informed them that they were fleeing before the English. They inferred from this that Sir Colin Campbell's encampment must be close at hand; and, after losing their way and again nearly falling into the hands of the rebels, they reached a grove about four o'clock in the morning, and Kavanagh, regardless of the remonstrances of the guide, threw himself on the ground to sleep for an hour. Before he had closed his eyes he was startled by the challenge, in a native accent, "Who comes there?" and sprang to his feet. Perhaps those three simple English words, pronounced by native lips, were the sweetest words he ever heard in his life. They had stumbled upon a picket of Sikhs, and the officer in command requested two Sowars to conduct them to the advance-guard.

Kavanagh was almost dead with cold and fatigue, but a kind-hearted officer of the 9th Lancers supplied him with clothes and refreshments. The adventures of the past night seemed to him like a fearful dream; now that they were past he could scarcely realize them. The whole English camp was struck with admiration of a deed unsurpassed in the annals of the heroic ages, and each vied with the other in doing honour to one whom they were proud to call their countryman. Even the stern and impassive old Scottish chief—usually so sparing in his praise, so severe in his reproof—was touched by the unselfish heroism of such a deed. In the darkened tent, unseen by human eye, Kavanagh knelt down and expressed his gratitude to Him who had taken him from the miry clay and conducted him in safety through the hosts of the enemy. His next thought was of his wife and children; and before lying down to rest he had the flag of the semaphore in the Alum Bagh hoisted as the signal of his safety. It was in vain that he tried to sleep; his over-excited brain refused to be lulled to rest. At eleven o'clock he was seated at Sir Colin's table, surprising his entertainer by the strangeness of his adventures and the strength of his appetite. His assistance was invaluable in explaining the plans drawn up by Sir James Outram, and in pointing out the best route for advancing through Lucknow. By exposing his own life he saved that of many a gallant soldier who would otherwise have been lost; and Sir Colin showed his appreciation of his conduct by retaining him near his person. Next morning the army of rescue was on the march, and after a feeble resistance reached the Alum Bagh. On the 14th of November they advanced against Lucknow, under the guidance of Kavanagh, who was familiar with the neighbourhood of the city. The cowardly Sepoys fled before our men, and sought refuge within the walls of Lucknow. On reaching the banks of the river the English army halted, and spent the night under arms, waiting anxiously and eagerly for the hour when the Massacre of Cawnpore was to be avenged. The night was dark and chilly; Kavanagh slept by the side of Sir Colin Campbell on the cold floor; the foe attempted nothing to disturb their repose.

With the earliest dawn Sir Colin was mounted on his charger, riding from post to post and giving his orders for the day. A new route proposed by Kavanagh, as preferable to that indicated by Outram, was at once adopted; but during the following night a heavy cannonade was kept up to mislead the enemy from the real point of danger. Next morning our men advanced rapidly through the tortuous lanes and thick plantations, meeting with little resistance from the enemy, who expected to be attacked in another quarter, till they reached the Secunder Bagh. Here a heavy fire of musketry was opened upon them, and the first man who tried to pass was shot in the hip and fell. Kavanagh leaped from his horse, took the poor fellow in his arms, and bore him in safety to a neighbouring hut. Others pressed forward and surrounded the building; the artillery seized an embankment which commanded the gate; the enemy were deprived of all means of escape. The Highlanders were the first who entered; arrested in their progress by a dead wall, they mounted the roof, tore off the tiles, and leaped into the midst of the mutineers. At the same time a breach was made in the walls of the Secunder Bagh; Sikh and Highlander vied with one another in being the first to reach it; many were hit, but nothing could resist their impetuous bravery. They forced their way in, and, maddened with resistance and the remembrance of Cawnpore, they showed no mercy; the bayonet did its deadly work till all was still, and two thousand of the mutineers were piled together in one gory mass as a monument of our vengeance. Humanity shudders at the remembrance of such a scene, but the murderers of helpless women and children at Cawnpore deserved no quarter.

Our men, worn out with fatigue and hunger, remained under arms the whole night, waiting anxiously for daybreak. Sir Colin slept outside the Secunder Bagh, with Kavanagh by his side; with the earliest dawn the whole army was on the move. The enemy, disheartened by their reverses, offered little resistance, and began to retreat; Kavanagh, who had advanced to examine their position, was mistaken for a spy, and had a narrow escape from being shot by his countrymen. Undaunted by the danger to which he was exposed from the peculiarity of his dress and appearance, he led a party of our men to the Motee Mahul, which was occupied by the enemy, and, finding that the wall could not be broken through without sappers, he returned to Sir Colin for assistance. After an amusing altercation between him and his impetuous chief the required aid was granted, and the British flag soon waved on the summit of the building. After this success Kavanagh pressed forward in the hope of being the first to reach Sir James Outram; he passed in safety through the fire of the enemy till he met a soldier of the 64th Regiment, who conducted him to the spot where a group of officers were standing. It was Sir James Outram and his staff; as soon as they recognised their former comrade in arms they shouted, "It is Kavanagh! three cheers for him! he is the first to relieve us." The warmth of this greeting was felt at the moment to be a sufficient recompense for all the dangers he had encountered; no wonder that tears rose to his eyes as he grasped the hands of those whom he had parted with a little before, doubtful whether he should ever meet them again. There was more joy in that meeting than falls to the lot of many men in the whole course of their lives—a joy such as can only be experienced by those who have risked their own safety in behalf of others.

After the first congratulations, he offered to conduct Sir James and his staff to the commander-in-chief. It was an undertaking of some danger, but the Bayard of India never knew fear. They passed unscathed through a shower of grape and bullets, and Sir James took shelter in the shade of a hut while Kavanagh went to announce his arrival to Sir Colin Campbell. The meeting between these two gallant men was like the meeting between Wellington and Blucher after Waterloo; but there was no time for empty compliments; they had to make good their retreat from Lucknow without a moment's delay. Havelock, the good Christian, the gallant soldier, tottered forward to welcome his deliverer; seven days later he was carried to his grave, lamented and respected by all who have learned to appreciate his heroic bravery, his humble piety. Three better or braver men than Havelock, Outram, and Campbell have never met; they have all passed away now; but such men can never die; they will live for ever in the memory and affections of their grateful and admiring countrymen. Nor was Kavanagh forgotten at that meeting. Sir Colin spoke of him in such terms of admiration as rarely issued from his stern lips, and expressed his sense of the value of his services in his despatch to the Government of India. "His escape at a time when the intrenchment was closely invested by a large army, and when communication, even through the medium of natives, was almost impossible, is, in Sir Colin Campbell's opinion, one of the most daring feats ever attempted; and the result was most beneficial; for, in the immediate subsequent advance on Lucknow of the force under the commander-in-chief's directions, the thorough acquaintance with the localities possessed by Mr. Kavanagh, and his knowledge of the approaches to the British position were of the greatest use; and his excellency desires to record his obligations to this gentleman, who accompanied him throughout the operations, and was ever present to afford valuable information." But dearer to Kavanagh than the praises of despatches or the congratulations of comrades were the tender reproaches of his wife, as she clasped him to her breast and wept her joy and admiration in his arms. The poet who sang the parting of Hector and Andromache could alone do justice to such a meeting; it lies not within the province of simple prose. He appeared in the midst of that beleaguered garrison as a bearer of safety—a messenger of mercy; the very soldiers blessed him as he passed, the heart of the widow and the captive sang aloud for joy, and many pressed into his house that they might "only have a look at him." Few rewards have been more justly earned or more gratefully paid.

After effecting the rescue of the garrison, Sir Colin Campbell retired by forced marches to Cawnpore, where his presence soon reassured the forces, disheartened by the attacks of the enemy during his absence. Kavanagh accompanied him to Cawnpore, and soon after started for Calcutta, where the refugees from Lucknow met with a generous and hospitable reception from the governor-general and the British residents. The guide who had acted such an important part in the enterprise was not forgotten; all met with much sympathy; but there was a ringing cheer, such as none but

English can give, when "Lucknow" Kavanagh (the name by which he has ever since been known, and a prefix as worthily gained as that which distinguished the Confederate general "Stonewall" Jackson) appeared with his wife and family. But such a restless spirit could not remain inactive at Calcutta while the fighting was going on in Oude; he no longer belonged to the uncovenanted service, and was at liberty to go wherever he pleased. He made his way up the country, formed the acquaintance of the *Times'* correspondent, Dr. Russell, who persuaded him to mount an unruly horse that nearly broke his neck, and at last joined the army of Sir Colin Campbell, then a second time advancing from Cawnpore to Lucknow.

During the subsequent fighting he exposed himself to the fire of the enemy with almost reckless bravery; his constant immunity from danger gave rise to a sort of half belief that he bore a charmed life, and this belief was almost justified by the result. Many a gallant English officer bit the dust at Lucknow, but the bullets of the enemy seemed to be turned aside by some invisible hand from the person of Kavanagh. If the old Greek mythology had not been obsolete, we should have been tempted to believe that some friendly god or goddess was watching over our hero, and guarding him alike from friend and foe, as Aphrodite and Poseidon watched over Æneas at the siege of Troy. More than once he was in danger of being shot by his countrymen as a deserter; he had hand-to-hand combats with the enemy, whom he was ready to meet at any odds; he was thrown from horses, precipitated from dog-carts, tumbled into wells, was shot through the shoulder, wounded in the ankle, and survived to thrill the world by the story of his strange adventures, which borders on the realms of romance. When fighting was over at Lucknow he resumed his civil duties, and used all his influence to protect the miserable natives who had returned to their homes, and to check the thieving propensities of the gallant Sikhs and savage little Ghoorkas. In June, 1858, he offered to proceed to the camp of the enemy with a flag of truce, to persuade them to lay aside their arms and submit to the British rule; but the authorities at Lucknow—wisely, as we think—

refused to expose his life to such a danger. Soon after this he was ordered to Muliabad, where he was intrusted with the command of a certain number of Sikhs and native police, whom he frequently led against the enemy. In these encounters he had many hair-breadth escapes; on one occasion his horse was disabled by a shot, and threw him to the ground. It was deemed a mark of merit on the part of Sir Hugh Widdrington that he could fight upon his stumps; Kavanagh was a hero of the same calibre; though dismounted he was not disarmed, and such was his determined bravery that he not only beat off his assailants, but seized one of them by the throat, and made him prisoner. At the fort of Birrwa he summoned the enemy to surrender, promising them their lives if they yielded without further resistance; they expressed their readiness to do so, if they could only have faith in his promises. On this he threw aside his arms, pushed past his own men who were between him and the enemy, walked into the centre of the yard where they stood, and thus placed his life at their mercy. They were awed by the courage of the act, and threw themselves at his feet in token of surrender; and thus, by yet one more daring deed, many lives were again saved by him. Such generous devotion was calculated to produce a powerful impression on the native mind; the Sikhs under his command looked up to him as a superior being, and once, when in great jeopardy, two of them saved his life at the expense of their own. After an absence of nine months he returned to Lucknow to rejoin his wife, who had suffered much uneasiness from the frequent reports of his death, and welcomed him almost as one from the dead. The joy of their meeting was scarcely over when he received orders to proceed to Sundeela and place his valuable services at the disposal of Brigadier Barker, who was advancing to attack two rebel chiefs who had shut themselves up within the fortresses of Birrwa and Rohya. He took an active part in reducing these strongholds, and in bringing back the Talookdars, or native barons, to submission to the British rule. It was only when all resistance had ceased that he returned to his civil duties, and reluctantly exchanged the sword for the pen. In

May, 1859, he returned with his family to England, and published a brief account of his adventures.

Such a man assuredly deserved the Victoria Cross, which has often been the reward of isolated acts of bravery. He merited it not only for acting as a guide to Sir Colin Campbell at Lucknow, but also for frequently exposing his life to danger in the field. Our readers, then, will learn with some surprise that, when Lord Canning recommended him for the Victoria Cross, the Court of Directors refused to forward his recommendation to the Queen, under the pretence that "he would be entitled to the medal which they anticipate her Majesty will confer upon the garrison and relieving army of Lucknow." They doubtless esteemed the Victoria Cross too great an honour for a member of the uncovenanted service. This was a last failure of expiring red-tapeism in the East; for Kavanagh had soon after the satisfaction of announcing a new *régime* in the capital of Oude, and of wearing the Victoria Cross on his manly breast. He was the means of saving 300,000*l.* of public treasure at Lucknow, and no one will say that he was too liberally rewarded by the gift of 2000*l.* and the appointment of Assistant-Commissioner in Oude. In one sense, the doers of deeds like Kavanagh's can never be adequately rewarded by gifts or offices: their richest recompense is to be found in the high esteem of their fellow-men and the grateful remembrance of posterity.

CHAPTER XIX.

LIEUTENANT BUTLER AND THE VICTORIA CROSS.

URING several years previous to the Indian mutiny the kingdom of Oude had been a source of much anxiety to the Governors of India. It was formerly an independent province, in which were about 3,000,000 people, but in 1856 it became a province of British India. The capital of Oude is Lucknow, one of the largest cities in India, containing at least 300,000 inhabitants; it is a straggling place, extending over nearly three miles, but contains many large important buildings, forts, &c. The streets are very narrow and winding, thus rendering it difficult for any troops to march through it when an enemy is in possession of the neighbouring buildings. A fine river—the Goomtee—runs past the town, and bounds it on one side.

It was on or about the 24th of May, 1857, that the first indications of an outbreak became manifest at Lucknow; at this date there were about 500 available European troops, whilst the mutineers of the native regiments numbered about 4000. In addition to these, the whole of the inhabitants of the district were in rebellion, being led by various leaders, and formed bands of brigands, whose principal object was to hunt down and murder Europeans.

Sir Henry Lawrence was at this time Chief Commissioner of Oude, and, being possessed of great foresight and skill, prepared to receive the coming shock. He put a portion of Lucknow, termed the Residency, into a state of defence, stored it with ammunition and provisions, fortified also a place termed the Muchhee Bhowun, and then waited the course of events.

After having defended himself in these two places from the

30th of May, he, on the 29th of June, sallied out in the hope o cutting off a party of mutineers, but, having ventured farther than he intended, he discovered a most powerful body of the mutineers, and was obliged to retreat with considerable loss, more especially as the artillery he had taken with him deserted their guns and joined the enemy. Shortly after this he found that, with his diminished numbers, it was imprudent to hold two places. Thus the Muchhee Bhowun was abandoned, and the whole garrison were brought into the Residency, and a defence commenced which was certainly one of the most marvellous that has ever been recorded in history.

The ruling mind in Lucknow was from the commencement that of Sir H. Lawrence, and many brave men were accustomed to look to him for advice or directions in various trying circumstances. When, then, he died, on the 4th of July, from the effects of a wound produced by a shell which burst in the room in which he was sitting, his loss cast a gloom on the devoted band within the Residency, and rendered for a time their position even more than ever perilous.

Day by day and night after night a continued fire of artillery and musketry was directed upon the Residency, and the only defence on the part of the besieged, in many instances, was to remain under cover, and thus to escape from the iron hail above them. Among the many singular events that occurred during the siege of Lucknow, there were none that were more exciting to those concerned than the underground combats. The mutineers, having been trained by our own Sappers and Miners, were thoroughly acquainted with the principles and use of mines, and they applied their knowledge in the present instance to the attempted destruction of their enemy. Let any of us imagine ourselves to be shut up in a fort surrounded by a merciless enemy, unable to show even a hand above the walls of the defences without having a shower of bullets aimed at it, and then to know that from several directions there were galleries being driven underground until a spot could be reached beneath us in which a sufficient quantity of powder could be placed to send us, our fort, and guns a hundred feet in the air.

Fatal as the mine undoubtedly is, it, like the deadly rattlesnake of America, invariably makes a noise before it strikes its blow, and thus it was impossible for the mutineers to work underground and yet make no sound; so that the garrison by watchfulness could hear the blows of the enemy's pickaxe and spade, and could then make what was called a counter-mine, and at the proper time blow up the work of the besiegers. In many cases the defenders broke their way into the galleries made by the mutineers, and shots were exchanged in the darkness underground. In only one instance did the mutineers succeed in their mines; this occurred in consequence of a mine being directed against an outer wall of the Sikh cavalry lines, the noise of the horses' feet preventing the sound of the miners from being heard. This mine, upon being exploded, buried half-a-dozen drummers in its ruins, and opened a breach large enough to have admitted the enemy, who were, however, too cautious to venture upon an encounter at close quarters, even with a foe which they outnumbered in the proportion of ten to one.

In many instances the counter-mines of the besieged produced most destructive effects on the enemy. In one case where the mutineers commenced a mine a counter-mine was immediately attempted, which, when exploded, blew up the enemy's gallery, a house near it, and some three dozen men.

In spite, however, of these successes, the condition of the besieged was bad enough.

During the whole of June, July, and August, this devoted band maintained themselves against their innumerable foes. The massacre at Cawnpore had shown them what they might expect if they surrendered, and thus, in spite of sickness, want of provisions, and other evils, they held their ground, until, on the 23rd of September, the firing of artillery in the distance informed them that help was at hand. So strangely are some constitutions framed and kept up by excitement that, as we were informed by an eye-witness, in many instances the besieged during several weeks took no other nourishment than a little water and a few mouthfuls of bread per day, feeling quite unable to touch any other food, and, in fact, having no appetite for it.

On the 25th of September, Generals Outram and Havelock commenced their attack upon Lucknow, and early in the morning the first brigade commenced its march. It was soon found that the enemy had made most extensive preparations to meet them, each suitable station being selected for cannon, which played with murderous effect upon the advancing troops. During six hours the gallant band of warriors, each member of which deserved a cross of honour, struggled forward to the relief of their comrades—the English women and children shut up in the Residency. During the afternoon a temporary halt was ordered under the walls of a palace termed the Fureed Buksh; but ere long darkness coming on rendered the next movement one of considerable importance. The Residency was yet half-a-mile distant, and large bodies of the enemy were between it and the palace. To delay till the morning the relief of the besieged might be an unwise proceeding, for the ferocious mutineers might during the night make a successful attack, and a massacre would be the result. It was therefore decided that the 78th Highlanders and another regiment should advance. This decision having been arrived at, a short half-hour only was passed before men, women, and children, who had almost ceased to hope, suddenly found themselves in comparative safety, delivered by the skill and courage of Havelock and his column of relief.

The besieged, who had during a hundred days been shut up in the Residency, were actually surprised by the arrival of succour. Although several intimations had been received to the effect that a relieving force was coming, yet there was no appearance of it even on the morning of the 25th, although considerable commotion was observable among the armed men and sepoys in the town. At about 5 P.M. volleys of musketry were heard in the streets, and the peculiar hiss of the Minié ball was audible. A few minutes later the English troops were seen fighting their way gallantly, and then from every loophole and embrasure, from hospital and house, arose a cheer and shout from every living being within that inclosure that had so long been a prison, and was so near being a grave.

Yet, after all, this relief proved to be merely "succour," for, as about 30 officers and 500 men were killed and wounded during the march through the town, and as also in the previous actions many men had been lost, the army of 3000 that had left Cawnpore to relieve Lucknow had dwindled into a mere handful. There was also a difficulty about food, for the increase in numbers caused a demand for more provisions, and already there was a scanty supply even for those who previously occupied the Residency.

Those who have been much exposed to "fire" have often experienced many hairbreadth escapes and singular incidents. Several are related in connexion with the defence of Lucknow. An officer was handing a glass of water to a companion, the glass being held low down, when a bullet struck the glass and smashed it to pieces, without, however, hurting either man. Three prisoners were brought in, and were being tried by a drum-head court-martial, when the proceedings were suddenly cut short by a round shot, which, without ceremony, killed the three prisoners, after which the court was dissolved.

It was soon found that the sepoys, having discovered how small a force had joined the garrison, were determined to pursue their attack with renewed vigour, and continued the siege until the intrenchments were deserted on the 19th of November.

We in England who live at home at ease, and perform our morning toilets with composure, can scarcely imagine the effect that would be produced upon us by an event such as the following, related with great coolness by a lady in her "Diary of the Siege of Lucknow:"—

"This morning an 18-pounder came through our unfortunate room again. It broke the panel of the door, and knocked the whole of the barricade down, upsetting everything; my dressing-table was sent flying through the door."

When the relief had overcome the various obstacles that had been opposed to its entrance into Lucknow, and had joined the besieged garrison, it was found necessary to give up the Residency. This was accomplished by a ruse, and during the night, when the women and children, the wounded and sick, were conveyed in safety to the Alum Bagh, thence to Allahabad, leaving Lucknow to be dealt with by men alone.

Lieutenant Thomas Adair Butler, 1st Bengal Fusiliers, at Lucknow.

It was not till early in March, 1858, that Sir Colin Campbell appeared with a large British force before Lucknow. At this time there were about thirty thousand Sepoys in arms in the city, besides which there were fully fifty thousand armed volunteers and irregulars. The commander-in-chief's preparations had been most ably planned and carried out. A bridge was soon thrown across the Goomtee, with very little opposition. On the 7th of March twenty-two guns, all of large calibre, were sent across this bridge, and joined Sir J. Outram's force on the opposite side. On the 8th a decided step was made towards the capture of the city. A heavy fire had been maintained all day on the Martinière, and Sir Colin determined to assault it very soon.

It was on this day that the officer whose exploit we this month illustrate gained the Victoria Cross. An officer, who also gained the Cross on the same day, had led a portion of his company against a two-gun battery and spiked the guns; thus the most advanced position of the troops was secure from artillery fire. It was of great importance that the skirmishers on the opposite side of the river should be made acquainted with this success, and Lieutenant Thomas Adair Butler, 1st Bengal Fusiliers, swam across the Goomtee, climbed the parapet, and remained for some time exposed to a heavy fire of musketry. He, however, gave the information that he wished, and was prominently mentioned by Major-General Outram in general orders. For this act of coolness and bravery he was allotted the Victoria Cross: an honour well deserved. There are many men who, in the heat and excitement of action, will take a prominent lead, and will then perform more than they would be disposed to do in moments of calmness; but when a man swims across a broad river in the face of an enemy, and remains by himself exposed to a severe fire, he must indeed possess those characteristics entitling him to be called brave.

Sir Colin Campbell was well acquainted with the peculiar style of fighting preferred by the mutineers. If behind stone walls, earthworks, or in buildings, the rebel sepoys would remain under fire all day. If, however, they were brought into close contact with cold steel, their courage deserted them, and they made the best use of their legs. In his orders for the attack on the Martinière, he particularly insisted on the application of cold steel. "The men employed in the attack will use nothing but the bayonet. They are absolutely forbidden to fire a shot till the position is won." The description of the Highlanders' advance is thus graphically given by Dr. Russell:—"Our guns were now thundering away, mortars, howitzers, and 24-pounders, at the pits, huts, and Martinière, from which the enemy kept up an incessant fusillade of the weakest sort, the only thing remarkable about it being its pertinacity. The time wore on, and at last the Highlanders and Sikhs came marching from their camp, and drew up behind the Dilkoosha. The enemy had remained steady in their trenches under the fire of six mortars and ten heavy guns and howitzers. But the instant they caught sight of our bayonets, and that the lines of the Sikhs and Highlanders came in view, we observed them, by twos and threes and groups, and at last in masses, running and marching at the double, as fast as they could clear out of the works, and moving to the rear, or stealing off under cover of their parapets. We saw the Highlanders, with skirmishers thrown out in front, advancing rapidly, without a sound in their ranks, towards the Martinière, while the Sikhs, on their flank, agile as panthers, ran at full speed towards the trenches, from which the enemy, firing a few hurried shots from their muskets, were flying so fast that not a man was left inside by the time our troops were within two hundred yards of the Martinière. In less than ten minutes we saw Highland bonnets among the trees in the park, and the Sikhs rushing through the vines in the rear, looking in vain for an enemy."

By the 19th of March the entire city was in our possession, being thus gained after sixteen days' fighting, counting from the first advance of Sir Colin from the Alum Bagh. Taking all things into consideration, the heat of the climate, the number of the enemy, and the fact of his fighting from behind stone walls or earthworks, this advance on and capture of Lucknow is a most marvellous achievement, especially when we consider the small loss that our troops suffered.

Every private English soldier in India at that time was worth a considerable sum, for his loss could not be easily replaced, and thus a wise and prudent general had to spare his men as much as possible, and to calculate previous to a battle whether even success could afford to be purchased by the loss of a given number of men.

When Lucknow was entered by our troops a scene was witnessed that baffles all description. The wealth of India has ever been known as immense, and much of this had been collected in Lucknow. The palaces of princes and private houses of rich natives were alike open to view, the owners having left them in the greatest haste upon the arrival of the English conquerors. Soldiers, whose spare pay amounted to scarcely more than a few pence per day, were able to lay hands upon gold and silver ornaments, watches, and jewels enough to buy a king's ransom. In one instance a box, which was being carelessly handled by some men, was stated by those well informed to contain jewels to the value of one hundred thousand pounds. Unfortunately, this fell into the hands of some one unknown, who shortly disappeared with the box, and neither was afterwards heard of. Camel and elephant loads of rich brocades were carried away from the city, whilst wealth of every kind was scattered about in wild confusion.

Not only in India and England, but in all Christian countries, the defence and capture of Lucknow caused great excitement and interest. The massacre of upwards of eight hundred men, women, and children at Cawnpore had sent a thrill of horror throughout Europe at such cruelty and disregard of life, and as our forces in India were comparatively few, it did not seem improbable that the brave defenders of Lucknow might meet a similar fate. Thus the encounters during the first two weeks of March, 1858, will be remembered by all; and those who on these occasions gained the Victoria Cross, must feel and be known as men who risked their lives in a great and glorious cause, not only for the honour of their name and country, but for the triumph of Christianity and mercy over cruelty and vice.

CHAPTER XX.

DR. HOME AND DR. BRADSHAW AND THE VICTORIA CROSS.

HEN the gallant Havelock effected his entrance into Lucknow on the 25th of September, 1857, a considerable number of our wounded men who were being conveyed in "doolies," or hospital litters, were left behind near the Motee Munzil under the charge of a military escort. As soon as the army of rescue had made good its position in the Residency, General Outram, who had assumed the command, despatched a party of 250 men to effect a junction with Colonel Campbell, of the 90th, and to assist him in bringing in the wounded. They ultimately succeeded in this object, but some idea of the dangers they had to encounter may be formed from the following narrative. The doolies containing the wounded remained during the night of the 25th of September in the passage in front of the Motee Munzil Palace without attracting the notice of the enemy. On the morning of the 26th the mutineers opened fire upon them, and numbers were killed by the shot and shells. The surgeons in charge of the wounded behaved with the greatest coolness and courage. One of them, an assistant-surgeon in the artillery, requested one of his brother officers to assist him in an operation. On their way to the spot they were exposed to a constant fire. "Well, Bartrum," said one of them, "I wish I could see my way out of this." "Oh," said the other, "there is no danger whatever." The words had scarcely passed the lips of the assistant-surgeon when he was shot down. Two minutes before he was speaking of his wife and child, and the pleasure he would have in meeting them in the Residency. They

were destined never to meet in this world. The position of the wounded now became critical; they were separated from the main body of the army by about a mile; they were surrounded on all sides by the enemy; their only hope of safety lay in forcing their way to the intrenched camp.

Such was the opinion of Colonel Campbell, of the 90th, who had charge of the escort. Addressing Dr. Home, whom he believed to be the senior medical officer present, he informed him that he had completed his arrangements for conducting the wounded to the Residency, and requested him to take charge of the party. It was of importance to secure the services of some one acquainted with the *locale* to act as guide. Mr. J. B. Thornhill, a gallant young civilian, anxious for the safety of his relative, Lieutenant H. M. Havelock, who was still among the wounded, expressed his readiness to perform this arduous duty, and the offer was at once accepted by General Outram. He reached the Motee Munzil in safety, and Dr. Home's party prepared to start under his guidance. Colonel Campbell informed them that after traversing a space of about 340 yards they would no longer be exposed to the fire of the enemy, as there was a way through the palaces skirting the river where they would be sheltered from attack. The military escort of 150 men was placed under the command of Major Simmonds, of the 5th Fusiliers, one of the best and bravest officers we have ever known. He subsequently died of his wounds, leaving a young widow in Mauritius to deplore his loss. No time was lost in collecting the doolies. When all was ready a rush was made for Martin's house, a stone building about forty yards from where they stood. The moment they left the gate the enemy opened fire on them from a battery across the river. No time was lost in reaching Martin's house, where they looked for shelter. Their position there was as unsafe as before; the round shot from the enemy's battery pierced the walls of the house in every direction. After a delay of half an hour they resumed their dangerous march. Major Simmonds advanced in front with the escort to clear the way, followed by the doolies in long procession. They continued their march for two hundred yards without suffering any loss, till they reached a "nullah," or pond, three or four feet deep, through which they had to wade. Some of the doolie-bearers and wounded were drowned or killed by the enemy's grape; those who succeeded in crossing reached a street where they were partly sheltered by a high wall.

Major Simmonds did all that could be done for their safety. The gallant escort were shot down right and left, but they kept up a steady fire and never ceased to advance. On leaving this street the guide lost his way; instead of pursuing the path by the river he led them into an oblong square lined on three sides with sheds, which is now familiarly known to every resident in Lucknow as Doolie-square. No sooner had they entered this square than the enemy, who had posted themselves on the roofs of the sheds and behind the walls, opened fire upon them and shot down many of the escort and doolie-bearers. Many of the latter threw down the doolies in despair, and no threats or entreaties on the part of the officers in charge could induce them to take them up again. They either fled or met their fate with stoical indifference; it was the the will of Allah, and to Allah's will they must submit. In the case of a few the instinct of self-preservation was stronger than their creed; they ran the gauntlet of the enemy's fire and escaped. The medical officers and those who accompanied them rushed through the square till they reached a covered archway opposite to a corner house occupied by the enemy, who fired into them with such destructive effect at the distance of a few yards that the same bullet often passed through several men. If they left the archway they were exposed to the fire of the enemy who were concealed on the roofs of the sheds; to remain there was certain destruction.

Mr. Thornhill, the guide, who had unwittingly brought them into this danger, now proposed that they should retrace their steps and turn the doolies back. This could no longer be done, as the doolie-bearers had abandoned the wounded already in the square, but an effort was made to prevent others from entering it. Dr. Bradshaw and Dr. Home's apothecary went back and persuaded the doolie-bearers in the rear to resume their burdens and to follow them along the path by the river which the guide had missed; in

Drs. Home and Bradshaw superintending the removal of the wounded to the Residency at Lucknow.

this way they reached the Residency in safety. Poor Thornhill in passing through the square was twice wounded; one of these wounds proved mortal. Those who remained beneath the archway looked out in every direction for some place of shelter. There was no time to be lost; armed soldiers were entering the square and murdering the helpless men in the doolies. It was a harrowing scene, but Dr. Home never lost his coolness or presence of mind; he stuck to the doolies as a young ensign would stick to his colours in the hour of danger.

On the right side of the archway was an open door leading into a house; here a small party sought for shelter. It consisted of Dr. Home, Captain Becher, of the 40th Native Infantry, Swanson, of the 78th Highlanders, nine soldiers as yet unhurt, and three wounded men. This small party of fifteen persons were hemmed in on every side by the enemy; their only chance of safety lay in holding out till assistance reached them from the Residency. It was now about ten o'clock in the morning; they might not have long to wait. They screened themselves as much as they could from the fire of the rebels, who crowded round the door and might have forced their way in had it not been for the gallant conduct of Private Patrick McManus, of the 5th Fusiliers. This heroic Irishman stood in the gateway as their guardian angel; ensconcing himself behind a pillar near the door, he kept up a steady fire on the enemy for half an hour, and thus prevented them from effecting an entrance. His hand was so steady, his aim so certain, that whenever he raised his piece the cowardly Sepoys fled from their loopholes or prostrated themselves on the ground. There stood McManus, a hero in the strife, keeping the whole multitude of the mutineers at bay. He had not even to fire; he had only to show his rifle, when all the cowardly wretches trembled before him—such was the influence exercised over them by the bearing of one undaunted man. The house at the gateway became the central point of attack; the mutineers assembled there from all quarters, and yelled like beasts of prey thirsting for human blood. As in the Homeric battles, the combatants were so close that they could revile one another. Sometimes the assailants would advance within twenty yards of the house. "The Feringees are cowards," they would say; "why do they not come into the street?"—an unreasonable question, considering that the Feringees were only fifteen in number and the enemy more than a thousand. On this the redoubted McManus would show his rifle, when the cowards became silent through abject fear. Ah, Patrick McManus, my boy, if the mother that bare you had seen you that day, her old heart would have been proud of you!

The leader of the mutineers abused them for their cowardice. "Come on!" he would say; "what are you afraid of? There are only three Feringees." On hearing this the gallant little party, wounded and all, would give a loud shout to make the enemy believe that they were more numerous than they really were, and Patrick McManus would peep out from behind his pillar. They also strengthened their position by barricading the door with lumber and with sandbags, to form which they stripped the dead Sepoys of their "cummerbunds," or waistcloths. The mass of dead bodies which had accumulated round the door served as a barrier to prevent the mutineers from entering. On finding that they could not force the house they directed their fire against the wounded in the doolies, and killed about forty of them.

At this moment an incident occurred which serves to prove what sacrifices our soldiers are ready to make for officers whom they love. In one of the doolies close to the beleaguered house lay Captain Arnold, of the Madras Fusiliers, a gallant officer who had been severely wounded. Among the holders of the house was Private Ryan, of the same regiment, who resolved to make an effort to rescue him from his dangerous position. As he could not do this alone he called for some one to assist him, when Patrick McManus stepped out from behind his pillar and offered to accompany him. He was already wounded in the foot, but a wound was nothing when danger had to be encountered. The two brave men cleared the barricade, rushed through the gateway amid a shower of bullets, and reached the doolie in safety. Here they had to encounter a new difficulty. Their united strength could not raise the doolie from the ground, so they took poor

Arnold in their arms and bore him to the house. It is a remarkable fact, that while the ground around them was torn with musket-balls, and Captain Arnold received a wound in the thigh which afterwards proved mortal, both of his deliverers escaped unhurt. Encouraged by their success, they ventured forth a second time and carried in a wounded soldier whose piteous cries had excited their compassion. The result was the same as before; they were safe, but the soldier received two mortal wounds and died before he reached the house. Such incidents almost justify the belief that the age of miracles has not yet passed away.

During this struggle the duties that devolved on Dr. Home, the only unwounded officer in the house, were most arduous. He had to direct and encourage the men by his example, to dress the wounded, and to assist in shooting down their assailants. In all this he was ably assisted by Private Hollowell, of the 78th Highlanders, who proved himself worthy of such a leader. When the rebels found that they could not force an entrance, they stole stealthily up to the window and fired through the plastered venetians. Our men lay down on the floor; the bullets thus passed harmlessly over them. The Sepoys then attempted to rush the house, when Hollowell, watching his opportunity, shot down their leader, an old man, armed with sword and shield, and dressed in white with a red waistband. One man was now told off to fire from each window and three from the door. Dr. Home kept watch and ward at one of the windows with his revolver in his hand; he could see all that was passing in the street through a hole made by a bullet. A Sepoy crept stealthily up to the window at the distance of three yards; the doctor shot him dead with his revolver. Hollowell gave another his quietus, and then for a time all was still.

About an hour elapsed before the attack was resumed. During this interval the beleaguered party broke through the plaster and took up their position in the outer room. Thus far they had made good their defence, but a still greater danger awaited them. As they were congratulating themselves on their success they heard a dull, heavy, rumbling noise. Home started up and shouted, "Now, men, or never! Let us rush out and die in the open air, and not be killed like rats in a hole. They are bringing a gun on us!" The men were preparing to act on this advice, when they observed that it was not a gun but a screen, moved on wheels, which the rebels pushed up against the door. A minié rifle fired at the distance of a few yards made no impression on it. On observing this our men retreated into the room they had formerly occupied, while the enemy mounted on the roof, broke through the plaster, and threw lighted straw down upon them. The house took fire; their position was no longer tenable, and death seemed to stare them in the face.

What were they to do? One thing was evident—they could no longer remain in the house; the smoke and heat had become intolerable. Raising the three most helpless and wounded in their arms, they rushed through the back door into the open square. At the distance of about ten yards they observed a shed on the north side of the square and made for it. During the passage the three wounded men were hit, and subsequently died of their wounds, while those who carried them escaped unhurt. Among the wounded was Lieutenant Swanson, of the 78th, whose name has been already mentioned. They found the floor of the shed covered with dead and dying Sepoys. This movement took the enemy by surprise; they had expected them to issue forth by the door, and not by the way they came; and though the little party was exposed to the fire of at least six hundred men, none but the wounded were hit. On rallying their forces they found that they had six men capable of bearing arms, and four wounded able to do duty as sentries. It was now three o'clock in the afternoon, and, though their position seemed desperate, no one dreamed of surrendering; they knew that they could expect no mercy from their ruthless assailants, and determined to hold out to the last. Their position must be known to the general; Havelock was not a man to abandon them in the hour of danger. Could it be that his gallant little army had been destroyed by the rebels, and that they were the last survivors? If so, their only resource was to hold out to the last and to sell their lives as dearly as possible.

Such were the thoughts that presented themselves to the minds of these heroic men. No time was to be lost; the enemy was already upon them. The shed, which was loopholed in every direction, afforded little shelter; it had been used the day before by the mutineers for the purpose of firing on our army. Two shots were suddenly fired on the little party through a broken passage in one end of the shed; a sentry was placed there to guard it against the enemy. Such was their cowardly terror, that the presence of one man was sufficient to ward them off. They now came creeping stealthily up to the walls, discharged their pieces through the loop-holes, and then made off. To guard against this annoyance a sentry was placed at every loophole; the wounded men cheerfully did their duty the same as the others. So long as they had remained in the house at the archway, they had been able to protect the doolies from the attacks of the enemy, but now that they had changed their position they could no longer afford them any assistance. On observing this, the Sepoys came rushing through the gate, and began to massacre the wounded men; some were burnt alive in the doolies; others were cut to pieces by their savage assailants. Their countrymen were saved the horror of witnessing this spectacle, as the enemy, while engaged in this massacre, kept on the other side of the doolies, so as to escape observation; but their blood was chilled and their own sufferings intensified by the piercing shrieks of the tortured men, who were now beyond the reach of all human aid.

At this moment a singular incident occurred. While the Sepoys were passing from doolie to doolie engaged in their ruthless work, they came to one which contained Lieutenant Knight, a wounded officer of the 90th Regiment. A Sowar drew aside the curtain and made a thrust at him with his sword. With that sudden energy which is often imparted to the helpless in the hour of danger, Knight sprang through the opening in the other side of the doolie, and ran off in the direction of the rear-guard, pursued by the enemy, who had witnessed his escape. He was already wounded in the leg, but, notwithstanding this drawback, he succeeded in distancing all his pursuers. More than fifty shots were fired at him, two of which struck him in the legs, making three wounds in all; he had strength, however, to continue his flight till he reached the rear-guard, where he found himself in safety.

On finding that the loopholes in the walls of the shed were guarded, the Sepoys mounted the roof, made holes through it, and began to fire on the party below. Though the muzzles of their pieces were only about four feet from our men, none of the latter were seriously wounded; in truth, the miraculous escapes that occurred on this occasion are so numerous and surprising as to be almost incredible, if they were not well authenticated. As the shed was no longer tenable, they bored through the wall into the courtyard, so as to escape for a moment from the heavy fire from the roof. Their position was desperate; the most sanguine had almost ceased to hope; the strongest were prostrated by hunger, heat, anxiety, and fatigue; the wounded, parched with thirst and terror-struck by the shrieks of the tortured, longed to escape from such misery, and prayed for death at the hands of their countrymen. We have heard men who shared in the horrors of this fearful scene declare that, if they had not been restrained by Christian principle, they would have laid violent hands on themselves, or courted death from the bullets of the enemy.

Such feelings may have sprung up in their minds as they listened to the shrieks of the tortured, and thought of their own fate if they fell into the hands of the enemy; but the love of life is strong, and they continued to defend themselves. Was there no other place of shelter than the shed they occupied? On looking out from the courtyard they observed the rear of a large building at the distance of thirty yards. Dr. Home and one of his party stole cautiously out to reconnoitre; night was setting in, and the darkness was favourable to their undertaking. They reached the building without attracting the notice of the Sepoys, and discovered that it was a large mosque, with an arched opening about eight feet from the ground. By mounting on the shoulders of his companion, Dr. Home was enabled to enter the building through this opening, and found himself in a spacious courtyard looking into a garden. No pious Mussulman was performing his devotions there; the place seemed to have been designed by Providence for their preservation; and Dr. Home, after advancing a short distance into the mosque, returned to the opening in the wall, and beckoned to the others to join him. They hesitated to do so, and during this delay Dr. Home and his companion were discovered by the enemy, who opened fire on them from the roof of the shed, and drove them back to their former position. Their enterprise was not altogether fruitless; inside the mosque they had found a *chatty* of excellent water belonging to the Sepoys—a prize at that moment far more precious in their eyes than all the gold of Ophir or the diamonds of Golconda. They had been biting cartridges all day; their lips were dry and cracked with thirst; but they thought of the wounded, whose sufferings were still more intense, and carried with them the *chatty* of water for their relief. All partook of the reviving draught, which, to borrow their own expressive language, "made them twice the men they were before." It is a common belief among physiologists that water only increases the sufferings of those who have long been unable to satisfy their thirst; but it was not so in this instance. It made them twice the men they were before, and thus enabled them to continue their resistance.

Sentries were told off for the night, and every man who could stand had to take his share of duty. Every loophole had its guardian; owing to the length of the shed none were left unemployed. The darkness which had now set in was favourable to our men; it prevented the enemy on the roof from watching their movements or observing the position they occupied, and enabled them to fire through the roof with the additional advantage of knowing from the sound of their feet where the Sepoys stood. On discovering this, the latter quitted the roof, and for a time all was still; it seemed as if they had given up the attack as hopeless. When the firing ceased, a reaction set in after the fierce excitement of the day; the stoutest hearts were almost appalled by a sense of their desperate condition. They had long since ceased to hope for deliverance; they clung to life with that instinctive feeling which leads the shipwrecked mariner to cling to a plank, though he knows that escape is all but impossible. If the shed was forced, their only thought was to rush forth and sell their lives as dearly as possible. As they listened to the shrieks of the tortured, they swore in their hearts that, come what might, they would never fall into the hands of the enemy. Death had lost all its bitterness; the grim king was stripped of all his dark imagery of terror. If he had come of his own accord, they would have welcomed him as a friend, but as Christian soldiers, whose lives were not their own, they were bound to wait for his coming. And all through the long, dreary hours of that night of horror they *did* wait for him, but he came not; those who retained their consciousness almost envied the wounded who had become delirious. Their ammunition was almost exhausted; there only remained about seven rounds for six men; if the enemy renewed the attack, all would soon be over. But the enemy did *not* renew the attack; they found it easier and safer to torture the wounded in the doolies than to dislodge or destroy a few resolute men driven to bay.

Sleep would at times overpower them; they sank down on the floor, but the mental tension was too great to permit them long to rest. Their fearful position was still present to their minds, and after a few minutes of troubled sleep, they would start to their feet with the impression that the enemy were upon them. No enemy appeared; on finding that it was a false alarm, they would keep watch for a time, till, overpowered by sleep and exhaustion, they again sank upon the floor. One desperate man proposed to his comrades to rush forth and fight their way back to the rear-guard; two offered to join him in the attempt; the others refused to leave the wounded in the hands of the enemy.

About two o'clock in the morning they were roused to a fresh life by the sound of heavy firing close at hand. Their hearts leaped to their mouths as they heard the sharp crack of the Enfield rifles and the rush of the enemy over their heads. Hurrah! Havelock had not forgotten them; it was their own countrymen advancing to the rescue. The revulsion of feeling made them wild with joy; they shouted with all their might, "Europeans! Europeans!" they cheered them on to the attack—"Charge them! charge them! Keep to your right!" The firing died away in the distance; in a few minutes all was silent. They listened for the advancing tramp of armed men, but no such sound was heard; again they gave themselves up to despair. Any fate was preferable to further suspense; they agreed to fight their way to the Residency or perish in the attempt; but on creeping forward under the shadow of the building, they observed a large body of men clustered round a fire in the archway. Escape in that way was evidently impossible; it would have been madness for a few starving men to attack a body of the enemy who had just repulsed our own troops; so they crept back to their former place of shelter. The bitterness of death was already past; they could meet their fate with indifference. The dreary hours passed silently on till a little after daybreak, when they heard the sound of distant firing; it failed to rouse them from their apathy; the hope of deliverance had died out within them. The sound came nearer and nearer, till at length they could distinguish the sharp crack of the Enfields, and the regular rattling volleys which told them that their countrymen were at hand. Ryan, the sentry, with the usual vivacity of his country, was the first to express the feelings of his comrades; jumping up with sudden energy, he shouted, "Oh, boys! them's our own chaps!" Ryan's language was far from being elegant or correct; but their position was too critical for weighing the niceties of speech, and we question whether Demosthenes himself could have spoken more to the point. Its effect was immediate and striking; those who were prostrated by despair sprang to their feet with renewed energy, and shouted to their deliverers to keep to the right. "Cheer together, men," cried Home. They cheered, and waited anxiously for the result. They had not long to wait; a ringing cheer came back from their countrymen, which told them that deliverance was at hand. They had still a few charges remaining; these were expended on the Sepoys, who were firing from the loopholes on our men. The enemy were soon dislodged; the party of rescue forced their way into the shed; Dr. Home received the congratulations of his countrymen on his successful resistance, and the wounded, whom he had defended to the last, were conducted in safety to the Residency.

When the report of their gallant conduct reached England, Home and Bradshaw were rewarded with the Victoria Cross. Mr. Desanges has assigned them a place in his Gallery. All who have read this simple narrative of their heroic defence of the wounded intrusted to their care, will admit that they were entitled to this honourable distinction.

CHAPTER XXI.

ROSS L. MANGLES, ESQ., V.C., BENGAL CIVIL SERVICE, ASSISTANT-MAGISTRATE AT PATNA.

THE town of Arrah, near which Mr. Mangles earned the Cross of Valour, is about twenty-four miles from Dinapoor, from which it is separated by the river Sone. It is the chief place in the district of Shahabad, and when the 7th, 8th, and 40th Regiments of Bengal Native Infantry mutinied at Dinapoor, on the 25th of July, 1865, they advanced against Arrah, where they expected to meet with little resistance, as there were no European troops at that station. It so happened, however, that the chief authority was vested in Mr. Wake, the resident magistrate, who proved himself equal to the occasion. He had not been trained to the profession of arms, but he possessed that calm courage and undaunted energy which most of our Indian civilians exhibited during the mutiny, and which contributed largely to the re-establishment of our power. Familiar with the manners and language of the natives, he had watched the progress of events with an anxious eye, and already foresaw the storm that was about to break forth; as he could not avert it, he prepared to meet it like a man. He had already warned the authorities at Calcutta that the licentiousness of the native press must sooner or later lead to an outbreak, and that symptoms of disaffection had already begun to appear in his own district; but the forces at Dinapoor, consisting of Her Majesty's 10th Regiment, two Companies of the 37th, and two Companies of Artillery, were deemed sufficient to overawe the natives. They would have been so, if they had been under the command of an efficient officer; but the major-general was an old man, too infirm to be able to mount his horse without assistance, and utterly unfit to cope with the difficulty. The consequence was that the mutineers, who might easily have been disarmed or imprisoned, were allowed to escape, and proceeded to plunder the neighbouring towns. There were few Europeans left in the town of Arrah; the workmen who were employed on the railway, frightened by the symptoms of mutiny around them, and apprehensive for their own safety, had deserted the place in the beginning of June; but Mr. Wake, who remained at the post of danger, induced them by his example to return. He applied everywhere for assistance, but no troops could be spared till the 11th of July, when he received a small detachment of Sikh police from Patna.

On the evening of the 25th of July, intelligence reached Arrah that the native regiments at Dinapoor had mutinied, and crossed the river Sone. There was no time to be lost; the fifteen Europeans in Arrah had to decide at once what course they were to pursue: in a few hours the enemy would be upon them. There was not a single soldier in the place; the local police had fled at the first intimation of danger; there was no fort or stronghold where the Europeans could find refuge. No one could have blamed them if they had consulted their safety in flight; but that band of brave civilians scorned the idea, and resolved to remain at their posts. Mr. Boyle, an engineer of the main-trunk railway, was the only one amongst them who had made some preparations to meet this emergency; he had anticipated the danger, and some weeks before had begun to fortify with stones and timber a detached two-storied house, about fifty feet square, which stood in the same compound as his bungalow, and to collect a store of provisions. Mr. Boyle's preparations for the coming danger had been the source of many a joke to his less thoughtful companions; but their levity gave place to gratitude on the 26th of July, when the mutineers were upon them. The ladies and children had already been sent away; the fifteen civilians who remained shut themselves up in Mr. Boyle's house, with the fifty Sikhs of Captain Rattray's police battalion. Their store of provisions was limited; their only weapons were rifles, revolvers, and hogspears; but they had abundance of ammunition, and an indomitable courage, which supplied every deficiency. On the morning of the 27th the mutineers marched into the town, released the four hundred prisoners in the gaol, and seized eighty thousand rupees which they found in the treasury. They then concealed themselves among the trees and buildings near Mr. Boyle's house, where they kept up a galling fire during the day, and invited the Sikhs to join them; but these brave fellows had the virtue to refuse the bribes which they offered. On the 28th they procured two small cannon, with which they opened fire on the house, which was now riddled with balls; but its brave defenders never dreamed of surrendering. One of the cannon was mounted on the roof of Boyle's bungalow, so as to enable the mutineers to fire into the house at the distance of sixty yards. "Nothing," says Mr. Wake, "but the cowardice, ignorance, and want of unanimity of our enemies prevented our fortification from being brought down about our ears." The gallant defenders offered something more than a passive resistance; every mine of the enemy was countermined; every new battery was met by a fresh barricade. The Sikhs, inspired by the example of the Europeans, vied with them in courage; when provisions ran short, they sallied forth one night and brought in four sheep. One of them was dangerously wounded; singular to relate, this was the only casualty that happened to the little garrison; all the others escaped with slight scratches or bruises. When the supply of water failed, the Sikhs dug a well underneath the house, and continued their labour till they found a spring; in short, the honours of the defence are equally divided between them and the Europeans. For seven days and nights the siege went on, and the gallant little band had to defend themselves against three thousand assailants. They looked for assistance, but they looked in vain; the authorities at Dinapoor seemed to have left them to their fate. They might have left their stronghold with all the honours of war; the mutineers, weary of the siege, and almost despairing of success, were willing to spare their lives, but all their offers were contemptuously rejected. They would never condescend to negotiate with rebels: they would rather fight it out to the last.

We must now direct attention to the steps which had been taken for the relief of the little garrison. As we have already mentioned, Major-General Lloyd was in command at Dinapoor; it was unfortunate that the control of military affairs, at such a moment, should have been vested in one who was worn out with years and infirmities, and should have been enjoying his well-earned pension at home. Arrah lay within his district, and it was his duty to take measures for the relief of its gallant defenders. This duty was peculiarly distasteful to a man whose culpable irresolution had already led to such disastrous results, and for two days nothing was done. Mr. Taylor, the civil magistrate at Patna, within whose district Arrah was situated, assembled all the European residents at his house as soon as he heard of the outbreak at Dinapoor, and invited them to act with him in case of an attack. This took place about one o'clock on the 25th; two hours afterwards a distant firing announced that the mutineers were engaged with the European forces; soon after, the report reached Patna that they had marched off in the direction of Arrah. Mr. Taylor at once improvised an expeditionary force of about one hundred men, made up of Sikhs, Nujeebs, recruits, and volunteers, and despatched it that same day in the direction of Arrah, to watch the movements of the mutineers. Mr. Mangles, who held the appointment of assistant-magistrate at Patna, joined this expedition as a volunteer, and accompanied them on their march till they were recalled by the commissioner, who had received alarming reports from the neighbouring stations, and deemed their presence necessary for the safety of the principal town. On the day after the mutiny, Mr. Taylor wrote to Major-General Lloyd, urging him to place a small body of European troops at his disposal; but the latter refused to comply with his request, on the ground that he had only six hundred soldiers under his command, and that he could render no assistance. Knowing the urgency of the occasion, Mr. Taylor resumed his application, and proposed to raise a corps of volunteer cavalry among the officers and gentlemen of Patna and Dinapoor, if the general would send two hundred men to cooperate with them for the relief of Arrah.

The general had already made an unsuccessful attempt to rescue the little garrison from their perilous position. He thought only of his own safety till the 27th of July, when, feeling more reassured, he sent a detachment of the 37th Regiment from Dinapoor toward Arrah, for the purpose of dispersing the mutineers. The troops embarked on board the *Horungotta* steamer, and might have reached Arrah in a few hours, but a sort of fatality seemed to attend everything which the general undertook. After three hours' steaming, the *Horungotta* ran aground, and as she could not be got off the troops quickly returned to Dinapoor. The general was now willing to accept Mr. Taylor's proposal, and a second expeditionary force, consisting of detachments of Her Majesty's 10th, and 37th Regiments, some native troops, and the corps of volunteer cavalry was organized, and embarked on the evening of Tuesday, the 28th of July, on board the steamer *Bombay*, which had arrived at Dinapoor in her downward passage on the Ganges, and was detained for the public service. If the defence of Arrah forms one of the brightest episodes in the history of the Indian mutiny, the disaster which overtook this ill-fated expedition may be regarded as one of its gloomiest pages: it was not the mere loss of men at a critical juncture, though that was considerable; it was the destruction for the moment of that *prestige* which has almost invariably followed our arms in India, and by which alone we have acquired our ascendancy in that vast peninsula. The expedition was placed under the command of Captain Dunbar, of the 10th Regiment. Mr. Mangles belonged to the corps of volunteer cavalry. The mutineers, who were cognizant of all their movements, had formed themselves into an ambuscade, and attacked them on the night of the 29th of July. Our soldiers fought with their usual gallantry, but were overpowered by superior numbers, and compelled to retreat. Captain Dunbar was killed; only a few of his men effected a retreat to the boats; the rest were butchered by the enemy, who gave no quarter. It was on this occasion that Mr. Mangles distinguished himself by his humanity, and thus became entitled to wear the Queen's Own Cross. He had been wounded, and would have been justified, under the circumstances, in consulting his own safety; but his generous heart led him to think more of others than of himself. A soldier of the 37th Regiment had been struck down by his side; wounded himself, and weak with the loss of blood, he was induced, from a feeling of humanity, and without any prospect of reward, to make an effort to save his life. If he left him in the hands of the enemy, his fate was certain; the murderers of helpless women and children would show no mercy: all this must have been present to his mind, as he hurriedly bound up his wounds, careless of the murderous fire to which he was exposed. Nor was this all. When he had dressed his wounds, he raised him on his shoulders and carried him for several miles, till they reached the boats in safety. When we consider that almost the whole detachment were killed or wounded, their escape seems to us to border on the miraculous, and no one will question Mr. Mangles' right to a place in Mr. Desanges' Gallery, or grudge him the Cross of Valour. The permanent record of his heroic conduct and tender-hearted humanity may stimulate others to imitate his example, and may thus exercise a beneficial influence on the rising generation. The Victoria Cross was awarded to Mr. Mangles in the Government *Gazette* of the 6th of July, 1859, and Mr. Desanges' pencil has conveyed to the minds of thousands a more vivid conception of the act by which he gained it, than we can expect to produce by this brief narrative.

We now turn from the disaster of the 29th of July, 1857, to relate how a second and far more successful attempt was made to relieve the beleaguered garrison. The name of Major Vincent Eyre will ever be associated with this event, as the instrument, in the hands of a Higher Power, for the rescue of those who must otherwise have perished. When the mutiny broke out, this officer was recalled from Burwah, and embarked at Calcutta for the Upper Provinces, on the 10th of July, having under his command No. 3 Horse Field Battery, with the 1st Company 5th Battalion Artillery attached. Allahabad was the rendezvous where the different detachments of the relieving army were to assemble, and Major Eyre reached Dinapoor on the evening of the 25th of July, the very day when the three native regiments had broken into open mutiny. He lost no time in placing himself and his men at the disposal of Major-General Lloyd, and at his request landed three guns. Next morning these guns were re-embarked, and Major Eyre resumed his voyage. As yet he knew nothing of the beleaguered garrison at Arrah: he only heard of their gallant defence on the 28th of July, on reaching Buxar, where the greatest anxiety was felt for their safety. If he had consulted his own feelings he would have hurried at once to their assistance; but a sort of panic had broken out at Buxar, from the idea that the mutineers were advancing to destroy the valuable stud property there, and he detained the steamer till the following morning, when, finding that there was no immediate danger, he started for Ghazeepoor, where a weak company of the 78th Highlanders had been stationed to overawe a half-mutinous native regiment. On reaching that town on the afternoon of the 29th, he placed himself in communication with Colonel Davies, of the 37th Regiment, who was in command; and at his request landed two guns under the charge of Lieutenant Gordon, Royal Artillery. He received in return a detachment of twenty-five men of the 78th Highlanders to aid him in the relief of Arrah; and the Honourable Captain Hastings, superintendent of the stud at Buxar, who happened to be at Ghazeepoor, volunteered to accompany him.

The steamer anchored off Buxar at nine P.M. on the evening of the 29th, where Major Eyre found a detachment of 160 men of Her Majesty's 5th Fusiliers, who had just arrived in the *James Hume* steamer. They were under the command of Captain L'Estrange, a gallant young officer, who, on this and other occasions, greatly distinguished himself. The 5th Fusiliers had been stationed in Mauritius, and were on their way to China; on landing at Calcutta, and hearing of the horrors of the Indian mutiny, Lord Elgin at once placed them at the disposal of the Governor-General, who lost no time in despatching them to the disaffected districts. Captain L'Estrange, on learning what had occurred at Arrah, entered warmly into Major Eyre's projected enterprise, and no time was lost in organizing a field force. On the morning of the 30th, three guns and 150 men of the 5th

Fusiliers were landed; the Highlanders would willingly have joined them, but their presence was necessary at Ghazeepoor, where they rejoined their company. During the day the little army was reinforced by fourteen mounted volunteers, who were placed under the command of Lieutenant Jackson, of the 12th Native Infantry. Captain Hastings was appointed staff-officer of the force: his local knowledge and unflagging energy enabled him, in the course of a few hours, to procure the necessary carriage and commissariat supplies. Every moment was precious; all were eager to start; no time was lost in extricating the waggons from the hold of the steamer; the artillery ammunition-boxes were mounted on light carts, which were found equally serviceable. India was not re-conquered by ordinary routine: every leader had to exercise his own judgment, and to trust in his own fertility of invention.

At five P.M. all was ready, and the little army commenced its march. Officers and men were inspired by the same chivalrous spirit; no knight-errant of old, hurrying to the rescue of injured innocence, could have been more eager for the fray. Our soldiers have their faults, but they cannot be taxed with inhumanity, or a want of sympathy with the sufferings of others; and the gallant defence of the little garrison had excited their sympathy as well as their admiration. After a march of six miles, they were joined by four elephants, which Mr. Ban, Civil Service, had induced the Dumraon Rajah, a native prince of doubtful loyalty, to send. With all their zeal their progress was slow: the roads were bad; the bullocks fresh from the plough; it was day-break before they reached their first encampment at Nya Bhojepoor, which is only fifteen miles from Buxar. The enemy had despatched a mounted spy to watch their movements, but the unerring aim of one of the volunteers closed his eyes for ever. He was recognised as one of the confidential men of Koer Singh, the brother of the Dumraon Rajah, who had always professed his warm attachment to the British rule, and lived on terms of intimacy with the English residents. He was a man of superior ability, and possessed of great influence over the Rajpoots of Shahabad; but his affairs were embarrassed, and his large estates heavily mortgaged. It was owing to this circumstance, and Brahminical influence, that he proved a traitor to our cause, and placed himself at the head of the mutineers at Dinapoor, who proclaimed him King of Shahabad. It was he who instigated them to revolt, and furnished them with boats to cross the river to Arrah, where he was now conducting the siege in person. The death of the spy prevented him from obtaining the information he so much desired.

The little army halted at their first encampment till the hottest part of the day was over; at four P.M. they resumed their march, and on the morning of the following day, the 1st of August, they reached the village of Shahpoor, where they received letters from Buxar, conveying the first intelligence of the destruction of Captain Dunbar's expeditionary force by the mutineers, who had entrapped them into an ambuscade. They learned, at the same time, that several of the bridges between Shahpoor and Arrah had been destroyed by the enemy in order to impede their progress; but the gallant little band, though far inferior in numbers to the detachment which had been cut off, resolved to proceed at all hazards. No time was lost; no fear or anxiety was expressed; at two P.M. they were already on the march. After advancing about four miles, they found a party of hostile villagers in the very act of destroying one of the bridges they had to cross, and an hour was lost in repairing it. They continued to advance without further interruption till darkness closed upon them, when they bivouacked for the night: a party of fifty of the 5th Fusiliers was sent forward to guard a bridge leading to the native village near which they were encamped. Meanwhile a party of mutineers had advanced from Arrah, and taken up their position in a thick, extensive wood about a mile from the village, with the intention of attacking them unawares, and cutting them off as they had done in the case of the other rescuing party. The line of march lay directly through this wood, which extended on either flank. At daybreak, when they were close upon it, they heard bugles sounding the assembly, and knew that the rebels were at hand. Major Eyre was too prudent to neglect the warning which the enemy had thus inadvertently given, and halted his force to reconnoitre. The enemy now appeared in overwhelming numbers, and extended themselves along the wood on either flank, with the evident intention of hemming in and destroying the little band opposed to them. On perceiving this, Major Eyre drew up his forces on the open plain to the right of the road, in the hope that the enemy would venture forth to attack him, and opened fire on them to the front and flanks with the three guns. They had not the courage to attack him openly, but sought shelter behind the broken ground between the two positions, where they could fire at our men with comparative safety. On this Major Eyre sent forward a party of skirmishers of the 5th Fusiliers to draw them from their positions, and, after a brief resistance, they fell back upon the wood where they had spent the night. The road, as we have already mentioned, lay directly through the middle of this wood, and Major Eyre concentrated his fire upon it with the view of forcing a passage. The enemy dispersed themselves right and left, leaving the road clear, the baggage and guns were moved forward under cover of the Enfield rifles, and our gallant little army pushed through the wood before the enemy had time to close their divided wings or renew the attack.

Having failed in this their first attempt to intercept the army of rescue, the mutineers fell back upon a village about two miles a-head, where they destroyed a bridge, and took up a strong position among the houses. Our men continued to advance along the road, which was a sort of elevated causeway with partially inundated paddy-fields on either side, till they were within a short distance of the bridge, when Major Eyre halted for refreshment, and sent out scouts to search for a ford across the river. During the engagement in the wood, the four elephants sent by Dumraon Rajah, after disembarrassing themselves of the soldiers' great coats and bedding with which they were loaded, went over to the enemy; it seemed almost as if they were possessed with the same spirit of disaffection as their master. The scouts returned without having discovered a ford, and Major Eyre diverged from his line of march toward the nearest point of the railway, which was only about a mile from the village. While the infantry and baggage pushed forward in this direction, the guns opened fire on the enemy, for the purpose of distracting their attention from this movement. This ruse succeeded for a time, but as soon as the enemy discovered that our men had changed their line of march, they advanced in great strength to intercept them at the angle of a wood close to the railway. The two armies pursued a parallel course on the opposite sides of the stream till they reached the railway, when Major Eyre attempted to dislodge the enemy from their position in the wood. Greatly superior in numbers, and sheltered by the cover of the wood, the mutineers fought with every advantage on their side; twice they rushed forward to seize our guns, which, in the heat of combat, were almost deserted; twice they were driven back by showers of grape. Pressed by superior numbers, and encircled by a wall of fire, the brave Fusiliers began to lose ground; it was one of those critical moments when all depends on the decision of one man. If Major Eyre had hesitated for a moment, the garrison at Arrah would have resisted in vain, and another disaster overtaken our arms; but he proved himself equal to the occasion. He knew that the British bayonet, wielded by manly British arms, has often turned back the tide of victory, and retrieved the honours of the day; when he gave the word "Charge!" the Fusiliers cleared the stream with a ringing cheer; at a single bound they were in the midst of the enemy, dealing death on every side. The mutineers were twenty times their number; but though they had been a thousand times stronger the result would have been the same: they have never been able to sustain a hand-to-hand combat with the fierce Feringees. Panic-struck by the sudden attack, they broke and fell back in the greatest confusion, while long lines were opened through the retreating mass by the crushing fire of our artillery. In a few moments all was over; the victory was complete; the ground was strewn with dead and dying; but not one of the five thousand, who an hour before threatened our little army with destruction, now stood up to oppose their passage. Our soldiers obtained the victory, but they fought for something more; they thought of the beleaguered garrison at Arrah, of their gallant and long-protracted resistance, of the fearful fate that awaited them if they suffered a repulse; all their hearts throbbed with such thoughts as they bounded across the stream with levelled bayonets, and carried everything before them. After these defeats at the railway the mutineers fled precipitately to Arrah, where they had barely time to remove part of their plunder to the jungle when the victorious little army marched into the town.

They did not arrive a moment too soon; the house, so gallantly defended for seven days and nights by sixteen Europeans and fifty Sikhs against three regiments of mutineers and Koer Singh's levies, was found to be so effectually ruined, that a few hours' delay must have completed its destruction. The deliverance of the little garrison from the worst of fates was little short of miraculous, and we can trace the working of a Higher Power in arranging the different steps by which that deliverance was effected. A leader less resolute and energetic than Major Eyre would have quailed before the difficulties and dangers that opposed his progress; nothing but their own unflinching fortitude could have enabled the little garrison to hold out so long. For more than a week they were harassed by the fire of the enemy, which was so close and continuous that not a loophole could be approached with safety, and yet they inflicted far more loss on their assailants than they suffered themselves. Only one of them was severely wounded, while no less than fifty or sixty of the enemy are believed to have fallen. This result is to be attributed to the precautions they used for their own protection, and their superior skill in the use of the rifle: the unerring aim of Mr. Littledale, a civilian, inspired the mutineers with a salutary dread, and drove them to seek shelter behind every available corner. The defence of Arrah must ever occupy a conspicuous place in the annals of the Indian mutiny.

A week was spent in restoring the country around Arrah to order; martial law was proclaimed; the people were disarmed; about thirty wounded Sepoys, and several native officials who had aided the mutineers, were hanged. Meanwhile Major Eyre had applied to the authorities at Dinapoor for some reinforcements to enable him to follow up his victory, and on the 8th of August a detachment of two hundred men of the 10th Regiment, under the command of Captain Patterson, arrived at Arrah. This regiment had suffered severely on the occasion when Mr. Mangles so greatly distinguished himself, and the men were burning with the desire to avenge their comrades, and obliterate the remembrance of that disaster. Major Eyre was not the man to balk them in their purpose; he resolved to lead them at once against Judgespoor, the stronghold of Koer Singh, where he and the mutineers had taken shelter. He was joined by eight of the garrison of Arrah, and the fifty Sikhs who had shared in the defence under the command of Mr. Wake, and by a further reinforcement of one hundred of Rattray's Sikhs, under Lieutenants Roberts and Powers. The attack on Judgespoor was generally considered to be a dangerous, if not a desperate undertaking, but at two P.M. on the 11th of August, Major Eyre marched forth from Arrah with the certainty of victory.

After a march of eight miles they reached an open plain, where they bivouacked for the night. The following morning they resumed their march, and found the road more difficult as they advanced. At ten o'clock they halted an hour for refreshment. Two miles farther on they came in sight of the enemy, who had taken up a strong position in the belt of jungle surrounding Judgespoor, with a river in their front. In their centre was the town of Dulloor, before which some breastworks had been raised; between it and our army was a native village, occupied by an advanced picket, which soon retired before the fire of our skirmishers. The mutineers lay so close in the jungle and broken ground as to be almost invisible; but a few discharges of grape made them shift their position more to the right. Now was the time for the 10th to wipe out the remembrance of the ambuscade, and such was their impatience that almost before the order to charge could reach them they rushed forward with a cheer, and charged to within sixty yards of the enemy, who broke and fled for refuge to the town of Dulloor, and the adjacent jungle. Meanwhile their left and centre had been repulsed by the detachment of the 5th Fusiliers under Captains L'Estrange and Scott, who now took part in the pursuit.

During the engagement Koer Singh's irregular lines on the left had moved round, and were threatening our right wing under cover of the jungle and broken ground, but they were checked by the fire of the Sikhs and volunteer yeomanry, and of a howitzer under the skilful management of Staff-Sergeant Melville, Royal Artillery. After an hour's resistance the whole body of the enemy fell back on Judgespoor, pursued by our men, who captured two guns during their flight, and followed them up to the walls of the stronghold, which consisted of an extensive mass of buildings, protected by lofty walls with loopholes for musketry, and capable of offering a protracted resistance if properly defended. The mutineers were seized with such a panic that they offered no resistance, and our men entered Koer Singh's fortress in triumph at one P.M., where they found ample accommodation and refreshment after their rapid march. Koer Singh had evacuated his stronghold only one hour before the triumphant entry of our men, and fled in the direction of Jutoorah, seven miles to the south, where he had another fortified residence in the jungle. He was pursued by eighty men of the 5th Fusiliers, under Captain L'Estrange, and the Volunteer Yeomanry, who, on reaching Jutoorah, found that he had continued his flight towards Sasseram with the remains of the 40th Regiment of Native Infantry, who alone of all the rebel army still continued to share his fortunes. Captain L'Estrange not having sufficient forces to follow up the pursuit, contented himself with destroying the place, and then returned to Judgespoor. Our troops found abundance of provisions there; the stores of grain alone would have sustained twenty thousand men for six months; they were distributed among the starving villagers, who had been plundered by Koer Singh and his followers. At two P.M. on the 15th of August, Judgespoor was evacuated, and the stronghold, including a new Hindoo temple, on which large sums had been expended, was blown into the air. Major Eyre then advanced as far as Peeroo in pursuit of Koer Singh, when he received instructions from Sir James Outram to return to Arrah, and to join the force which was now on its march for the relief of Lucknow. Major Eyre's battery and the detachment of the 5th Fusiliers shared in all the honours and dangers of that successful enterprise, and suffered severely while forcing their way into the town. The gallant L'Estrange, whose name has occurred so often in the course of this narrative, and who was known to us as a young officer of superior intellect and studious habits, was mortally wounded; three of his brother officers shared the same fate. Mr. Mangles still survives to enjoy the reward which he earned by his courage and humanity.

CHAPTER XXII.

CAPTAIN HENRY EVELYN WOOD, 17TH LANCERS.

NO young officer in the service has had greater opportunities of distinguishing himself than Captain Wood, or earned a better title to the distinction of the Victoria Cross. He is a son of Sir John Page Wood, Bart., of Rivenhall-place, near Witham, Essex, and a nephew of Sir W. Page Wood, Vice-Chancellor of England. Our readers, on reading this simple record of his numerous acts of bravery, will be surprised to learn that he has not yet completed his twenty-eighth year; in truth, his name became familiar to the world at a period when most boys of his age and position are still seated on the benches at Eton, mastering the intricacies of the Latin grammar and reading of the deeds which similar heroes in ancient times performed. He was intended at first for the sister branch of the service, and entered the navy as a midshipman. During the Crimean War he had an opportunity of serving on board H.M.S. *Leander*, under the command of the gallant and much lamented Sir William Peel, who had the rare faculty of inspiring all around him with the same heroic spirit by which he himself was animated. Henry Evelyn Wood soon secured the confidence and won the admiration of the captain of the *Leander*, whom we find writing to Sir John Page Wood, on the 18th of April, 1855, in the following terms:—"You will be glad to hear that not only has your son shown the most beautiful courage in battery, but his conduct and his manners are as exemplary as his courage."

Such tributes of praise are the most precious reward of parents whose sons are fighting the battles of their country. Our young hero had soon an opportunity of justifying, in the eyes of the public, the praises bestowed upon him by his leader, to whom, at his own request, he was appointed aide-de-camp—no mere honorary appointment, as the sequel will show. On the 18th of June an attack was made on the Redan, and young Wood, who was foremost in the fray, was wounded by a grape-shot in the arm. Such a wound would have placed most men *hors de combat*, but the young sailor thought only of his duty. With the huge grape-shot protruding from his arm, he assisted in placing one of the scaling ladders against the walls of the Redan, and continued on the scene of combat throughout the day. His gallant conduct and patient endurance of physical suffering excited the admiration of all who took part in this affair, and called forth the warmest approval of our leaders in the Crimea. The following day Sir Stephen Lushington wrote to his uncle, Captain Mitchell, R.N.:—"You will be sorry to hear that your young nephew, Wood, has been wounded in the arm by a grape-shot. The shot struck the bone obliquely, and was cut out when he got into camp. I saw him in the trenches, and he bore it like a hero. He was Peel's aide-de-camp, and Peel endeavoured to keep the boy from the murderous fire into which they plunged with the scaling ladders; but he would take no refusal, and went out with the rest. Wood will be at Razatch to-day, in Lord Raglan's carriage."

Lord Raglan knew how to appreciate such conduct: not satisfied with placing his carriage at the disposal of the wounded sailor, he thus marked his sense of approval in one of his despatches:—"Amongst those who greatly distinguished themselves were Captain Peel, Mr. Daniels, and Mr. Wood." Official etiquette prevented Lord Raglan from alluding more particularly to Wood's conduct in a public despatch, but on the 21st of June he wrote the following kind note to Captain Mitchell:—"I am very glad to have had the opportunity of being in any, the smallest degree, useful to your nephew, Mr. H. E. Wood, whose distinguished career cannot fail to enlist everybody in his favour. I am rejoiced to hear that he is going on well. I am assured that the bone is not injured." It was by such little acts of kindness that Lord Raglan endeared himself to all who had the honour of serving under him, and such tributes of praise are naturally cherished by their relations as the most precious relics.

Nor was Sir William Peel backward in testifying to the distinguished valour of his gallant aide-de-camp. Writing to his brother, Frederick Peel, Esq., M.P., on the same occasion, he says:—"Would you let Sir Page Wood know that his gallant son behaved with extreme intrepidity? He was, or is, my aide-de-camp, and received a severe wound from a grape-shot, but will not lose his arm. I can assure you I thought more of that boy than of anything else, and tried in vain to plead some excuse for getting him out of the way, but he would be my aide-de-camp, and it would have been a worse blow to have denied him. Thank God he is safe, and it was such a relief to me." This letter gives us a keen insight into the character of both. No one can read of the ardent impatience of the young sailor-boy to share in the dangers of the field, the reluctant consent wrung from Peel by his importunity, the consciousness of the latter that a refusal would have been more keenly felt than the wound itself, his anxiety about his safety throughout the day, and his gratitude to God for the preservation of his life, without feeling that the most heroic courage is often accompanied by an almost feminine tenderness of heart. We admire Peel for his bravery shown on many a battle-field, but we love his memory for the care with which he watched over the sailor-boy placed under his charge on the 18th of June, and the joy he felt and expressed on finding that his wound was not mortal.

Others besides Peel testified to his gallant bearing on this occasion. Sir Stephen Lushington, Commander of the Naval Brigade, writes:—"I can strongly recommend this young officer for his gallantry and good conduct during the whole time he was under my command. He was severely wounded on the 18th of June, when conveying the ladders." Lord Lyons also thus alludes to him in a speech which he made at the Mansion House:—"Nothing in the annals of chivalry contains a brighter instance of devotion than was exhibited by Captain Peel and his aides-de-camp, one of whom,

Mr. Wood, when wounded placed the scaling-ladders against the walls of the Redan." On the 6th of September, 1855, Captain Peel addressed the following letter to Sir John Page Wood:—"Your son was only known to me through his gallant behaviour. On the 17th of October he volunteered, with Mr. Daniels, my other aide-de-camp, to bring up powder from the rear, through a fire which daunted others; and the spirit he showed on that occasion was not exceptional, but was maintained throughout. It was the more noble as there were no spectators. The names of these two heroes are known through the whole army; and I almost thought it inconvenient having two such spirits around me. I trust his wound is doing well. It must be very tedious and painful."

Owing to the severe wound he had received at the attack on the Redan, Wood was obliged to return to England to recruit his health. For reasons which need not now be specified, he was induced to transfer his services from the navy to the army, and in September, 1855, he received his commission as a cornet in the 13th Light Dragoons. The Lords Commissioners of the Admiralty testified the value of his services in the navy, and their secretary, Mr. Phinn, addressed the following letter to his father in their name:—"In accepting the resignation of your son, Mr. H. E. Wood, I am to express their Lordships' regret that so gallant an officer is lost to the naval service." It might have been expected that Mr. Wood's gallantry at the Redan would have been at once rewarded with the Victoria Cross; in the age of chivalry many knights had earned their spurs by less heroic deeds. But our young hero had yet to wait for years, and to perform still more daring deeds of valour, before his claim to wear the symbol of his sovereign's favour upon his breast was recognised. He had not yet completed his eighteenth year, and it may be that his youth stood in the way of his obtaining this honourable distinction. Be that as it may, it formed no obstacle to his being enrolled in the Legion of Honour, and an effort was made by those who knew how to appreciate his gallantry to procure for him the Cross. Sir Stephen Lushington forwarded his name, and wrote to him:—"I still hope to see the Victoria Cross on your breast." Admiral Richards, one of the Lords of the Admiralty, supported his claims, and was so sanguine of success, that he wrote to his father as follows:—"You may rely upon it that none of *his class can be recommended for the Cross of Valour without your brave boy being one.* His is now a world-wide fame, and requires no certificates, no testimonials, to bolster it up. It is difficult to imagine *what* kind of naval merit can include if his excludes."

Our readers will experience the same difficulty in discovering the grounds on which Mr. Wood's claim was disallowed, and his name omitted from the list of those who received the Cross of Valour. Political considerations ought to have no influence in deciding the claims of those who aspire to this honour; where all are equally brave, all ought to be equally rewarded. But it was not so in this case. It was in vain that his friends remonstrated, and Sir Stephen Lushington wrote thus strongly in his favour:—"It is still my opinion that Mr. Wood deserves the Victoria Cross as much as any one that I recommended at the same time, not excepting his gallant chief, the late Sir William Peel; and it will afford me much pleasure to hear that he has received the much-desired honour. . . . . He was one of the first officers I recommended for it, and certainly one of the most gallant in the Naval Brigade." The writer of this letter went even so far as to remonstrate with the authorities on the omission of Mr. Wood's name, but all this led to nothing; and our young hero, tired of inaction, and longing for other opportunities of distinction, exchanged into the 17th Lancers, and embarked for India.

His indefatigable perseverance in mastering the native languages, aided by the high character he had already attained in the field, soon procured for him the favourable notice of his superiors in India. After a residence of one year and nine months, thirteen of which were spent in fighting and hard marching in pursuit of the rebels, Lieutenant Wood passed the examination for interpreter in Hindostani, thus justifying Sir Joshua Reynolds's remark, that genius is only another name for perseverance. Young men of Wood's indomitable courage and perseverance must ultimately attain to distinction in any career; the world may be careless at first, but it cannot always ignore their claims. We have the testimony of a distinguished Indian officer, Major-General Beatson, that, after a residence of eighteen months, he already knew more of the native languages than most officers who had spent ten years in India. The continuance of the rebellion afforded him opportunities of proving that intellectual effort is not incompatible with the highest courage. During the action at Sindwaho, he greatly distinguished himself. Owing to the paucity of officers in the 3rd Bombay Cavalry, he had volunteers to command, a troop of the 3rd Light Cavalry, during the campaign; and in the hottest of the fight he rode up almost single-handed and attacked a body of the enemy. His gallantry on this occasion was recognised by His Excellency the Governor-General of India, whose attention had been directed to it by Lieutenant-Colonel Curtis, 1st Bombay Lancers, and Colonel De Salis. He had continued to act as brigade major to Brigadier Somerset, and on the breaking up of the field brigade under his command, the latter recommended him in the strongest terms to the favourable notice of the Assistant-Adjutant-General. Some idea may be formed of the value of Lieutenant Wood's services at this period, from the following extract from Brigadier Somerset's letter: — "It only remains for me to say, that, in the various duties which have devolved upon Lieutenant Wood, as my only staff officer, while under my command he has shown the most unwearied zeal, particularly on occasion of the rapid pursuit of the enemy—calling for the utmost exertion from all—especially from one whose position did not admit of his taking advantage of a few short hours that others had for rest—as well as the highest intelligence and facility for the management of native Indians, quite unusual in one so recently arrived in this country."

Brigadier Somerset concluded by recommending him for employment upon the staff of the army, or with native cavalry; and this recommendation was not without its immediate effect. In times of peace such appointments are usually given to those who are backed by the strongest influences; but such are the exigencies of the service during the prevalence of war, that merit cannot be altogether overlooked. A general, in the selection of his staff, consults only his own interests in striving to have the right man in the right place. General Michel at once appointed him to the command of a troop of irregular cavalry, and in August, 1859, he was acting as Brigade Major under General Beatson, who thus alludes to his abilities in the command of native troops:—"In this officer I have a strong proof that it is not having passed a long time with native troops which alone renders an officer fit for irregular cavalry. Lieutenant Wood's knowledge of his duties as a cavalry officer, his zeal and energy in all situations, render him more valuable as a staff officer with irregular troops than most officers I have met with in India, who have been all the period of their service with native corps. . . . . He has all the qualifications of a first-rate soldier, in addition to the highest principles of a gentleman."

Lieutenant Wood's services in the Crimea and India were of such a nature that they could not be altogether forgotten, and though they were overlooked for the moment, circumstances eventually occurred which brought them fresh to the remembrance of the public, and enabled him to secure that honourable distinction to which he had never ceased to aspire. At the commencement of the year 1860 the Indian mutineers, disheartened by repeated reverses in the field, broke up into detached parties, and concealing themselves in the jungle, endeavoured to protract the contest by plundering the inhabitants of the surrounding districts. Among those who had suffered most from their depredations was a potail of the name of Chemmum Singh, who resided in the vicinity of the jungles between Beora and Muksudnugger. The rebels who had taken refuge there committed frequent depredations in the Barseah district, and though frequently attacked by different parties had always contrived to escape. Chemmum Singh, whose loyalty was doubtless intensified by personal loss, was naturally anxious to get rid of such unpleasant neighbours, and made known their movements to the commander of the district. Intelligence of this reached the ears of the rebels, who resolved to have their revenge. Issuing forth at night, they seized the unfortunate potail and carried him and his relations off to the jungle, with the intention of reviving that species of trial which, in the old Border warfare, was known as Jedburgh or Jeddart justice. They meant to hang him first, and try him afterwards.

It would have fared ill with the poor potail if it had not so happened that Lieutenant Wood arrived at this juncture, after a long march, at Sindhora, the post where his regiment was stationed. Though worn out with his long march, he no sooner heard of what had happened than he resolved at once to attempt a rescue. Hastily collecting a Duffadar and four Sowars of his own regiment, and a Naick and six Sepoys of the Bareilly levy, he started with this small body of men in search of the rebels. He knew that success depended not so much on the numbers as the courage of his men, and forced his way into the jungle in the direction where the rebels were supposed to be concealed. After proceeding twelve miles from Sindhora, without perceiving any traces of the enemy, his practised eye detected the glare of a fire in a dense part of the jungle. He at once suspected that this had been kindled by the robbers whose lurking-place he was trying to discover, and made up his mind to attack them before they were aware of his presence. He dismounted, and leaving three Sowars to take charge of the horses, advanced through the jungle on foot with the other two of his party. For three miles they crept through the dense bush, using every precaution so as not to attract the notice or excite the alarm of the robbers. At length their perseverance was rewarded: at one o'clock P.M. Lieutenant Wood witnessed a *tableau vivant* in the dense jungle of Sindhora, which he is not likely ever to forget. There, in the midst of the bush, at the distance of twenty-six feet from the place where the party of rescue lay concealed, were the whole of the robbers, stretched on the ground, and fast asleep, some five of their number, who kept drowsy watch over their comrades, and the unfortunate potail, who was waiting his doom with all the calm indifference of Oriental fatalism. They were roused up in a manner they little expected. The party of rescue fired a volley; and Lieutenant Wood rushed forward into the nullah amongst the rebels, followed by the Duffadar and Sowar of his regiment. The latter, inspired by his example, followed him into the thickest of the danger; but the Naick and six Sepoys of the Bareilly levy consulted their safety by remaining in the rear. If he had been properly supported, the whole body of the rebels might have been killed or captured; as it was, they were seized with a panic and fled into the jungle, leaving their arms and several of their comrades who had fallen, behind. Thus one brave man, with two native followers, routed and put to flight a body of seventy rebels, who were well armed and familiar with the country. While such a deed may not be altogether unrivalled in the annals of the suppression of the Indian Mutiny—a period when our countrymen seem to have vied with one another in the display of the most daring courage—it may at least be affirmed that it has never been surpassed, or accompanied with more excellent effect. The band ot robbers, routed and put to flight, never ventured to return to the scene of their former depredation, and the inhabitants of the surrounding country were indebted to Lieutenant Wood for the safety of their lives and property. Chemmum Singh and his relatives were restored to liberty, and the party of rescue having accomplished the object of their expedition, returned to Sindhora. Lieutenant Wood's services on this occasion were honourably mentioned in a despatch by Colonel Sir Richmond Shakespeare, and gratefully acknowledged by the Governor-General of India.

It might have been expected that such distinguished conduct, on repeated occasions, would now have secured for this gallant young officer that Cross of Valour which had ever been to him an object of honourable ambition. Fresh difficulties, however, arose, and the authorities at home were slow to recognise his claims. General Sir J. Michel, who had ever taken a warm interest in his career, and had the best opportunities of studying his character, had already, in April, 1859, addressed a letter to the chief of the staff, recommending Lieutenant Wood to his favourable notice. By the regulations of the service, he was precluded from general promotion; but Sir John Michel recommended him for a brevet majority, as soon as he should obtain the rank of captain. "His services under my command," writes Sir John, "are as follows:—

"On marching from Mhow, in August, 1858, the left wing, 3rd Bombay Cavalry, being deficient in officers, he volunteered to take charge of a squadron, and whilst in command was present at the actions of Raggurh, where his squadron did excellent service; he also commanded these men at the actions of Sindwaho and Kerai.

"On the formation of a light column under Lieutenant-Colonel Benson, on the 8th of November, 1858, he was named staff officer, and was present at the different rapid pursuits under Colonel Benson and Colonel Somerset, and present at the fight of Baroda, 1st of January.

"His extraordinary activity, zeal, energy, and judgment, together with his utility, from having rapidly passed in the Hindostani language, combine to render him a most valuable officer, and one whose services deserve reward, and whose promotion would be an advantage to the service.

"This young officer's career has been so brilliant, that I trust I may be permitted to attach to this letter a former memorial of his in reference to the Victoria Cross, that his lordship may be able to judge of his antecedents."

The important services enumerated above were performed previous to the successful attack on the band of robbers. After this brilliant affair, Sir J. Michel again intervened in his favour, but without success, as we learn from the following note addressed by him to Lieutenant Wood:—

"You are doomed to be, in respect to the Victoria Cross, unlucky.

"However, go on as you are doing, and your steady good conduct and gallant bearing will eventually bring fruit.

"Recollect, in your military career, as long as I hear well of you, of which I have no doubt, you will always find me a sincere friend.

"I will never apply to any one to do anything for you as a favour, but with the strength of my position will support your wishes, on the grounds of your merits and your services."

Circumstances occurred in 1860 which induced Lieutenant

Wood to resign his appointment in the Indian service. It is not our intention to dwell upon the causes which led him to abandon the field of labour in which he had so greatly distinguished himself. It may be sufficient to mention, that he had threatened a treacherous rajah with arrest, and this incurred the censure of his former chief, Sir R. Shakespeare. Every one acquainted with the facts of the case will admit, that if he erred it was an error of judgment, springing from excess of zeal for the public service, and therefore deserving to be leniently dealt with. Censure proceeding from such a quarter deeply wounded his highly sensitive spirit, and, notwithstanding the remonstrances of his friends, he retired from the Indian service, and prepared to return to England. His departure elicited the sincerest expressions of regret, and the most cordial recognition of his services from those who had witnessed his brilliant career. Major Mayne, the well-known commander of Mayne's Horse, whose painful duty it had been to convey to him the censure of Sir R. Shakespeare, wrote to the latter, on the 7th of August, 1860, as follows:—

"Lieutenant Wood has, in consequence, sent in his resignation of his appointment, which I forward for your consideration. I have remonstrated with Lieutenant Wood, but he is too discouraged to remain under present circumstances.

"I greatly regret that there has been cause for his incurring your censures, but it is my duty to report to you the essential services that this officer has rendered since he joined me, in carrying out the harassing details of organizing the second corps of my horse: his unwearied energy; his close attention to details; his admirable temper; his strict discipline; the physical activity he daily exerts to teach his men the use of arms and horses; his unceasing intercourse with his officers and men; his unremitting endeavours to make himself thoroughly acquainted with their habits and language; his disregard of self and personal trouble, and the critical knowledge he has obtained of his profession, form a very long list of high qualifications.

"But I have daily noticed them with intense satisfaction—I may say hourly—for from where I write I can see—hardly avoid observing—all that passes at Lieutenant Wood's quarters.

"I have never yet met with an officer of Lieutenant Wood's age (not yet twenty-three years) who gave higher promise of making a brilliant soldier. His whole heart and soul are in his work, and he is an impersonation of Sir Charles Napier's *beau idéal* of an Irregular horseman, for he is intent on his duty in eating, drinking, and sleeping, while his gallantry and devotedness in the field have won for him the recorded praise of Lord Raglan, Sir William Peel, and all who knew him in the Crimea, where he was recommended for the Victoria Cross, and all under whom he has served in India. . . . . Lieutenant Wood is much loved in the brigade, and I consider his resignation as a loss to the public service."

Major Mayne also recorded his sense of his merits in Brigade Orders, and such proofs of esteem must have been soothing to his spirit as he bade adieu to the shores of India. That he did so with sorrow the reader will readily imagine; no one can renounce the prospect of a brilliant career without regret. Kind and appreciating friends were waiting to welcome him to his native shore; home, with all its endearing ties, was waiting his return; and yet, even at the last hour, he turned a longing eye to the scene of his former labours, and began to think of accepting employment in the Indian service at some future period. On the 4th of October, 1860, immediately before embarking for England, he wrote to Colonel Travers, Commanding Central India Force, requesting him to keep him in view if a vacancy should occur, and stating that he would rather command the 1st or 2nd corps, on the present system, than any other regiment. This letter produced a kind reply from Colonel Travers, who expressed the warmest admiration of his qualifications as an officer, and promised to place him in command of the first cavalry regiment where a vacancy occurred, provided that he could do so without injustice to others. Satisfied with this assurance our young hero set out for England, where he found that fame had preceded him, and won for him the tardy recognition of his services. In truth, the Victoria Cross had been awarded to

pacity, mismanagement, and the reckless sacrifice of valuable lives; and while such charges can have no effect upon those who are on the spot, and have had frequent opportunities of witnessing his capacity for command, they have doubtless tended to injure him in the opinion of those who have only an imperfect knowledge of the circumstances of the case. Though we were not present at the attack on the Gate Pa, we have derived our information from some of the principal actors in that unfortunate affair, so that the following narrative may be safely accepted as a faithful account of what occurred. We shall confine ourselves to the simple facts of the case, and leave our readers to draw their own conclusions.

Tauranga is the native name of a district on the east coast of New Zealand, about a hundred miles south of Auckland. It has long been the site of a missionary establishment under the charge of Archdeacon Brown, who has laboured among the natives during more than twenty years, and remained unmolested at his field of duty during the progress of the present war. A few British settlers had established themselves there for purposes of trade, and a resident magistrate was appointed to watch over the interests of justice. The Maoris of Tauranga are and always have been a warlike race, but there was no reason at first to question their loyalty. During the prevalence of the war in the Waikato district, the principal seat of the late campaign, the Maoris at Tauranga remained faithful in their adherence to the British Crown. It was only after the hostile tribes, driven from their land in the Waikato by the advance of our army, had dispersed themselves in the south, that symptoms of disaffection appeared among the natives of Tauranga. The fugitives excited the alarm of their countrymen by asserting that they also would be stripped of their lands, and thus inciting them to revolt. The effects of these incentives to rebellion became so marked, that the 68th and 43rd Regiments, which had recently arrived from India, were sent to Tauranga to overawe the disaffected. This movement brought matters to a crisis; a small portion of the natives remained faithful to the British Crown, while the great majority left their homes and joined the insurgents. Our forces encamped on a small peninsula called Te Papa, which is connected with the mainland by a narrow isthmus: the command was intrusted to Lieutenant-Colonel Greer, of the 68th Regiment. The hostile natives continued to hover round our camp, cutting off our supplies, and seizing the commissariat cattle within a few hundred yards of our sentries, without any attempt on our part to punish their audacity. Emboldened by our supineness and their own success, they resolved at length to erect a pa, and the site they selected would have secured the approval of Vauban, if he had been still alive. In truth, the Maoris of New Zealand, though they have never studied at Woolwich, are adepts in military engineering; instinct in their case has supplied the want of science. The sites of their pas, which are simply redoubts built of earth and inclosed with a wooden palisade, have always been chosen with the double intention of inflicting the greatest possible injury on their assailants, and securing their own retreat when their position becomes untenable. No attempt was made to restrain the natives from erecting a pa at Tauranga; the work went on for weeks, and our men quietly looked on. It is a far easier matter to prevent the erection than to effect the capture of a pa, but there may have been causes for this inactivity unknown to us. Be that as it may, the pa was built without interruption on the narrow slip of land which connects the peninsula of Te Papa with the mainland. This isthmus is the gate which commands the entrance to the whole district; hence the pa erected on it was known as the Gate Pa. On either side was a swamp extending to the water, so that it was impossible for our men to force their entrance into the interior without dislodging the enemy from their stronghold. An order had been issued for the 43rd Regiment to proceed to Auckland, but Colonel Greer, in the exercise of a wise discretion, retained them at Tauranga, in the belief that their services would soon be required.

On the night of Thursday, the 28th of April, General Cameron, who had arrived at Tauranga with his staff some days before, commenced his preparations for attack. The forces under his command seemed to be amply sufficient for securing success: they consisted of the 68th Light Infantry, the 43rd, the Flying Column, made up of detachments from the 14th, 65th, and 70th Regiments, and the Naval Brigade, consisting of more than two hundred sailors from the different men-of-war stationed there. The attacking party were strong in artillery, having with them eleven Armstrong guns, besides two howitzers and six mortars. The only arms possessed by the enemy, whose numbers did not exceed six hundred men, were their rifles and tomahawks; but this inferiority was compensated for by the advantage of fighting behind the walls of the pa.

The general's object was to intercept the enemy in the rear, and thus cut off their retreat. Under cover of the night, the 68th Regiment and thirty men of the Naval Brigade forced their way through the swamp, and took up their position in the rear of the pa, without attracting the notice of the insurgents. April is one of the brightest and sunniest months in New Zealand, but the morning of the 28th was dark and lowering; heavy rains began to fall, and the rays of the sun were obscured by the murky atmosphere. By the imperfect light of dawn the 68th could be seen extended in skirmishing order behind the pa, so that the enemy were completely hemmed in. They might hold out for a time, but it was only a question of time; the general's arrangements were perfect, and no doubt was entertained of our ultimate success. At half-past seven o'clock the cannonade began; the artillery, officers and men, displayed the greatest courage and skill in working the guns; shot and shell continued to be poured upon and into the redoubt without intermission till four o'clock in the afternoon. The few natives who had appeared in the rifle-pits at the commencement of the attack were soon dislodged, and retreated into the pa by a hole not larger than an ordinary covered drain. During the cannonade they seldom returned our fire; the general impression was, that the shot and shell had done their deadly work so effectually as to leave few of them alive. The general, however, delayed his attack till a breach had been effected in the walls sufficiently large to admit the storming party—a fact which seems to have been wilfully ignored by his assailants at home, who have unjustly accused him of recklessly sacrificing the lives of his officers and men by commanding them to mount an impracticable breach, when his proper course would have been a mine or a distant cannonade. All that could be done by a distant cannonade was already effected; the breach was there staring them in the face; the storming party had only to enter in and take possession. The wanton sacrifice of human life is the last charge that would be brought against General Cameron by those who have taken part in this campaign; in this respect he resembles his friend and countryman Lord Clyde, who never exposed his men to unnecessary danger. If human skill could always command success, he had a right to count upon victory; but we need not anticipate. At four o'clock in the afternoon the storming party, consisting of the Naval Brigade and the 43rd Regiment, were formed into line, while the covering party advanced within a hundred yards of the pa, and opened fire. The enemy showed themselves on the walls, and briskly replied. The storming party, led by Commander Hay, of the *Harrier*, now advanced swiftly in column; the men were in the highest spirits, and rushed forward with a ringing cheer. Nothing could withstand the impetuosity of their attack; in a moment they had cleared the ditch, scaled the embankment, and plunged through the breach into the redoubt. The reserve party thought that the day was won; for a time no sound was heard save a straggling shot or an occasional cheer. But this silence was not to last; it was only the treacherous lull that precedes the storm. That storm soon burst forth with the greatest fury; all at once the pa, the supposed grave of its Maori defenders, became instinct with life; volley succeeded volley in rapid succession; in the intervals might be heard savage yells such as never issued from any British throat. It was a moment of intense interest to the spectators, who for a time could see nothing but the clouds of smoke that rose from the pa after each volley; enough, however, soon became visible to show that our arms had met with a sudden reverse. Soldiers and sailors, mixed up in confusion, came thronging through the breach, plunged into the ditch, and rushed forward in the wildest disorder; some sudden panic had seized them, but there might still be sufficient time to turn the tide of war and retrieve the honour of the day. General Cameron at once ordered the supports to advance; a braver officer than Captain Hamilton, of the *Esk*, could not have been found to lead them on. If a single arm could have changed the fortune of the war, the disaster of the Gate Pa would never have occurred; but the supports came too late. The gallant Hamilton sprang upon the embankment, waved his sword in the air, and shouted, "Follow me, men!" Scarcely had the words passed his lips when a bullet struck him on the head, the sword dropped from his hand, and he fell to rise no more. The death of their leader increased the panic of the men; the supports became mixed with the fugitives; all discipline was forgotten; all remonstrance on the part of the officers was unavailing; *sauve qui peut* became the order of the day. The enemy, profiting by this panic, took deliberate aim, and poured a destructive fire into the retreating mob, whose only thought was of escape. The day was lost; the instrument had broken in the hands of him who knew how to use it so skilfully. It was too much for even the strongest nature to bear with equanimity; the general dashed his field-glass on the ground, turned his back on the fugitives, and retired to his tent to conceal his emotion.

Various causes have been assigned for this disastrous retreat. It has been affirmed that the storming party, on entering the pa, met with no resistance, and saw no traces of the enemy, except a few wounded Maoris lying on the ground, apparently abandoned by their comrades. Believing that the redoubt was evacuated, they threw aside their arms, and began to help themselves to the plunder which was scattered about. It may be that the Maoris had recourse to this artifice in order to throw them off their guard, as they are already familiar with the looting propensities of the British soldier; it is certain that they had not all evacuated the pa. A considerable number had done so; but the majority had concealed themselves in chambers dug out in the ground, and covered with boughs of trees and earth. They had remained there during the cannonade, and it is a singular fact, worthy of the notice of military strategists, that the storm of shot and shell which descended upon the pa for upwards of eight hours could not reach them. The killed and wounded were those who exposed themselves on the walls; no shot or shell could reach their more prudent comrades, who with heroic patience awaited the result in their subterraneous retreat. When the defenders of the walls retreated before the impetuous onset of the storming party, and tried to escape by the rear, the others remained in their hiding-place, and bided their time. When they saw through the thin covering of boughs and earth that the storming party had abandoned their arms and given themselves up to plunder, they opened a destructive fire upon them. The effect was much the same as if a volcano had suddenly opened beneath their feet, and begun to pour forth volumes of smoke and flame; many of our men were killed and wounded at the first discharge; discipline might have done much, but all discipline was at an end; mere courage could avail nothing against this invisible foe. Our officers behaved with their usual coolness and bravery, but every effort to restore order was unavailing; the confused mass staggered and reeled like a drunken man, as volley after volley was poured into them from beneath. Meanwhile the insurgents who had striven to escape by the rear, repulsed by the steady fire of the 68th, returned to the pa, and increased the panic by the suddenness of their attack. The cry rose among our men that the enemy were being reinforced by the arrival of fresh troops: some one, it is said, gave the order to retire. Be that as it may, the day was already lost; the panic became general; soldiers and sailors rushed in a confused mass to the walls, and precipitated themselves into the ditch below. It was at this moment that Captain Hamilton came up with his supports: he came soon enough to find a death of glory on the walls of the Gate Pa, but too late to turn the tide of war. The supports were borne back by the flood of fugitives, and the Maoris remained masters of the field.

The soldiers blame the sailors as the cause of this disastrous retreat, and the sailors are ready enough to retaliate. It is matter of regret that they should have been mixed up together during the attack. Both fight well in their own way, but they fight best apart. The soldier has not the dash of the sailor, and the sailor is wanting in the steadiness of the soldier. It is certain that on entering the pa both became mixed up together, and the confusion which thus ensued prevented the officers from exercising that authority over the men which they might otherwise have done. When a panic once sets in, all discipline is at an end. The officers encouraged the men by voice and example; they remained at the post of duty when those under their command began to retreat; this fact alone is sufficient to explain the great disproportion between officers and men killed and wounded. It is painful to relate that our soldiers and sailors abandoned their wounded officers to their fate, and left them in the hands of the enemy; but there was one honourable exception. Samuel Mitchell, captain of the foretop of Her Majesty's ship *Harrier*, who formed one of the storming party, did all that could be expected from the British sailor in the hour of danger. He entered the pa with Commander Hay, and when that officer was mortally wounded he refused to leave him, though repeatedly urged by him to consult his own safety. The gallant sailor listened to the voice of humanity, and refused to leave his dying officer; raising him in his arms, he carried him outside the pa amid a shower of bullets. There must have been a cherub aloft watching over his safety and sheltering him from danger; no hostile bullet reached his person; the body of his leader was rescued from falling into the hands of the enemy. Mitchell, on this occasion, was doing duty as captain's coxswain, and his heroic deed was not overlooked or forgotten. It was reported to Commodore Sir William Wiseman, who recommended him for the decoration of the Victoria Cross, and we are glad to observe, from the *London Gazette* of the 26th of July, that this honourable distinction has been awarded to him. Long may he be spared to wear it!—a living witness that England can appreciate and reward such acts of gallantry. We were glad to learn that the services of Dr. Manley, R.A., had met with the same recognition. The duties of an army surgeon rarely afford him an opportunity of displaying gallantry in the field; but he has often to exhibit a moral courage as worthy of our admiration as the dashing bravery of him who heads a forlorn hope. It requires no usual amount of courage to minister to the wants of the wounded and dying on the field of battle amid the bullets of the enemy, and this was done by Dr. Manley with as much *sang froid* as if he had been performing an operation in St. George's Hospital.

It has often struck us how little faith can be placed in the best historical narratives, when we consider the difficulty, if not the impossibility, of attaining to the truth regarding an affair of recent occurrence, even when we have an opportunity of consulting the principal actors. The storming of the Gate Pa is no exception to this rule. The fugitives assert that an officer gave the order to retire; the officers deny that such an order was ever given. We have mentioned above that the panic originated from the return to the pa of the Maoris who had endeavoured to escape, and were driven back by the fire of the 68th; we have heard it strenuously urged that the Maoris never left the pa, but had merely concealed themselves in the subterraneous chambers, where they lay *perdus* till they heard the approach of the storming party. It went the round of the papers that the 68th Regiment three times in succession endeavoured to storm the pa, and were as often repulsed. It was not the duty of the 68th to storm the pa; they were assigned their position in the rear to cut off the enemy's retreat; they indignantly deny that they ever attempted an assault or suffered a repulse. Their trifling loss in killed and wounded renders it impossible that they ever quitted their position. We merely mention these discrepancies to show that a little scepticism is not out of place in the study of history, and that the future historian of the war in New Zealand will find some little difficulty in arriving at the truth.

The night of the 29th of April was, in the British camp at Tauranga, a night of deep humiliation and mutual reproach. The men were disgraced in their own eyes, and what would the people of England say? There is not a more gallant regiment in the service than the 43rd; Napier, who belonged to them, has commemorated their deeds of valour in the Peninsula, and the memory of the numerous engagements in which they have taken part is preserved on their colours. But now where were all the laurels they had won in the Peninsula and India? Soiled and trampled in the dust, and by whom? Not by forces equal to them in arms and discipline; not by foemen worthy of their steel; but by a horde of half-naked, half-armed savages, whom they had been taught to despise. They erred in despising them overmuch; they forgot, or they had never learned, that the defenders of that pa belonged to a race reckless of life, loving war for its own sake, who were then fighting, as such a race ever will fight, for their homes, their lands, their liberty, their all.

The time may come when the Maori race will be subdued, but that will only be when the Maori race has been extirpated. Would that the people of England knew this as well as the colonists of New Zealand! A disgraceful chapter in the future history of our country might then have never to be written. The storming party learned when it was too late that the courage of despair rises superior to all human calculations of success, and that no bounds can be assigned to the heroic powers of endurance of men fighting for their liberty. It could be no ordinary race that waited patiently for eight hours, with no other shelter from the descending hurricane of shot and shell than a few boughs of trees covered with earth, till the moment had arrived for rushing forth and rolling back their assailants like a broken wave. It adds nothing to our glory to detract from the virtues of our adversaries. In the Maori character there is much to condemn, but much also to admire and to imitate. If, instead of being exterminated, they were embodied into regiments, commanded by men who spoke their language and studied their character, they would be found as useful as the Sikhs in India; and, on the ground of public expediency as well as of Christian principle, it would be better to save than to destroy. The Maori race once extinguished can never be restored, and it would be impious to imagine that any one race has been created in vain.

But what was the fate of the wounded and dying officers left in the pa? Night closed over them and concealed them in impenetrable darkness. No less than seven officers of the 43rd were there, besides others belonging to the navy. They were in the hands of those who cut off Captain Lloyd's head, and sent it round among the other tribes as a trophy of victory. The vanquished soldiery could hear the yells of triumph from the pa; some even imagined that they heard the shrieks of their tortured countrymen, but this was only the work of the imagination. The Maoris remembered mercy in the hour of victory, and treated our dying officers with humanity worthy of the imitation and admiration of all civilized nations. No hostile hand hastened on the hour of death, already fast approaching. Their persons and their property were alike respected. An effort was made to relieve the sufferings of those who were still alive. Lieutenant-Colonel Booth, commanding the 43rd, was shot through the spine and the arm. His wounds, though mortal, did not produce immediate death. He stood leaning against the wall of the pa, suffering intensely from thirst; around him lay his slaughtered officers. Our pen shrinks from recording the sufferings he endured throughout the night of horror which he survived. He had risen rapidly to command, and was in the very prime of his strength and manhood. Tall, erect, and powerful, he looked like a man who could ward off death for half a century; he had done so in India and elsewhere, but now he had met his fate at the Gate Pa at Tauranga. This was the first time that he had led his regiment into action, and had they behaved in a manner worthy of their high reputation? Alas!

There lay the two Glovers, the sons of an English clergyman, on the field of gore, but not of glory. They were lovely in their lives, and in death they were not separated. We had seen the elder fall in the foremost of the fray, and the younger, who loved him with more than a brother's love, rush forward with a loud and bitter cry. A brother's love may do much, but it cannot reverse the iron decrees of fate, which take no account of human affection or sorrow. It was in vain that he raised him in his arms, and strove to bear him from the field—a hostile bullet brought both the brothers to the ground, and left them side by side, with the tide of life ebbing fast away. If there is a mother in some distant English rectory weeping, like Rachel, for her children, because they are not, or a father lamenting their loss, let us comfort them with the assurance that in life and in death they were all that the fondest parent could wish.

We have read of a martyr's sufferings at the stake: we question whether in intensity they equalled those endured by Colonel Booth during that fearful night. He never lost his consciousness, and an occasional groan escaped from his lips. An armed Maori stole up to him. There was no sorrow in the thought that he had come to give him the *coup de grâce;* but it was not so. The heart of the half-savage man was touched by the spectacle of woe. Colonel Booth read this feeling in his face, and muttered, "Water." The Maori shook his head, to show that there was none in the pa, and slipped out in search of some. He never returned, but next morning his body was found at the brink of the swamp, with a pannikin by his side. A soldier of the 68th, ignorant of his purpose, had fired at him with fatal precision, and arrested him on his errand of mercy. The will must be taken for the deed. The exposure of his life to all but certain death from the humane desire to give a cup of water to a dying enemy shall not be without its reward.

In the course of the night the insurgents abandoned the pa, and made good their retreat by the rear, without suffering much loss from the 68th, who had been placed there to intercept them. No blame can be attached to the 68th; no regiment has ever been able to prevent the Maoris from effecting their escape. They pass with ease through swamps where the British soldier could never gain a footing. Amphibious in their habits, they are as much at home in the water as on land. Their loss on this occasion was trifling: it certainly did not exceed thirty men, while ours amounted to 104 killed and wounded, including a larger portion of officers than on any other occasion where British troops have been engaged. The causes of this disproportion are already known to our readers.

For a time it was not known in the British camp that the enemy had evacuated the pa. The frantic yells had died away—no sound was heard to disturb the stillness of the night. Tempted by the long-continued silence, Major Greaves, of the 70th, stole up to the ditch, mounted the breach, and found the pa empty. Returning to camp, he reported what he had seen, but no attempt was made to enter the pa till daybreak. The enemy had fled, carrying their wounded with them. Colonel Booth was still alive, but the surgeon told him that his hours were numbered. He was borne to the camp, where he survived till the following day. Before his death he was visited by General Cameron. "I endeavoured, sir, to carry out your orders; I am sorry that I have failed. I at least tried to do my duty." "You have done so nobly," was the general's reply, as he pressed the hand of the dying soldier, in whose breast the sense of duty was stronger than the love of life. It is pleasing to record the virtues of men who, in this inglorious warfare, have gone down to the grave unwept, unhonoured, and unsung, because England takes little interest in a war with savages, and dismisses the subject for others more attractive. The other dead or dying officers were removed from the pa. Captain Hamilton, of the 43rd, breathed only once after his body was found. A bullet had passed through his head, and so altered his features that it was difficult to recognise the handsome face with which we were once so familiar. We had known him years ago in the East, when he was an ensign in the 10th Regiment. During the interval he had served throughout the whole of the Indian campaign, and followed Havelock to Lucknow. He belonged to a race of soldiers, and was every inch a soldier himself. Poor Hamilton! we think of him still as he sat at the mess-table, expatiating on the capture of Lucknow, or some cognate subject, to a group of admiring ensigns who loved him for the dangers he had passed. He served in the 10th Regiment with the present Sir Henry Havelock, now on the staff in New Zealand, who always spoke of him with respect as a gallant soldier, and betrayed the deepest sorrow on learning that he had fallen.

The cause of the sudden panic which seized our men at the Gate Pa will never be known with certainty. It would be easy to show, from ancient and modern history, that the best troops are subject to such panics, which often spring from the most trifling causes. Terror, like courage, is sympathetic; it spreads like an infectious disease, from man to man, till all are swept away before it. At the battle of Fridlingen, fought on the 14th of October, 1702, between the French and Austrians, the former almost lost the day through a sudden panic which seized their ranks. The infantry had reached the summit of a hill to dislodge the German cavalry, and had succeeded in doing so, when a voice suddenly exclaimed, "*Nous sommes coupés!*" On this every regiment turned and fled. It was fortunate that in Marshal Villars they had a leader equal to the occasion. "*Allons, mes amis!*" he cried; "*la victoire est à nous! Vive le roi!*" "*Vive le roi!*" replied the soldiers, still retreating as fast as they could. With some difficulty Villars rallied them, and led them back to victory; but if a single regiment had attacked them at that moment the result would have been the same as at the Gate Pa. The most trifling incident may make a whole army retire in confusion. Such an incident occurred during the Indian campaign. A body of our men were on the march, preceded by some of their officers on horseback. A horse became restive, and threw its rider; other horsemen rushed to his assistance; clouds of dust were raised; the cry rose from the ranks that the rebels were upon them; a sudden panic was the result, and our soldiers fled when no one pursued. It was fortunate no enemy was at hand to profit by the confusion and terror occasioned by the nowise remarkable incident of a surgeon falling from his horse.

The 43rd Regiment have already atoned for the disaster at Te Papa. A few weeks after that event they again encountered the enemy at Te Ranga, and proved themselves worthy of their Peninsular fame and the glorious names inscribed on their standards. A temporary reverse is no proof that a regiment has degenerated; it is often the occasion, as in this instance, of eliciting the display of a higher amount of courage than might have attended ordinary success, and of teaching a deeper respect for those whose military spirit and capacity we have been disposed to under-estimate.

CHAPTER XXIV.

ENSIGN M'KENNA AND THE VICTORIA CROSS.

LITTLE is known in England of the war which has been carried on in New Zealand. Despatches are occasionally published, and the names of those who have distinguished themselves in the field are honourably mentioned; but the seat of war is too remote for the people of England to feel anything but a passing interest in a contest which they entered upon with reluctance, and would gladly see finished. And yet in this struggle between British soldiers and hostile Maoris, deeds of valour have been performed which history will not willingly let die; and the name of McKenna will be as gratefully remembered in New Zealand as those of the heroes of the Victoria Cross Gallery in England. We hope the day is not very far distant when he will figure in that gallery with the other brave men who have carved their way with their swords into Mr. Desanges' temple of fame.

We listened to McKenna's simple narrative the other evening in a rude hut at the camp of Awamutu, in the very centre of the seat of war. We have heard some of the most brilliant speakers of the day, and been enthralled by the magic power of their eloquence; but the interest excited by the charms of such oratory was less thrilling than that produced by the soldier's plain story of deeds in which he himself was the principal actor. Before submitting that narrative to our readers, which we shall do as much as possible in McKenna's own words, we may simply premise that, while of Irish descent, he is a native of Leeds, and has served seventeen years in the 65th Regiment, the greater part of that time as a non-commissioned officer. He is an intelligent, well-educated man, in the very prime of life, well adapted to occupy the rank which has been assigned to him, and worthy to wear the Queen's own Cross on his breast. He has always borne an excellent character in a regiment which is distinguished for the excellent conduct of its soldiers, and the strong feeling of attachment which they cherish to their officers, from the kindness and consideration with which they have been treated during eighteen years' service in this remote island. This is McKenna's story.

"In the beginning of July, 1863, the 65th Regiment was stationed in Auckland. We were all expecting immediate orders to embark for England, and our hearts beat high at the thought of seeing our native land, which, after the absence of many years, had never been forgotten, and was now dearer than ever. The 2nd Battalion of the 18th Royal Irish had just landed, and were daily expecting to receive orders to embark, when, to our great surprise, we were told to hold ourselves in readiness for active service in the field. It was no use grumbling, so in a few hours we were ready. Some of us, I dare say, liked the excitement of a campaign more than the monotony of a long sea-voyage; and a few inspiriting words from the colonel made us forget all thoughts of home in the excitement of the coming struggle. On the 9th of July we marched from Auckland, and, though I say it myself, a better regiment than ours never was, and never will be, seen in this country. We bade farewell to our wives and children, and camped for the night at Otahahu, nine miles from Auckland. Thence we proceeded to the Queen's Redoubt, which 300 of our men left on Sunday, the 12th of July, for Tuakan, under the command of our dear old chief, Colonel Wyatt, C.B. Tuakan is about sixteen miles from the Queen's Redoubt. It stands on a precipitous cliff overlooking the Waikato river. It is the site of an old Maori fortification, and is naturally a place of great strength. The road was difficult and dangerous, with the dense bush on either side, but we reached Tuakan in safety, where we soon cleared the ground and erected a redoubt, which, in honour of our dear young Princess of Wales, was named Alexandra. If she saw it she would not be ashamed of it, for there is not a better one in the island. Well, perhaps the Queen's Redoubt is a little better, as in right it ought to be; but in strength and beauty of design ours is next best.

"It was nearly finished on the 19th of July, when Colonel Wyatt withdrew one-half of the men, and left the other 150 under the command of Captain Swift. He is dead now, poor fellow, and no words of praise from me can reach his ear; but a better officer never carried sword or wore the Queen's uniform. God bless him! I was only a poor sergeant; but if I had been his own brother, he could not have been kinder to me. His example told upon us all; we all liked our duties, and tried to do all we could to suppress the rebellion. His first act was to seize a number of rebel canoes and to man them with crews from his own detachment; in this way we contrived to seize large quantities of potatoes and other provisions from the hostile natives. But he did more than this: he extemporized a body of Forest Rangers, who scoured the dense bush around the redoubt, kept the natives at a distance. He had heard of atrocities they had committed on defenceless women and children, and longed for an opportunity of meeting them in the field. Poor fellow! he little dreamed that his first meeting with them would be his last. But such are the chances of war. If he had lived, the world would have heard more of him, for there was never a braver or a better officer in the British or any other service.

"Well, things went on as usual till the 7th of September. On the morning of that day we had a visit from Mr. Armitage, the resident magistrate of the township of Havelock. He had charge of five large canoes, manned by natives, and loaded with forage and provisions, which were proceeding from Camerontown, a friendly Maori pa, to the Queen's Redoubt. The forage had been brought up from the Waikato Heads; the barque *City of Melbourne* had conveyed it there from Auckland. The river transport had been established in consequence of the difficulty of transporting stores by the great South Road; and as the canoes were paddled by friendly natives, no one imagined that there could be much danger of their being attacked.

"I shall never forget the morning of the 7th of September. Captain Swift was asleep in his tent when Mr. Armitage arrived. He wanted one of the large canoes we had seized, and I had to go three times to the captain's tent before I could wake him. He was usually a light sleeper, but it was different on this occasion. It did not strike me much at the moment, but I have often thought of it since. Well, Mr. Armitage left, and nothing unusual happened till about eleven o'clock. I was down at the landing-place superintending some work, when all at once I heard the report of several shots. I stood and listened. The shots were followed by successive volleys, which gradually subsided into the regular, or rather irregular, firing of a smart skirmish. This went on for about a quarter of an hour. I knew from the direction of the sound that the fighting was going on at Camerontown. I hurried to the captain, and told him I was sure the rebels had attacked Mr. Armitage's party. While I was speaking, all at once we saw a large volume of smoke curling up in the air close to the pa. We both came to the conclusion that the rebels had set fire to a house which had been recently built for Mr. Armitage.

"About half an hour after this we saw a canoe, paddled by four natives, coming up the river. We knew from the way they used their paddles that something was wrong. Their faces were as green as the French Emperor's at Solferino, and their teeth were chattering with terror. They were so panic-struck that it took some time before we learned from them that the rebels had formed an ambuscade, and attacked them while off their guard. Mr. Armitage and two white men had been killed, and all the friendly natives dispersed or slain; these four only survived to tell their fate. Thirty or forty men, women, and children, had perished.

"We are pretty well used to such things out here, so no time was wasted in idle words. In half an hour we had a party, consisting of Lieutenant Butler, myself, two sergeants, one bugler, and fifty rank and file, under arms, the whole under the command of Captain Swift. We were all too eager for the fray to care much for eating, so we snatched a hasty dinner and were off by one o'clock. People at home can have no idea of a march through the bush. We had to cross nine or ten miles of swamp, intersected by rivers scarcely practicable for regular troops, so as to strike the foot of the wooded range of hills on a spur of which stands the pa of Camerontown. We had to creep through the dense bush, but there is no difficulty persistent pluck may not surmount. We were all tired enough when we reached a small clearing about half-past four o'clock in the afternoon, and felt the need of the evening *tot* of rum which was now served out. One sergeant and ten privates, on receiving theirs, were sent on in advance; the main body followed a little after. On proceeding a few hundred yards they discovered that the advanced guard had strayed from the right path, and we could not shout without attracting the notice of the natives. We felt it rather hard to be deprived of their services, as we had no men to spare, but it was decided that we should go on. Our force was now reduced to two officers and forty-three men, but Captain Swift was a host in himself; we would have followed him anywhere and against any odds.

"It was at this juncture that I had an opportunity of showing some qualities which have brought me under the notice of General Cameron, and procured for me such honours as have rarely, if ever before, been bestowed on a British soldier. There are as good men as I am in the ranks, unknown to fame, but time and chance happeneth to all. I never dreamed of honours—my only desire was to do my duty. I asked and obtained leave from Captain Swift to advance forty or fifty yards in front of the men to act as scout, an office for which I was well qualified from former experience. I took a direct course through the bush towards the spot where the natives were supposed to be. About five o'clock I reached a large opening, where I could plainly see the rebels' encampment in the bush, about four hundred yards in advance. Crossing the clearing in a stooping position and at a smart pace, I again made for the bush, followed by the whole detachment. Five minutes after we could distinctly hear the sound of the rebels' voices, and Captain Swift, imagining that they were advancing by the same path to attack us, threw his men into ambush. On finding that they refused to advance, I crept stealthily up to within a few yards of them. Unlike most Maori war parties, they were laughing and chattering, which led me to think they had been making free with the rum they had seized in the canoes. I returned and reported this to Captain Swift, who came to the same conclusion as myself, that they were all drunk. The order was at once given to fix bayonets and charge. Our men advanced, led by Captain Swift, Lieutenant Butler, and myself, three abreast, the path not admitting more. When we had stolen up to within a few yards of the rebels, our leader gave the word 'Charge!' The word had scarcely passed his lips when, as if by enchantment, the whole bush was lighted up with a terrific volley. It seemed as if one of the extinct volcanoes so common here had suddenly opened its crater and begun to belch forth flames. The enemy were so close when they fired that some of their coarse powder was actually found sticking in the faces of our soldiers. For a moment our men staggered beneath this heavy fire, but it was only for a moment, for, immediately recovering themselves, they closed up in a line of skirmishers in the bush, and brought their rifles to bear on their dusky foes. I had taken cover behind a tree close to Lieutenant Butler, for the purpose of reloading my rifle, and even in that hour of danger I could not help admiring his bravery. He stood at the left front, a little in advance, cheering on the men by his voice and still more by his example. I saw him discharge his revolver right and left; three Maoris fell beneath his fire, and were dragged into the bush by their friends. I was still admiring his heroic courage and gallant bearing, when all at once I saw him sink slowly to the ground, as if his spirit were struggling against some mortal blow. I sprang forward with two others to his assistance, and on raising him in my arms he said, 'Lead on the men, McKenna.' Surprised at such an order, I looked round to see where the captain was, and there he lay by his side mortally wounded. No language can express the anguish I felt on seeing one who, though my superior officer, had always treated me with the greatest kindness, in this condition. If he had been my own brother I could not have felt it

Captain Swift directing M'Kenna to take command of the detachment

more. Poor Captain Swift! I shall never forget the last look you gave me, or cease to regret your loss.

"'Are you wounded, sir?' was my first exclamation.

"'Oh, yes, McKenna; very severely,' he replied.

"On seeing me loading my rifle, he said—

"'Never mind loading. Take my revolver and lead on the men.'

"These were the last words this good and gallant soldier ever spoke to me. I mechanically took up the revolver, gave one last look at my dying officer, and then shouted, like one possessed—

"'Men, the captain is wounded; charge!'

"I rushed on at the head of the men, and we drove the natives before us like sheep. We now found ourselves in a small opening on the crest of the hill. The natives found shelter in the bush to our left and front, where they opened fire on our little band of thirty-eight men. Our position was critical. One of our officers was mortally, the other severely, wounded; ten miles of swamp and bush lay between us and any succour; around us were three hundred savages thirsting for our blood. I think it was God who gave me strength to act as I did that day. Assuming an air of coolness (which, in my heart, I was far from feeling), I ordered my men to extend in skirmishing order across the clearing, and to keep up a steady fire. My object was to hold the place for a time, till the advanced guard, attracted by the firing, should join Corporal Ryan and the four men left in charge of the wounded officers, so as to have them carried well on to the redoubt before the approach of night compelled us to retire.

"The Maoris had been encamped on the spot now occupied by our party, and had left a great many things, such as tents, sacks and kits of potatoes, behind. These our men formed into a sort of breastwork, and kept as well under cover as they could. Several of the natives climbed up the trees in order to fire over the breastwork, and one of them was brought down in splendid style by Private Smith of ours, his fall causing a *thud* like the fall (though louder) of a plump partridge. After waiting till about six o'clock,

I resolved to retire by the way we came; but I had scarcely given the order when we were met with a tremendous volley from the very quarter by which we intended to retreat. The enemy took deliberate aim, and three of our men fell badly wounded. I then brought the party back to our former position, and sent for my brother sergeant to consult with him as to what should be done. His proposal was to run the gauntlet through the Maoris, and to make for Mr. Armitage's pa, which was about 150 yards farther on in the bush. He thought we could establish ourselves there and hold out till we received assistance; but I knew that the thing was impracticable. The pa was commanded by a hill from which the enemy could have amused themselves by shooting us at leisure; in short, the place was untenable.

"A poor fellow of the name of Stephen Grace being close at hand when I put the question, and always ready to offer his advice, proposed that we should form three sides of a hollow square, and retire down the hill to our rear, which was not wooded. I could scarcely help smiling at such a foolish proposal, when all at once I heard a deep sigh at my elbow, and on turning round saw poor Grace rolling down the hill in mortal agony, till his head lodged in a fern-bush, and all was over. I ordered the bugler to take his rifle and belt, and to cover him over with fern. I had no stretcher, and it was impossible for the men to carry his body with safety to themselves; he was now beyond the reach of harm, and we left him there with the green fern as his mort-cloth.

"At a quarter past six o'clock, I ordered the wounded to be taken down the hill to the rear by a path that led across the valley to the dense bush on the other side. I felt sure that a native path in that direction would lead to the Mauku or Pa Kekoe, both military posts. I knew that all depended on our coolness and self-possession. If we fell into confusion, or showed any signs of fear, we were lost; so I told the front rank of skirmishers to fire a volley and retire down the hill, giving at the same time a ringing cheer as if about to charge. As soon as they were established below, I ordered the rear rank to do the same thing. Nothing could be better than the conduct of the men at this trying moment; the movement was executed with as much steadiness as if they had been on parade. On reaching the foot of the hill we found, to our infinite delight, a beautiful stream of clear water. We saw by the footprints on the bank that the Maoris had been there; we knew it to be them because they turn their feet inward when walking, and spread their toes out like a duck in crossing swampy ground. They soon gave us clearer evidence of their presence by rushing out of the bush and opening a heavy fire on our men, who as readily returned it. The cowardly villains had not courage to descend from the crest of the hill, but kept up their fire there till our party entered the bush.

"About eight o'clock we began to make our way through the bush, but soon discovered that we had lost the path. On this I told my men that we must remain where we were till next morning. I then formed them into a square, and ordered every man to *speak* his name, so as to ascertain whether any were missing. Two men failed to answer; both were wounded — Private Whittle slightly, across the scalp, and Private Bryne severely through the right hand. On inquiry, I found that, after drinking at the stream, they had pushed on by themselves instead of waiting for the main body, and diverged from the path without being missed; but we shall have more to say of their adventures presently. I then gave my orders for the night: every man had to put on his great-coat (all had brought them with them folded across their right shoulders); to sit with his rifle ready in his hand; no pipes to be lit; not a word to be spoken. I knew that this was the only way to elude the enemy and to reach the redoubt in safety. Under the tender mercies of Divine Providence, my efforts proved successful. About four o'clock next morning I placed myself at the head of my men, and we resumed our march through the bush. We pushed our way with difficulty through the dense masses of supplejack and creepers; we crossed over hills thickly covered with wood; we descended ravines that were almost perpendicular. No word of complaint was heard—all struggled on for their lives. At length, at eight o'clock A.M., our gallant little band emerged from the bush and found themselves in the open country about seven miles from the redoubt, which they could see in the distance. Rushing straight ahead, they met Colonel Murray with a hundred men of the 65th Regiment coming to their assistance. We now knew that we were safe, and it would have done your heart good to have heard the hearty English cheer that burst forth from both parties on first seeing one another. I know, too, that many a heartfelt, grateful prayer was breathed to Almighty God for having preserved them through all their dangers.

"Our joy was mingled with tender regret on learning that Captain Swift was no more. He died at seven o'clock the previous night. Corporal Ryan and Privates Talbot and Bulford remained with him to the last. They carried him in their arms for some distance after he had received his death-wound, but the agony he suffered was so intense that he requested them to lay him down on the ground. They placed him behind a fallen tree and concealed him as well as they could; they then crept down beside him. On hearing the heavy firing, he said to Corporal Ryan, 'I am sure McKenna has gained the pa.' Soon after they heard the natives coming through the bush; the report of firearms told them that the Maoris had attacked the advanced guard who were hastening to their assistance.

"After a short skirmish the advanced guard had to retire to make for the redoubt, which they reached about nine o'clock the same night. In this affair the natives, in firing, actually came behind the tree under which Captain Swift was lying with Ryan, Bulford, and Talbot. He begged of them not to leave him. They assured him that they never dreamed of doing so; they would stay by him till the last; they were ready to die with him if necessary. They told him that his moaning might attract the notice of the enemy. On hearing this, the poor fellow placed his hand on his mouth to restrain his agony till the Maoris retired. His last words to Ryan were, 'Give me your hand.' He pressed it, and then died as quietly as if he had fallen asleep, which I am sure he did in Jesus.

With reverent and loving hands they covered the body with fern, and started for the redoubt at break of day. On their way they met the party sent to their relief.

"I must now return to Lieutenant Butler. Privates Thomas and Cole remained with him all night in the bush. He suffered much from his wound, and complained bitterly of the cold, though the men had thrown their two great-coats over him. There is no sacrifice a soldier will not willingly make for an officer he loves. Private Thomas took off his blue serge shirt and put it over him, remaining all night in his cotton shirt and trousers. Well, I agree with you it was a generous act; but so great is the attachment of our well-commanded regiment to their officers, that they would go through fire and water to serve them.

"I sent back a guide with Colonel Murray's party to conduct them to the scene of action, and pushed on for the redoubt, which we reached at eleven o'clock A.M. We were much worn out, but grateful to God for our deliverance. In the evening Colonel Murray's party returned; they brought in Captain Swift's body, but could find no traces of the two men who were missing. They gave up the search as hopeless, and, embarking on board the steamer *Arrow*, returned to head-quarters. About ten o'clock next morning 100 men of the 70th Regiment marched into the redoubt; they had been guided through the bush from the Queen's Redoubt by that most efficient officer Captain Greaves, of the 40th. We left the Alexandra Redoubt under their charge, while 100 of our men, under the command of Lieutenant Warren, started in search of their missing comrades, Captain Greaves accompanying the party. We reached the scene of action about four o'clock P.M., but found that the Maoris had disappeared. In a subsequent despatch Captain Greaves estimated that they must have amounted to little short of 300 men, and, judging from their number of sleeping-places and other indications on the spot, I am inclined to think that this estimate was not beyond the mark.

"I struck the tracks of the missing men at the bottom of the hill where they had last been seen. A little farther on we found one of their pannikins in the road. Darkness setting in we were obliged to return, but not before we had visited the pa at Camerontown, where we found quantities of maize, bran, and oats scattered about the beach, partly burned and rendered unfit for use. We found a canoe on the beach which I wished to destroy, but was prevented by Captain Greaves, who thoughtfully observed that it might be the means of saving one or both of the poor fellows who were missing. We now made for the redoubt, bearing with us the body of Private Grace, which we found on the same spot where we had left it. We reached the redoubt at half-past twelve o'clock the following morning, when we learned that Whittle, one of the missing men, was on the other side of the river calling for help. From our long residence in the colony we have many skilful paddlers in the ranks; in a few minutes a canoe was manned, and in half-an-hour the poor fellow was inside the redoubt, carefully attended by Assistant-Surgeon Styles, of the 40th Regiment. He had been exactly sixty hours without food, and was much exhausted.

"When sufficiently recovered, he informed us that after leaving the party on the 7th, he and Bryne took the path to the left, instead of following the one to the right as we did. He had not proceeded far when he became unconscious; how long he remained in that state he could not tell. On being restored to consciousness by the drops of rain falling on his face, he found himself alone; Bryne had gone on. For two days he wandered about the bush, trying in vain to find an opening; at one time, while following a native path, he nearly fell into the hands of a party of rebels. He was close upon them, when, warned by the sound of their voices, he crept back into the bush without being seen. A still more singular incident occurred to him the previous evening. He heard the footsteps of our party at Camerontown, and, rushing forward, caught sight of them as they were entering the bush on their return from the canoes. Such was the impression produced by this sight that all his faculties, bodily and mental, were completely paralysed; he could neither speak nor move; when he recovered from his temporary prostration the party had disappeared. For a moment he was tempted to believe that he was labouring under some mental hallucination, the result of over-anxiety and bodily weakness, but it was not so. Finding no traces of our party, he hurried down to the river, where he found the canoe which Captain Greaves had the foresight to preserve. Using a rough piece of board as a paddle, he contrived to make his way up the river till he found himself within four hundred yards of the redoubt, but on the opposite side. Here he had the misfortune to drop the piece of board, and could only save himself from being swept away in the canoe by clinging to the long weeds in the shallow part of the river till his cries brought his comrades to his assistance.

"Poor Bryne, the other missing man, was less fortunate. He wandered about in the bush till he was surprised by a party of the enemy. We learned afterwards that he begged hard for his life, but he had to deal with wretches who knew no mercy. Five balls were lodged in his body, and he was stark and stiff when we found him. My story is now told; every one admits that it was one of the most desperate affairs that have occurred in the course of this war.

"I arrived at the Queen's Redoubt, and was immediately sent for by General Cameron. I found him surrounded by his staff, but the moment he saw me he advanced and shook me warmly by the hand. 'Sergeant,' he said, 'you have done well.' 'And I am amply rewarded by this honour,' was my immediate answer; 'not to myself alone, sir, but to the brave fellows who were with me, is the credit due.' 'I know it,' said the general; 'there is not another corps in the colony could have done as the 65th.' Nor was this all; in his despatch to Governor Grey, General Cameron expressed his admiration and approval of our dear old regiment in the most complimentary terms, and it was on his recommendation that I received my commission and the Victoria Cross. Corporal Ryan was also gazetted for the Victoria Cross, but never lived to wear it. His death was in keeping with his life; he was accidentally drowned near Tuakan while trying to save a drunken comrade. Three months after their gallant conduct, Privates Bulford, Talbot, Cole, and Thomas received the medal for distinguished conduct in the field, the first two for remaining with the body of Captain Swift, and the two latter for waiting on Lieutenant Butler and conveying him towards the Redoubt."

"In all this desperate affair did you ever think of your wife and children, McKenna?"

"Not once, sir. She asked me the same question the first time we met, and seemed a little put out when I gave her the same answer, but she understood it all afterwards. In the excitement of an engagement a soldier can only think of immediate duty; when the danger is past he feels how grateful he ought to be to Him who has preserved his life for those who are dearer to him than life itself."

CHAPTER XXV.

SERGEANT-MAJOR LUCAS, OF THE 40TH REGIMENT, AND THE VICTORIA CROSS.

E had the pleasure, a few weeks ago, of seeing Lieutenant-General Sir Duncan A. Cameron, K.C.B., the officer commanding the forces in New Zealand, attach with his own hands the Cross of Valour to McKenna's breast, and declare, in the presence of his own regiment, that a more chivalrous soldier had never been invested with this symbol of his Sovereign's favour. Sir Duncan, at the same time, expressed his regret that he who had shared in the danger could not share in the reward, but rejoiced to think that Corporal Ryan's death was in keeping with his life, which he had lost in trying to save a comrade from drowning. Three cheers were given for Ensign McKenna, and none joined more heartily in those cheers than Sergeant-Major Lucas, of the 40th Regiment, who had received the same decoration from the hands of the general at the close of the Taranaki war in 1861.

A brief sketch of the island, and the causes that have led to that and the present war, will not be without interest. The aboriginal inhabitants of New Zealand are known by the name of Maoris—a word which in their language signifies indigenous to the soil—and are about 60,000 in number. They are supposed to have emigrated, about four centuries ago, from the Society and Sandwich Islands, and to have dispossessed another race, many traces of whose existence are still to be found in New Zealand. In appearance they bear a striking resemblance to those gipsies who may still occasionally be seen in the neighbourhood of Norwood and the Crystal Palace. They are a fine, powerful, muscular race, naturally fond of war, and possessed of great energy of character. They have made great progress in civilization since the island was first discovered, in 1642, by Abel Tasman, a Dutch navigator, who named it after his own country. It was visited in 1769 and 1777 by Captain Cook, who took possession of it in the name of the English Government, and suggested that it should be used as a penal settlement. He introduced pigs, cabbages and turnips into the island, and his name is still familiar to the natives as one of their greatest benefactors. Their are several fountains known as Cook's Springs, and the rum he occasionally distributed among them is gratefully remembered as "Te wai toki a rangi"—Cook's sweet water of heaven. While the natives were kind and hospitable to those who treated them well, they were ever ready to revenge any injury they received, and murdered the crews of several vessels of whose misconduct they had reason to complain. Thus, in 1809, the sailors on board the *Boyd*, an English ship, under the command of Captain Thompson, were massacred at Wangaroa. This melancholy event was the result of the captain's imprudence. Among the passengers was a Maori chief, who had visited Sydney, and was now on his way to his native land. Being short of hands, the captain requested him to assist the sailors in working the ship. On his refusal to do so he was tied to the mainmast and flogged. This degrading punishment roused all the savage passions of his nature, but, disguising his feelings, he persuaded the captain to visit Wangaroa, of which he was the leading chief. All suspicion was disarmed by the friendly bearing of the natives, who were only biding their time. Watching for a favourable opportunity, they attacked the ship, and murdered the captain, the crew, and many passengers. A similar calamity had overtaken the crews of two French vessels, in consequence of their having unintentionally desecrated the place set apart for the burial of the natives.

When the Maoris were plundering the *Boyd's* cargo, they came upon some boxes of seed, which was scattered about as useless. It took root, however, and in a few years the surrounding district was overgrown with garlic and parrot's-bill acacia (*Clianthus Puniceus*), which yields a beautiful flower used by the natives as an ornament for the ear. After this the island was little visited except by whaling ships (the captains of which were sometimes so accommodating as to lend their ovens to prepare the banquets of human flesh so much relished by the Maoris) till 1839, when the New Zealand Land Company obtained a charter and began to form settlements in the south. It is worthy of remark, that so early as 1835 Great Britain formally recognised the independence of the natives and bestowed on them a national flag; but no sooner had the new company begun to buy extensive tracts of land from the natives, than the missionaries interfered and induced the home government to send out a governor. As a governor over an independent race would have been a contradiction in terms, the difficulty was obviated by inducing a number of natives to assemble at Waitangi, and to attach their signatures to a treaty in which they acknowledged the supremacy of our Queen. Rum and blankets were liberally distributed among the natives, who were ready to sign anything. Such was the origin of the treaty of Waitangi, on which alone our claims to the loyalty and obedience of the Maori race can be said to rest. It was a mere farce, unworthy of the ministers of religion who originated it—equally unworthy of the great nation who sanctioned it. As well might the nine tailors of Tooley-street, who dubbed themselves the men of England, have undertaken to dispose of the liberty of their countrymen, as the signers of the Waitangi treaty to barter away for rum and blankets the future independence of the Maori race. And yet it is in virtue of this worthless document, the authors of which in any civilized country would have been liable to an indictment for conspiracy, that we profess to treat the Maoris as a subject race, and make war against them as rebels when they try to assert their independence.

Notwithstanding the treaty of Waitangi, the Maoris continued to retain their own customs, manners, and laws, and to act in every way as an independent people. Their chiefs, far from acknowledging the supremacy of the British crown, frequently waged war against us and with one another. When they fell into our hands they were never treated as rebels. In short the Maoris tolerated our presence in the island because they found our colonists useful for purposes of trade; but when they discovered that the British population was constantly on the increase, and their lands fast slipping from their possession, they resolved to assert their ancient independence, and to pass such laws as would prevent the alienation of their property. They were willing that the colonists should remain subject to their own Sovereign and laws, but they claimed the same right for themselves, and in the exercise of that right elected one of their chiefs to be Maori king, and formed themselves into a league to prevent any lands from being sold by any individual member of a tribe without the consent of the whole. Such a league would at once be pronounced illegal in England, where it is a recognised principle that every man has a right to do as he likes with his own; but the Maori tenure of land is different. It rarely belongs to a single family or to a single individual; it is the property of the whole tribe, much in the same way as a common in England is the property of all whose lands are adjacent. Every member of a tribe has the right to hunt and fish over the land which belongs to the whole community; no man, not even a chief, has a right to dispose of any part of that land without the consent of the whole tribe. When a piece of land is sold the money is distributed equally among all who are entitled to a share, the chief rarely retaining anything for himself. The only way in which a piece of land can become private property is by an individual selecting and cultivating it with the consent of the tribe; it then belongs to all the descendants of the original cultivator, who may be dispersed among other tribes, and it cannot be sold without their consent. Now this peculiar tenure of land was the cause of the Taranaki war of 1860-61, and of the present war in which so many valuable lives have been lost. The establishment of a Maori sovereignty would have ended in nothing; the Maori king was a mere puppet in the hands of a few ambitious chiefs; the great body of the nation would never have acknowledged his supremacy; and the movement would have covered its originators with ridicule. But when the local government interfered with the rights of property, and violated the first principles of Maori law by purchasing from an individual land which belonged to the whole tribe, and enforcing possession by violence, they struck at the root of Maori independence, and brought on that fierce struggle of which we have not yet seen the end. The Maoris are fighting for their lands and liberty, while we are fighting for British supremacy. The settlers have already more land than they can cultivate, but this has not prevented them from coveting that which belongs to the natives. If they had waited patiently, a period would have arrived when the Maoris would have seen it to be to their own advantage to part with lands which they cannot turn to any profitable account, but they were unwilling to wait, and endeavoured to compel the natives to enter into their views. Such a policy was as imprudent as it was unjust; there were few troops in the colony; and when the natives flew to arms in 1860, the government had to appeal to the Australian colonies for assistance.

The appeal was not made in vain; all the troops that could be spared were despatched at once to the seat of war, including four companies of the 40th Regiment, detachments of which were stationed at Melbourne and Hobart Town. Sergeant-Major Lucas, who then held the rank of colour-sergeant, arrived in New Zealand in 1860, and took part in all the engagements we had with the enemy till the temporary cessation of hostilities in 1861. The Maoris do not fight in the same way as Europeans; it is part of their policy to avoid giving battle in the open field. Their mode of warfare is to conceal themselves in the bush, and to fire upon our men when off their guard; or to erect pas or redoubts, surrounded by a ditch, and surmounted by wooden palisades. Inclosed behind the walls of these pas, they coolly await the approach of our men, and pour upon them destructive volleys while they are advancing to the assault. When their position is no longer tenable, they evacuate the pa, and such is their perfect knowledge of the country that they often contrive to escape through the ranks of our men with little loss. The evacuation of a pa is not considered a defeat; they select a favourable site, and proceed at once to erect another, which has also to be stormed. Many valuable British lives are thus lost, and the war would be interminable, were it not that we may cut off their supplies and ultimately starve them into subjection.

The late war was carried on in the Province of Auckland; but it was in Taranaki, the capital of which is New Plymouth, that Sergeant-Major Lucas won his laurels. He is a fine, soldierly-looking man, a native of the South of Ireland. He entered the army at an early period of life, and has served eighteen years in the same regiment. One of his brothers, a soldier of the 40th, was severely wounded in the Taranaki war, and allowed to retire from the service with a pension: he himself, though he took part in every engagement, escaped unhurt, and now occupies the highest rank that a non-commissioned officer can attain. The war in Taranaki had been carried on with varying success till March, 1861: the British forces under the command of Major-General Pratt had erected a series of redoubts for the purpose of keeping the enemy in check and protecting the town of New Plymouth. These redoubts were occupied by detachments of our men, and skirmishing parties were daily sent out to scour the neighbouring bush, where the enemy were known to be lurking. On the 18th of March, 1861, a party consisting of about thirty men of the 40th Regiment was sent out in front of No. 7 redoubt, situated on the river Waitara, in search of the enemy. Between the redoubt and the bush there intervened an open space of some eight hundred or nine hundred yards in breadth, over which our men were allowed to advance without resistance; but no sooner had they entered a narrow defile, surrounded on either side by bush and fern, than a heavy fire was opened on them by an invisible foe. Captain Richards, who was in command of the party, threw out his men in skirmishing order, and ordered them to fire in the direction whence the smoke proceeded. The enemy being concealed in the bush had the advantage of being able to take deliberate aim, and several of our men were killed or wounded. Lieutenant Rees, who was next in command to Captain Richards, seized a rifle which a wounded soldier had dropped, and encouraged the men by his example to keep up a steady fire. At the same time he requested Colour-Sergeant Lucas to send two men to remove two of the wounded who were badly hit. As the men were preparing to execute this order, a fresh volley from the enemy placed one of them *hors de combat*, and a bullet hit Lieutenant Rees in the right groin. He staggered and fell, when Colour-Sergeant Lucas, with much presence of mind, ran up to his assistance, and sent him to the rear under the charge of the soldier who remained unhurt. Three wounded men and four stand of arms still remained on the field, and the gallant sergeant resolved to present a bold front to the enemy till he was relieved. Sheltering himself behind a tree, he opened a brisk fire on the enemy, and kept them at bay. So long as he remained behind the tree he was safe, but whenever he left this shelter to take aim, he became exposed to the fire of the enemy, who, deterred from advancing by his gallant resistance, endeavoured to shoot him down. Two soldiers had the courage to stand by him, and for a quarter of an hour they kept the enemy at bay without being hit, though they were exposed to a constant fire from a distance of only thirty yards. Several of the Maories were wounded, and carried off by their companions; the brave little band, anxious but not discouraged, still continued to hold out.

The amount of danger incurred by Sergeant Lucas may be learned from the following incident:—The tree behind which he found shelter had several creepers suspended from its top; a bullet from the bush hit one of these creepers and cut it in two at the distance of a few inches from his head. If the Maoris had been better marksmen the whole of the little party must have perished, and the wounded men have fallen into the hands of a relentless foe; but in moments of excitement the natives fire wildly, without taking aim at any particular object. It was to this fortunate circumstance that Sergeant Lucas and his two followers owed their lives; the enemy were excited, and so fired without precision. As it was, they were enabled not only to continue their resistance, but also to inflict considerable loss on the enemy. For a quarter of an hour the unequal combat was kept up till a party under Lieutenants Gibson and Whelan came up to their assistance, on which the enemy retired. Only one of the three wounded men recovered, and Lieutenant Rees, in consequence of the severity of his wounds, was obliged to return to England. It would be difficult to overestimate the importance of Sergeant Lucas's gallant conduct on this trying occasion; he prevented the bodies of his wounded comrades from falling into the hands of the enemy, and saved four stand of arms. Nor was this all: the moral consequences of his heroic resistance were soon evident. The next morning the white flag was hoisted by the natives, and this was the last engagement in the Taranaki war.

In August, 1862, Colour-Sergeant Lucas was appointed sergeant-major of his regiment, and has continued ever since to discharge the duties of that office in such a way as to secure the confidence and esteem of his superior officers. His conduct was not overlooked or forgotten by the general in command. A full account of the affair was transmitted to the authorities at home, and the following notice appeared in the *London Gazette* of the 19th of July, 1861:—

"Colour-Sergeant John Lucas, 40th Regiment.—On the 18th of March, 1861, Colour-Sergeant John Lucas acted as sergeant of a party of the 40th Regiment, employed as skirmishers, to the right of No. 7 redoubt and close to the Huirangi Bush, facing the left of the position occupied by the natives. At about four o'clock P.M. a very heavy and well-directed fire was suddenly opened upon them from the bush and the high ground on the left. Three men being wounded simultaneously, two of them mortally, assistance was called for in order to have them carried to the rear; a file was immediately sent, but had scarcely arrived when one of them fell, and Lieutenant Rees was wounded at the same time. Colour-Sergeant Lucas, under a very heavy fire from the rebels, who were not more than thirty yards distant, immediately ran up to the assistance of this officer, and sent one man with him to the rear. He then took charge of the arms belonging to the killed and

Sergeant-Major Lucas, 40th Regiment, defending a position against the Maoris, on the 18th of March, 1861

wounded men, and maintained his position until the arrival of supports under Lieutenants Gibson and Whelan."

On the 2nd of November, 1862, all the troops in garrison at Auckland were assembled on the racecourse to witness the decoration of Sergeant-Major Lucas with the Cross of Valour. The soldiers formed a square, in the centre of which stood General Cameron and his staff. The sergeant-major took his stand in front of them, and the gallant old general, after expressing his admiration of his conduct, which he invited his comrades to imitate, placed on his breast that distinctive mark of his Sovereign's favour which is dearer to the soldier's heart than any other. Our readers will feel with us the hope that Sergeant-Major Lucas may long be spared to wear it, and to take part in other wars reflecting more credit on our arms and our honour as a nation than the present struggle in New Zealand.

CHAPTER XXVI.

THE HEROES OF THE VICTORIA CROSS IN NEW ZEALAND.

E have already described some of these heroes, and the gallant deeds by which they earned the Cross of Valour. We have shown how Sergeant Lucas, of the 40th, defended two of his wounded comrades from the attacks of the Maoris till a party was sent to his relief; how McKenna of the 65th stood by his dying officer to the last, and proved himself worthy of the command that had devolved upon him, by conducting his comrades through the fire of the enemy and the intricacies of the bush to the redoubt which they had left; how Samuel Mitchell, that true-hearted sailor, stood by Commander Hay, of the *Esk*, in the Gate Pa at Tauranga, and refused to leave him till all was over.

Since that time we learn from the *London Gazette* that the Victoria Cross has been awarded to Lieutenant-Colonel McNeill, of the 107th Regiment; to Assistant-Surgeons Temple and Manley, and Lieutenant Picquard, of the Royal Artillery; and to Ensign Down and Drummer Stagpoole, of the 57th Regiment, in recognition of gallant deeds done in New Zealand. The bestowal of the Cross on Assistant-Surgeon Temple, R.A., was a tardy act of justice; it was awarded to him by the unanimous voice of the army for humanely exposing his life to almost certain destruction in hurrying to the assistance of Captain Mercer, R.A., who was mortally wounded. This occurred during the attack on Rangiriri, the great pa or stronghold of the Maoris on the banks of the Waikato river, about sixty miles from Auckland. The Taranaki war began in

1860, and was carried on with various success till 1862, when it was supposed to be over. There was no truce or peace concluded with the enemy, but the settlers indulged the hope that they might now live in peace. On the 4th of May, 1863, they were roused from this state of false security by the report that two officers and eight men had been fired upon by an ambuscade, and all, with one exception, killed; this act was denounced as murder, but we must remember that they were marching through the enemy's country with arms in their hands, and were thus almost inviting their fate. General Cameron wished to take precautions against such attacks, but the governor assured him that there was no danger, as the war was over. Then came the abandonment of the Waitura, the disputed territory, and, a month later, the battle of Kuitikara, in which twenty-five Maoris were slain. After this the province of Auckland became the seat of war. The governor issued a proclamation denouncing all the natives as rebels who should not surrender their arms and take the oath of allegiance within a week: the result was such as might have been expected; the Maoris cleared out with all their valuables, and fell back into the interior. Their forces were concentrated at Pokewu, or the Queen's Redoubt, a place thirty-five miles south of Auckland, close to the Waikato river. Our troops advanced against them, and a battle was fought at Roheroa, a mountainous ridge, two miles south of Pokewu, where the insurgents had encamped and fortified their position with a series of rifle pits, from which they opened a heavy fire on their assailants as they ascended the steep declivity. The regiment opposed to them consisted of young recruits who had never been under fire before; for a moment they hesitated, and all might have been lost, if General Cameron had not rushed forward in front, waving his riding-whip and cheering them on to victory. He thus saved the character of a young battalion. The Maoris dispersed, and found refuge in the neighbouring swamps, leaving twenty-two killed on the field of battle. Their loss was not great, considering that the force opposed to them was as three to one. On the same day a Maori ambuscade attacked an escort under the command of Captain King, of the 18th Royal Irish, in the neighbourhood of the Queen's Redoubt; our men, who were straggling along the road, smoking and chatting, with their rifles uncapped, resisted as much as they could, and escaped with the loss of four men, twelve rifles, and the carts and horses left on the field. If any of the Maoris fell, their bodies were removed; no traces of them were to be found the following day.

Redoubts were then erected for the protection of Auckland; the bush was cut down for hundreds of yards on either side of the Great South Road; a Commissariat Transport Corps of nearly 1000 men was raised; four regiments of Militia were recruited, chiefly in Australia and the South; the strength of the Imperial forces was raised to 10,000 men; including local corps, we had about 25,000 men under arms to cope with the enemy, who have never been able to bring more than 600 men into the field. If the country had been open, the war would soon have been brought to a close; but our men had to pass unfordable streams and to force their way through the bush. The enemy fell back to a place called Mere Mere, situated on a rising ground on the Waikato, about nine miles from the Queen's Redoubt. The enemy's only artillery consisted of two old ship's guns loaded with tenpenny nails; but the place was believed to be impregnable, and our men remained in camp there for three months. It was the old story of Sir Richard Strahan and the Earl of Chatham. General Cameron was longing to be at them, but he had to wait for Sir George Grey, and Sir George Grey was waiting for nobody knows what. The expense of supporting such an army in the field is enormous; three millions of money have already been expended. At length our troops advanced to attack the Maori stronghold; the preparations were as elaborate as Uncle Toby's for the siege of Dunkirk, and something brilliant would doubtless have occurred if the Maoris had been a little less impatient. They evacuated Mere Mere, and fell back to Rangiriri, where they had a strong pa on the summit of a rising ground situated midway between the Waikato and an inland lake. If we were too slow at Mere Mere, we were a little too fast at Rangiriri; because the former was a place of no great strength it was inferred that the latter was the same. A rush was made;

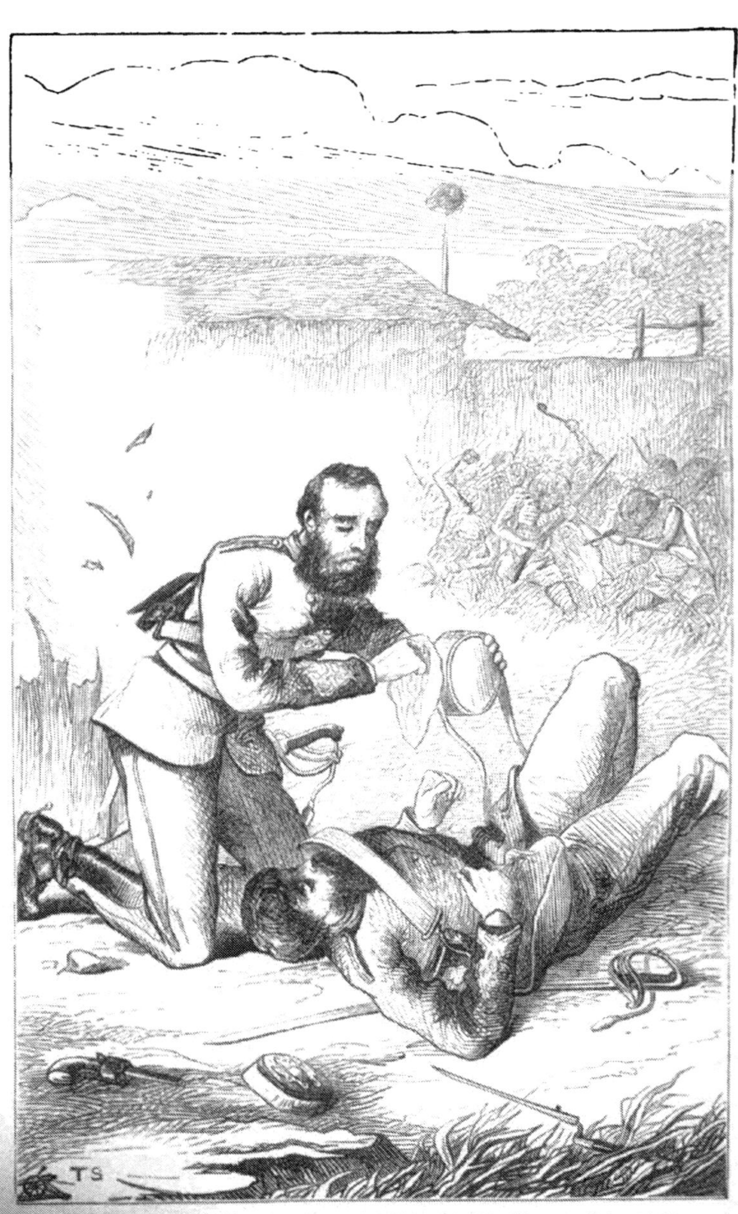

Assistant-Surgeon Temple, R.A., assisting Captain Mercer, R.A., at the attack on the Pa of Rangiriri.

the outer works were carried; but the attacking party fell back on finding themselves confronted by other works of still greater strength. To retreat was to lose the *prestige* of our arms, and to invite the neutral tribes to rebellion. The place must be taken at all hazards; a second rush was attempted; the officers advanced in front, and cheered on the men, but the men refused to stir. The general then turned to the fifty artillery men who accompanied him, and, armed with swords and revolvers, they rushed forward, stopped to breathe for a moment in a gully, and reached the parapet, which some of them mounted. They were led by Captain Mercer, R.A., one of those brave, gallant, God-fearing men who are an honour to the service and to humanity itself. He had a presentiment that he would fall, but he was prepared to die; like Havelock, he had been preparing for death for years, and it did not take him by surprise. A Maori bullet struck him in the jaw, carrying away the lower part of the face; he rolled backwards on the ground mortally wounded. His party was repulsed. Was there a man there brave enough to advance to his assistance? He must hold his life cheap; he will have to pass through the double fire of the enemy. But what sacrifice will our soldiers not make for an officer they love? First one soldier advances, and then another and another, but it was only to meet with speedy death. It was at this moment that William Temple, an assistant-surgeon of the Royal Artillery, learned that his friend Mercer stood in need of his aid. Without balancing chances, or hesitating for a moment, he went where duty called—it might be to death, it could not be to dishonour. He reached the spot so fatal to the others; the most sanguine could scarcely indulge the hope that he could escape. For a moment he was enveloped in smoke; every eye was strained till it cleared away. A sort of sigh of relief rose from many a breast as he was seen by Mercer's side, doing all that could be done to alleviate his sufferings. From instinct more than from intention, he stooped when exposed to the fire of the enemy, and thus their bullets passed harmlessly over his head. General Cameron, who had witnessed his devotion to duty, only expressed the desire of the whole army in recommending him for the Cross of Honour, which was awarded to him in the *Gazette* of the 23rd of September, 1864. Lieutenant Picquard, R.A., obtained the same honour for carrying water to the wounded at the risk of his own life.

The Artillery having failed, the general sent for the blue-jackets, told them his only hope was in their courage, and pointed to the pa. "Go on, my lads," said their leader, "I'll not be far behind you." It would have been better, perhaps, if he had been a little before them; as it was, they advanced to within fifty yards of the pa, and then retired below the crest of the hill. One poor little middy of fourteen was shot through the head while in advance of the others. What could be done? The general was ready to receive any suggestion. The officer commanding the Engineers proposed mining, which was attempted; but the fuse was damp, and refused to explode. The Engineers then advanced under cover, and effected a breach in the wall. On perceiving that their position was no longer tenable, the Maoris hoisted a white flag, and surrendered at dawn. William Thompson, the great chief of the rebellion, had escaped, with most of his followers: only 183 prisoners fell into our hands. They could easily have escaped if they had chosen, but they had waited on in the hope of being reinforced. The loss of the Maoris was about forty-five killed, while ours amounted to six officers killed or died of wounds, and nine wounded; forty men killed, and eighty wounded. The attacking force amounted to 1000 men; about one-seventh of them were killed or wounded; the defenders of the pa could not have amounted to more than four or five hundred men; forty-five were killed on the spot; the wounded were carried off.

One or two steamers were placed on the Waikato river, and our troops advanced to Ngaruawahia, the royal residence of Potatau II., whose palace of reeds may still be seen there. This town is situated about twenty-six miles to the south of Rangiriri, at the confluence of the Waipa and the Horatiu, whose united waters form the Waikato river. The governor had promised to meet W. Thompson, the Maori king-maker, here, and to settle the conditions of peace; but for reasons unknown to us he failed to appear, and our troops pushed on till they reached Piko Piko, a strong pa on the summit of a hill overlooking the Waipa, about thirty miles to the south of Ngaruawahia. We remained encamped opposite this stronghold for three weeks without attempting an assault; our experience at Rangiriri had taught us to be cautious. We had 3900 men under canvas; the defenders of the pa could not have exceeded one-fourth of that number; but, notwithstanding this disproportion, no attempt was made to dislodge the enemy. At the end of three weeks we turned their position, and advanced to the villages of Awamutu and Kilu Kilu, from which they derived their supplies; on this they were obliged to evacuate their stronghold and retreat into the interior. A skirmish took place at Rangiawahia, a native village three miles from Awamutu, during which a venerable Maori lady distinguished herself by coolly occupying a chair in her verandah, and firing deliberately on our men, who retaliated by burning down a native *wharze*, or hut, which contained some warriors who refused to surrender, and were consumed in the flames. We then constructed a line of redoubts, extending from Maugautautari, a stronghold on the Horatiu, which W. Thompson had evacuated, to Te Rori on the Waipa, for the purpose of keeping the enemy in check. This was not so easily done as we imagined. In March some three hundred natives advanced to Ohapau, a village five miles from Awamutu, and began to construct a pa in the midst of a grove of peach-trees. It was captured on the 2nd of April, but Rewi, the ringleader, escaped.

On the 30th of March the incident occurred which procured for Lieutenant-Colonel McNeill the honour of the Victoria Cross. He holds the appointment of aide-de-camp to General Cameron, who was then at Pukerimu, and had occasion to communicate with Brigadier Carey, who was in command at Awamutu. The distance from Pukerimu to Awamutu is eighteen miles; midway between these two stations stands the redoubt of Ohapau, occupied by a detachment of the 40th Regiment. Rough bridges have been erected at the different creeks, but there is no regular road, merely a native path leading through the bush. Near Ohapau is a clump of trees admirably adapted for an ambuscade. Lieutenant-Colonel McNeill had no other escort than a private of the Defence Force (a colonial corps consisting of 250 troopers) of the name of Vosper, who acted as his orderly. Nothing remarkable occurred during the journey till they had occasion to pass the clump of trees near Ohapau, when a party of insurgents opened fire upon them. Private Vosper was thrown from his horse, and Lieutenant-Colonel McNeill succeeded in catching him. Vosper then remounted, and both rode off. The fire of the Maoris is said to have been very close and very severe; under such circumstances the escape of the horses and riders without being grazed by a single bullet is little short of miraculous. It is unfortunate, perhaps, that there were no other spectators of the scene than the immediate actors. Private Vosper has to vouch for the gallantry of Lieutenant-Colonel McNeill, and Lieutenant-Colonel McNeill for the danger incurred by Private Vosper. When the affair was reported to General Cameron, he recommended his aide-de-camp for the decoration of the Cross of Valour; and he was duly invested with it on the 6th of December, in the presence of all the troops that could be assembled to witness this interesting ceremony.

Lieutenant-Colonel McNeill is a good and gallant soldier; he proved himself to be so during the Indian campaign, when he served on the staff of Sir Edward Lugard, and was honourably mentioned in public despatches. It is right that these services should be known to the public, as they have contributed to procure for him the honour of the Victoria Cross, the wearer of which, like Cæsar's wife, should be beyond suspicion. We should be glad to see some public recognition of the bravery displayed by a sergeant of one of the colonial corps near the same spot, five days before Lieutenant-Colonel McNeill and his orderly were attacked. On the 25th of March this sergeant had left Pukerimu in company with a civilian who had been visiting his brother there, and was now on his way to Awamutu. Both were well mounted, and nothing remarkable occurred till they were within four miles of the camp, where the road passes near the first of the lakes lying between Ohapau and Te Rori. The two horsemen were riding quietly along, thoughtless of danger, when an ambuscade of some thirty or forty Maoris opened fire upon them from the bush; the sergeant felt that his horse was hit, and spurred him on with all his might, in the hope that he might still be able to carry him beyond the reach of danger. On the first impulse of the moment he had thought only of his own safety; but he had only proceeded a short distance when he became anxious for the fate of his companion. On turning round, he saw his horse lying dead on the road: in another minute the civilian would have been lifeless beside him. He was rushing along with all his might, pursued by a Maori, who was rapidly gaining upon him, and had already poised his spear to strike. The sergeant wheeled his horse round, and with the rapidity of thought rushed to the rescue. One shot from his revolver laid the Maori prostrate; in another minute the civilian was mounted behind him, and then away for their lives. The noble horse seemed to know what results depended on his speed, for, though wounded and weak from the loss of blood, he never halted till he reached the rising ground that overlooks Awamutu, when he fell down dead. He had carried them three miles with seven bullets in his body, till they were beyond the reach of the Maori rifles. When the danger was past he lay down and died. The incident created much sensation at the moment. The sergeant's coolness and courage excited the admiration of the whole camp; but many months have passed away without bringing with them any public recognition of his heroism. This, doubtless, has arisen from oversight. We shall be much gratified if our present remarks lead to further inquiries being made. Civilians have obtained the Victoria Cross in India; there is no reason why it should not be bestowed on those who are equally worthy in New Zealand.

Our readers are already familiar with the attack on the Gate Pa at Tauranga, on the 29th of April, when our soldiers and sailors, after effecting an entrance into the Maori stronghold, were seized with a sudden panic, and retreated in the greatest disorder. It is rare indeed for our soldiers or sailors to desert their officers in the hour of danger; but on this occasion terror was more powerful than the sense of duty. It was not so with all, however; there were one or two honourable exceptions. When Commander Hay fell mortally wounded inside the pa, one gallant sailor stood by him, and refused to leave him, though frequently urged to do so. It was right that such an act of distinguished devotion to duty should be recognised as an encouragement to others to imitate his example, and Samuel Mitchell now carries on his breast the Cross of Valour as a memorial of the humanity and courage he displayed at the Gate Pa. On the same occasion, Assistant-Surgeon Manley, of the Royal Artillery, distinguished himself by exposing his life to great danger in entering the pa with the generous intention of offering assistance to Commander Hay. That unfortunate officer was beyond the reach of human aid, but this detracts nothing from the praise due to Assistant-Surgeon Manley, who remained with him to the last, and did all that human skill could suggest to alleviate his sufferings. Nor was this all; on learning, after his return to the camp, that there were other wounded officers in the pa who might require his aid, he offered to proceed to their assistance. To have done so would have been to expose his life to certain destruction, as the insurgents had now resumed possession of their stronghold; the service cannot afford to lose such men as Assistant-Surgeon Manley. While this generous offer was refused, it was felt that he had already made good his title to the distinction of the Victoria Cross, which has now been conferred upon him. Assistant-Surgeons Temple and Manley belong to the same branch of the service, and it is honourable to the medical profession that two of its members should have attained to the same distinction in the course of one year.

While the province of Auckland has been the principal seat of the present campaign, a sort of desultory warfare has been carried on at the same time in the district of Taranaki, where the 57th Regiment is stationed. This district, which has been often described as the garden of New Zealand, extends along the western coast of the North Island; its capital, New Plymouth, is situated at the base of Mount Egmont, a solitary, snow-capped mountain, about 10,000 feet high, rising out of a densely-wooded plain. There is no harbour, and the loud roar of the waves breaking on the inhospitable shore is constantly to be heard. An English settlement was formed there in 1841, but at this time there were only ninety natives, living for security in the cliffs around Mount Egmont, or in holes among the sugar-loaf rocks; the rest had fled to Cook's Straits or been carried off into captivity. The whole district was a waste, and Governor Hobson bought for 400*l.* the right which Te Whero Whero, a native chief, had acquired over it in virtue of conquest; after it had passed into our hands the fugitives began to return, and nothing could equal their surprise on finding their lands parcelled out among strangers. Twisting their long arms round the gigantic trees, which had long been *tapu* or sacred, they besought the woodmen to spare them; their spirit was broken by conquest; as yet they offered no open resistance. It was only when our arms had suffered reverses in other parts of the island that the natives of Taranaki began to show a more independent spirit, and to reclaim the lands which had now passed from their hands. The matter was referred to Governor Fitzroy, who decided that the settlers were only entitled to 3500 of the 60,000 acres to which they laid claim; the natives resumed possession of the rest. This decision increased the bitterness of feeling which had already sprung up between the two races, and has been the cause of all the subsequent disturbances at Taranaki. The settlers are anxious to purchase, but the natives refuse to part with their lands. "Money," they say, "soon melts away, but the land remains." In order to preserve and sustain this conservative feeling, they formed themselves into the Anti-Land-Selling League, the nature of which may be learned from its title, and absolutely refused to part with a single acre. The war of 1860-2 and 1863-4, which is not yet over, originated from an attempt on the part of the Colonial Government to suppress this league by purchasing lands from any of the natives who were disposed to part with them. If these purchases had been confined to the actual possessors of the soil no objection could have been made to them, every man having a right to do what he likes with his own, but no man has a right to sell what belongs to his neighbours. This was actually done at Taranaki, and unfortunately the Government, in order to assert a principle, took possession by force of the land thus purchased. This brought the two races into immediate collision, and the war has been lingering on for years. It would be foreign to our purpose to describe its leading events; it is sufficient to remark that it has been carried on with various success, and that the 57th Regiment, under the command of Colonel Warre, C.B., has taken an active part in the Taranaki campaign. An engagement took place at Poutoko on the 2nd of October, 1863, during which Ensign Down and Drummer Stagpoole, of the 57th Regiment, distinguished themselves by carrying off two wounded men who would otherwise have fallen into the hands of the enemy. Stagpoole had already attracted the notice of his commanding officer by volunteering to rescue a wounded soldier on a previous occasion, and the announcement in the *London Gazette* that he and Ensign Down have had the Cross of Valour awarded to them has given general satisfaction in New Zealand. Courage is not the exclusive property of any one class; it is to be found among all ranks in our army and navy; it is right, therefore, that that Cross, which is intended expressly to be the reward of courage, should be bestowed impartially upon every one who has made good his claim, whether he bear her Majesty's commission or be merely a drummer-boy. Chivalry admitted none to its ranks save those who were of noble birth, but many of the most chivalrous deeds of modern times have been done by men who have no claim to illustrious descent, and owe everything to themselves. The Cross of Valour is a standing recognition of this fact; it is far more precious than garters and ribbons, or the other gewgaws of rank; it is the special reward of the brave, and none but the brave deserve to wear it.

Peace will never be established on a solid basis in New Zealand till the settlers and aborigines have learned to treat one another with more respect. At present they regard one another with mingled feelings of hatred and contempt. The Englishman thinks that he has a right to despise brown-skinned men who were once cannibals, who know nothing about title-deeds, live in dog-kennels, feed on fern-roots and putrid fish, and render their faces hideous by tattooing. He hates them as the only obstacle between himself and those valuable lands with which they refuse to part; he is tempted to believe that the only way to pacify New Zealand is not to leave a single Maori alive. "The black fellows," or "niggers," as they are contemptuously called, conscious of the existence of these feelings, are ready enough to retaliate. They have the firmest belief in their own superior courage. "You white people," said a native chief, "are very good for building houses and ships, for buying and selling, for making cattle fat, and for growing beans and cabbages; you are like the rats, always at work; but as to fighting, you are like them also, you only know how to run."

During this war they have had occasion to revise their opinion regarding our courage; they have also taught us to respect their heroic powers of endurance, and to believe that many virtues may be found beneath a brown skin. If the experience of the past prevents us from looking forward with too much confidence to the future destiny of this noble race, who have decreased to one-half of their number since they welcomed the Anglo-Saxon race to their shores, we have at least a right to expect that they shall be treated with justice, and nothing be done to hasten on that fate which seems already to be impending over them. England will thus be saved the remorse of wilfully neglecting to take any measures to avoid those calamities to which the contact of civilized with semi-barbarous races has hitherto given rise, and the Maori may yet become a sharer in those blessings which civilization and Christianity can alone bestow.

CHAPTER XXVII.

THE NAVAL BRIGADE IN INDA.

HILE a few of our sailors have forced their way into Mr. Desanges' Gallery, and made good their title to the Cross of Valour, it must be evident to the most casual spectator that the "blue jackets" have not been so fortunate as the "red coats" in securing this reward of gallantry. It would be unfair, however, to infer from this fact that our sailors are inferior to our soldiers in courage; both belong to the same race, and are animated by the same warlike spirit: but of late years sailors have not had the same opportunity of displaying their valour as in the days of Nelson, Jervis, and Duncan. Since the conclusion of the great French war in 1815, we have not been brought into collision with any of the great maritime powers. The battle of Navarino, where the united fleets of three European nations combined to destroy the naval power of Turkey, and to release Greece from the chains of slavery, redounded but little to our credit; and Russia, during the late war, afforded us few opportunities of gaining laurels by sea. It is true, that during the Crimean war some of our sailors earned themselves a name to live in the annals of fame; but it was not on that element peculiarly their own that they acquired this honourable distinction. It was not at sea, but on land, fighting side by side with our soldiers, that they proved themselves the worthy successors of the men who conquered at Trafalgar and swept our enemies from the ocean. If only a few obtained the Victoria Cross, the reason was that comparatively few were permitted to take any active part in the Russian

war, and that no man can prove himself to be a hero unless he has the chance of doing so.

Sailors have a natural taste for fighting, and they felt it very hard during the siege of Sebastopol that the soldiers should have the largest share. When any of them, by good conduct, became entitled to a holiday, it was not an unusual request to be allowed to spend it ashore, "to have a day's shooting with them 'ere red coats." They regarded such an event with as much interest as the keenest sportsman does when he talks of the 1st of September and looks forward to its arrival, and their ambition was equally great to make a good bag. It was the same during the suppression of the Indian Mutiny: the sailors who composed the Naval Brigade, led by the gallant young Peel, marched up the country with as much alacrity as if they had landed merely to enjoy themselves.

When, about the middle of May, 1857, intelligence reached Calcutta of the disasters at Meerut and Delhi, Lord Canning, the Governor-General, telegraphed immediately for aid to Bombay, Ceylon, and Madras. He knew that Lord Elgin and General Ashburnham were on their way to China, and urged in the most pressing manner that some of the troops under their command should be sent at once to Calcutta, to assist in suppressing the mutiny. It was fortunate for our future interests in India that Lord Elgin was generous enough to take upon himself the responsibility of diverting to the shores of the Ganges part of those troops which were intended to aid in the attack on Canton. About the middle of July, while he was waiting at Hong-Kong for the arrival of reinforcements, he received a despatch from Lord Canning, announcing that the revolt was spreading on every side and asking for farther aid. Lord Elgin at once started for Calcutta, taking with him a force of fifteen hundred seamen and marines, most of whom belonged to the two war steamers, the *Pearl* and the *Shannon*. These active, hardy men were organized into "Naval Brigades," and rendered the most important services under the command of their gallant chief, Captain Peel.

This distinguished officer was a younger son of the late Sir Robert Peel, and his brief but glorious career shed additional lustre on the name he bore. He loved his profession for its own sake: he delighted in the excitement of war; he was never more in his element than when he had planted one of those immense guns he knew how to handle so skilfully against the walls of Sebastopol and Lucknow, where he would continue to work it amid a shower of shot and shell. Genius is only talent directed into one particular channel, and the talent he inherited from his father was devoted to the noble profession he had adopted. He had already distinguished himself in the Crimea, and had accompanied Lord Elgin to China in command of Her Majesty's ship *Shannon*, when our sailors and marines were organized into naval brigades. He was placed at the head of the one which was intended to aid in the relief of Lucknow, and nobly did he discharge the duties which then devolved upon him. His was that daring but thoughtful courage that wins the confidence as well as the admiration of all who witness it; the earnest force of character that surmounts every difficulty and triumphs over every obstacle; the gentle, kindly bearing, the courteous manner, which tells more upon our soldiers and sailors than words of stern command; the influence which a noble nature exercises on all around. It would be difficult to over-estimate the value of his services during the seven months he commanded the Naval Brigade in the north-west provinces. We cannot trace his whole career; it is sufficient for the present to remark, that he died at Cawnpore, on the 27th of April, 1858, of smallpox. He had been wounded in the thigh during the last attack upon Lucknow, and was on his way to Calcutta when he was attacked at Cawnpore by the dangerous malady to which he succumbed. The recent annals of the British Navy can show no name which has better claims to be remembered than that of William Peel, of whom it may be truly said that he died too soon for his country but not for his own fame.

Lord Elgin arrived at Calcutta early in the month of August, 1857, bringing with him two war steamers, the *Shannon* and the *Pearl*, which were placed at the disposal of the Indian Government. Peel, who had so gallantly managed a naval battery in the Crimea during the siege of Sebastopol, was commissioned to organize a naval brigade, and entered on the task with his usual energy. Aided by the resources of the two war steamers, he succeeded in forming a splendid naval brigade, the most effective, perhaps, we have ever possessed, consisting of four hundred able British seamen, and ten of those enormous 68-pounder guns which such seamen can handle so skilfully. They started from Calcutta, up the Hooghly and the Ganges; their progress was necessarily slow; the half of August and the whole of September passed wearily away on this most tedious voyage. The ardent spirit of the seamen would have chafed and fretted beneath this compulsory delay, if they had been under the command of a leader less esteemed and admired; as it was, his presence and example told upon all. Week after week elapsed; the gallant band made but slow progress against the stream; their ponderous guns rendered it still slower. On the 30th of September, Peel reached Benares with 286 of his brigade. Without waiting for the arrival of the rest, he hurried on to Allahabad, which he reached on the 3rd of October, with 94 men; he remained there four days when he was joined by the others, with their enormous guns and stores of ammunition. These guns—the chief cause of delay—were now found to be useless, as no means of transport could be found for conveying them across the country, and they were abandoned at Allahabad with regret. They had still their 24-pounders to trust to, one of which was proudly named the *Shannon*, after the war steamer to which she belonged. Urged by the authorities at Patna to afford them some relief, Peel formed a small naval brigade, which was placed under the command of Captain Sotheby, to be employed against the insurgents in the neighbourhood.

The wearisome voyage up the Ganges was now concluded, and on the 4th of October, soon after his arrival at Allahabad, Peel received the following telegram from Sir Colin Campbell, then at Calcutta:—"In the course of about a week there will be a continuous stream of troops, at the rate of about ninety a day, passing on to Allahabad, which, I trust, will not cease for the next three months." Peel was now in his element, and the Naval Brigade under his command found abundant employment in facilitating the passage of troops and artillery from Allahabad to Cawnpore. Their strength was increased by the arrival of 126 naval officers and seamen under the command of Lieutenant Vaughan, who joined them on the 20th of October. This reinforcement was composed of sailors of the merchant service at Calcutta, who volunteered to join the brigade, and rejoiced in the opportunity of serving under such a distinguished commander. On the 23rd, four siege-train 24-pounders were on the way to Cawnpore, under the charge of 100 men of the Naval Brigade; on the 27th, other four 24-pounders and two 8-inch howitzers were despatched with an escort of 170 seamen; and on the same day a large amount of ammunition was forwarded. Peel infused something of his own energy into every seaman under his command, and personally superintended every arrangement; so that on the 28th of October he was ready to start for Cawnpore, and was joined on the way by Colonel Powell, with the head-quarters of Her Majesty's 53rd Regiment. On the 31st they reached Shured, where they received the alarming intelligence that the Dinapore mutineers had crossed the Jumna with three guns, and were preparing either to attack Futtehpore or to force their way into Oude. The soldiers and sailors under the command of Powell and Peel did not exceed 700 men, while the number of the enemy did not fall short of 4000; our men, moreover, were encumbered with the charge of a large and valuable convoy of siege and other stores, the loss of which at such a juncture would have been irreparable; still it was of the last importance that something should be done to arrest the progress of the rebels, and the two leaders, Powell and Peel, resolved to offer them battle.

As a general rule, it is injudicious to allow sailors and soldiers to be mixed together during an attack, and frequent disasters have resulted from overlooking this fact; but on this occasion, from our inferiority in numbers, we had no choice. On the evening of the 31st our men reached the camping ground at Futtehpore, where they were joined by a small detachment of the 93rd, or Sutherland Highlanders, who were also on the way to Lucknow. The following morning a column, consisting of 500 soldiers and sailors, marched to Kudjna, a distance of twenty-four miles, to attack the enemy. The latter had taken up a strong position, with their right occupying a high embankment screened by a grove, and their left extending on the other side of the road, which was commanded by their artillery. Our column was divided into three parts: one advanced to attack the enemy's guns, while the other two supported it on either side. Our soldiers and sailors rushed forward with their usual impetuosity; but the rebels, having every advantage of position, maintained their ground for two hours, and kept up so severe a fire of musketry that many of our men, including Colonel Powell, who received a musket-ball in the forehead, were killed. At this moment, Captain Peel, on whom the command devolved, displayed such coolness and presence of mind as proved that, though a sailor, he was fitted for the highest military command. Perceiving that the enemy could not be dislodged without incurring the loss of many lives, none of which could well be spared, he changed the mode of attack by marching his men round the upper end of the embankment, and their forces being thus divided, they were driven from all their positions, leaving their camp equipage and two of their tumbrils in our possession. If there had been a small body of cavalry to follow up this success, the whole body of the enemy might have been dispersed or destroyed; but no pursuit could be organized, as our men had marched seventy-two miles in three days, and exhausted nature could do no more. The column, after collecting the dead and wounded, returned to Binkee, and after a little rest resumed their march to Cawnpore. The enemy are supposed to have lost about one-fifth of their number, and abandoned the idea of marching into Oude: that terrible column of blue jackets and red coats had shown them what they might expect when they dared to cross bayonets with the redoubtable Feringees.

We need not trace the advance of the Naval Brigade, which was now reduced to 250 men, from Cawnpore to Lucknow: it is sufficient to remark, that they and their gallant leader reached the Alum Bagh early in November, and placed themselves under the command of Sir Colin Campbell. Our readers will bear in mind that Lawrence maintained his position in the Residency until his death, early in July; and that the command then devolved upon Inglis, who continued the defence until September, when he was relieved by Outram and Havelock. It was known that the small garrison was hemmed in on every side by the rebels, and every effort was made to relieve them; it was with this object in view that Sir Colin Campbell had concentrated his forces around the city of Lucknow on the 14th of November. The name of this gallant veteran will ever be dear to the people of England. The son of a Glasgow tradesman, he obtained his commission while still a boy through the influence of an uncle, and had served forty-nine years as an officer of the British army. Being unable to purchase, he could not look for rapid promotion, but, like Havelock, he had learned to labour and to wait. He had shed his blood freely in the service of his country; his gallantry had been acknowledged in public despatches; but many years elapsed before he obtained his company. In the course of nearly half a century he had fought in almost every quarter of the globe; he served in the Walcheren expedition; then in the Peninsular war, including the battles and sieges of Vimiera, Corunna, Barossa, Vittoria, San Sebastian, and Bidassoa; then in North America; then in the West Indies; then in the first Chinese war; then in the second Sikh war; and lastly, in the Crimea. When the news of General Anson's death reached England on the 11th of July, Sir Colin was offered the post of Commander-in-Chief in India, which he at once accepted. When the question was put to him, "When will you be ready to start?" his reply was "To-morrow." He kept his word: the next day he was on his way to India, taking very little with him but the clothes on his back. Sir Charles Napier was wont to say, that two towels and a piece of soap was ample luggage for an officer serving in India: Sir Colin Campbell seems to have held the same opinion. He travelled by the quickest route: by rail to Folkestone, steam to Boulogne, rail to Marseilles, steam to Alexandria, rail and other means to Suez, steam from Suez to Calcutta. How his ardent spirit must have chafed during the many weeks he was detained at Calcutta! But that time was not lost. He attended to the minutest details; he remodelled the whole system of military machinery in India; he arranged with the Governor-General the plan of the ensuing campaign. He admired with all the unselfish admiration of a true soldier the heroic resistance of the garrison at Lucknow; the struggles of Havelock's little army; the combined efforts of Havelock and Outram. At length, on the 28th of October, he left Calcutta, travelling like a common courier, and caring nothing for the pomp and glitter of military rank. After several narrow escapes by the way, he crossed the Ganges on the 9th of November, and commenced his attack on Lucknow on the 14th, with a miscellaneous force of 4000 men.

The gallant old chief had one guiding principle throughout the whole Indian campaign—never to sacrifice the life of a British soldier unnecessarily. He was resolved that Lucknow should be taken, but with the least possible expenditure of human blood. Knowing that Havelock and Outram had suffered severely in cutting their way through the town two months before, he formed a plan of approach through the south-western suburb, and trusted to his artillery and the Naval Brigade to batter down the enemy's defences step by step and day after day, so as to open up a passage for his infantry with comparatively little loss. To this plan he steadily adhered, and for several days there was a series of partial sieges, each directed against one of the enemy's strongholds. Our army pushed its way slowly, but success was certain in the end. On the first day he drove the enemy, after a running fight of two hours, from the Dil Roosha Park, and then from the Martinière College, an institution for the education of half-caste children, founded by Claude Martin, who came out to India as a private soldier, and rose to the rank of major-general. During these operations the heavy guns of the Naval Brigade served to keep the enemy in check, and rendered important assistance. After completing his preparations on the 15th, and exchanging signals with Havelock and Outram, Sir Colin crossed the canal on the morning of the 16th, and advanced to the Secunder Bagh, a high-walled enclosure about a hundred and twenty yards square, loopholed on every side, and strongly garrisoned by the enemy, who fought with the greatest obstinacy. In vain the guns of the Naval Brigade thundered against the walls; the noise grew deafening; the ardour of our troops could no longer be restrained; two companies of Highlanders, with fixed bayonets, reached a plateau, and rushed forward till they were stopped by a dead wall. "In at the roof, Highlanders!" shouted the old chief, whose blood was now up; "in through the roof; tear off the tiles. Go on!"

They needed no second order; in a moment the plumed bonnets and tartan kilts vanished through the tiles and broken bamboos, and the enemy, driven from their position, retired with the loss of two guns.

At length the breach in the main building was declared practicable; the hole was barely large enough for a single man to pass, but all were impatient of further delay. The gallant old chief thought of Badajoz, where he was the first to storm the breach, and would willingly now have been the first to pass through the fiery opening if duty had permitted; as it was, he uncovered his grey hairs, and waved the Sikhs and Highlanders to the assault. Then followed a gallant race between the mountaineers of India and of Scotland: a Sikh is the first to enter and—to die. He is followed by a Highlander; a bullet passes through his body, the plumed bonnet rolls from his head, and he sinks lifeless to the ground. Another and another press forward and meet the same fate, but their comrades step across their bodies and make good their entrance. The gate was violently forced, and the whole body of Sikhs and Highlanders poured into the Secunder Bagh, and then came the hour of retribution. "Remember Cawnpore, boys! No quarter! Think of our women and children! Mercy? no mercy for you!" Such were the cries that rose from our men as the bayonet did its deadly work. No quarter was given, and many of the enemy threw themselves into the flames which were now spreading through the building. The massacre of Cawnpore was avenged at the Secunder Bagh; two thousand of the enemy met their death within its walls.

The Naval Brigade, under the command of the gallant Peel, was then ordered to the front, and advanced toward the Shah Nujeef—a domed mosque with a garden, which had been strongly fortified by the enemy, with the intention of arresting the progress of our army. The walls of the garden had been loopholed on every side; the entrance was built up, and the summit of the building crowned with a parapet. On the left was a village held by the rebels; Brigadier Hope and Colonel Gordon drove them from this position before the Naval Brigade opened fire on the Shah Nujeef. Peel was aided by a field battery and some mortars, but the enemy defended the post with the greatest obstinacy, and kept up an incessant fire of musketry from the mosque and the loopholed walls of the garden. It was on this occasion that three members of the Naval Brigade displayed such conspicuous bravery as attracted the notice of the Commander-in-Chief, and secured for them the distinction of the Cross of Valour. The *Shannon* 24-pounder, which bore the name of the war steamer from which it had been taken, was entrusted to the charge of Lieutenant Young and William Hall, A.B., who proved themselves worthy of the confidence reposed in them. Though exposed to a heavy fire of musketry and assailed by hand-grenades thrown from the walls, they led up their heavy gun to within a few yards of the building, and opened fire on it with as much coolness as if they had been alongside an enemy's frigate and fighting on their own element. It was, to borrow the words of Sir Colin Campbell, "an action almost unexampled in war," and excited the admiration of all who witnessed it. For three hours a heavy cannonade was kept up against the walls of the mosque, and our sailors would have suffered more at the hands of the enemy if they had not been covered by the withering fire of the Highlanders in the rear. Sailors always like to mingle a little fun with fighting, and Lieutenant Nowell Salmon, of the Naval Brigade, who was known as an unerring marksman, had recourse to an ingenious expedient to arrest, or at least to weaken, the enemy's fire. Close by the walls of the mosque stood a lofty tree, whose spreading branches overlooked the building, and offered a tempting cover to any one who was venturous enough to climb it. Lieutenant Salmon perceived at a glance all the advantages of such a position, where he could see without being seen and shoot without being shot. Having obtained the necessary leave, he mounted the tree in true sailor fashion, and, sheltered amid its leafy recesses, took deliberate aim and picked off the enemy's sharpshooters when they ventured to show themselves in the mosque or the garden. He was ably seconded by a private of the 93rd Highlanders, who, standing below, received the discharged rifles, loaded them, and handed them up again. We can conceive the surprise and consternation of the rebels as they saw their ranks thinned and their comrades shot down by an irresistible foe, and the enjoyment of the reckless sailor as he witnessed the effect of his unerring fire. At length Sir Colin, impatient of delay, gave orders to storm the place, which was done in the most intrepid manner by the soldiers and sailors, who forced their way through the garden and drove the rebels from the mosque. The gallantry of the Naval Brigade at the capture of the Shah Nujeef was acknowledged in a public despatch; Lieut. Young, William Hall, A.B., and Lieut. Salmon, who was badly wounded, were decorated with the Victoria Cross; and Captain Peel became Sir William Peel.

It would be foreign to our purpose to follow the army of rescue in all their operations till they effected their entrance into the Residency, or to describe the emotions of Campbell, Outram, and Havelock, as they grasped one another's hands and felt that their work was done. All the three have now passed away; but they did noble service to their country, and their names will not be speedily forgotten. The early struggles, the patient discharge of duty in a subordinate position, the perseverance and the final success of Campbell and Havelock, ought to be a lesson and encouragement to the young men of England who have to tread the same path and aspire to reach the same goal.

Wherever the Naval Brigade served during the Indian campaign, they displayed the same coolness and courage as at the capture of the Shah Nujeef. It was part of Sir Colin's tactics to employ artillery as much as possible so as to save his infantry, and whenever walls were to be battered down he had only to summon Peel and his now famous brigade to the front. Their gallant achievements in Oude must ever occupy a prominent place in Indian history, and the name of Peel received additional lustre from the brave young sailor who perished in his prime. In the scarcity of regular troops, they occupied a middle position, and did the work of soldiers and sailors with equal readiness: well-drilled and accustomed to active movements, they were ready to march at a moment's notice, and moved their heavy guns with a rapidity and ease hitherto unknown in field operations. They were favourites wherever they came; their unfailing good-humour and almost boyish exuberance of spirits were contagious, and spread to all who served by their side. When the campaign was over and the mutiny suppressed their services were not forgotten; the residents of Calcutta did honour to themselves by honouring them with a public reception and a grand banquet. We can conceive the hearty enjoyment of the blue jackets as they partook of the delicacies which had been prepared for them, and listened to the kind, graceful words in which Outram, their fellow-guest, told of their services as witnessed by himself at Lucknow during the previous winter. "Almost the first white faces I saw, when the lamented Havelock and I rushed out of our prison to greet Sir Colin at the head of our deliverers, were the hearty, jolly, smiling faces of some of you *Shannon* men, who were pounding away with two big guns at the palace; and I then, for the first time in my life, had the opportunity of seeing and admiring the coolness of British sailors under fire. There you were, working in the open plains, without cover or screen, or rampart of any kind, your guns within musket range of the enemy, as coolly as if you were practising at the Woolwich target. And that it was a hot fire that you were exposed to, was proved by three of the small staff that accompanied us (Napier, young Havelock, and Sitwell) being knocked over by musket balls in passing to the rear of those guns, consequently further from the enemy than yourselves."

Such words, spoken by the Bayard of India, must have been grateful to the Naval Brigade after all their toils and privations. When the banquet was over, they were dispersed among the different vessels to which they belonged. Peel and his Naval Brigade have ceased to exist, but if England should require their services other Peels and other brigades will spring up to prove that our sailors have not degenerated—that they belong to the same race and inherit the same qualities as those who in former times secured for Britannia the empire of the waves, and the enjoyment of that freedom which we still prize as our noblest birthright.

CHAPTER XXVIII.

THE VARIOUS RANKS IN THE BRITISH ARMY, AND HOW TO DISTINGUISH THEM.

HE civilian is often wofully puzzled when trying to make out the rank of a military man in uniform. He sees a venerable, soldier-like man, in scarlet or blue, marching beside a body of men. This personage is crowned with a cocked hat with white plumes, with all the pomp of sword, &c., and is immediately selected as "the General." Impressed with the appearance of the hero, his importance and rank, the speaker inquires who the general officer is, and in reply will be informed "that is the quartermaster, who has just been promoted from the rank of serjeant-major." Again, a ferocious-looking man, who, with long beard and moustache, *walks* (not *marches*) in rear of the regiment, with cocked hat and trailing sword, is neither a fire-eating general nor dashing colonel, but our kind medical friend, who looks at our tongue and feels our pulse. A quiet-looking man, in a dark frock coat, who is the least conspicuous of a group of officers, is General Sir Blank Blanco, K.C.B., the hero of so many battles.

The two principal points by which rank is indicated are the collars and sleeves of the various coattees and jackets. A crown and star, used either singly or in combination, denote three different degrees of rank. Commencing at the highest rank, viz., Field-Marshal, we will now describe the principal peculiarities of dress, so that the reader may be able to form a generally correct opinion of the rank and occupation of each member of the military service.

ARMY DRESS.

A Field-Marshal's dress consists of a single-breasted scarlet tunic, the collar laced round with inch lace. At each end of the collar are two batons, crossed, and formed of crimson velvet and gold, worked on a wreath of laurel embroidered in silver. The cuff, which is three inches and a quarter deep, has two rows of inch lace round the top, and there is a scarlet pointed slashed flap on the sleeve, laced with inch lace. On the left shoulder is a double gold cord, with a small button to retain the sash.

The buttons are gilt, and have on them two batons, crossed, and encircled with laurels.

Cocked hat, with a plume of long white swan feathers, drooping downwards and outwards, with scarlet feathers underneath.

The trousers are dark blue, with oak-pattern gold lace two and a half inches wide down the sides.

The sword is scimitar shape, and contained in a brass scabbard. The hilt is gilt, with an ivory grip, two batons crossed, and encircled with oak leaves on the handle. The sword belt is of Russian leather, one and a half inches wide, embroidered with three rows of gold embroidery. A sash of gold and crimson silk net is worn over the left shoulder, the ends of fringe hanging downwards.

The above is the full dress. The undress consists of double-breasted frock coat of dark blue. The collar and cuffs of blue velvet with cross batons on the collar, a double gold cord on the left shoulder to retain the sash. The trousers are dark blue, with a broad red stripe down the side. A forage cap with gold embroidered peak, and band of gold oak leaf lace two inches wide round the cap.

The full dress of a General is the same as that of a Field-Marshal, except that on the collar there is, in place of the cross batons, a silver embroidered crown and star an inch and a quarter long. The buttons are gilt, but instead of cross batons they have on them a sword and baton crossed. The handle of the sword also has on it a sword and baton crossed.

The undress of a General is blue frock coat, with sword and baton on collar; in other respects like a Field-Marshal's.

The dress of a Lieutenant-General, a Major-General, and a Brigadier-General is the same as a General's, with the exceptions that a Lieutenant-General has on his collar a crown only, instead of a crown and star. A Major-General has on his collar a star only, whilst a Brigadier-General has the collar plain, without star or crown.

We now come to the three principal divisions of the remainder of the regular officers, viz., Field Officers, Captains, and Subalterns.

Field Officers are all those above the rank of Captain and below the rank of General; they consist therefore of Colonels, Lieutenant-Colonels, and Majors. The distinguishing mark of a Field Officer is the lace or embroidery on his sleeves, which comes to a point up the arms; the annexed illustrations show the sleeve of a Field Officer of the Artillery.

In all line regiments and in several others, the Full Colonel may be known by his wearing the dress of his regiment, and having on his collar a crown and star. A Lieutenant-Colonel has a crown only, whilst a Major has a star on his collar.

The sleeves of Line Officers are not embroidered, but the collar trimmings also indicate their rank, the Field Officers having lace round the top and bottom of the collar, down the edge of the skirts behind, on the edge of the skirt flaps and edge of the sleeve flaps, and two rows of lace round the top of the cuffs.

Officers below the rank of Field Officer have lace on the top only of the collar, one row round the top of the cuff and none on the edge of the skirts. Then on the collar a Captain has a star and crown, a Lieutenant a crown, and an Ensign a star.

When the frock coat is worn, the collar will indicate the rank of the Field Officer. The crown and star being the mark of the Colonel, a crown for Lieutenant-Colonel, and the star for the Major.

The same marks are used for the various ranks when the shell jacket is used; but in both these cases there is in the Line no difference between the dress of a Captain and a Lieutenant or Ensign, but in the Royal Artillery and Engineers the cuff lace will indicate to which rank the wearer belongs. *a*, Field Officer's patrol jacket; *b*, Captain's sleeve for full dress; *c*, Lieutenant's sleeve.

a.

b.

The distinguishing marks on the collar and sleeves of the majority of the army serve to indicate the rank of the various officers, but we have also to deal with other details.

c.

DRESS AND RANK.

Commencing with the Medical Department, we shall be able to distinguish the Surgeon and Assistant-Surgeon principally by the belt, which is of black leather. They also wear the black shoulder-belt and instrument case; in other respects their uniform is the same as is that of the other officers of the regiment to which they belong, with the exception of wearing a cocked hat with a black cock's-tail feather, drooping, and five inches in length.

When medical officers belong to what is called the "Staff," and not to any particular regiment, their full-dress is a scarlet tunic with black velvet collar and cuffs, blue cloth trousers with gold lace, two and a half inches wide for a Director-General or Inspector-General, and one inch and three quarters for officers below that rank; cocked hat with black cock's-tail feathers, shoulder-belt and sword-belt of black morocco.

In undress a double-breasted blue frock coat, two rows of buttons down the front, trousers of dark blue with scarlet stripe, the breadth of the stripe varying according to the rank, the same as the lace.

The forage cap consists of blue cloth with black leather peak and chin strap, black silk oak leaf pattern band, surmounted by a crown embroidered in gold on the front. A shell jacket is also worn in undress, and is the same as for infantry officers, the collar and cuffs of black velvet.

The various ranks in the Medical Department are—

Director-General of the Army Medical Department, who ranks as Brigadier until he has served three years in that rank, when he ranks as Major-General. The latter rank is distinguished by inch lace round the collar with a star at each end, whilst a crown and star in silver with half-inch lace on the collar indicate the former rank.

A Deputy Inspector-General ranks as a Lieutenant-Colonel until he has served five years, after which he ranks as a Colonel; he has the same lace, with a crown at the end of the collar. This also is the dress of a Surgeon-Major, who ranks as a Lieutenant-Colonel in the army.

A Staff-Surgeon ranks as Major, and has half-inch lace round the top and bottom of the collar, with a star in silver at each end.

An Assistant-Surgeon ranks as Lieutenant until he has served six years, when he takes rank as Captain. He has the same lace on his collar as a Staff-Surgeon, but has a crown only at each end.

All the Medical Staff who rank equal to or above a Major have two rows of half-inch lace round the top of the cuff, whilst officers below that rank have one row only bound on the cuff.

The officers equal to the rank of Major or above it have the badges of their rank as a crown or star on their collar, whilst officers below that rank have their collars plain. Thus the Medical Department generally may be recognised by their cocked hats with black plume, the black belt, and also by the buttons, which have **V. R.**, with a crown, and "Medical Department" written round.

With every regiment there are, besides the medical officers, a Quartermaster and a Paymaster. The Quartermasters wear the dress of their regiment, but wear also a cocked hat, this being the insignia of what is termed the Staff of an Army, viz., of General Officers, Aides-de-Camp, Surgeons, Quartermasters, Adjutant-Generals, &c. The Paymasters also wear the dress of their regiments with cocked hats, the Quartermaster's hat having a white cock's feather five inches long, mushroom shape, with red underneath, whilst the Paymasters wear no feathers. The waist-belts are black for both these departments.

In almost all the Cavalry Regiments, including the 1st and 2nd Life Guards, the ranks are distinguished as follows—

All Field Officers have a row of embroidery round the collar and cuffs, whilst those below that rank have none. A Full Colonel has a crown and star in silver at each end of the collar, with embroidery; a Lieutenant-Colonel a crown only, with embroidery; a Major, with star and embroidery; a Captain, crown and star; Lieutenant, crown; Sub-Lieutenant, star. The Veterinary Surgeon has a cocked hat with a red feather.

We next come to a long list of Staff Officers, among whom are Adjutant and Quartermaster-Generals with their Deputies, Assistants and Deputy-Assistants, Brigade Majors, Military Secretaries, Aides-de-Camp, Staff of Garrisons, &c. The general principles of these dresses are the same. The tunic is scarlet or blue, edged round with gold cord; on each side of the breast four loops of the same cord with caps and drops.

The ranks of Staff Officers are distinguished by the knot on the cuff and the crown and star. All the Staff wear the cocked hat, the general form of feather being upright, with white and red swan feathers.

In many cases officers of the rank of General or Field-Marshal are Colonels of particular regiments. The present Commander-in-Chief, for example, being Colonel of the Royal Artillery. When this is the case, and any duty specially concerning Artillery is carried on, it is usual for an officer not to attend in the dress of a General or Field-Marshal but in that of the Colonel of the regiment to which he belongs.

RANKS.

Next to Field-Marshals come Full Generals. After a General comes a Lieutenant-General, and then a Major-General. The civilian usually makes a mistake in the relative rank of these two officers; for as a Major is higher in rank than a Lieutenant, so he considers a Major-General must be higher than a Lieutenant-General. The principle by which to remember this, however, is to deduct from General the prefix, and the remainder indicates the rank thus, deducting Lieutenant from General we have a larger remainder than if we deduct Major.

Colonel and Lieutenant-Colonel come next; then Major, Captain, First Lieutenant, Second Lieutenant, and Cornet or Ensign.

A Second Lieutenant takes precedence of a Cornet or Ensign.

These ranks being fixed and known, we can now compare the staff and civil branches of the army with them. The great advantage of "rank" to the civil branches is not merely the position, but the power of choosing quarters in garrison, cabins on board ship, &c., before officers who are junior in rank. No nominal rank allows any person except a regular officer to have any military command; thus, if an Ensign were on board ship with troops, as also an old Surgeon and Paymaster, the Ensign would command the troops, though the Surgeon and Paymaster both rank as Captains.

The following are the relative ranks of the Staff Officers named below:—

Paymasters	Rank as Captains.
Surgeons	Rank as Captains.
Assistant-Surgeons	Rank as Lieutenants.
Veterinary Surgeons during the first ten years of their service . . .	Rank as Cornets.
Ditto after ten years	Rank as Lieutenants.
Ditto after twenty years	Rank as Captains.
Quartermasters	Rank as Lieutenants.

In the Medical Department there are various titles, each of which ranks according to the following list:—

Inspector-General	Ranks as Brigadier-General.
Deputy Inspector-General . . .	Ranks as Lieutenant-Colonel.
Staff Surgeon, 1st Class	Ranks as Major.
Regimental Surgeon and Staff Surgeon, 2nd Class	Ranks as Captain.
Apothecary	Ranks as Captain, but junior of that rank.

Assistant-Surgeon	Ranks as Lieutenant.
Deputy Purveyor	Ranks as Lieutenant.
Medical Clerk	Ranks as Ensign.

COMMISSARIAT DEPARTMENT.

Commissary-General	Ranks as Brigadier-General.
Deputy Commissary-General, if of three years' standing . .	Ranks as Lieutenant-Colonel.
Ditto under three years' standing	Ranks as Major.
Assistant Commissary-General .	Ranks as Captain.
Deputy Assistant Commissary-General	Ranks as Lieutenant.
Deputy Clerks	Rank as Ensigns.

WAR DEPARTMENT.

Storekeepers, Barrackmasters of 1st Class . . . . ,	Rank as Majors.
Deputy Storekeepers, Barrack-masters, 2nd Class	Rank as Captains.
Barrackmasters of 3rd & 4th Class	Rank as Lieutenants.
Clerks	Rank as Ensigns.

Chaplains attached to Brigades rank as Majors, whilst those attached to Regiments take rank as Captains.

RELATIVE RANKS OF ARMY AND NAVY OFFICERS.

An Admiral of the Fleet . . .	Ranks with Field-Marshal of the Army.
Admirals	Rank with Generals.
Vice-Admirals	Rank with Lieutenant-Generals.
Rear-Admirals	Rank with Major-Generals.
Commodores	Rank with Brigadier-Generals.
Captains after three years . .	Rank with Colonels.
Captains during first three years	Rank with Lieutenant-Colonels.
Commanders	Rank with Majors.
Lieutenants, Masters, and Pay-masters	Rank with Captains.
Mates	Rank with Lieutenants.
Midshipmen	Rank with Ensigns.

The givers of dinners in country places where relative ranks are not well understood may take a hint from this list, for they not unusually commit a breach of etiquette in ceding the first honours to an army Major when a navy Captain is present, being unaware that the latter is the officer of the higher rank. It is not, of course, expected that every lady or gentleman is to be a perambulating Army and Navy List, but a glance at either publication and a comparison with the invitation list may often prevent an officer from feeling snubbed—we having ourselves frequently seen a grey-headed veteran naval Captain put on one side, whilst a young army Major was requested to conduct the lady of the house from the drawing-room; the reason assigned being that military and naval men were so punctilious and scrupulous about ranks, and Major ranks above Captain.

In no case, however, can a naval officer command a military officer on shore, or a military a naval officer at sea.

We next come to that valuable branch of the army termed the Non-Commissioned Officers, and dealing first with the Cavalry we have the following ranks :—

LIFE GUARDS AND HORSE GUARDS.

Non-Commissioned Officers.

Schoolmasters.
Regimental Corporal-Major.
Quartermaster Corporal.
Corporal Instructor of Musketry.
Armourer-Corporal.
Saddler-Corporal.
Farrier-Majors.
Troop Corporal-Majors.
Bandmaster.
Trumpet-Major.
Corporals.

Corporal-Majors rank with Sergeant-Majors, and Corporals of the Life Guards and Horse Guards rank with Sergeants of Cavalry and Infantry.

IN THE CAVALRY.

Schoolmaster.
Regimental Sergeant-Major.
Quartermaster-Sergeant
Sergeant Instructor of Musketry.
Paymaster-Sergeant.
Sergeant-Armourer.
Sergeant-Sadler.
Farrier-Major.
Hospital Sergeant.
Bandmaster.
Troop Sergeant-Major.
Trumpet-Major.
Sergeants.
Corporals.

In the Royal Artillery there are as follows for each Brigade and Battery, and each rank is distinguished by the following marks on the sleeve:—

Brigade Sergeant-Major and Brigadier Quartermaster-Sergeant's sleeve.

Assistant-Instructor in Gunnery.

Battery Sergeant-Major's and Quarter-master-Sergeant's sleeve.

Trumpet-Major's sleeve.

Farrier-Major's sleeve. Horse-shoe on stripes.

Collarmaker-Major's sleeve. Bridle on stripes.

Wheeler-Major's sleeve.

Orderly Room Sergeant, Staff-Clerk, Hospital-Sergeant, Paymaster-Sergeant.

Farrier-Sergeant.

Collarmaker-Sergeant.

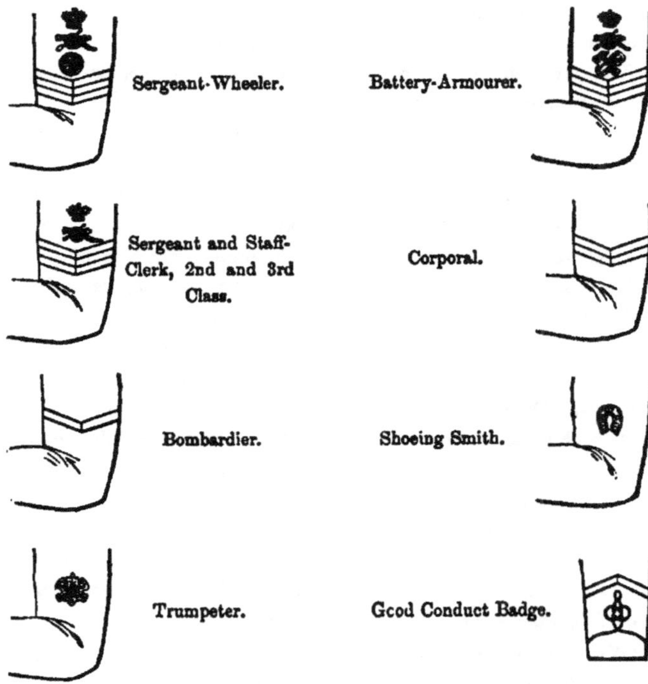

It will be seen that the badges on the cuffs indicate a higher rank than when placed on the arm above the elbow: thus for Brigade Sergeant-Major and Orderly Room Sergeant the badge is the same; but one is on the cuff, the other above the elbow.

A man whose conduct has been good, and who has not received any punishment for a certain period, is granted a good conduct badge, which entitles him to one penny a day. Some Soldiers have three or four of these on their arm, but to distinguish these men from Sergeants, the peak of the badge points upwards, whereas that of the Sergeants, &c. is downwards.

The distinguishing marks for other branches of the army, although not strictly the same as those given above, are yet sufficiently alike to enable us to decide the rank and occupation of the various non-commissioned officers that we meet.

We now come to the general dress of the various branches of the army, commencing with the

LIFE GUARDS, who, when in full dress, wear a scarlet tunic, with polished steel cuirass, steel helmet with a white plume, jack-boots and white leather breeches. The farriers wear blue tunics and a black plume. The HORSE GUARDS have a blue tunic, but in other respects the dress is the same except the plume, which is red.

The seven regiments of DRAGOON GUARDS wear scarlet uniform (with the exception of the 6th Dragoon Guards), brass helmets, with white horsehair plumes.

The 6th Dragoon Guards wear a blue tunic, as also the 17th Lancers. Other Lancer regiments wear blue jackets, and Hussars have blue tunics. The trousers of all the cavalry are blue, except those already named as having leather, and the 11th Hussars, whose overalls are crimson.

In head dresses, the HUSSARS wear a black low sable head dress like a short bearskin, termed a "busby," with plume and bag. The 2nd Dragoons wear a bearskin cap with white hackle feather. The LANCERS wear a square top black leather skull cap.

When cloaks are worn the 1st Life Guards wear a red cloak with blue cape; 2nd Life Guards scarlet cloak with blue cape; Horse Guards, blue with scarlet collar. The remainder of the cavalry blue cloaks, with collars the same as the facings of their regiment, which are as follows:—

REGIMENT.	UNIFORM.	FACINGS.
1st Dragoon Guards . .	Scarlet . .	Blue.
2nd " . .	" . .	Buff.
3rd " . .	" . .	Yellow.
4th " . .	" . .	Blue.
5th " . .	" . .	Dark Green.
6th " . .	Blue . .	White.
7th " . .	Scarlet . .	Black.
1st Dragoons	" . .	Blue.
2nd "	" . .	"

REGIMENT.	UNIFORM.	FACINGS.
3rd Dragoons	Blue	Blue.
4th "	"	"
5th "	"	Scarlet.
6th "	Scarlet	Yellow.
7th "	Blue	Blue.
8th "	"	"
9th "	"	Scarlet.
10th "	"	Blue.
11th "	"	Crimson overalls.
12th "	"	Scarlet.
13th "	"	Blue.
14th "	"	"
15th "	"	"
16th "	Scarlet	"
17th "	Blue	White.
Madras 18th Hussars	"	Blue.
Bengal 19th "	"	"
" 20th "	"	"
" 21st "	"	"

The Royal Artillery.

The uniform for the Royal Artillery is dark blue with red facings. The Horse Artillery wear a jacket in full dress; the Foot Artillery a tunic. The jacket of the Horse Artillery is braided in front with yellow horizontal stripes; the head dress is a black busby with white plume and red bag (the full dress), and for undress a forage cap with gold band.

The Royal Engineers.

The Royal Engineers, or Sappers and Miners, as they are also called, wear a red tunic or jacket with blue facings, Oxford mixture trousers with red stripe; the head dress a fur busby of black seal skin, white plume, and blue bag.

The Military Train.

A dark blue tunic or jacket with white facings; shako of black cloth with black horsehair plume, dark blue trousers with white stripe.

INFANTRY.

There are 109 regiments of Infantry, without the Rifle Brigade. The uniform of each is as follows :—

Guards wear scarlet tunic single-breasted, black trousers with scarlet welt, and black bearskin cap. The Grenadiers wear a white plume; the Coldstreams a red plume; the Scots Fusiliers no plume.

THE LINE uniform consists of single-breasted red tunic, black trousers with scarlet welt for winter, and dark blue trousers in summer; shako, dark blue cloth with red and white ball tuft. Undress a jacket and forage cap, the number of the regiment being in front of the cap.

RIFLES wear tunic and trousers of rifle green cloth.

LIGHT INFANTRY have the shako surmounted by a green horsehair plume instead of the ball tuft; in other respects the uniform is the same.

Fusiliers have a white horsehair plume instead of the ball tuft, except the 5th, where the plume is red and white.

Five of the Highland Regiments wear the kilt, viz., the 42nd, 78th, 79th, 92nd, and 93rd. Three, viz., the 71st, 72nd, and 74th, the trews. The kilted regiments, as also the 72nd, wear a bonnet of black ostrich feathers, with tartan plaid skull, with white or red feather. The facings of the regiments vary; a so-termed Royal Regiment having blue facings, the others consist of different colours, yellow, white, red, buff, and green being the variations.

Commissariat.—The dress of this service consists of dark blue tunic, blue velvet facings, dark blue trousers, red stripe, dark shako and tuft.

The Medical Department wear scarlet tunic, black facings, blue trousers with gold or red stripes, cocked hat and black plume.

The Army Hospital Corps wear dark blue with grey facings.

Among the extras to be seen in uniform in most garrison towns, are Bandmasters, Bandsmen, Drummers, &c., and Schoolmasters.

The Bands of the Infantry have white tunics with regimental

or scarlet facings. The Bandmaster usually wears a black frock coat in undress, and the regimental dress with gold in full dress.

Schoolmasters wear a blue frock coat with shoulder knots, crimson silk sash, oilskin cap, black trousers in winter, blue serge in summer.

The Militia of Great Britain consists of Artillery and Infantry, and is equipped in the same manner as is the regular army, except that the lace is silver instead of gold, and the buttons white metal instead of brass.

In the present day, when soldiering is popular and when each town or district sends forth its volunteers, we naturally see an endless display of uniforms, some of which are difficult to identify. Taking, however, the preceding remark about gold lace and silver, red and blue uniforms, numbers on caps, &c., any non-military man may be able to form a very good estimate of the branch of the service and the rank to which each person belongs, a little practice being sufficient to soon train the eye to mark the various peculiarities.

When regiments are formed on parade for reviews or any similar purpose, they are usually placed in the order of their precedence. This order being as follows:—

The Life and Horse Guards have the precedence of all other corps.

The Horse Artillery, whether mounted or dismounted, take the right of all other cavalry.

The Cavalry always take the right of Infantry.

The Royal Artillery take the right of Infantry.

The Royal Engineers take rank next to the Royal Artillery.

The Foot Guards follow next to the Royal Engineers.

The Regiments of the line follow in the order of their number.

The Royal Marines take rank after the 49th Regiment, and the Rifle Brigade after the 93rd.

When Militia regiments of different parts of the United Kingdom meet, that regiment takes precedence which belongs to the county in which the meeting occurs.

CHAPTER XXIX.

A GRAND REVIEW.

REVIEW of the armies of Europe, Austrian, Prussian, French, Russian, British, Italian, Turkish—is only to be achieved on paper. According to a recent calculation it appears that the numerical strength of the armies of Europe is 4,735,782, and, however brilliant the spectacle might be, it would occupy a weary while to see so many men pass by in marching order. On paper it may be done, and so in imagination we take our stand by the reader, to point out the finest troops, or call attention to this or that particular regiment, as the living panorama of disciplined men sweeps on before us. The air resounds with the strains of martial music; the earth seems to shake beneath the feet of the legions, and the eye is dazed with a blaze of colour.

The Austrians—the standing army of Austria is the oldest in Europe — lead the van. The neatly-made white tunics of the infantry, collars and facings marking the distinction between the regiments, and their straight-peaked shakos made of black cloth, present a very noble appearance. The sergeants and corporals are distinguished by woollen stars on their collars, broad black and yellow cords on their shakos, and sword-knots of the same unvarying colour made of wool. The knapsacks of the men are of dark brown calf skin, and their cloaks are fastened on the top of their knapsacks. The men are armed with short light muskets, but to every regiment there are a certain number of grenadiers. The officers, you observe, are fewer in comparison than those of so large a body of men in an English army. To command this body of infantry we should have at least two generals, four colonels, some ten lieutenant-colonels, majors, and fifty-five captains; here the duty is performed by one colonel, six field officers, and thirty-two captains. Perhaps, say you, it is too few. Perhaps. But these fellows march in excellent order—tramp, tramp! and the drummers play with wonderful precision.

These fellows in the light grey tunics are rifles—a good colour, grey. How much better than the old invisible green, which was always visible! And how well the men look in that Swedish felt hat with one side turned up and fastened by a brush. They are some 32,000 strong, these men of the rifle, and the regiments are justly regarded as the finest in the service.

Next in order of march come the border infantry, raised originally in the reign of Maria Theresa; you may know them by their coffee-brown tunics and black cross-belts. Disciplinary companies follow close upon them. They march well, but if you look closely at some of the fellows you may notice a rollicking daring in them quite foreign to the regular troops. These disciplinary corps are established for the purpose of drafting in those untamed spirits that have not yet learned how to obey, and the discipline is pretty sharp. *You* would not like it! *you* would be writing to the *Times* about it, if you dared!

General Discipline in the Austrian army?—Well—almost as unpopular an officer as Corporal Punishment—pardon so dull a joke on so bright a day—well, the discipline is not so sharp as it used to be. We don't hear so much of the stick, and running the gauntlet has quite gone out of fashion. That running of the gauntlet was terrible work. Stripped to the waist the culprit was marched through the ranks of his comrades, every soldier armed with a cane, every soldier striking a blow—a punishment so severe that many a time a man having endured it has asked for a draught of water, and died before the water could be brought. Now they do these things better: imprison the culprit, put him to shot piling or on extra drill, but—

Oh these men of iron! Hardy and brave as the men of iron who served under old iron-handed Charlemagne! These are the Austrian heavy cavalry—these the cuirassiers with their breast-plates of black polished iron, but *no back-plates*. They wear low leathern helmets and a brass crest; they have white tunics, and grey trousers covered with leather to the knee. Powerful horses carry these powerful men, but we doubt whether the grey-clad riflemen could not bring them down, notwithstanding their iron breast-plates. Amid a cloud of dust the Cuirassiers and Dragoons ride on, and close in their rear come the Lancers with their short dark green tunics, with red collars and facings, richly decorated with yellow epaulettes, aiguillettes and cords, green trousers with red stripe, white cloaks and low-crowned chapkas of various colours with a tuft. Each man carries a long lance decorated with a black and yellow pennon. These Lancers are followed by the Hussars, wearing tightly fitting tunics and trousers; and after that, thundering over the ground, the Artillery—an Artillery equal to that of any in Europe. The gun carriages and limbers are painted yellow with black wheels, and the men are riding on long jaunting cars, their uniform consisting of brown tunics with red cuffs and facings, light blue trousers, long grey cloaks, and felt hats with one brim turned up and fastened by a black and yellow tuft. Their belts are white, and they carry a short infantry sword.

A small company in dark brown tunics with blue facings, and small low shakos, follow next. These form the Land Transport Corps. After them come the Engineers, with a special corps for Pontoons, and another Special Corps for Flotilla purposes; and, lastly, 19,000 strong, march the Gendarmerie, as fine a body of men—to look at—as ever trod the ground.

The oldest standing army in Europe is that of Austria. Its history is indissolubly connected with that of the Empire; but, while there is no army in Europe which displays stronger traces of the Middle Ages, no pains have been spared to make it the most efficient by a ready adoption—since 1850—of all modern improvements.

The army, like the Empire, is a strange compound of nationalities. Germans, Sclavons, Hungarians, Wallachs—all are included, the army being made up by conscription through all the provinces of the Empire, and all classes, with some few very exceptions, being subjected to it. The army belongs to the Emperor and not to the Empire, and hence an officer may serve in it for years without having any claim to the protection of the State. Foreigners, ever since the period of the Thirty Years' War, have held high rank in the Emperor's army, and it is asserted that one-half of the officers now holding commissions in the Austrian army are not Austrians by birth.

By the latest returns it appears that a considerable reduction is taking place in the numerical strength of the Austrian army. The expenses, which in 1863 were estimated at a sum equivalent to 10,000,000*l.*, were reduced in 1865 to 9,000,000*l.*, and the estimates for 1866 are no more than 8,000,000*l.*

You notice that the men are marked by strange contrasts of physiognomy; they are marked also by strong animosity to each other, not as individuals, but as nations. The troops raised in one dependency of Austria hate with a thorough hatred troops raised in another, and it is very difficult sometimes to keep peace between them. It is a rule also that troops raised in any particular district should never be permitted to garrison that district; and, in fact, that no troops should remain long in any one place. By this means all familiarity with civilians is cut off; the men must associate together—the officers must associate together. As to the men, they are tolerably well paid—always enough to secure them a good breakfast, dinner, and supper, with twopence or threepence over for a dram. The officers—especially those holding high rank—are nothing like so well paid as officers similarly commissioned in England. They do not meet at mess, but each officer dines where he pleases, and thus—

But here come the soldiers of Prussia, the soldiers of the Great Army, which bears something of the impress of Frederick the Great.

Here are the Prussian Rifles, in dark green tunics, with red collars and facings, grey infantry trousers, and a shako with a peak before and behind, and a horsehair brush. Their belts are of black leather, and the *couteau de chasse*, which can be used as a bayonet, is worn on the same belt as the cartouche-box. They are all capital marksmen, and rapidity of firing is regarded as a *sine quâ non*.

The Rifles are closely followed by the whole body of Prussian infantry, on a war footing, 360,436 strong. They wear short tunics of blue cloth, the collars red in the front and blue behind. Why blue behind? Because the helmet would soon wear the other colour dirty. The head covering—*pickelhaube*—is a round helmet with projecting pike, the line wearing the regimental number in front, while the Guard is distinguished by a star. The Guard is also distinguished by horsehair plumes. Who are those who wear a cross in front of their helmets? These are the Landwehr Infantry. There is, if you will look closely, something in the uniform to distinguish the corps: the regiments of Prussia Proper and Pomerania have white shoulder straps; those of Saxony and Brandenburg, red; those of Posen and Silesia, yellow; those of Westphalia and the Rhine, light blue. The trousers of the men are of dark grey cloth with a red piping down the side; they all wear boots, but on march put gaiters over them; their cloaks are of dark grey cloth, and their belts are of black leather.

This strong body of cavaliers—every horse a model—forms the Prussian Cavalry. Here are the Garde du Corps and Grand Cuirassiers. They have back and breastplates of polished steel, and wear short white tunics with red, blue, green, yellow, black, or orange colour cuffs and collars, according to their regiments; their trousers are of dark grey cloth; their helmets of polished steel; their principal weapon, the long cut-and-thrust sword, worn in a white buffalo belt.

Here come the heavy Landwehr Regiments, in dark blue tunics and bright helmets; in their rear ride the Italians, their dark blue jackets, all picked out with red, are armed with long lances with black and white pennons. These are followed by the Dragoons, in light blue tunics with different coloured facings; Hussars, with black fur shakos and cloaks, and trousers of light grey. And after them thunder the Artillery, on a war footing, with some 34,000 horses and a proportionate number of men.

In time of peace the Prussian army is only 122,260 strong, with

5500 officers; while on a war footing it numbers 299,401 men, who can take the field, while 95,957 men are left behind for home contingencies. The difference between the peace and war establishment of Prussia is greater than in any other European nation.

Universal service is the rule in Prussia, and every healthy man, without distinction of rank, must personally perform military duty; but the period a soldier remains in the standing army is short. The majority only serve three years—from twenty-one to twenty-four; after which they are enrolled for two further years in the reserve, and then pass to the Landwehr of the final levy. The Prussian is aware from his earliest years that he will have to enter the army, and hence even his childish amusements bear a military stamp, and military drill forms part of his common education. It is no small thing to demand of a nation that its entire population must belong to the army up to the thirty-fifth year, and be ready at any moment to quit home and family and to march wherever it is commanded. But so it is in Prussia.

The non-commissioned officers of the Prussian army as a body are probably the best in the world. They have the privilege before them of a civil appointment after twelve years' service, and they would rather work hard for this than obtain a commission. There is a striking difference between them and the French sergeants, whose only ambition seems to be to rise from the ranks—to pluck at the bâton which is found—with how much of difficulty!—in every man's knapsack.

The French! Well, the French, you know, are an enthusiastic people—they lead, in civil as well as military circles, rather stagey lives. Have you seen Gustave Doré's admirable pictures illustrative of the life of a certain Captain Castagnette? Now he loses an eye—now an arm—now two legs; now he has a bomb in his back which cannot be extracted; and now, finally, *sans* everything, he dozes by the fireside, sets fire to his wooden leg, expels that ugly lodger, the bomb in his back, and is himself dashed into a thousand or more pieces, nothing remaining but the Cross of the Legion! All is lost, save honour! It is very French.

But here are the Frenchmen, ready to fight for honour and glory. *Vive l'Empereur!* Here are they, 500,000 strong. "*L'Empire c'est la Paix*," is it? Every Frenchman is a soldier by birth. Born in the purple were the imperial children of Rome—born, or cradled in the buckler are these children of the modern Empire! It may serve the turn of a Russian or a German to aver that the most stupid soldiers are the best—that it is not a soldier's business to think, but simply to obey. Not so think the Frenchmen. Intelligent, active, independent, are these brave Gallic heroes. "Your hand, brave comrade—nay, never apologize. If the right hand has been knocked off in fair fighting, give me your *left* hand."

Here are the Infantry, in light blue tunics, longer and wider than those of Prussia, a black belt, to which is attached cartouche box, bayonet, and sabre sheath; knapsack of brown calf-skin; large fringe epaulettes, red trousers, small low shako of blue cloth, with a brass shield in front, short half-boots, and gaiters. Here are the buglers and sappers, armed with short rifles, and here are twenty battalions of light infantry, each battalion numbering more than 1200 men. There are the Chasseurs, consisting entirely of picked, active, strong soldiers—hardy mountaineers of Auvergne, the Vosges, the Ardennes, the French Alps, the Pyrenees, and Corsica. Here are the bronze-visaged sons of Algeria, the Zouaves, their ranks recruited by a vast number of Frenchmen, and a sprinkling of Germans, Poles, and Italians, attracted by the fiery impetuosity, almost boyish fun, and Oriental costume of the band. They number about 8000 men. They are closely followed by battalions of Light African Infantry, four battalions of Native African Skirmishers, wearing the Zouave dress; and these, again, by the old Foreign Legion, made up of Germans, Prussians, Bavarians, Poles, Hungarians, Spaniards, and Italians. Next come the Disciplinary Corps, 1600 strong; and, lastly, six companies of Hospital Orderlies, amounting to 1600 or 1700 men.

The helmeted men who ride those powerfully made horses, that you might swear were raised in Normandy, are the Cuirassiers. They are all tall, athletic men; so also are the Carbineers, who follow them. Next come the Dragoons, forming a total of seventy-two squadrons, who can take the field with 13,000 horses, and forty-eight squadrons of Lancers, with 8,000 horses. The Light Cavalry consists of twelve regiments of *Chasseurs à Cheval* and nine Hussar regiments—on a war footing, 24,000 or 25,000 strong. The Hussar and Chasseur are only distinguished from each other by their gay and overladen uniform; their arms and horses are very much alike. They ride little, strong, but terribly ugly horses, reared in the mountainous parts of France. Next come the *Chasseurs d'Afrique*, numbering about 3,000. They wear light blue tunics of the Polish cut, red shakos, and white capote cloaks. They are armed with long rifles and light sabres. The Spahis—numbering about 3,000 men, principally natives of Algeria, mounted on Moorish stallions, their uniform, armament and horse equipment perfectly Oriental in style—next pass in review; and then the eye is dazzled by the splendid spectacle of the Cent Gardes. Their uniform is magnificent, and every man is fit for a sculptor's model. And lastly, there is a large body of the Imperial Guard—the Cuirassiers—splendidly built fellows, mounted on sturdy horses of the Norman breed.

Here's the Artillery—the finest arm of the French service. Has not the Emperor himself written a hand-book on artillery practice? The uniform of the men is tasteful and richly decorated; red-fringed epaulettes and red-bordered shakos, short dark blue jacket with red facings, trousers of the same with a broad red stripe. All the foot artillerymen are armed with a short straight sword; all who serve on horseback carry cavalry sabres. The guns are horsed by country-bred horses—compact, strong brutes, not particularly attractive to the eye, but useful, and well able to stand any climate. If the French Artillery were placed on the war establishment, it would number 60,000 strong, with 49,000 horses and nearly 1200 guns. The Commissariat troops and the indispensable Engineers, in their blue tunics, come next, and while they pass before us we may offer a few words on the army in general.

The French army on a full war establishment is represented by 580,000 men, 82,000 cavalry horses, and 1182 guns; there is also a reserve, made up of old non-commissioned officers and conscripts, whom it has not been found necessary to call out, amounting to at least 150,000 men. All the men are thoroughly in earnest; they don't wear the "Emperor's coat," but the uniform of their country; the regiments do not bear the name of any varying possession, but has its own number and permanent place in history. "We did so and so at Austerlitz," say the men to this day, in speaking of the regiment to which they belong. In France, too, any good soldier can become a corporal, any corporal a lieutenant, and so on in military rank. The words of the Great Emperor will never be eradicated from the minds of the French troops: "Every soldier of France carries a marshal's bâton in his knapsack;" and indeed many a man who entered the service in a blouse has died in a General's uniform.

Ah, my friend, I see you are inattentive. I know what means that glow upon your cheek and sparkle in your eyes; I hear the strain as well as yourself:—

"Our plumes have waved in combats
 That ne'er shall be forgot,
Where many a mighty squadron
 Reel'd backward from our shot.
In charges with the bayonet
 We lead our bold compeers,
But Frenchmen like to stay not
 For *British Grenadiers*.

"Once boldly at Vimiera
 They hoped to play their parts,
And sang fal lira lira
 To cheer their drooping hearts.
But English, Scotch, and Paddy-whacks,
 We gave three hearty cheers,
And the French soon turned their backs
 To the *British Grenadiers*.

"And what could Buonaparte,
 With all his Cuirassiers,
In battle do at Waterloo
 With British Grenadiers?
Then ever sweet the drum shall greet
 That march unto our ears,
Whose martial roll awakes the soul
 Of *British Grenadiers!*"

You know the old colours, and the old familiar music of the "spirit-stirring drum" and "ear-piercing fife" is a welcome sound. Hurrah for our soldiers! One, two, three! and a ringing one over the young recruits. Now for another one after that. What is that for? The Volunteers, of course.

The number of effectives in the British army by the last return was 204,057. They are scattered all over the world, scarcely more than 30,000 being at any one time at home; and under so many varied temptations as they must be exposed to, both abroad and at home, it says much for the men that during the last year there were only 1438 deserters and 466 cases of corporal punishment. As to what British troops have achieved—is not the history of England full of it? The sheer pluck they have displayed under all sorts of disadvantages has made them famous through the world. All sorts of disadvantages—at home not over well paid, not over well cared for in garrison; not incited to exertion by the prospect of promotion above that of a non-commissioned officer; not encouraged to feel himself a man as well as a soldier; exposed to a degrading punishment; clad in a costume totally unfitted for the field or the march; armed with heavy and cumbersome weapons; sent to all parts of the globe in precisely the same uniform; no proper provision made for his comfort or convenience; not taken care of by the authorities, not allowed to take care of himself; not——

> "Upon the plains of Flanders
> Our fathers long ago,
> They fought like Alexanders
> Beneath old Marlborough!"

I know it, my friend, but they fought under great disadvantage. They were ill-provided with everything; they were badly paid, and their pay, small as it was, was kept; their sheer pluck, as we said before, won the battle——

> "And still in fields of conquest
> Our valour bright has shone,
> With Wolfe and Abercrombie,
> And Moore and Wellington."

I am aware of it all, but they would have thrashed their foes as surely, and certainly with less inconvenience to themselves, had they been better cared for. "If you had to fight the battle of Waterloo again, how would you like to be dressed?" said the Prince Regent to a Guardsman. "In my shirt sleeves, your Majesty!" was the highly practical reply. Do you remember what use they made of the Grenadiers' bear-skin caps in the Crimea? They filled them with mud, and found them excellent building material. Do you remember the outcry there was when the stiff dog collars were taken off our half-strangled soldiers? Do you recollect how Miniés and revolvers were ridiculed by plethoric old officers? "I'll tell you what, sir, our men didn't want Miniés and revolvers and such new-fangled bosh at Waterloo, sir. They won without them, and can do it again, sir."

I observe that you are observing the march of the British soldiers, more than my observations. Well—'tis a grand sight. Chobham and Aldershott have done something for them. Those are the Guards: the Household Brigade, composed of the Grenadiers, of three battalions, the Coldstream, of two, and the Fusiliers, of two battalions: forming a total of seven battalions, each with a strength of 900 men. They are fine, tall, powerful fellows—picked men. How bravely they bestirred themselves that foggy morning at Inkermann, when the Russians dropped in before breakfast! Who can forget that soldiers' battle? The men who follow are the Infantry Regiments of the Line, all armed with rifles. There are 100 regiments, numbering somewhere about 130,000 men. There are the Rifle Brigade, in their uniform of dark green cloth and dull metal buttons; then a company of Amazons—no, the Highlanders, in their national garb. The pibroch tells of their coming:

"Think on Scotia's ancient heroes,
Think on foreign foes repelled;
Think on glorious Bruce and Wallace,
Who the proud usurpers quelled!

"See the northern clans advancing!
See Glengarry and Lochiel!
See the brandished broadsword gleaming!
Highland hearts are true as steel."

And now the Cavalry appears on the scene—the so-called "Heavies" more lightly, however, mounted than the French, Prussian, or Austrian Cuirassiers; counterbalanced, perhaps, by the extreme heaviness of the Light Dragoons when compared to continental Hussars. The Heavy Cavalry is composed of three regiments of Guards, nine Heavy Dragoon regiments, one Carabineer regiment; altogether thirteen regiments, comprising a strength of about 6,000 men, with the same number of horses. The Guards form Her Majesty's Body Guard, and there is not a finer body of men in the world. The English Light Cavalry is composed of Dragoons, Lancers, and Hussars.

The Artillery consists of what is called the Royal Regiment of Artillery, which has a strength of about 800 officers, 1500 non-commissioned officers, 1900 rank and file, with 4200 horses. In addition to this Artillery Regiment, there is a brigade of Horse Artillery, comprised of 70 officers, 150 non-commissioned officers, and 2200 rank and file, with 1900 horses. All the material is excellent, no expense being spared to raise this branch of the service to a proper degree of efficiency. The Engineer Corps is an important addition to the army.* At Woolwich there is a splendid school for the non-commissioned officers.

And here are the Volunteers!

"Altogether," you say, "a splendid show, these British fellows. Only a small item in this grand parade of European armies, but clearly there is the might of men in them. They afraid!

"'Come, if you dare!' our trumpets sound.
'Come, if you dare!' the foes rebound.
'We come, we come!'
Says the double beat of the thund'ring drum.
Now they charge on amain!
Now they rally again!
The gods from above the mad labour behold,
And pity mankind that will perish for gold.
The fainting foemen quit their ground,
Their trumpets languish in their sound—
They fly! they fly!
Victoria! Victoria!"

---

* See article on the Engineers, p. 24.

Ah, my dear friend, when your enthusiasm has a little cooled will you kindly direct your attention to the troops *now* passing under your Roman—no—I mean your British—nose. These are Russians. How stolidly they march, and how alike they are. There is a company of the Guards, and all the men have light hair and blue eyes; there's a company of the Guards again, and all the men have black hair and dark eyes. Order is Russia's first law, and, this confest, all are and must be very like the rest. One day a ship, with many officers and men on board, went down in the Neva. The order was passed to the soldiers to save in the first place the officers of the Guard. They therefore anxiously inquired of each officer they got hold of if he belonged to the Guard? The poor fellows could not answer, as their mouths were full of water, so they were allowed to drown. On another occasion, as it was very dusty, the soldiers were ordered to water the field for exercise. While employed in this duty it came on to rain heavily, but they continued the task with the utmost gravity. They had been ordered to do it, and that was enough. During the siege of Warsaw a young grenadier addressed a veteran, and pointing to the entrenchments, said, "Do you think, comrade, we shall take them?" "I do not think we shall," the other replied; "they are too strong." "But," said the young man, "if we are ordered to take them?" "Oh, that will be another thing; if we are ordered to take them of course we shall do so."

Out of 65,000,000 to 70,000,000 men subject to the Czar, 40,000,000 to 45,000,000 are liable to the conscription. The infantry of the Russian Imperial Guard consists of five grand infantry divisions, each composed of two brigades, and these again subdivided into four regiments. The Grenadier Corps is divided into six brigades or twelve regiments. There are also attached three Carabineer regiments. There are six Infantry Corps, each consisting of three divisions of six brigades, or twelve regiments. One rifle regiment is attached to each division. The Circassian Corps is subdivided precisely like the line infantry, but the regiments are much stronger. The Finland Corps only consists of one division of two brigades, subdivided into twelve battalions, equal to 12,600 men. The Siberian Corps is composed of one division; the Oremberg Corps also comprises one division. The total strength of Russian infantry amounts to about 540,000 fighting men. The total strength of the Russian cavalry is estimated at 80,000 men. Those magnificent fellows that just now rode by, in their white uniforms and black helmets and cuirasses, are the picked men—the Cuirassiers of the Guard. The Russian Artillery is formed of nine foot and two horse divisions—14,000 guns and 44,000 men.

Who are these? These are the Italians, just drawing long breaths of liberty; and these, soldiers of Spain and Portugal; and these, sons of Mohammed—weak descendants of a mighty race, who set the world aflame from Delhi to Grenada!

All the colours of the rainbow, all the tongues of Babeldom, all the varied physiognomies of all the races in all the world—they troop past us: the wild, weird Cossack, with his tremendous lance; the dapper English Volunteer, with his rifle sure as David's sling; the Zouave, with his cat upon his knapsack; the Prussian officer, very bare in pocket, but proud of the "King's coat"—here they pass before us; the air resounding with the strains of military music, the rat-a-plan of the French troops, the clash of Turkish cymbals, the ringing sound of the English bugle, the shrill note of the Highland pibroch. Yes—here are our fighting men, ready to—— well—may Heaven grant that their swords may rest in their scabbards, and that their artillery shall thunder only to usher in —with soldiers' music—a Millennium of Peace!

CHAPTER XXX.

A SOLDIER'S FUNERAL.

HEN a soldier dies notice is at once given to the officer in command of his troop or company, and an inventory is taken of his effects.

The coffin is made (and paid for by means of the effects of the man, which are sold by auction in the garrison after his funeral), and this, with a few trifling fees, is the only expense. The coffin is carried to the grave either on a gun carriage or by men belonging to the man's company, according to the service to which the man belongs.

The band, or the drums and fifes or bugles, of the regiment to which the man belonged attend the funeral, and lead, playing the dead march; then come a firing party, which are provided with three rounds of blank cartridge; then the coffin and pall bearers, after which the mourners.

When any of the relatives of a soldier attend his funeral they follow immediately behind the coffin; then come the men of the troop or company, the order at a funeral being, that the juniors march nearest the coffin, the seniors last. In all cases of the funeral of private soldiers there is an officer in attendance, usually a subaltern officer, who commands the party, and in the march follows in rear.

The firing party mainly indicates the military rank of the deceased soldier. A private soldier or corporal being entitled to thirteen rank and file; a sergeant to nineteen; a cornet or ensign to thirty; a lieutenant to forty; a captain to one hundred; a major to two hundred; a lieutenant-colonel to three-hundred, and a colonel by his own regiment.

When an officer above the rank of colonel is buried, there are cannon employed instead of small arms. A brigadier's funeral is attended by two squadrons and one battalion, and a salute of nine cannon is given. A major-general's is attended by three squadrons and two battalions and eleven pieces of cannon. A lieutenant-general's thirteen pieces of cannon, three battalions and four squadrons. A general's with fifteen pieces, four battalions, and six squadrons. And a field-marshal's saluted with seventeen pieces of cannon, and attended by six battalions and eight squadrons.

When a general or flag officer is being conveyed to the grave, minute guns are fired; but these are not to exceed the number to which the officer was entitled when alive.

When an officer dies in any garrison town, it is customary to send round with the orders, which are read by every officer each evening, a notice to the effect that the funeral will take place on a particular day, and any officers wishing to attend are to be at a place named at a given hour. It is usual for every officer belonging to the regiment or corps of the deceased in the garrison to attend, if not otherwise occupied, and personal friends of the deceased follow also.

All officers who attend funerals appear in full dress with a piece of black crape above the elbow of the left arm, this being the only mourning allowed in the army. The pall-bearers, who should be of the same rank as the deceased, usually wear a crape scarf in addition to the crape on the arm.

When the officer belonged to the royal artillery or cavalry his charger is led to the grave, saddled and equipped, the boots of his master being suspended on each side of the saddle, the heels turned to the front. On the coffin, the busby, helmet, or shako is placed, and the officer's sword-belt and gloves.

There are few things more imposing in outward appearance than a soldier's funeral. The slow, measured beat of the drum, the firing party marching with their arms reversed, a position highly emblematic of grief, the strange mixture of uniform and black pall, invariably tend to make the bystanders feel that a soldier's funeral is far more solemn and impressive than is that of a civilian.

When the procession approaches the grave the firing party file to the right and left, and thus form on either side; they then rest upon their arms reversed, whilst the coffin is borne between the ranks. When the coffin has been lowered into the grave and the service completed, three rounds of blank cartridge are fired in the air as a *feu de joie*—a somewhat inappropriate term for the occasion—but modified by an old corporal who instructed us in the goose step, and who used to order us to fire a "*few de joy*—as for the Queen's birthday," or "a *feu de wo* for a *funerial*."

A soldier's life is, when on service, passed amidst scenes of danger, and thus probably he to a certain extent becomes indifferent to death; to say the least, he has not time to grieve very long. Thus no sooner has the ceremony of depositing his comrade in the earth been accomplished, than the band, or drums and fifes, which so solemnly performed the dead march when proceeding to the burial place, strike up a cheerful quick march, and the soldiers return to barracks to the tune of "Here we are again," forgetful of the scene in which they have lately been actors, and regardless of the probability of themselves being the next claimants for six feet of earth.

The most important military funeral of late years, and one which everybody went to see who could do so, was that of the Duke of Wellington. Famed throughout the world for his brilliant military and civil career, as well as for the genius which characterized all his acts, the nation with one voice called for a public and gorgeous funeral, as a last tribute of its estimation of so far-famed a chieftain.

It was on a dark November morning that hundreds and thousands of persons, long before dawn, wended their way through the streets of London, intent on obtaining a good position on the pavement or to be sure of reaching the house and thence the window, which had been previously secured and from which the procession could be best seen.

Even as early as six o'clock in the morning, large bodies of cavalry and infantry are marching through the streets, whilst officers in uniforms ride up and down, giving orders and arranging the positions for various bodies of men who are yet to make their appearance. In all the principal open spaces troops are mustering; behind the Horse Guards and in St. James's Park, all branches of the service being represented, from the little known uniforms of Indian soldiers to that of our own guards; for the Great Duke had culled his first laurels on the fields of India, and soldiers from the then East India Company's service attended as representatives of that branch of our army.

The course taken by the procession was from the Horse Guards to St. Paul's, and an enormous number of troops were required to keep the ground along the course, this crowd being immense. Not only were the streets crowded, walking being almost impossible, but it was estimated that upwards of two hundred thousand seats were sold to sight-seers.

In the actual procession were six battalions of infantry, nine guns from the field batteries, five squadrons of cavalry, and eight guns from the horse artillery.

The Duke's regiments were of course represented on the occasion, and gave an additional interest to the scene. There was the "Brigade," of which Arthur Duke of Wellington was Colonel-in-Chief, and also the regiment in which young Arthur Wellesley learned the goose step and how to "shoulder arms."

The military, however, formed only a portion of the procession, for the Great Duke was a man of many honours; for Russia, Prussia, Spain, Portugal, Hanover, and the Netherlands had conferred upon him the marshal's bâton, and these nations were each represented on the occasion. Besides these foreigners, many of whom had served with the Duke, there were men of our own country, whose names were well known, and whose reputation would have shone brighter had they not been dimmed by comparison with that of the Duke. In the procession and around the grave there might be seen one of our most far-seeing and able Generals, Sir Charles Napier, the man whom the Duke had selected to go to India at a period of emergency, and to whom he looked as one alone capable of playing the requisite part at that time. Near him was the dashing gallant Lord Gough, who loved to fight side by side with his men; Lord Seaton, Viscount Combermere, Sir W.

Cotton, Sir A. Woodford, &c., names familiar as household words, were grouped around the grave of their loved chief.

The contrast on this day was marked indeed between the grandeur and brilliancy that appeared in St. Paul's, and the silent deserted appearance of Apsley House, where every blind was down and every shutter closed.

It was remarked that as the procession wended its way through the streets, and as the somewhat gorgeous-looking vehicle that contained the coffin passed, every person from the highest to the most humble, bared his head and seemed to be awe-struck, and reminded that fame, rank, and genius are no more free from the call of death than are poverty, misery, and insignificance.

The Duke's titles having been repeated by Garter, King of Arms, the ceremony was concluded, but will long be remembered by those who were witnesses to the imposing scene.

On the 6th April, 1864, a military funeral took place at Woolwich which was attended by a large body of officers, and was a good specimen of a military funeral.

Colonel Bingham, the Deputy Adjutant-General of the Royal Artillery, died at Brighton, to which place he had gone for change of air. His body was conveyed to Woolwich for the purpose of being interred with military honours, and he was buried at Old Plumstead Church. In consequence of the rank of the deceased officer, but more especially from the great respect in which he was personally held, every officer who could obtain leave from out-stations was present on the occasion. Not only did every officer of his own regiment attend, but very many from other branches of the service, so that altogether upwards of three hundred officers followed in the procession.

The weather on the occasion was fine and bright and well-suited for a military display. At one o'clock the troops in garrison paraded, and a large body was told off to line the road from Woolwich Common to the Church, a distance of nearly three miles. At two o'clock the coffin was brought from the house and placed on a gun carriage, covered with a Union Jack, the drums in attendance giving muffled rolls. On the coffin were placed the Colonel's cocked hat and sword, and the carriage was drawn by six horses. The procession then moved on in the following order—

Detachments of Horse Artillery, mounted.
Eight Batteries of Royal Artillery, on foot, with arms reversed.
The Royal Marine Band, playing the Dead March.
Nine Guns of Royal Horse Artillery.
The Royal Artillery and the Bugle Band.
The Garrison Chaplains.
The Corpse.
On either side of the Coffin, four Colonels Royal Artillery as Pall-bearers.
The Deceased's Horse.
Private Mourners.
Officers of the Adjutant-General's Department.
The Gentlemen Cadets.
The Clerks of the Adjutant-General's Departments.
The various Officers who attended.
Mounted Detachments of Royal Horse Artillery.
Private Carriages.

The procession altogether extended considerably over a mile, and at the slow pace at which the march was carried on nearly an hour and a half elapsed before the church was reached.

The small church of Plumstead had rarely if ever been filled by so many military celebrities as on this occasion. Among those whose names are familiar to the public were Field-Marshal the Duke of Cambridge, Sir Richard Airey, Sir J. Scarlet, Sir Edward Lugard, General Foster, General Bloomfield, and others.

The troops were formed in the churchyard and in a field near. The nine guns were drawn up on a higher portion of ground, and at some distance from the church, for the discharge of a cannon not uncommonly breaks windows, and thus these implements of warfare were removed to a safe distance. When the funeral service had been read and the body lowered into the grave the Armstrong guns fired their salute, and the last offices were paid to a good and noble soldier as well as to a most just and honourable man.

The funeral of a soldier who dies amidst scenes of civilization, where the last honours can be paid to him in the manner just described, is certainly an imposing scene, but to some minds it seems less solemn than it might be, and too much of a show. The high probability that among many of those who attend such a funeral there are several who knew little or nothing personally of the man whose body they are following to the grave, may possibly tend to do away with a portion of the real grief which some people are accustomed to see habitually displayed at a funeral. The gaping crowd also, who are usually free critics on the dress and personal appearance of the various members of the procession, render a large military funeral by no means that quiet scene which we all thirst for when the heart has been saddened by the departure of a loved friend. But we can conscientiously state that at those funerals of which we have been eye-witnesses the conduct of those personally engaged, as well as of the lookers-on, has been such as to harmonize with the sensitive state of those who were nearly allied by blood or friendship to the deceased.

When a soldier meets a soldier's death, and is buried "with his martial cloak around him," and when no band of music attends his funeral, or other pomp is added to his last honors, the last offices are not less solemn, the whole scene not less impressed on the memory, and the sudden reminder that in the midst of life we are in death not less efficient in its results. When we see a friend gradually sicken and day by day become weaker, whilst doctors shake their heads and relatives despond, we are prepared at last for the final scene. When, however, we breakfast with a comrade, walk with him to the parade, march beside him as we approach an enemy's position, hear him suddenly cease speaking when in the middle of a sentence, and look round to see him sinking to the earth lifeless; and when, after a smart brush with an enemy, we return to attend the funeral of this comrade, who has been to us perhaps more than a brother for months or years—we seem to be nearly allied to death, for *we* may on the following night be consigned in the same way to six feet of ground, our security for life being no greater than was our comrade's.

In many cases, where the number of slain can be counted by hundreds, the day following a great battle is a sad one. Experienced was the general who exclaimed—"Nothing but a defeat is more sad than a victory, for the losses of the latter are only exceeded by those of the former." To give each man a separate grave, or to pronounce a funeral service over each man, would occupy more time than could be spared; thus, a large hole, and a funeral service for 100 men, who are rapidly covered with earth, and who, shroudless and coffinless, are thus disposed of, is the other side of the scene of pomp which we have described as a soldier's funeral at home.

FINIS.

LONDON:
SAVILL AND EDWARDS, PRINTERS, CHANDOS STREET
COVENT GARDEN.

www.ingramcontent.com/pod-product-compliance
Lightning Source LLC
LaVergne TN
LVHW012111170826
845678LV00001BA/7

* 9 7 8 0 3 5 3 4 8 3 3 2 3 *